CIVIL BULLETS

THE FINAL WAR

CHRIS ROCKWELL

ISBN softback:978-1-64184-458-1
ISBN hardback:978-1-64184-459-8

TABLE OF CONTENTS

FOR THOSE ABOUT TO...

I was born in a small Northern California town where the Sierra Nevada Mountains and the Pacific Ocean meet and named for the "gold" that was found there. Gold miners, lumberjacks, pioneers, and outlaws were the real men and women who settled our town. Once here, my family toiled for the land and business barons, making a good life out of what they were dealt.

Out of the pages of a Steinbeck novel, my dad's family came out West from upstate New York in search of work in the 1940s. They experienced life in migrant camps and worked in the fields picking fruit, hoeing tomatoes, and picking cotton. My dad was seven years old, working alongside his family in the fields. Over time they made their way to Northern California and settled into a logging camp in the Sierra Nevada Foothills, where my grandpa drove logging trucks and drank a lot. My grandmother, Dorothy, homeschooled her five children and worked nights as an LVN at the county hospital 25 miles into town.

As Dad and his family made their way across the harsh and bleak country, fighting to survive, my mom was born in Santa Monica, California, into a working-class German-Irish family. They lived about a mile from my grandpa's job as an LA detective, and less than a mile from the beach, where famous Hollywood millionaires lived in luxury. Mom went to school and hung out with kids with famous parents, surfed on her lunch break, and saw the Beatles at Dodger Stadium and the Doors at a small private venue. As a teenager, she spent her afternoons with an eccentric artist and a glass of beer, rode the horse Red Skelton gifted to her, and even had a call with Elvis. My parents' lives were very different, but when Mom ended up here because her father had taken a job as the first ranger at Lake Oroville, it was only a matter of time before they would meet. Mom was working at the county hospital as a new RN where Grandma Dorothy worked as an LVN. Dorothy made the introduction, and my other grandma, Ethel Anne, found them the perfect property to buy. The rest is history.

I grew up in this blue-collar town in Northern California, playing organized sports, working in lumber yards, and even married my high-school sweetheart. I came from teachers, nurses, truck drivers, construction workers, and cops who worked hard and then went home to focus on their family. I observed people who were conscientious about showing up every day with a good attitude and work ethic that added value to the team. Their mindset was rooted in the working-class American family. They pulled their weight but were being deceived into believing that most people thought and worked like them.

The more I went out into the world, the more I discovered that a large majority of people don't actually think about team above self. I observed the divided ideology between being an employee versus being the boss. That's when I realized that most people base their views on rigidly preconceived ideas, assumptions, and a flood of media clips with fragmented and disconnected information, starting with their parental examples.

As I began writing this book, I was experiencing the beginning of my crash. It started during the Great Economic Recession of 2008 and lasted years, testing the very fiber of my being. This life-changing chapter in history—coupled with my lifelong fascination with human nature, entrepreneurship, and revolutionary and economic history—drove me to ask how we got to such a dysfunctional and divided nation.

After many nights overdosing on drugs, booze, and polarizing talk show hosts spewing wax poetic nonsense like Ron Burgundy slave puppets, I wanted to figure out how we could resolve the situation we found ourselves in.

I had reached a hopeless state of mind that either manifests in the savage end or a new beginning. Through my darkest and most painful days, I chose to believe that things would work out. Despair stripped me of the final layers of pride and ego, and that's when I shed the fake armor that was keeping me from my true self and purpose. I believe I'm here to see inspiration and possibilities in others and share my experience and hope. I began to explore some things about life I didn't understand.

As I finish this book in the summer of 2020, we are experiencing a global crisis due to COVID-19; race riots followed by Seattle's example of divide with the creation of "CHAZ", a "nation" ironically created with borders, protected by armed guards or soldiers, and run by a drug lord and an economic depression.

It's been ten years since I began this journey, and my life looked very different. I thought very differently. I use my lived experience as a parallel to the current state of America, helping to span the bridge that divides ourselves and our country into blue and red, black and white. My original plan for the book was to draw a parallel of my life experience and the manic social distortion of America. As I was finishing this massive project (basically two books in one—macro/micro), after years of research and a lot of writing, I read Tucker Carlson's book, *Ship of Fools*, and was thoroughly impressed. I realized that he had written a similar book to what I was writing, about the socio-political and economic state that we were living in. Tucker and I are both Gen Xers from California and saw a state and country morph from similar perspectives.

In a strange twist, Tucker Carlson's book made my book better. It allows me to simply let my lived experience be the focus of the book. The overlap that I will keep in is the Silicon

Valley case study of Yahoo that Tucker covered with expert journalistic research. I actually lived the experience and figured it would provide added color to the story. *Civil Bullets* and *Ship of Fools* combine to provide the parallel—the micro (individual lived experience) and macro (US socio-political). I will be writing other pieces on leadership, entrepreneurship, society, the economy, and more that will be available as premium content to subscribers at civilbullets.com.

I do not endorse extreme or hate ideology, political correctness, and people with selfish financial, political, or ideological agendas that threaten the founding principles of the United States of America and the average working person's way of life. I am not running for political office. I am not an extremist or a commercial sellout trying to be the next Tony Robbins self-help guru or landing a gig with Fox or MSNBC. My ideas will invariably continue to evolve as I experience and learn more about the world around and inside me. But at this point, my principles are steadfast and true. It's up to me to live them every day, or not.

I was tired of listening to people around me and in the media talking about things related to race, economics, and politics that were based on disconnected sound bites, or a deep-seated and usually unfounded and out-of-date ideology handed down to them by their paycheck or their knee-jerk oppositional defiance towards their parents or mainstream views. People develop fiercely passionate beliefs based on fundamentally flawed information and perspective; not studying the facts nor having diverse lived experiences, and inherit fear to honestly explore the true root of the challenges we face individually and as a nation, lest it disrupts our cozy life of leisure.

My journey will share a very personal window into the multifaceted life I have lived and the experiences, successes, and failures that shaped my thinking. My personal story will share real-life anecdotes to our most controversial and dividing issues like race and socioeconomic ideology. I will include humor as well as personally tragic experiences and discovery with the intent to connect people to the similarities our country is going through and will invariably go through again; to laugh at some of the little differences, and seethe at some of the outrageously egregious ones.

Americans, by nature, are suspicious of people in power. I mean, we told the king of England to fuck off and fought for independence and won! My parents and grandparents shared a respect and disdain for leaders. They never held the role of leader in their careers. They resented the leaders while at the same time worked their asses off to please them. They aren't unique. It's an American cultural contradiction. Living on both sides, mixed with a diverse lived experience, has provided me with a lens to share the bigger picture of our greatest strengths and our most fundamental and predictable pitfalls, individually and as a nation.

Many blindly assume and puke nonsense just to be heard, expounding on worlds they think they know, but don't, when they should be spending more time listening, asking why, and exploring the worlds they haven't lived. How can someone truly understand the mindset of a CEO if they have never led an organization responsible for fiscal viability and people? How can someone really talk about fixing education or healthcare when they have never experienced what it's like to work inside a classroom or hospital? Seriously. Think about it.

Making a decision based on mainstream media is not an answer. Nor is refuting all new ideas like an ignorant grunt from the Stone Age, saying you have a college degree and a white-collar job in Silicon Valley, therefore you have some sense of expertise about every subject under the sun. As I listen more and speak less, I'm amazed at how many fucking "experts" there are!

At the time I started writing this book, I was the CEO and founder of King Duce Records, producing platinum hip-hop artists, and a hired-gun executive in Silicon Valley, helping a team of Stanford stars and legendary artists build an innovative company that gave them the power to create print-on-demand products to make more money and build their brand without the up-front cost and loss of creative control. It was 2009, right after the 2008 real estate crash that tidal waved my real estate investment business, the economy, and most people and businesses in its way. With my eye on the silver lining, I'm thankful my partner and I closed our business profitably in October of 2007 because of the trends we were tracking. When most businesses connected to real estate were filing bankruptcy to cover their debt crunch, my partner and I were paying off our investors with a profitable return. We built and ran a good business.

The entire world was changing dramatically. The first black president was taking office, and I got my first DUI and landed in jail. My job, money, wife...everything seemingly vanished all at once. I had worked so hard to build a life, and now it was gone. I was beyond bitter.

I went from the top of the game to a dead man walking around my hometown with only a backpack to my name. It would take ten years to find my way out and into a new life beyond my wildest dreams. Over time, I came to realize that the purpose of my book is to openly share my lived experience of success and, probably more importantly, overcoming life-altering setbacks.

I wrote the book in a style that is in line with my literary heroes. They are no different than the cowboys, athletes, and rock stars I grew up idolizing. Jack London, Ernest Hemingway, Mark Twain, and a few others are my favorites because they were not just great writers, but they were dreamers, explorers, and conscientious observers of how the world is both crazy and amazing. They tried to provide real lived context to what most people consider fantasy, intellectual theory, or unreal experiences of other people. I always found those kinds of artists to be intriguing, authentic, and entertaining. I admired their courage and flair to test the boundaries and taboos of life, taking the risks that very few ever would dare to seek the truth.

I have lived my life with passion, curiosity, and unwavering desire to learn—to test the boundaries of what is possible for me, and to reach my potential in every aspect of my life. I'm an explorer at my core. That's where the discovery is. And the most challenging exploration, especially in these times, is the inward exploration of self: the good, the bad, and the ugly to discover truth. To test self against the competitive markers in the world while focusing on the eternal loving relationships of friends and family. To get the truth on how and where we fit in life, and then to develop our mental tools to improve and self-actualize. I owe that to my family, to myself, and to the world.

I hope this book offers a little hope to someone struggling in this crazy game of life. I now realize it is the reason I spent ten years writing it. It was worth every drop of blood, sweat, and tears.

Fearless, grateful, and free!

Chris Rockwell
October 17, 2020

2

GOLDEN CHILDHOOD

Golden Childhood

OCEAN BABY

The ocean was a part of me before I was born; it's in my DNA. My mom was a Catholic schoolgirl growing up in Santa Monica back in the golden era of the 1960s when the Beach Boys ruled the radio waves, and Hollywood sold the dream she lived. She spent her days surfing all the major hot spots, breaking boards against the rocks as she pressed her fate by riding closer to the pier than most of the guys. She would free-dive for abalone in Malibu during wave breaks and spend afternoons having lunch and talking art with an older bohemian artist she knew from her neighborhood. Her avant-garde lunch came served with a beer when she was fourteen years old. My mom was not a typical teenager; she was not living in a typical place or time. She was living her teens in the epicenter of modern-day enlightenment, spawned by the pop culture scene of artists and surfers leading the world in song, film, and fashion. She was probably 5'10" by then and had a wiser and more graceful way about herself than most in motion, words, and thought. Simply put, she was a classic Southern California surfer girl you'd see in the movies.

Mom grew up with the stars of Hollywood and the LA music and surf scene, observing fame and fortune from interestingly close proximity but living on the edge of Brentwood in a modest working-class home on Gorham Avenue in Santa

Monica. I was able to see her childhood house just before it was leveled and replaced with a $4.5 million manor. It was located down the street from the LAPD police station, where my grandpa served as a South-Central Watts detective. Mom could've signed on for a star-studded ride easily with her abounding beauty, intelligence, and creative talent. She spent her time either working at the Arrow Theater and the surf shop at the west end of Sunset Strip or watching famous friends perform around the bonfire. Often, she was hanging out with her best friend Valentina Skelton at Red Skelton's Bel Air mansion. She saw the dark side to that world with all the drug overdoses and destroyed lives that the fame machine spits out or kills. I think that experience gave her some conviction about how she was going to live; she chose to ride the wave and enjoy life raising a family in a slower NorCal country pace.

My parents started free-diving in 1969 on the Northern California coast, known for its abalone diving, spearfishing, and rugged beauty. It also happens to be the breeding ground to the infamous great white shark, a region known as the "Red Triangle." They were conscious of the danger but lured to the ocean by an intrigue and sense of adventure that transcends fear.

Navarro Beach is a big expanse of sand, constantly shifting and changing with the force of the Navarro River joining the Pacific Ocean. There are magnificent rock outcroppings, including a fifty-foot rock just offshore called the Shark Fin, because it looks like the dorsal fin of the deadly predators that frequent the area. One of my earliest memories was at about three years old, standing naked at the edge of the water, looking out to the horizon where the men were diving, dreaming that one day I would join them on the great hunt. I spent much of my early life experiencing the morning sunlight touching the surface of the water with soft pastel pinks and purples and brushstrokes of yellow, gently awakening the ocean and all life that calls her home. The distant sounds of seagulls and crashing waves muted by the hundred yards of sandy beach and scattered driftwood give character and soft acoustics to the soundtrack.

My parents would cross this river to dive the rocks just north of the beach. They would literally pack my playpen above their heads with me on my dad's shoulders as they crossed the raging spring river. Adventure was built into me. Fifteen years later, I would witness my first great white shark attack diving this very spot. Keep reading; I share that story later in the book.

The vast expanse of sand and driftwood made the perfect bonfire beach for the locals and the gypsies passing through in their Grateful Dead-painted school buses adorned with a message on the side that read *God is Green*. Navarro was a pioneer's boom and bust lumber port and mill during the gold rush, and later supplied much of the lumber to rebuild San Francisco after the great earthquake of 1906. After surviving a few catastrophic fires and floods that leveled the lumber mills, as well as the entrepreneurs that bet their life savings and dreams building them, Navarro became the beach the locals frequented. They came to fish, dive, and gather driftwood for fuel. It hid the turbulence of a past, not so far gone, of crazy sailors raising hell up and down the coast while they waited the typical three days for the lumber schooners to reload fresh rough-cut redwood headed for its destination south to San Francisco Bay and on to other destinations around the globe.

There were bars and brothels like Navarro by the Sea, the hotel built on the south hill just inland from Navarro Beach, and still standing thanks to local fundraising efforts to renovate it. There was the Caspar Inn right up the road, built on the Mendocino coast in a tiny patch of oceanfront bluff. The bar is still a local favorite for live music and a night's stay in old brothel rooms upstairs that overlook the ocean and sunsets. I had the opportunity to stay a week in the west guest room with a window to the ocean, enjoying the music and libations, except I didn't have to pay for the fun. The place has an unreal history, and you can feel it, especially with the rugged north coast setting. These places were famous for their debauchery and violence. Sailors, lumberjacks, and miners together with cash, whores, and whiskey is a Molotov cocktail made of enriched uranium. I think I'm drawn to those times and chaos because it mirrors parts of my personality and lived experiences.

The 1970s overflow with nostalgic childhood memories of camping at the coast, riding in the back of the truck with my younger brothers and friends, and heading out of camp for a day of fun and adventure at the beach. Our families camped at Paul Dimmick State Park, a campground within the protected forest of giant old-growth redwood trees donated by the old Union Lumber Company. Some of the trees were as tall as three hundred feet, towering like living skyscrapers cradling the gently rolling Navarro River as it made its way to its namesake beach and the Pacific Ocean.

In annual springtime tradition, the Brandts pulled in with their old rusted orange Dodge truck followed closely by my parents with a load of kids in the back of our 1966 Chevy stepside long bed. That truck was proudly used during the construction of the Oroville Dam; it even had a bed liner made from a piece of the giant conveyor belt used to transport gravel and clay to the dam site from pits ten miles away. Grandpa Rockwell worked on the project driving giant dump trucks. My dad said the Oroville Dam project was the best job his father ever had; said it was during that time he was a happier guy to be around—and he drank less. Grandpa felt like somebody because he was making good money and was a part of such an ambitious project. I think my dad bought the old Chevy truck because it connected him to his father, despite its beat-up body and bad flywheel, kind of like their relationship.

After a campfire breakfast of egg, abalone, cheese, and garlic pasta topped with J. Lee Roy's Dippin' Sauce, we would migrate eight miles west to the beach. Everyone jumped out of the vehicles, excited about the adventure ahead of them, as they packed up and began the hike across the long beach to reach the river mouth that must be crossed to get to the dive spot, a rock outcropping just north of the massive beach. Watching my dad and the older guys put their wet suits on and prepare their masks, fins, weight belts, and other diving necessities for the hypothermic water that usually hovered at a bone-chilling 54 degrees was exciting. The pre-dive ritual was a time of anticipation and serious preparation for the perils that awaited the divers. It was kind of like watching warriors preparing for battle. I was watching men getting ready for the hunt as a tribe. I witnessed a bonding and focus of pursuit that was powerful, and a legacy I desperately wanted to carry on.

While most of the other dads I knew played golf or maybe went rifle hunting for deer in the fall, I was very aware that diving for abalone and spearing fish off the north coast, with its violent ocean, jagged rocks, and great white sharks, were certainly no passive experience like golf. It's a different mindset and usually a different personality. My dad and his friends were clean-cut, athletic, blue-collar guys who admired tough men who worked and played in the natural world, hunting, fishing, and exploring. They wanted to test themselves against the forces of nature and other men. The experience of watching Dad set out into the dangerous ocean is probably some of the most powerful imprinted messaging that I still reference for my identity and sense of adventure.

My dad was a gladiator in the ocean. Watching him take on giant crashing waves gave me a sense of pride and confidence within myself, knowing that my dad was doing something very few men were willing to dare. And not only did he do it, but he was also one of the most prolific free-divers I've ever encountered. He could out-dive my brothers and me well into his sixties. I'm not kidding. He was and always has been the warrior I looked to for my concept of what a man is. As I would later discover, my dad's courage facing the mighty ocean would symbolize the way he challenged conventional thinking and living throughout his life. More than ever, I appreciate the passion and commitment my dad gave to everything he did. He wanted to truly test his limits. That's an unconventional and elevated mindset, in my opinion, one that I choose to believe and use as my formula for living.

As my dad and the other men hiked down the beach, across the Navarro River, and then disappeared around the rocks on the north side where they would dive, my brothers and I would fantasize about what adventure the men were off on. We would just as soon lose track and be off on our own adventure, pretending to be great warriors like those we had just witnessed. We would build forts out of the shards of driftwood that washed up all over the beach. Sometimes the river would deposit entire redwood and oak logs washed up from a high tide after drifting in the ocean for years. Some logs on the beach were over fifty feet long and weighed tons. It was easy to lose ourselves in an ancient time and a world far away.

A typical day at Navarro beach was a mellow image of young mothers wearing bell-bottom Levi's and red and white bandanas worn like Joni Mitchell. They played guitars on the beach while children ran around the edge of the swiftly moving river and merciless ocean. Classic white and red checkered tablecloths laid out on the sand with wicker picnic baskets revealed a traditional Italian lunch of salami, cheese, rolls of freshly baked French bread, and a couple bottles of red wine. The Mastelotto brothers always provided the bounty for lunch and made the annual trip because they grew up next door to the Brandts. The women would talk and laugh while they made sandwiches, occasionally gazing out towards the ocean to check on their husbands and sons diving in the trough.

After a few hours of playing, then eating a quick lunch, we would run back down the beach to eagerly await the hunters returning with their catch of the day. I had so much anticipation of the trophies they would bring back to shore, always hoping the great adventure story of the day went to my dad. The guys would appear from around the rocks with a diving float, usually a netted big-rig tire tube that could hold twenty abalone, a stringer of Cabazon rockfish, and occasionally a few Dungeness Crab. With excitement, we watched them carry their catch and gear chest-high through a raging river to reach us on the other side. With proud smiles, they presented us young boys with their bounty.

I remember feeling so proud, especially when curious tourists would congregate around the returning hunters and their strange catch of sea creatures. It was usually a nice suburban family on their annual "car-cation," taking five billion pictures of the same abalone and living vicariously through our families' adventure. I got a kick out of the interaction my dad and Sonny Brandt would have with these folks from different towns and countries. They would often end up giving them an abalone, at least back in the old days.

There's a legendary story around the campfire about Jimmy Mastelotto. The Mastelottos made money in cattle, oil, gold—you name it. They were the original hustlers. They didn't talk about it; they did it, and they did it with style and guts. Now Jimmy, the wealthiest and most gregarious of the Mastelotto brothers, is said to have gotten into a heated exchange with an associate about which pair of divers could get more abalone in a given time frame. They had another bottle of wine and then started talking bigger and louder. Ultimately, Jimmy bet this guy thousands of dollars that my dad and Sonny Brandt could beat his two diver friends. No one knows for sure if that wager ever happened, but I would bet that it did, knowing the gambling entrepreneur that Jimmy Mastelotto was.

Our dads didn't escape for "men only" weekends. They lived the adventure, explored, and journeyed with their wives and kids, experiencing the world together as one. That is a bygone era that is sorely missed in our society. Talk about symbolism and family values. I realize how fortunate I was to have this upbringing and lived experience as a child.

At the end of every great day diving and playing at the beach, we would return to camp soaked, coated with sand, and frozen from the ride back to camp in the back of the old Chevy. Still shivering from the ride, we would pack up the cleaning knives and cutting boards and head down to the river to clean the fish and abalone. The men would carry a big redwood picnic table into the ankle-deep shallows to sit and clean their catch, drink beer, and recap the dramatic highlights from the day. The young kids and babies would play at the edge of the gentle and shallow river as the mothers watched from close by; the sounds of the river, the echoed talking and laughing of the men and women, and the occasional bird singing gave the scene a soft nostalgic feel. The light getting low, the forest growing still, and the smells of the campfire blending with the sounds of laughter would have everyone feeling good and connected.

THE ROCKWELL RANCH

I'm a typical small-town boy from the foothills of Northern California, with bigger than typical dreams. I was very fortunate to be born into a family that gave me the attributes, awareness, and freedom to chase the visions in my mind. The early years were all about me roaming the property, half the time naked, swimming in the creek, working and dreaming in dad's tool shed, and wanting to be like the hardworking, good family men who surrounded me. Dad was a high school counselor and psychology teacher. Mom was a nurse. Both were equally liked and respected in our small town.

Similar to church, we spent fall evenings assembled in the living room, eating dinner and watching Monday Night Football. My younger brother, Nick, and I would patiently wait for a commercial break to wrestle with Dad while our baby brother Dan waddled around with a ten-pound diaper and blond hair sticking out like he'd been electrocuted. Mom was in the kitchen cooking an old German family goulash of macaroni-style noodles with tomato sauce and hamburger. The familiar smell of oregano and onions simmered their way into the living room and blended with the oak and pine logs burning in our old Ben Franklin cast-iron fireplace.

Nearly leaning out of the couch and into the TV, Dad analyzed and coached the football game with noticeable intensity: "Do you see why that receiver dropped the ball? He didn't want the ball bad enough. Boys, don't ever wait for the ball to come to you. Go get it and score!"

Our dad has always been an amazing observer and teacher to young people, which made him an excellent coach to his three young boys. He was very sensitive and intense, like I am, and led by a child's heart. He made everything an adventure, learning with us and never telling us to try something he wouldn't be willing to try himself. For example, he never played soccer, but he would dribble a soccer ball on a narrow trail with us through an undeveloped swath of rolling oak-covered terrain filled with natural obstacles including hidden roots, rocks, and gopher holes scattered like landmines, waiting to throw the ball into the surrounding poison oak and blackberry bushes. The goal was to challenge ourselves; to better what we were capable of the day before. It wasn't just about winning, but we understood that it was important. We were raised with the belief that winning was a byproduct of being a well-prepared athlete and that winning in life is all about preparation as well.

There's a half-time break that begins with a classic Miller Lite commercial with John Madden and the pro athletes of the 1970s era of machismo decadence. Dad's thought trail continues with his diatribe on modern marketing and consumerism. He was a man's man and a total athlete, but he didn't drink or smoke and believed modern advertising was exploiting people's insecurities and primal desires for profit.

"How can our government allow big corporations to promote alcohol to minors by using sex and sports celebrities during primetime TV?"

Mom, sensing Dad's growing intensity, softens the moment with, "Okay, babe…"

"Well, honey…!" and with that distraction, Dad turns his attention to his boys, smiles, and starts wrestling with us.

Mom keeps the focus on the stable and pragmatic, "Boys, did you get your homework finished? Otherwise, you're not going to your dad's basketball game tonight."

As the screams of the kickoff to the second half of the game can be heard, my brother Nick and I respond respectfully exasperated, "Yeesss, Mom!"

I remember gazing out our large 1940s rectangle living room window as the sun set, creating deep oranges and purples, a beautiful finale to a cool fall October night. My mind faded away with the sun and the sounds of the football fans in the background coming out of our old Zenith TV. I dreamed I was playing for the Raiders and making the big game-winning tackle. My surroundings of love, physical sports, and hard work gave me the mental visionary platform to believe it was possible in a practical sort of way. I didn't just dream about it as a disillusioned reality. My childhood was like a dynamic incubator for athletes or start-up companies in Silicon Valley, but with more dimension and nuance, thanks to my family's understanding of nature's wisdom.

My parents believed in giving their children the proper environment to thrive in every way. Of course, their utopian commune wasn't free of glitches, but the overall formula was an amazing world of security and love that fostered happiness, freedom to dream, learn and explore with confidence, and work ethic to persevere through adversity. I spent the first years of my life running around naked on our four acres, exploring the property as if it were my own personal planet. I was totally safe and free to try things and explore anything and everything. Failing or "wrong" wasn't something I consciously heard or understood. My parents gave me the encouragement and real-life attempts at figuring things out on my own. It was all one big adventure. My days were filled with discovering new things, which usually meant being outside interacting with Mother Nature. I was encouraged to chase my interests with unbridled enthusiasm and openness to learn how to do things I didn't yet know.

Something was different...

We had this giant stainless-steel water distiller on the back porch and a big industrial juicer. It wasn't one of those Infomercial Juice Tiger machines made of plastic. Our juicer had a grinder that could've been used as a tree chipper. The grinder turned the fruit and vegetables into a wet pulp that was spit into a canvas bag then pressed by a hydraulic steel piston that extracted every drop of moisture from the pulp. We fed the dry pulp to our chickens and rabbits, and we always had fresh juice. My dad tried all kinds of crazy shit...and we drank it. Beets, onions, potatoes, celery, parsley, and other things that would make us gag sometimes. At least that's how I saw it back then. The reality is that most of the time, we had freshly pressed carrot juice with some fresh lemon juice, and depending on how my asthma was, Dad would blend some celery juice in to help reduce my breathing struggle, which I dealt with throughout my sports career.

Breakfast at the Rockwell house was like a training hall for athletes and a fascinating comedy show to most of our friends. My dad loved cooking and taking care of us every morning. *Every* morning! My dad was not a slipper-wearing Mr. Rogers. He was a man's man but was also able to show his feelings to his children with almost complete vulnerability and openness. Every morning before school, Dad would sit at our bed and wake us to the new day with a gentle rub on the chest or head, quietly telling us good morning and how much he loved us. As I write this, I'm dumbfounded by how amazing he was with us. Another case in point for people who claim they can't change because of what they came from. My dad's father didn't show him affection and tell him he loved him or thought he did anything good. So, how did my dad make that monumental shift in behavior? Choice and action.

He gave us a solid and safe reality that allowed us to develop and flourish in many ways. He was always up before daylight like the old-timers and already had the Ben Franklin fireplace lit and the coffee boiling. The combination of those timeless smells of burning pine, coffee, and breakfast simmering and summoning me downstairs will always be nostalgic for me. After he woke us up (except my brother, Nick, who always overslept), Dad would run back downstairs to check on my special needs baby sister, Nicole, who he was hand-feeding simultaneously while preparing our breakfast of pancakes, eggs, juice, and cod liver oil poured onto the spoon.

Drinking cod liver oil in the morning is another one of those funny in hindsight childhood memories that was totally fucked up at the time. For you young folks out there, people used to take a tablespoon of fish oil out of the bottle every morning. Nowadays, it comes in a pill and is tasteless. Not back then. The stuff smelled and tasted like the bottom of the holding tanks on the fishing boats in Noyo Harbor. Disgusting. We all gagged most of the time, but watching Nick try and get it down was like watching stand-up comedy. He was gagging walking down the stairs before breakfast just thinking about it. He just had a queasy stomach, whether it was on a boat or in a car. Cod liver oil first thing in the morning was like trying to eat a dead rotting fish carcass.

My brothers and I would sit at the breakfast table while Dad would cook us eggs, wheat pancakes with wheat germ, and, like our friend Danny McCall would say, raisins the size of prunes. These pancakes were like eating a giant and very dense energy bar for breakfast. The original Clif Bar! Except the size of the cast-iron pan he cooked them in was about 12 inches in diameter. Dad would dump extra eggs and wheat germ into the batter, to the point that the pancakes would weigh as much as the plates they were served on. I'm not kidding! All our friends got a kick out of seeing how the Rockwell boys ate.

This was just another aspect of my identity that made me different. I literally remember being embarrassed because I ate healthy food and not the "cool" food all my friends were eating—shit like Kellogg's Frosted Flakes, Pop-Tarts, and Hostess Cherry Pies. I mean, that just seemed cool. The commercials sure made it appetizing and hip. I would get frustrated once in a while by the lack of shitty food in our cupboards. It's probably the same reason I dressed down with old Levi's and shirts in elementary school. I wanted to adopt the ways and be part of the average kids. I wanted to blend in. I just knew, regardless of how hard I tried, I was growing up in a different environment. Not better or worse, at least to me, just different. Nonetheless, I always wanted everyone to get along, despite the differences.

Another thing that felt strange was being one of the only kids in school who had parents who didn't believe in God. Well, my mom was technically agnostic after a decade of private parochial school. My dad had searched black Baptist churches and Pentecostal tent revivals observing devout folks speaking in tongues and falling on the ground to come to his conclusion that there was simply too much suffering for there to be an intelligent force behind humans and the universe.

Our home was laden with musical instruments that were played during evenings just before bed or when my mom's parents would come over for dinner. They would sit around the piano and sing songs with harmonies after dessert and coffee. My parents had a couple of old acoustic guitars that they would fingerpick classic folk songs on. My dad would sit at our bedside and play and sing an old hobo folk song called "Woodchuck" as if he were on a children's television show. It was like Roger Miller singing "Kansas City Star" about being a star of a kiddy show. Every time Dad played it, we giggled with amusement at his antics and comedic style and performance of the song.

My parents listened to a wide mix of music, laying the foundation of curiosity and interest in the different sounds and dialects of composition. Mom's musical experience included her formal piano lessons growing up but also the laid-back strumming on her acoustic guitar on the beach sitting around the fire with her famous schoolmates.

I remember the day my dad brought me a single tom drum off a set from the music department at the high school where he worked. Jim Christensen, the music teacher and my dad's friend, gave it to my dad to give to me. I was always banging on things. I used to beat the hell out of that drum. I would walk by my mom's upright piano and stop, strike some keys, glance at the Scott Joplin sheet music, and mess around with some impromptu performance. I liked exploring a wide range of sounds, rhythms, and moods, and didn't realize that I was off on my musical journey…I was always exploring it with an innocent naked ear of curiosity. I never had any interest in learning a song that already existed. In my mind, it had already been done. I just explored sounds and would interpret what I felt from inside.

Paradise found... the old-fashioned way

There was an old irrigation canal that ran through our property. It was built in the mid-1800s to feed the gold mining sluices and then repurposed to water the countless square miles of orange and olive orchards that still dot the golden belt of the Sierra Nevada foothills. We spent summers wading in and floating down the creek, stopping off along the way to thaw out from the frigid high sierra water and fill up on blackberries that lined the creek during the hottest time of the year. It felt timeless and a million miles away from the hectic day-to-day lives of so many people on this planet.

We didn't have much money; we were barely middle class. Dad was just starting his teaching career, and Mom spent most of her time at home with us kids. My dad came from hardworking poor parents who believed in the American Dream as they toiled to eke out a living with five kids. My dad was smart, aware, and could see the universe and Earth's wonderment, but he could also see the true absurdity of mankind's destruction and hypocrisy. I saw him triumph out of real poverty without welfare of any kind. No excuses, people.

There just are none. I'm not saying it's not difficult. My dad made it out and created a pretty damn healthy environment and way of life for himself and his family, starting from poverty living in logging camps and labor camps, picking cotton and fruit like the classic Steinbeck novels. My own father did this! So please, do not sit there and tell me I'm speaking from a disconnected reality. Watching a father conquer his negative examples and work hard with a positive attitude without any government handout reinforces my opinion and attitudes about America and what it takes to be a man.

My grandparents never took welfare of any kind, either. They just slaved away for shit pay, providing their children the example of hard work to realize the post-WWII middle-class American Dream that I was raised in. My grandmother, Dorothy Rockwell, was kicked out of nursing school as a young woman because she got pregnant, despite being married to my grandfather, Robert Rockwell. That's how it was. Wanna talk about inequality and prejudice? She worked nights as an underpaid LVN for over forty years while she tended to five kids, including teaching them at home while they lived in the logging camps. She provided a security and wisdom that was crucial to keeping the family together through tough times. What a woman!

My mom chose to spend most of her time with us in our early years, so I experienced the things we strive to find in this world: security, love, fulfillment, adventure, and happiness. I can honestly say that I don't ever recall my parents telling me that any of my ideas weren't possible. They encouraged me to develop those ideas into practical form by the example of their work ethic and determination to produce conscientious work. I guess in hindsight, that's what gave me character—my individuality, attitude, and outlook.

From the time I could walk, I was following my dad everywhere around our property as he built things, fixed fences, fed the horses, rebuilt our Chevy truck engine, or spent hours trying to study to complete his master's degree in psychology from Chico State. I was always fidgeting about, trying to be like him, to help him with his undertakings, but would inevitably be off on some new adventure of my own within minutes. My dad would take each interruption as an opportunity to be with me. He never yelled at me for my curiosity, and he always included me in his. When my dad decided to build a basketball court when I was 18 months old, I was helping him drill holes in the boards. The story is family folklore because just as I was managing the power drill on my own, my grandmother drove up and about had a fucking heart attack! I shake my head in amazement to this day at the freedom and encouragement my parents gave me to try new things.

I didn't leave the property much before I started pre-school except for an occasional Oroville High School basketball or football game. I was the official Tiger mascot at two years old and even had a write-up in the local newspaper with a picture highlighting my golden shoulder-length locks and the tiger costume jumpsuit, makeup and all, which my mom put together with creative ease. Looking back at the old newspaper article, I was already full of limitless confidence, and every step I took, I was being showered with accolades just for showing up with a smile.

Although local public excursions were limited, they exposed me to my parents' working environments. They were celebrated by the people around them. I felt the respect they earned by the way they lived their lives as an active part of our small town. It seemed like everyone liked my parents. They were good, solid human beings, with impeccable records of conduct and behavior within the community. They lived that behind closed doors for the most part, too.

My world existed on those four acres nestled in the golden belt of the Sierra Nevada foothills, in a small town forged from gold, lumber, and a hardworking pioneering spirit. Our home was built by the widowed Dr. Tucker, the town's most esteemed dentist and respected businessman. The original Tucker home across the creek from my parents' home was built back around the turn of the century. He owned hundreds, if not thousands, of acres of land around that area, mostly for raising mandarins, oranges, and olives. He was also known to speculate on the stock market, with often successful results. When his socially upward conscious wife passed, Mr. Tucker married his assistant, a brilliant yet unpretentious woman who truly knew and understood Tucker. They built their simple dream home, the home I was raised in, just up the hill from the original home. Tucker's assistant and life partner placed the home with southern views highlighting the bend in the creek and valley views all the way to the coastal mountain range from the living room window.

By the time my parents moved onto the Tucker Ranch, it was a dilapidated postcard from a bygone era marked by overgrown plants, trees, and decomposing barns and outbuildings built back in the 1940s. My grandmother, "Mud," found the place, conveniently just down the road from where my grandpa built their home after retiring from the LAPD. Seeing lots of negative social changes, he decided to hang up his gun and become one of the founding state rangers on the newly created Lake Oroville. The Oroville Dam is still one of the world's largest earthen dams. It was even dedicated by then-Governor of California, Ronald Reagan. Dad and G'Pa would work on the house when time permitted, but my parents chose to give us an upbringing of adventures rather than be tied to honey-dos and home-improvement weekends. It was more important to them to build healthy and confident children than to build a palace and accumulate stuff. When we would leave the property, we were heading out on an adventure: camping, diving in the ocean, skiing, or hunting deer in the Eastern Sierras.

As kids, we would crawl under the house through a latched screened door that was about three feet tall by three feet wide. We would play in the cool dirt and dig up old dental equipment, syringes, and orthodontic tools that looked like torture devices from the medieval period buried under a veil of moist dirt that had the distinct smell of soil hidden for decades under an old house. It was like our own personal clubhouse with only a four-foot ceiling, a creepy cave dimly lit by the yellow-tinged light bulb at the entrance. Some days we felt like we were Indiana Jones and his crew from *Raiders of the Lost Ark,* complete with the threat of rattlesnakes and black widows that called the dank crawl space home.

On the northwest side of the house, lining the side of the creek, was our Bamboo "forest." I'm sure the second Mrs. Tucker planted it as a visual buffer to the old Tucker home sitting just on the other side of the canal. We spent hours hacking away at the giant stocks of bamboo to clear a trail just wide enough to be shoulder width. There is something exciting about cutting your own trail!

Both Tucker homes, although very different in design, shared an equally breathtaking view west towards the valley and coastal mountains, including the Sutter Buttes that sometimes peek out on foggy mornings in the valley like a tropical island floating on an ocean of clouds. My parents still live there today, and it is back to what we imagine Dr. Tucker and his assistant originally built, with the same craftsmanship and beautiful views watching the sun disappear over the coastal mountains.

I experienced visual beauty in my daily life and had a mother who taught me to see through the lens of life creatively. At the same time, Dad was showing me an example of a real man, challenging what it meant to be a sensitive, intelligent, athletic man's man and father. I was afforded the luxury of waking up as a kid and walking outside to pee while I slowly woke to nature's harmony and possibility. Most days of my young life began with a new canvas and unlimited ways to imagine, interpret, and create the fantasy before me, or in my mind. I lived in an environment that allowed the time, security, and wonderment to ponder ideas, operating in tune with nature's rhythm. My parents understood the concept of organic development way before that word was popular.

Along with all the wonder, encouragement, and freedom, there was also a sense of respect for all things and a commitment to doing good, thoughtful work. My parents viewed life as a fleeting moment to live with passion, love, and adventure. I had parents and grandparents who lived with purpose and heart. I watched them get up early to take care of their children and prepare for their job, with the intent to suit up and show up to make a positive difference in the lives they touched. And when they came home after work, their attention and total purpose were my siblings and me. It sounds almost like a thing of the past when you look at the modern state of all things sacred. My overall takeaway is immense gratitude for the love and commitment my parents gave to me.

SCHOOL DAZE

I had nothing to compare my reality to until I left the ranch to start preschool—and boy did I have a hard time with the confinement of the classroom walls. My parents had not expected any backlash to their child-raising strategy of freedom of thought and expression. I felt like I was being sent to boarding school or internment camp in Siberia. It was the first time I wore clothes full-time and had to sit inside for hours. I was confused, frustrated, and wanted to get back to exploring the world I had known for the entirety of my young life; it looked nothing like this. I fucking hated it, and I had a very challenging emotional time dealing with the forced sentence that had been handed down to me. My parents had made zero mention of this type of life, and then all of a sudden, they expected me to shift out of the freedom of a commune child to become a pragmatic mainstream kid. What the fuck?!

I learned the extremes of human nature back in preschool. As my first solo social experience, I learned very quickly that it was all about king of the hill or the climbing gym...and girls. I would pull four girls around in a red wagon, making them laugh and then kissing them in the boys' bathroom. I loved the high of it all. There was a big industrial trash bin behind the school building. I got the idea to show off by swinging off the top of it and ended up pulling the steel box on top of me, which snapped my left femur. I was trapped under five hundred pounds of steel and about a hundred pounds of garbage! The little girls went screaming, like little girls do, in every direction. Finally, Mrs. Macketty and the overweight, sweaty, and kinda creepy janitor dude lifted the bin with the help of some random guy. After getting free, I had my pants pulled off in front of the entire class by my dad, who was there almost instantly because he worked one block up the street at the high school.

I realized quickly that this was a stunt that ended up bad but created shock and awe. I liked it. I was all in, no matter what the outcome. Facing the fire and going for it was where I was always going to go. That 220 volts at 18 months old probably started it, or maybe the time I jumped on the back of my dad's tailgate as he was heading back to work from lunch. He suddenly saw me hanging on to the tailgate and flopping like a pennant in the wind through the rearview mirror as he was flying out of the gravel driveway and down our dirt road. He slammed on the brakes and watched in horror as I flew with a full flip to land on my stomach on the bed of the truck. He told me that he jumped out of the truck, thinking he killed his firstborn, only to find me on all fours making a revving engine sound and saying, "Vroom, Vroom Daddy! Do it again!" I wasn't two years old yet, but this feat just fed the adrenaline rush and attention that made me feel alive.

I basically had a three-phase childhood. The first phase was magic, the second was challenging, but the ending was pretty cool. Nonetheless, to this day, I'm still struggling to get back to the life I lived as a very young boy. I simply want to live in nature and create music and art barefoot and half naked. Nothing different from my most crucial developmental years. I spent a good portion of my adult life denying and flying directly away from that life, to achieve the publicly expected milestones set in front of me that collided ideologically to the free, easy living adventure that shaped me. Graduating from college and venturing out into the business world was like going to preschool all over again. Feeling the need to prove to the idiotic robots that I could do what they preached…and do it BETTER than even they ever had. To be placed into a different environment for long, excruciating periods of time is like a brutal brainwashing, a dumbing down of all the senses I was given by the environment I was developed in before being sent to linear land.

KINDERGARTEN KISS

I was in my first week at my new school and second kindergarten class. My first teacher, Miss Claiborne, blew her brains out after hitting rock bottom as a gold-digging coke bitch the week before school started. I remember thinking, *I don't blame her…I fucking hate school too!* As I got older, I knew what kind of chick Miss Claiborne was because I grew up with girls like her, who are now teaching kids in my hometown. They are the exact fake plastic shell of a once kind-of-pretty but very insecure girl from a small town. The kind who move one whole hour away to the "big city" of Sacramento to leave behind the simple country town and all she hated about herself. As my buddy Matt Brandt says, "Wherever you go, there you are."

After that strange false start to kindergarten, my parents moved me to a new school just across the street from where I was imprisoned at preschool. I didn't know many kids there and just wanted to go back home and play outside. My new teacher and principal were super cool, warm, and encouraging. They called me out if I needed it, too. They were friends with my dad, who was still working one block away at the high school as a psychology teacher and guidance counselor. Although I was at a new school, I was surrounded by people who were kind and encouraging to me, thanks to my dad's reputation and personal friendships.

I was shy and quietly eating my Friday pizza lunch when Michael Christensen landed next to me in the cafeteria. Mike was this hyperactive kid who played drums and listened to all the cool music. He had a drum set in his bedroom that looked like it had just come off the stage of an AC/DC concert. Mike was like a brother since our dads worked together at the high school; his dad was the music teacher who gave me my first drum. He had a hot older sister in the fourth grade named Chris Anne Christensen that all the boys were secretly in love with.

"Hey Chris! Did you eat the tater tots? Did you eat the salad? I love strawberries. (Humming something.) Kinnygarden sucks. Hey, have you heard of KISS?"

Firing questions and thoughts at me with his machine gun mind, I didn't even know what to respond to "…huh?" I muttered with a look of *What the fuck are you talking about?* but trying to be nice and follow his nonsensical chatter.

Without hearing me, he continued his barrage. "This is where it's at." He quieted to a whisper. "I heard he cut his tongue to make it longer. I also heard that he drinks his own blood. I swear on my drum set!" Mike whips out a cassette from his backpack and hands it to me like it's a bag of drugs.

Mike got serious, as if he were about to give me the secret of the Machiavellian world order. "Listen to it and join the devil's family. Haha. Just fucking with you! But seriously, KISS stands for Knights in Satan's Service. Listen to this tonight and bring it back tomorrow. It will change your life forever. You'll see skulls when you dream… Nah… Just fucking with you… Ha!… Detroit Rock City…Detroit Rock City. That song is forever. Listen to it with a black light. Scary man! Mother Mary is bleeding and cats are screaming. Nah. Just fucking with ya! Ha!"

My first week of kinnygarden was off to a trippy fucking start!

I still picture myself at home, placing the KISS cassette into the tape recorder that my dad borrowed from his friend, the high school librarian Bill McCutchen. As the electric guitars, bass, drums, and singing creatures reached through the four-by-four-inch speaker, I was transported to a new world. Like a heroin junkie shooting up for the first time, I was hooked. As the songs played, I was in a fantasy world. I unfolded the cassette cover to discover the photography and stories that brought the band of aliens from another planet to life. I was completely mesmerized and lost in a fantasyland of rock & roll. I never wanted to leave. Mike was right; my life changed that day. I knew somehow that music would be my future.

I give my dad a ton of credit for being a strong enough man to allow his firstborn son to talk about guys wearing makeup and playing rock & roll and how I wanted to be like them. He sincerely could sense how serious this was to me. He handled it with elevated understanding and gave me his blessing to explore strange music and worlds that he was not familiar with or necessarily personally interested in. He wanted to support what I was passionate about, even at that early age. That's why I'm writing this book today. My dad told me I could...a long time ago.

I don't remember much more about kindergarten except for a Christmas play where I was Joseph or Jesus, can't remember to save my ass. I do remember Mom trying to apply a beard of my own hair from an earlier hair cut at the house. As you can predict, the hair didn't come off because of the type of glue we used. The only other memory is our stupid fucking "graduation." What is the point? Honestly! I remember being told that we were all equal and successful as we showed the class our thesis on the subject we chose. Basically, we had to pick an animal or something to "study." I remember standing in line towards the back next to Sara Richards. We were the same size; well, she was definitely more muscular and better built than me at that age. She asked me what I was sharing for my animal.

"Great white sharks," I quietly replied.

HOT BLOODED

My dad worked with a Spanish school nurse named Louise Spittle. She would invite us up to swim at her place during the summertime when we were kids. She was always very nice to us and was excited to have our company when we came up. Now that I think about it, her husband was out there, and she was probably happy to have some normalcy.

Dad would take us up to the Spittles' house for a swim after we watched *Dukes of Hazzard* and *Fall Guy*, had breakfast and got some work done with him around the house; either pulling domestic duty and cleaning bathrooms or the kitchen while Mom worked at the hospital, or working outside building something or pulling star thistle from the horse pasture. By our early years, we understood that leisure was a reward, not a right. Nonetheless, my dad allowed us to enjoy much of our days off to relax and just be kids. He knew how fleeting and special that time was. He was cool that way. He blended nurturing and leisure time with teaching us to help around the house.

"Barry! Boys! Come on in!"

The Spittles' place was a classic adobe brick Spanish-styled house that had a pool perched in the back with a western view of the valley and coastal mountain range. The summer smells of gardenia flowers, dry grass, and pool chlo-

41

rine filled the air. Louise took the opportunity to give Dad a friendly hug, then she guided us through the house towards our destination. Big French doors opened onto the beautiful deck, glowing from the afternoon sun glistening on the pool and the landscape surrounding it. Elton John's "Philadelphia Freedom" played on the patio stereo, and windchimes floated with soft summer sounds in the background. Louise sauntered around the pool edge by my dad with her white swim wrap loosely hanging off her intense brown skin. My younger brothers and I just looked for the cue to jump in the pool.

When you grow up without a swimming pool, the opportunity to go to someone's house to swim is a special treat. The anticipation and fun of the upper-class swimming experience only comes around once in a while. Don't get me wrong, I loved growing up swimming in nature's lakes, rivers, and oceans, but a jump into a beautifully toxic chlorine pool represented wealth in my mind, even at a young age. That made swimming pools, and the people who had them, embody a status and success that seemed like something I wanted. For the time being, though, I was excited to enjoy someone else's swimming pool.

When we had to pee, we would find our way through the house to the restroom. One time I walked out, and I could hear loud music coming from down the hall. It was so loud that the family pictures were rattling against the wall like they were dancing to another big California earthquake. The physical vibrations put me in a curious trance, and I began walking towards the origin of the pounding and screeching sounds. I inched towards the doorway, and I felt my heart pound. I was shy, and fear told me to stop walking, but I couldn't. I was hypnotized by the music, almost like aliens were abducting me. I peeked my head into the room to see what was creating the eruption of sound. I saw the Spittle boys practicing their rendition of Van Halen's "Fire." It was 1978, and Van Halen's debut album had exploded onto the LA and national airwaves, changing the entire landscape of rock and pop culture. They stopped and stared at me standing in the doorway.

Mike Spittle, the younger brother behind the drums, saw me staring at all of the musical instruments around the room, "Hey, dude! Do you want to play the drums?"

I don't think he could hear my response, but he could see me smile and nod my head. He patiently set me up behind his drum kit and began teaching me the basics like he'd been teaching it for years, "So, you hit the stick to this top hat and step on the kick drum and hit the snare. That's basically it. Try playing to this."

As his older brother Greg practiced Van Halen's "Eruption" quietly in the background, Mikey puts on a vinyl record of Foreigner's hit "Hot Blooded." The song starts, and I try to keep beat with the song as he guides my arms. It started out awkwardly, like trying to turn the crank to start the engine on our old plow tractor, but by the second chorus, I was figuring out the three moving parts of the snare, top hat, and kick and was picking it up pretty quickly. Once I got it, I didn't ever want to stop playing. I smiled at Mikey for the gift he had given me. He smiled back at me like a proud older brother.

Everyone liked the Spittles. Their look and temperaments reminded me of the Van Halen brothers when they were about the same age. They even shared a semi-exotic look with long black hair and the threads to match their rock idols. Mikey was a cross between Alex Van Halen and the Beach Boys drummer Dennis Wilson in terms of his kinetic energy, cool, friendly personality, and effortless great looks and natural skills to be good at anything he kinda felt like doing. Greg, the oldest, was born with a speech impediment and a slightly deformed right ear rendering him painfully shy and quiet but driven as a guitarist and student. His long hair covered his disfigurements and insecurities. He was a gentle creature with so much heart and talent.

I remember walking outside, looking beyond the pool to the west, still consumed with the music scene I had just experienced. Everything looked different.

I was out of my mind. "Dad, someday I'm gonna play rock music. I'm gonna play drums like Foreigner or KISS. Did you hear what Mikey and Greg were playing? It was amazing!"

My dad was genuinely happy for me. "That's great, Son!" And he meant it. That moment reinforced my truth: music was my universe.

I ran into Greg decades later, and he was the same kind guy I remember as a starry-eyed seven-year-old, except now he was a pharmacist at Walgreens giving me advice on itch cream! I had the opportunity to thank him for encouraging me that day. He smiled, trying to recall that specific day, but I saw him drift back to those summer days jamming with his brother without a care in the world and endless possibility. I hugged him and walked out of the store, smiling, remembering the day the Spittle boys changed my life.

DAD'S CITY LEAGUE BASKETBALL

G oing to my dad's city league basketball games on a school night was pure adrenaline and excitement. It was a streetball show, on and off the court. It felt natural for my brother and me to trail our dad into the auditorium and hang out with him and the other athletes. Many of them he once taught and now played city league basketball with and against. I was intrigued by the multi-cultural social scene, black and white, and I watched the athletes' every move. Dad always came prepared and dressed with style, starting with his Adidas sweatsuit, Converse All-Stars, and a basketball, looking like Rick Berry, the legendary Los Angeles Lakers point guard. The double doors to the gym would open to an explosion of lights, loud voices, and the chirps of sneakers cutting on the parquet floor. As a little kid, it felt like a rock concert or an NBA game.

It was always the same scene on game night. The two teams are warming up and doing layups. There is a mix of a few middle-aged white guys and a whole slew of younger black guys in their mid-twenties, some looking like they were just released from prison. The crowd is mostly black apart from the occasional middle-aged and middle-class white wife sitting there with a forced smile to conceal the fact that she is totally out of her element. A few old-timers are talking about how the kids don't have the same fundamentals as they used to. Most conversations are barely decipherable except for a few of the funny one-liners that can be heard above the crowd.

I remember the night my dad introduced me to Carl White, the town's basketball star destined for the pros. He was recruited to play at Cal, but quickly dropped out and did time in prison for selling drugs. Our town is known for producing great athletes that self-sabotage their destiny. But at the time, he was it. This large black man with an afro and goatee looked at me and started walking towards me, dribbling the basketball, an emotionless expression on his face.

"Hey, little Rockwell, you gonna be a player when you grow up?" Carl shook my hand lovingly, but still hood. I was excited and nervous. It was like I had just met a pro athlete. I responded with a shy smile.

After my brief interaction with Carl White, my brother and I walked across the court, navigating through guys doing layups and a referee laughing it up with one of the players from my dad's team. I felt cool. Standing on the other side of the gym playing with a ball was the even cooler Matt Brandt.

"What's up, Larry?"

Matt was a mischievous and cool young aspiring stoner James Dean with freckles. He was only a few months older than me, but the youngest of four boys. He developed a swagger and toughness early on, trying to keep up with his older brothers and their friends. Matt was the ringleader of our young crew. He was like our big brother, the leader of the pack. He would be tough at times, socking us in the chest or calling us out for being a "pussy," but he always looked out for us, coached us, and handed down any newfound knowledge on fighting, sex, hunting, girls, sports, sex…

"Hey…" I responded, trying to be cool, but noticeably trying too hard because I was nervous.

My younger brother joins in. "Hi Matt!" Nick says, excitedly.

Matt disregards our vain attempt at matching his level of cool and immediately leads us off to sneak around the stage to climb the rafters and find trouble. It was like a makeshift secret clubhouse, a stage with curtains that hung from the rafters 15 feet up on each side to manage the lighting and props for theater shows. To us, it was a hidden dark hang out. We climbed the permanent wooden ladder up to our perch. Matt pulls out a can of Copenhagen, takes a dip, and spits off the rafter. I always thought he looked cool taking a chew.

We would sit up on the wooden platform with a flimsy railing, our feet dangling off the edge, spitting to watch it fall and splat on the wooden stage floor below. We'd listen to Matt's tales, handed down by his older brothers, like old miners. He was an elementary schoolkid at a tougher school, and his brothers were high-school star athletes. He had stories that would blow our minds. Anecdotes of things that seemed to come from faraway lands compared to our protected Mayberry upbringing.

Matt broke the spit contest silence with, "I bet you don't know what French kissing is."

I confidently respond with, "Yea..." but blew my cover with "...well, I think so..."

Matt gave me the *You don't have a fucking clue!* look then said, "It's when a guy and girl stick their tongues in each other's mouths and twirl them around."

I still tried to pretend like I knew what it was but was enthralled by the concept. It seemed awesome and scary. The experiences Matt had at his elementary school were a little more street edgy than my school, kind of like Matt's family compared to mine.

My brother's eyes and mouth were wide open in shock. "Whoa..."

Realizing he had a captured audience, Matt contin-ued with momentum, "I saw Holly Driver French kiss Scott Spencer at the bus stop last week."

Dying to understand more, I naively asked, "How long do they do it?"

My brother, sitting quietly and in deep thought about this new and somewhat frightening information he had just acquired, whispered, "I bet for hours."

Like a frustrated big brother, he scolded us. "Nah…more like a minute or two."

Through the crack in the stage curtain, I could see Dad running down the court against a noticeably better and pre-dominantly black team, even though half the guys are drunk or stoned. The crowd is getting loud, and spirits are good.

A young Reggie Parker is yelling out to someone on the court, "Man, Cedrick, you need to quit shooting! You make yo whole team look sorry!"

Everyone laughs as Cedrick runs down the court frown-ing at Reggie after bricking an easy shot.

Malika steps in to defend her cousin. "Reggie Parker, you need to quit eatin'! You fillin' out those sweats like the Michelin Man!" Everyone laughs, and the volume increases.

At this point, the game and the crowd are in full effect and the place is humming.

Reggie fires back, "I know you shame girl…you need to keep it down with yo loud self. Whatchu talkin' bout with those bottle-cap popping teeth!"

Defending her friend, Tamisha stands up among the nine black girls crowded together on a row of rollout bleach-ers. "Reggie Parker, you sorry ass nigga!"

There are a couple of nervous white middle-aged players' wives sitting next to the group of black girls. They're feigning amusement with the banter but would rather be home in bed with their doors locked.

The back and forth heckling continues until the final buzzer. We climb down from our adventure in the rafters and meet our dads on the sidelines as they high-five and shake hands with players from both teams. The aroma of sweat and competition is thick, but the atmosphere is rich with camaraderie and friendship. Every time we entered that world, I got a deeper understanding of people and of men.

3

TEEN SPIRIT

Teen Spirit

FACE-TO-FACE WITH
A MOUNTAIN LION

T he dry sagebrush-covered Eastern Sierra Mountains is more than just a place we journey to every year to deer hunt; we're called there. It is a grand cathedral of wild and rugged millennia, cradling and rejuvenating our souls. Like deer that migrate up the mountain for summer to cool down, stock up on food, and reproduce, we return here every year to our inner sanctum, to a far ago time that feels more natural than our modern daily life experience.

Sonny Brandt was my dad's close friend and small-town star athlete, homecoming king, and outdoorsman. He was a cross between Davey Crockett and Mickey Mantle. Sonny was built of wild and free pioneering blood. My dad identified his kindred spirit in Sonny, and they became friends years after high school through city league basketball. They gave each other the validation that men need. It made them better. Sonny and the Mastelotto brothers ran together in high school and came together for hunting, fishing, and diving trips. They all grew up working on old man Mose's ranch working cattle, growing and harvesting grapes for wine, and tending to all the chores of a full running ranch. The boys grew up working hard in the hot summer sun, playing sports, and sneaking off to drink wine and moonshine behind the watering pond. They had rifles, shot everything in sight, and killed deer and bear year-round for food.

Sonny was the social king of the group with his all-American blue-eyed good looks and athleticism. He had the social skills that won him the heart of the head cheerleader, Jackie Miller, daughter of Ol' Red Miller, the whiskey-drinking Irish fireplug that made his money in gold, heavy equipment, and real estate. He was known for his philandering and fiery temper. These were the real characters I grew up around. They were real men, and they didn't fuck around when it came to life...or money; it was hard to come by.

My dad first invited Sonny to join our family on a diving trip, then Sonny invited Dad for a bowhunting trip when I wasn't yet two, although my Oshkosh overalls were size four and hemmed up to my knees because I was a "filled out" boy. The adventure started one night in an old mining town in the Sierra Nevada Mountains. We pulled up just as Sonny came staggering out of the Cutthroat Saloon into the middle of the street in downtown Markleeville fighting some bikers. He had just knocked a guy down, and he turned to greet Dad and Mom with a bloody smile and a torn shirt, the lights shining on him like the winner of a championship boxing match.

We camped at the top of Monitor Pass, a summit of over 8,000 feet above sea level, connecting California to Nevada. There wasn't another human near us, creating the feeling that we were settlers crossing the continent to discover a better and more exciting life, the California Spirit. The view to the west embraces endless possibilities of purples and greens and the ocean but turn to the east, and it's a vast Nevada desert of stripped naked mountains bearing chalk-white scars from millions of years of extreme heat and erosion. At one point, not long ago, a massive lake called Lahontan spanned much of Northern Nevada and as far east as Utah. Supposedly it was home to dinosaur fish the size of blue whales that would make a great white shark piss itself.

As a younger man, my dad killed some big bucks with a rifle and walked away feeling sick about the unfair advantage. Once he discovered bowhunting, he was reunited with an ancient art that pits man and beast on fair ground, requiring extensive hiking, patience, persistence, and deadly accuracy under high anxiety caused by an adrenaline surge called buck fever. Growing up roaming the mountains alone as a young boy, bowhunting fit my dad's philosophy towards nature and all living creatures handed down by his parents. He is an intelligent, searching modern man, and hunting was not a simple decision for him. Maybe his internal struggle with hunting and killing stems back to his social class experience growing up poor and seeing the unfair advantages the spoiled good ol' boys got through money and small-town family connections.

The hunt is so much more than the kill. The love is in the search, the chase, the discovery; it's about the adventure in pursuit of the trophy and the stories we share with friends and family for the rest of our lives. As a kid, I felt like I was a cowboy back in the Wild West days, hiking around the hills with my bow and arrow, trying to emulate my dad and the Brandts. Blue-Collar All-American guys with a passion for sports and the outdoors. Bowhunting challenged us and gave us a connection to nature that was revitalizing to our wild spirit.

Before I even had a license, I got to drive the hunters around the dirt back roads as they stood in the truck bed, peering out over the cab and scanning for signs of game. On less fruitful days, we would just spook up dust and sage hen. Dad taught my brothers and me to drive on dirt roads during hunting and wood cutting trips by the age of ten. Dad was smart and believed in teaching us by giving us real tasks; he knew how to guide us until we figured out the concept. He was patient beyond belief and gave us encouraging instruction and gentle constructive criticism to build our confidence. He did this with everything—driving, hunting, ocean diving, sports, working with equipment, and building stuff. My dad lived on go all the time, with his clean living and hunger for adventures that challenged his physical and mental capabilities and showed him nature's wondrous beauty and magnitude. He passed this on to his boys and gave us the tools and confidence to become men.

It became a tradition to hunt in the mornings and then rest and head for a soak in the Grover Hot Springs down in Markleeville or spend the afternoon fishing or swimming in the Carson River. Heading back up the hill to camp always brought anticipation of an evening hunt. There's a fire lookout station perched on top of the highest peak of rocks that rise above camp to the southwest. You can drive up to the top using the rough switchback road primitively carved out of the mountain. It was customary for the men to hit the lookout just before turning in to camp to chase deer and watch the hot August sunset fade beyond the mountain range to the west. It's an intense, lonely, exciting, ancient view.

I was always fascinated with the lookout station. It was like an ominous and mysterious fort on top of the world. I would imagine camping out in there during a lightning storm with my brothers and the Brandt boys. Lookout Mountain, in actuality, is an 8,000-foot mound of old volcanic rocks perched high above the surrounding peaks and spotted with the shades of green and blue lichen, a type of simple plant that grows on and out of the cracks and indents caused from the erosion of extreme weather swings of hot and freezing throughout millions of years. I can still feel the wind sandblasting our faces with tiny rocks.

One evening, Dad and I decided to hunt on the drive back up. Mom and my younger brothers and sister passed us in the VW bus headed to camp to get dinner started. I remember my brothers making goofy faces at me as they went by us. I smiled and started to giggle but caught myself and straightened up, trying to be a tough hunter. In reality, I was still just a boy full of innocent dreams and silly fun; I certainly wasn't wired to kill yet. Dad slowed down as we reached the

Monitor Pass granite monument on the south side of the road nestled in between Aspen quakies lining the sparse mountaintop. There's something about this area; spirits whisper through the flickering light green and white aspen leaves. I noticed Dad peering up at the lookout as we drove towards it, carefully navigating the steep switchbacks leading to an 8,000-foot drop-off into the scorched white Nevada desert below.

"Do you want to drive up to the lookout? We spooked a few bucks this way a couple days ago."

I smiled at that, and we shifted gears out of the relaxed hot springs mindset and into serious, focused adrenalin-sparked hunting mode. Dad stopped the truck as he pulled onto the lookout road. He jumped out so I could drive and he could stand in the back to scan for bucks, giving him a better opportunity to exit and shoot more quickly. I loved driving my dad's truck for the hunt. I was just a kid, but as always, he had total faith in my abilities. By this time, I had driven for a few solid years on the hunting roads. I had learned to drive with finesse, so I didn't jar the hunters or spook deer unnecessarily. Few roads were smooth and free from the billions of volcanic rocks just below the topsoil.

I gently dropped the truck into drive and slowly crept forward up the steep, rocky switchback. I was excited and anxious with anticipation, and a little nervous, wanting to do a good job of driving for my dad. We drove up the first stretch, and just as we were approaching the switchback, my dad tapped on the roof, our sign that he had spotted a buck. I gently let off the gas and applied the brake with a feather touch until it stopped. Dad was out of the truck with a quiet stealth that eluded both myself and the giant buck standing about 65 yards up the hill and in front of the grove of buckbrush dotting the horizon; he was big, and his rack was symmetrical, a legit four-point Mulie known to live in the Eastern Sierra. I felt adrenaline surge through me as the buck looked back at us with surprise but held a bold stance to let us know this was his territory.

At that instant, an arrow pierced his chest, and the beast jumped, kicked his back legs out, and took off into the dense and thorny buckbrush. I sprung out of the truck to celebrate my dad's amazing shot, nearly forgetting to put the truck in park. Dad was totally focused on retrieving this magnificent animal. We ran up to the spot where he shot the buck and immediately spotted a blood trail and the arrow that had gone clean through his body. The question was, did the broadhead slice a vital organ or just glide through without causing fatal injuries? Sometimes you can tell by the color of the blood and the amount. But this time, the blood trail didn't give my dad a confident answer.

The sun was setting and snuffing out the evening light. We stood there as the wind gusted past us. My dad was lost in thought, wondering what the buck's evening was going to look like. He took great care and responsibility when he shot a deer. If it weren't a kill shot, he would dedicate days hiking the most inhospitable mountains to search for them. And before you animal rights activists get all ruffled, there is no waste either way. A deer's natural death options are oftentimes less than humane. They may die a slow and painful death of disease, or have their throat ripped open by a mountain lion, or break a leg and starve to death.

My dad tries to retrieve the buck out of respect for the animal. That's the kind of outdoorsman and man my dad is. I saw some of my friends and their dads act redneck stupid about hunting and killing animals. These idiots took a false arrogant pride from killing either a great trophy or a truckload of ducks. That destructive and wasteful attitude was something my dad hated; he believed everything had an equal right to life. "Well," he said half-jokingly, "except great white sharks, rattlesnakes, and black widows."

He wondered if he would get to it in the morning before the coyotes or bear or mountain lions ate it. It was a race against time and light. He was going to have a long sleepless night ahead of him. When we got back to camp, dad was cautious and reserved in telling Mom and the guys he shot a buck because he knew the hunt wasn't over. So, we quietly ate dinner and turned in. It got cold on the summit at night, and we slept outside under the stars. I loved it.

My dad woke me up with a firm shake and a whisper. The cold, dark cobalt sky was glowing from the flickers of morning light not quite visible.

"Chris, Chris!... Wake up! I shot a fucking mountain lion!"

I jumped out of my old Army sleeping bag and threw my clothes on as fast as I could, locked onto dad's eyes to get more of the story in the frigid silence. I could see that he was serious and focused. I knew this was going to be a wild adventure. We slipped out of camp just as light was thawing the icy dark. It took us about 15 minutes to drive back to the spot where he shot the buck the night before. He gave me the summary of what had happened as we drove over, explaining that he got up early and was looking for the buck when he unknowingly walked directly into the path of a mountain lion, her cubs, and a fresh kill. The mountain lion was in pounce position behind a log that exposed only her head and massive paws with razor-sharp claws. He knew he was in trouble and had to think through his options real quick before the lion decided to strike first. If you interfere with a predator and her babies after they just killed their meal, you aren't dealing with a soft cuddly innocent cartoon animal; they are killing machines.

My dad told me how he drew his bow back and shot the mountain lion's head, the only target he had. The arrow struck with a loud cracking pop, like his old Winchester 30/30 lever action rifle, piercing the lion through her right eye. It stuck halfway out of her eye and halfway out of the back of her skull. Instead of dropping dead from the arrow lodging through the center of her brain, the lion flipped around in the air and took off through the sagebrush like a screaming banshee, trying to free herself from the arrow. As it ran through the sagebrush, it sounded like a bicycle flying down the street with a card machine gun snapping in the back spoke.

When Dad and I showed up with Sonny and Matt, we began our search in the eerie quiet of dawn. We immediately began searching for a blood trail. This was now the top priority over finding the buck from the night before. Shooting a lion was illegal, and even though my dad was defending his life, California Fish and Game would've had his ass nailed to a post. Sonny brought along a holstered 357 Magnum pistol in case the lion was alive and still looking to put up a fight. We started combing the side of that hill, looking for any signs that could lead us in the right direction. I searched the ground with the intensity of a bounty hunter. With all the excitement and anticipation, I nearly stepped on a small pool of blood. I wasn't sure if it was from the deer or the lion, but I immediately yelled out to Dad and Sonny, "I found blood!"

They ran over to me with anticipation that you could see. It was as if, just for a split moment, I was the adult and the two men were reduced to children, helplessly searching for something they lost. Before they could reach me, something took over me, and I followed the blood trail that ended at a giant cedar tree about 15 feet away. I had to discover the story at the end of the blood trail. I approached the tree and got on my knees and crawled through the low-hanging branches that touched the ground and formed an impenetrable barrier to light. I didn't have time to be scared. It didn't matter, because I was young and immortal. I wanted to prove myself to the men I respected. Boys and men have died for that since the beginning of time. I thought of the glory I would receive from discovering the animal for the elder hunters. That's all I could think about.

As I crawled into the branches on my hands and knees and peeked through, I came face-to-face with the panting lion. The broken arrow was sticking out of her eye, and dried blood painted her face like the warrior she was. The moment seemed like a living still-shot image from the *National Geographic* magazines we had on the coffee table back home. It was a once-in-a-lifetime moment in the wild that seemed like a dream. The lion looked right at me. She panted and seemed almost calm; it was like she was telling me something. Then, as fast as I could absorb what I was experiencing, she darted out from under the tree and we never saw her again, yet she has forever lived on in me. I was twelve, but I felt like a man.

Years later, while I was hunting at the lookout with my dad and brothers, I found the skeleton of a mountain lion, its skull and spine fully intact. I took the skull home, knowing from the scar on the right eye socket that this was the majestic creature I had experienced a moment with. Two creatures, one living and one dying. I have always held her in the greatest respect, as does my dad. The moment under that tree with the lion was something that added to my sense of adventure and the circle of life, death, and love. Truth.

THE CATWALK

We were your classic tanned thirteen-year-old boys riding our BMX bikes down an old country blacktop road that cuts a path through a golden field on a hot July morning. Shirtless and wearing cut-off Levi's with boxers hanging out and old Converse All Stars with no socks. A faded Copenhagen can outline on the rear pocket marks the coming of age as a boy in our small Northern California foothill lumber town. My idols and Matt's older brothers, the Brandts, had this look down. Hell, they might have invented the look, as cool as they were. Long '70s hair; trim, scrappy, and athletic. They could party and fight their asses off and weren't afraid of shit. Matt and I did anything his older brothers would tell us to do in order to earn a moment of respect, even if that meant jumping off a forty-foot train bridge into icy black water.

The path we took was dotted with nostalgic houses and barns on the outskirts of town. We made our way to the far side of the bridge by walking side by side down the tracks, talking and laughing to ease our fears. I felt like we were on a mission like soldiers, focused on the fact that we were about to jump into the unknown.

The Brandt boys were like a timeless pioneering family who came out West 150 years ago for gold and a life of adventure. They were competitive, fearless athletes and men who loved hunting and fishing in the great outdoors. I idolized these guys and would always step my game up when I ran with them. They were constantly challenging each other to the next daring test of manhood. It usually meant fighting or jumping off something really fucking high.

"Jump Meat!" were the first words out of Russ's mouth, directed at his little brother, Matt. Matt looked over at his big brother with a cocky smirk, spit, and dove off the forty-foot-high train bridge we called the Catwalk. He obeyed his big brother as if he were taking indisputable orders from General Patton. I remember gasping and being in awe of his fearlessness as he disappeared beneath the surface. A few seconds later, he appeared from the river, his victorious plunge having pumped him up, and he made his way back to me and the other guys who were contemplating jumping, or maybe just running. Matt grabbed his can of Copenhagen and put in a dip.

We also looked up to and followed the lead of his big brother, Nick, who was soon to be drafted by the Atlanta Braves as a left-handed pitcher with speed and junk. Matt looked out at the water below and spat off the bridge again, almost in defiance of the fear he just triumphed over and broke the silence with, "I heard that some kid dove right into a chunk of concrete and rebar."

I peered down into the cold black water and looked back at Matt in horror.

"Shut up, Matt! That's a story some fucking drunk hobo made up", Nick wearily muttered, as if he has said it a thousand times to his little brother over the course of their lifetime.

"It's true! Clutch told me," explained Matt. The older boys laughed, and I laughed with them, hoping they were right. Meanwhile, I was clinging to the outside of the railing—terrified, stiff, and transfixed to the water below. Matt was getting impatient and yelled, "Jump, biscuit, before the sun sets." I jumped. My guts left my body in midair, and the world went into slow motion. I hit the water and felt alive, more alive than ever. I came up, shocked by the icy water yet euphoric from the jump. It was like a classic Mountain Dew commercial from back in the day; young people doing crazy stunts in the outdoors and enjoying the exhilaration of being wild and free.

SOCIAL DIVIDE AT THE LAKE

I grew up swimming on the lakeshore with my brothers and friends, just hanging out, fishing, and goofing off like kids do. It was from our vantage point that we would see people wakeboarding on their big fancy boats, celebrating their silver spoon "success" with loud music, laughter, and the total disregard for people not in their little clique. Us kids swimming and fishing on the shore were usually the target of their arrogance. It represented a common socioeconomic divisive power. These idiots would drive their dads' boats as close to shore as possible, with the full intent to show off and show us what we didn't have. It would leave a bad taste and a lower self-identity in my mind as the rolling waves from the boat wake would muddy our little beach, and my confidence, as they roared away in laughter. I remember feeling as worthless as the driftwood slamming up against the rocks as the boat got close enough to shore so I could make eye contact with the spoiled kids I went to school with. I didn't even like most of them. They were arrogant, based on the pseudo success of their parents. It was the opposite of how I grew up, including the manners they lacked and the general unawareness or consideration of others.

Even though I knew I should be bigger than my petty feelings (and they were painfully real), it burned me to feel less than them when I didn't even hold them in high regard.

I would be enjoying a perfect summer day swimming off the rocks and boundary logs of the Oroville Dam, and I would get mad at myself for feeling less than them. I hated it. I wanted what they had, mainly because I was conditioned by social and competitive pressure to think it was success. In my mind, I was a failure because we didn't have a pool, boat, or new car, even though I had more love, encouragement, and intellectual curiosity than any of those kids. My young and competitively trained outlook made me face the reality that money separated not just how we had fun, but how we lived and thought.

Well, there was this girl on a boat one day. She was beautiful and full of life, and she didn't act like the rest of them. She was the cutest girl out of all of them by far, and although I didn't know what it was at the time, she carried herself with real self-confidence and a rare awareness. She was not typical. I remember the way she waved to us on the shore. The others would act like they didn't see us, or at best, looked down at us. But not this girl. I heard her reprimand the driver for getting too close to our swimming spot. The driver immediately changed course. Who was this girl?! They dropped the throttle and disappeared out of sight as they headed up the middle fork of the lake for what I imagined would be a long day of fun. With the boat speeding away and her blonde hair dancing on the wind and sunlight, I wondered if I would ever see her again. She waved as our eyes connected. I ended up marrying that girl, but at that moment, I just stood there embarrassed, standing up to my waist in the water as the muddy waves repetitively punched me in the stomach to remind me of where and who I wasn't.

I don't think I directly correlated money to happiness. I knew it wasn't that clean-cut, even back then. My parents lived against the grain when it came to material wealth, religion, health, and parenting. I refer to them as pragmatic hippies because they were hard workers and educated, but they railed against the modern materialistic concepts of success and happiness. Nonetheless, money and worldly success was something I wanted to have, simply so I didn't feel like I was on the outside. Deep down, I honestly just wanted to explore and learn and build and not worry about money and social competition. It was draining.

Feeling different made me dig deeper into discovering and challenging myself and the status quo around me. I know a lot of those same ski-boat kids today, and I can say without question, that very few of them excelled at anything. Why? Because, like most people, they didn't grow, and they ended up thinking and acting in a way that showed they didn't appreciate what they were freely given. They end up doing whatever it took to get more of what they were given, without ever truly taking a moment to think about how, why, what...

JUNIOR HIGH AFTER-SCHOOL SPECIAL

The first week of junior high, I was hanging at Matt's house on a beautiful fall afternoon after school. I was so excited to be hanging with the older guys. They were all chewing and talking about chicks, fishing, and football. We made our way around the side of the house to the back entrance of the converted basement that was Matt's room. As we entered the room, I could hear Twisted Sister playing "We're Not Gonna Take It" as I focused on the creepy but cool Iron Maiden poster Matt had above his bed. He also had some Dodger nostalgia, a mounted fourteen-pound nine ounce German brown trout with a Budweiser lure hanging off the fish's lip, and an Olympia Beer neon sign with a lit-up mountain stream picture behind it, making it look like real running water. There was an old Coors can with the pull-off tab and some other antiques related to hunting, fishing, alcohol, tobacco, and RC Cola.

Junior high was my crash course in sex, drugs, and heavy metal. I teamed up with Matt, and I quickly started running with the eighth-grade stoners and athletes. It was one of the best times of my life. Matt and his friend, Donald Legg, were the epitome of cool to me. Everyone called Donald Blue Sky because he looked Native even though he wasn't. It was a name Matt came up with, and it stuck. Donald was the biggest stoner of all but by far the best student thanks to DNA from a Japanese mom and a scary-smart white Hells Angels biker dad. Mike Christensen was still hyper and beating up the drums. Johnny Huffstetler was the Danny Bonaduce of the crew. He was a feisty redhead with an Irish fighter's temper. Next thing I know, the guys are into a game of knee football, and Blue Sky runs over Mike with a crushing blow. Johnny dealt the verbal assault.

"Ohhhh!!! Christensen, you just got ran the fuck over!!"

Trying to play off getting slammed to the concrete foundation below the veil of shag carpet in the basement that was Matt's lair, he said, "It didn't even hurt. Fuck it! Let's do it again!"

Most of us suffered multiple concussions before we ever strapped on a football helmet. I grew up with tough kids. Broken bones, stitches, and contusions were proud scars of our passage into manhood.

"Mike, you long-haired albino bitch!" Johnny chided.

Everyone laughed.

Mike tried to fight back. "Look at you! Raggedy Ann fucker!"

"Hahahaha. Huff, you do look like a Raggedy Ann...." Blue Sky said in his classic stoner dialect.

"Fuck both of you!" Johnny fired back. "Mike, I'll kick your ass!"

Johnny kept his scrap with Mike, respecting Donald's size, smarts, and cool. Donald had long black hair, sold pot, and drove a Nova when he turned sixteen. He always looked out for me because he was Matt's best friend.

Matt changed the tone of the room, constantly looking for that little something to get somewhere else.

"Hey Blue," he whispered, "you got the joint?"

Coyly and coolly, "Ohhh, thiss?"

Smiling as he presents the joint to the room and lights it up, Blue Sky takes a hit and passes it to Matt. Matt passes the joint to me. Everything slowed down as I inhaled and blew out the smoke. The scene from my seat within minutes was a trip to the next dimension of my life. I was listening to Twisted Sister and Motley Crue, tripping on the posters of Iron Maiden's creepy fucking mascot Eddie, and feeling the freedom of the buzz settling in.

Johnny piped in, changing the focus of the conversation. "Hey Matt, are you going to Renee's party tonight?"

"No. I'm grounded for another week for getting caught drinking in Mr. Glasscock's class."

Mike jumped in like the ADD spastic cartoon character Tigger from *Winnie the Pooh*. "I'm going! That's supposed to be the best party of the year! Renee's mom is totally cool! I heard she bought a keg! I'm gonna try to finger bang Sandy Cook!"

Blue Sky raises the obvious question. "Oscar?! You know why they call her Oscar, right?" Mike stared blankly back at him. "Jesus, Mike! She's called Oscar because she tried fucking herself with an Oscar Meyer hot dog and ended up at the emergency room to have it removed!"

Everyone laughed while Mike looked angry and confused as to why that was an issue.

"Hey Blue, are you going?" Johnny asks.

"Yeah. My sister Diane is giving me a ride. How about you, Rockwell? Stoned? Haha..."

I could hear Blue Sky talking to me, but I was still in deep thought about the Iron Maiden "Trooper" poster of Eddie charging the bloody battlefields with a bayoneted rifle brandishing the remains of the British flag. I tried to gather my thoughts, so I didn't give the guys the impression that this was my first time.

"Ummm...yeah. I think... I gotta check...with...my..."

Matt turned into a big brother and gave some instructions. "Hey Blue, keep an eye on Rock tonight."

"No problem," Blue assured Matt. "He's in safe hands."

FIRST JUNIOR HIGH PARTY

Mom pulls up right in front of Renee's house to drop me off in our Volkswagen van. The party is in full gear, and there are people out front smoking and drinking. The lawn is already a battlefield of sin littered with beer cans, cigarette butts, whiskey bottles, and a passed-out chick named Wendy, a pure Mormon girl from my English class. My mom surveys the situation like a seasoned veteran of Los Angeles house parties during the age of the Doors and the Beach Boys back in the '60s. Even with that history, my mom looked concerned.

She handed me a pack of condoms and gave me her sex talk as she was dropping me off at my first real junior high party. "Chris, remember: Use a condom if you choose to have sex."

I was so embarrassed. "Mom! Bye!"

She is yelling out of the passenger window as I'm about five steps away. "Call me when you're ready, and I'll pick you up. Be safe and have fun!"

There are kids, some high school-aged, standing around taking the opportunity to give me shit as I walk towards the front door of the poorly kept-up house. The porch light casing was missing, and its yellow light beamed through the foggy night like a lighthouse guiding me to her jagged rocks of debauchery. I was bright-eyed but trying to adapt to the cool mannerisms of the characters around me.

Right then, Blue Sky came out the front door, taking the last few drags from a Marlboro Red, and saw me walking up like a deer in the headlights. "I see Mr. Rockwell could make it. Very good. Shall we venture into the party?" Donald spoke in a laid-back stoner dialect but would joke around sounding like a sophisticated American blue blood. He was very smart and aware, and he downplayed how much he learned and contemplated. With that, Blue tossed his cigarette butt into the Folgers can ashtray on the front porch, half full of butts and a crushed Budweiser can. We made our way through the dark entrance. There were beer bottles littered on the tables and floor. A young couple was making out in the corner. We continued into the living room where the music was playing; people were coupled everywhere, drinking and making out.

The song playing on the stereo was Motley Crue's "Shout at the Devil." I had never heard it before, and it set the tone of a darkly lit rock concert, with the smell of teenage perfume, beer, cigarettes, and the anticipation that something amazing was about to happen. I remember the feeling like it was yesterday. I was surrounded by things I had never seen before. The kitchen was a classic disaster of alcohol and trash everywhere; the front living room of the broken down two-bedroom house was littered with bodies twisted together like a mass grave of sex-crazy teens locked together in eternity. A girl stormed out of the bathroom with mascara running down her eyes and her friend chasing after her because she kissed her boyfriend.

"Wait! Sarah! It's not what you think!"

Jennifer pleaded with Sarah as she grabbed her former friend's arm to stop her in the middle of the room.

Sarah was distraught, like a typical 13-year-old girl who just caught her boyfriend making out with her best friend. "Let go of me, you fucking slut!! How could you kiss my boyfriend!! You're a dirty whore!!"

Jennifer turned from pleading to denigrating in one blink of an eye. "Well, you're a conceded bitch! And Scott thinks so too!"

Sarah punched Jennifer, and a catfight erupted for a flash. Scott walked out of the back room with a dumbshit look of *I fucked up* on his face, "Sarah! Wait!"

They ran past me standing in the doorway to the kitchen. I turned to go back into the living room and ran into Candy Black, a seventh-grade cutie that lived in a foster home and ran with the faster stoner girls. She had long feathered black hair, wore a black leather jacket, and carried a big pink comb in the back pocket of her super tight jeans. Candy had a sexy raspy voice that crackled softly when she talked. She was petite and beautiful and had these killer blue eyes and a shy mystery to go with them.

"Hey, Chris. What's up?" Candy said with a soft laugh, acknowledging the drama of a drunk cheating junior high couple breakup.

With the grace of a rookie, I managed to spit out the question about as bad as "How's the weather?"

"Hey... What are you doing here?" I asked.

At that moment, Blue Sky unknowingly but brilliantly interrupted my smooth talk. "Hey Rockwell, I have to go handle some business. I'll be back."

Blue Sky was approached by a few guys looking to buy some weed and obliged by reaching into the front pouch of his black and blue windbreaker to pull out the joints and deposit his cash.

Candy smiled casually. "Nothing...just hanging out with Amy Brighton. I'm staying with her tonight."

"Oh, cool. I'm here with Donald."

"Blue Sky? Cool."

I thought the gypsy life she led was mysterious and intriguing. I had no idea what it was like living out of a fucking backpack as a kid. I did at forty, but not when I was just starting to figure out life. I think we gained strength from

75

both worlds we came from. Candy was good at downplaying her situation, but she was always living with someone or back at her group home with all the other girls who walked through their days feeling rejected by their parents and society.

Candy continued. "I heard Darcy Hill is your girlfriend."

Acting embarrassed but somewhat proud, knowing the hot popular eighth-grader gave me some respect with girls like Candy, even though I was still shy about the whole physical thing at that point.

"Who told you that? I don't have a girlfriend. I heard you were going out with Darren Weinhard."

"He's cute but too much of a fighter. Not my type."

"Who's your type?" I lightly pressed.

Suddenly, Darren Weinhard walked up to me and got in my face to intimidate me. This guy haunted me from the first day I showed up to pop warner football a month earlier. I had just hit him in a practice scrimmage, and his pride was still reeling from it. The fact that I was talking to his ex-girlfriend didn't help his small man's complex.

Darren went into his flared nostril psycho mode. "What're you doing talking to Candy, Rockwell?"

"Leave him alone, Darren. We're just talking. Besides, you aren't my boyfriend."

That just made Darren angrier at me. So, he proceeded to push me up against a wall and started breathing heavily like a pit bull ready to attack. I remember his breath smelled like a wine cooler and thought to myself, *What a fag!*

"Rockwell, you don't know who you're talking to. Candy's not for you."

I mustered up the courage, with the entire crowd in the room watching to blurt out, "She's obviously not for you either."

With that, Darren punched me square in the left eye and stood their hyperventilating with rage. He held back a second punch because he saw Blue Sky standing right beside me,

76

not wanting to intervene yet but letting Darren know that he would pummel him if he continued.

Candy was visibly angry and embarrassed. "You're a fucking asshole, Darren!"

Darren marched off, staring at me with a threatening message. "I'll see you on the football field. And next time, I'm finishing you!"

I'm not a dick out to hurt people to feel better about myself, but I did end up breaking Darren's shoulder pads in half when I tackled him during a scrimmage when he was a senior in high school. I broke him that day like the younger alpha male in the wild beating the old alpha. That pretty much shut his fucking mouth for good. But that night at the party cemented his bully-centric relationship with me until he left high school. Truth be told, I felt kinda bad for him. I knew his dad drank and put a lot of pressure on his boys to succeed in sports.

Besides being embarrassed and in a bit of pain, I was trying to act like it didn't hurt. Candy got close to my face to assess the damage. Concerned and feeling more connected because of the violent sparring over her, she looked into my eyes. "Are you okay, Chris?"

I smiled with an embarrassed laugh. "Yeah, I'm cool."

Candy gave me a soft kiss, and the pain was gone. Then she continued our conversation without missing a beat. "To answer your question, you're my type."

Blue Sky walked up to check on me, putting his arm on my shoulder and smiling, looking out on the sea of drunk and twisted bodies trying to score. "Well, Rockwell, how do you like your first party so far?"

I was hooked.

BOY MEETS GIRL

I remember meeting Becky for the first time on a perfect summer evening down at Brandt Field, our town baseball and softball field complex. It was a place where teens could hang out with their buddies a few feet away from their parents' watchful eyes of security and check out the girls playing softball. I remember walking back to the baseball field after doing a loop through the softball fields. We caught each other's eye by the grass, and I saw that she was with a girl I knew. We were both still in uniform; each of us had just finished pitching winning games.

My friend Randi Fitzgerald hugged me and introduced us. "Hey Chris! Have you met Becky?" I remembered her from the lake that day. She was on the ski boat. She caught my eye then, and I instantly liked her. I could tell she dug me too. I mustered a somewhat confident, "Hi."

She responded with a cool, "Hi."

I blurted out something brilliant like, "How'd you guys do?"

Becky modestly said, "We won, but I didn't pitch great."

Randi sold Becky's star performance like a lesbian Jerry McGuire, "She struck out like ten batters, and she had three hits and 2 RBIs! I had a double and got into a fight." Randi would go on to marry a nice Italian woman and currently lives happily in Northern California.

I wasn't listening to the stats; I couldn't even remember my stats from that night. I've never been able to remember that kind of stuff. I measured my performance beyond stats. It was about winning, sure, but I also had an inner diagnostic that analyzed my every play with intense scrutiny and algorithms to improve the future. So, I was sometimes happy with myself after a team loss, and I've been devastated after team victories because I didn't meet up to my own high expectations and the expectations of the leaders I worked for. I was locked on to Becky while Randi continued about the details of the game.

I obliged Randi's social interference and forced a polite, "Cool."

I focused back to Becky and asked, "So what'dya get at the snack bar?"

"Snickers and Watermelon Bubblicious."

Trying to flirt a little, I jokingly said, "Lemme have some."

She showed me her big, beautiful smile and energy with a strong but flirtatious volley. "Yeah, right."

It felt like a gravitational force pulled us together as I tried to grab the candy bar from her. She turned and we began to wrestle around affectionately for it.

Randi stepped in like any good lesbian sidekick friend would. "Well, we gotta go!"

I felt an instant loss and yearning, fearful that we might never meet again. "See ya…"

Becky replied, looking directly at me with her big green eyes and a smile. "Bye."

As we departed and walked away in opposite directions, we both glanced back and smiled at each other like we had known each other for a long time. Right then, my heart swelled because I no longer feared I wouldn't see her again. I knew I would be with her someday. She just had a spark and a different style and a deep confidence I recognized and was drawn to. There was a connection. Sometimes it just is.

SPIN THE BOTTLE AND TP MEANS I LIKE YOU

Spin the Bottle

Since all our town's elementary schools merged for seventh and eighth grade into one school, Central Middle School, it wasn't until then that my friend, Paul Wilson, and I started hanging out. The middle school assimilation brought us face-to-face with kids we had never seen before, except maybe occasionally for sports stuff. Paul had gone to Wyandotte School in Southside; it was a lower-income school, and most of the black kids in town went there. My elementary school was a quaint little school safely tucked away in the rolling foothills and attended by middle- and upper-class kids.

Paul's parents were both teachers and nice, thoughtful, intelligent people. Paul's mom, Mary Lou, was a hip animal-loving lady who taught at the elementary school he attended. It was a rougher school, and her calm demeanor worked well with the at-risk population there. His dad was a creative brain that struggled with day-to-day emotional processing but was a great artist, teacher, and golf coach at Butte Community College. Randy Wilson was unique and quietly quirky but a refined and distinguished gentleman. At home, Randy was in his own world, both high and low. He was creatively messy, which suited Mary Lou just fine. Between the roaming animals of all kinds in the home and the hoard-eresque quality of finished and unfinished artwork—framed, unframed, or partially framed; the scattered shrapnel of oil paints, watercolors, inks, canvases, and brushes that filled each room—it was a curious obstacle course of intrigue and colors. It worked with the way my brain worked. In many ways, the Wilsons' house was more like mine than different. It felt comfortable and familiar.

Paul lived on the same side of town as me. It was only about a mile and a half from my house to his, so I would ride my bike over to his place to hang out on weekends.

Paul was the youngest with two older sisters and an older brother. Adam was a truly kind human and was always nice to me. He was almost five years older than us, making him a junior or senior in high school. He and his buddies would usually be over playing three-on-three basketball. I always liked the energy of the older guys. His sisters were also kind and patient with the two of us. These guys were more like family than friends to me, and still are.

One Saturday, Paul called to invite me over to hang out with a couple other friends...girls. I finished my chores in record time and jumped on my BMX bike and pedaled my way to his house as fast as I could go. Looking back, I must've been a sweaty mess when I showed up, smiling like I had no sense.

Donna was Paul's neighbor a few houses down, and she was bringing her friend Becky over with her. I recalled meeting Becky at the softball field earlier that summer, and I remembered her smile. I was excited but nervous to see her again. I had seen her around Central's campus at breaks a couple of times, but we were running in different groups.

The cool autumn night set the stage for youthful antic-ipation. What the hell were we gonna do when the girls arrived? The whole plan was to play spin the bottle. I think I was supposed to be excited, but I was more nervous about the possibility of being outed for not being good at this sex stuff. I was thirteen and had no idea because I had never done anything, not even a French kiss to my name. I was truly a shy kid in so many ways. Paul was about as inexperienced as me, but he had been around older siblings and a different culture every day in elementary school. Paul *knew* more than I did but shared my notch-less bedpost. I think maybe he had kissed Consuela Barnes, a black chick from Oakland.

When the doorbells chimed, it shocked my mind to the fact that the girls were here! Paul and I made our way to the front door, leaving a Hansel and Gretel-scented trail of cheap Adidas cologne, or was it Stetson? Both were poor attempts at smelling attractive, but it was what the "older" kids were using in eighth grade, so it had to work!

Paul opened the door and welcomed the girls in as if we were at the Wilson Country Club. He had a tongue-in-cheek wit that was on par with my dad. Nonetheless, Paul was a true gentleman though his extremely youthful and slight 4'9" junior-high build that made him seem younger in some ways. Girls felt safe around Paul, not because he didn't have game, but because he was a gentleman in a sea of dogs.

My anxiety was replaced with a relieved smile and laugh when I realized Becky and her friend Donna had dressed in multiple layers of tops and bottoms in preparation for our game. I mean, they looked like they were twenty pounds heavier from the layers of sweats and shirts. I was kinda happy to know they were just as nervous about the oncoming freight train of sex and relationships. We all felt safe enough to be kids just one more weekend without the pressure and stress of going further than we were ready for.

Later that night, after some laughs at our lame attempt at spin the bottle, we walked down the street to Donna's house so she could introduce us to her parents. Donna's house sat perched twenty feet above the road and had a brownstone retaining wall that made it look like a blue-collar castle compared to most of the houses on the street. Donna's stepdad had a blacktop business and had a few bucks, but his greasy, unkempt behavior and overall being wreaked of alcohol and half-ass living. He was chasing money and missing the big picture while he tried raising four wild stepchildren lacking a dad and discipline.

Donna's parents loved Paul and Becky because they were the kind of kids any parent would want their kid influenced by. Donna was typical. She was cute-ish but spoke hick and was clueless that she was half the version of her mom's coddled lies. I could quickly see the striking difference in Becky. Becky was alive and real in a way that people could feel. She was beautifully feminine but also a tomboy, riding ATVs with Donna and the guys after school and playing a mean game of softball. Her energy was just different. She was okay just being a kid and was not trying to be older than she was. She was grounded and comfortable in her own skin and truly a kind person. It was something I did not understand until much later. I discovered too late just how rare that is in this world. I even wrote in her yearbook, *I hope you grow some boobs this summer!* What an insecure punk I was! I liked her and was being flirtatious...but my God...boys can say the stupidest shit to girls they like!

Anyway, after we met Donna's parents, we went outside to figure out something to do. I don't know how it came up, but someone got the idea to throw eggs at cars that were driving by the house. Next thing I know, we were posted up with a dozen eggs, crouched behind the brownstone retaining wall that rose about three feet above their little patch of front lawn and shrubs. It was dark, and the only streetlight around was right in front of Donna's house. The battleground was set, and we impatiently waited for our first unassuming motorist to pass by. This was in the 1980s, and our town was still quaint, and the streets were relatively quiet. That meant we could wait a while for a car to go by. We got lucky and only waited a few minutes until we saw the oncoming lights of our first victim.

As the station wagon appeared in the spotlight, we all threw our eggs at the same time and completely missed the car. We laughed at how far off our aim was. Within five minutes, though, another car drove by, and we unleashed our ammo. This time only three were total misses, but Becky's shot was dead on. She threw a line drive that exploded on the driver's side windshield. The car screeched to a panicked stop, and the driver jumped out of the car.

"Holy Shit! Run!!" we all whisper-yelled at each other. The guy was fucking pissed. He looked up at the fortress that had just launched the surprise attack and charged up the driveway to get the enemy that scared the shit out of him and left an eggy mess on his windshield. We hauled ass to the back of the house and up a steep embankment. We could hear the young twenty-something dude in Donna's driveway cussing at us and pissed off. We were scared and huddled together like a pack of young pups. After a few minutes, we heard the car screech away into the night. We could finally breathe, and we began to laugh and retell the harrowing experience as if we barely survived.

Not unlike anywhere else in the USA, our first year in junior high meant meeting new kids, beginning new friendships, and experiencing first loves. Although I was hanging out with older eighth-grade girls and running with the eighth-grade guys as I was playing my first year of Pop Warner football, I was still very innocent and was drawn to Becky because she was okay being who she was. That night at Paul's was only the second time being around Becky, but I realized that I really enjoyed her. She had a smile and way about her that was different than the other girls. She was striking in looks and personality, but beyond that, Becky possessed a depth of intelligence, humor, and self-confidence that was not the typical junior-high masking to protect fear and insecurities. Becky was actually okay being a kid; she wasn't in a rush to grow up into something different and be something she wasn't.

TP Means I Like You

A couple of months later, I toilet-papered Becky's house as a teenage gesture of modern courting. I remember riding my bike over to Paul's house that night. I pedaled out into the cool night, not realizing there was no moon until I ran into a telephone pole and crashed into blackberry bushes. I wasn't hurt, and it was pitch-black, so I was safe from humiliation. I brushed myself off, laughing out loud as I shook my head clear.

I jumped back on my bike and coasted the remaining three hundred yards to Paul's house on Foothill Blvd. The warm glow of the living-room lights invited me up their clean black driveway bordered by oak trees to the south. Oleander bushes lined the north side of the driveway, creating a wall of privacy to keep the nosy neighbor, Mrs. Simpson, at bay. The front yard was soft and sloping with an occasionally tended front lawn. It was the classic three-bedroom two-bath working-class home that dotted the landscape of town. Just like my parents and many others in our neighborhood, the Wilsons added on to their simple house over the years to accommodate their growing family. They even converted the garage into a bedroom. They had a small in-ground vinyl pool and wooden deck built in the back for the family, but besides the pool and deck, the remainder of the backyard was a giant field with a few dilapidated barn-type outbuildings used as makeshift corrals and enclosures for their horses, goats, and chickens. They always had lots of animals around.

Paul greeted me at the door with a sincere smile that turned devilish as he whispered, "I have the contraband." Paul led me to his room and closed the door. He looked around slyly as if to make sure no one was hiding in his little bedroom before uncovering his two newspaper boy vests. He used two vests to carry his load of rolled papers every morning on his paper route, but that night the vests were to be loaded with rolls of toilet paper. Paul disappeared out of the room for a second and returned with armloads of new packs of toilet paper and a big smile. He quickly and quietly closed the door and began to rip the plastic wrapping apart to get to the TP so we could load the vests full. Paul's parents were in the living room, reading and listening to the radio; they didn't watch much TV. We said goodbye and headed out the front door. Paul ran up to the garage to grab his bike, alerting the dogs to Paul's parents' unconcern since he was the last of four well-behaved kids. They weren't the least bit concerned with us getting into trouble. In fact, at that point in their life I'm sure they were just happy to have a few moments to themselves.

Paul and I pedaled out into the night. He led me north onto Foothill. We reached Donna's house, the only street light for a mile, and turned west onto some street, the name of which I can't remember to this day, even though I ended up driving that route a billion times over the years Becky and I were together. I had never been to Becky's house, so I had no idea where we were going. I remember feeling nervous but cool because I knew if we pulled off this stunt it would make for a pretty good story Monday at school. I trusted Paul and the plan and followed his ghostly figure as we rode across a field covered with a low fog as if we were in a scary movie.

Within a few hundred yards, Paul stopped and dismounted to the bushes on the right side of the road. I hit my brakes and they screeched so loud it could've awoken the entire neighborhood. I coasted another few yards and then jumped off to walk the bike next to Paul's bike. I was nervous and had second thoughts, but there was no turning back with all those rolls of toilet paper! I followed him up towards the front door. We ditched the bags in the bushes so Paul could check to see if anyone was there. Multiple attempts at polite but loud enough knocks. No answer. Paul looked back with a big smile and two thumbs up. Game On! We proceeded to create a toilet paper tapestry of the trees and home, giving it a sort of angelic feel. Until it rained later that night.

COWBOYS, CAMPFIRE
TALES, & THE YETI

The Mastelotto Brothers were legendary outlaw Italian cowboys that settled in Oroville not long after the turn of the century. They had a heavy equipment and construction business, but the truth is that running cattle was in their blood. Their legend was solidified when they played outlaws in the legendary Clint Eastwood western *The Tale of Josie Wales,* filmed in our hometown. It was around the same time, during their heyday in the 1970s and '80s, when the Mastelottos built the Oro West Racquet Club. It was *the* club in town. I spent my youth running around the racquet club with my younger brothers and Matt Brandt while our dads competed against each other on the courts. I loved it! My dad was part of the "cool guys," and it gave us a sense of belonging and confidence to raise our game.

Roy was like a living legend to me. He was the Mastelotto known for his cooking and famous dipping sauce and brand. It was like a sweet and hot ketchup that we used on everything from baby back ribs and chicken to pasta and eggs. His brothers called him J. Lee Roy, so it became known as J. Lee Roy's Dippin' Sauce. Roy was a natural salesman and self-anointed as the "Cookin' Cowboy." To back this up, he won the gold medal at the John Asquaga's Nugget sponsored "Best in the West" BBQ cook-off back in the early 1990s. That put Roy on the map and his dipping sauce in stores throughout the greater Northern California region, including a private label deal with Bay Area brand Nobb Hill.

I guess you can say Roy and his brothers were the first entrepreneurs I knew. And they did it with a gambler's style. There's a picture of Roy and Clint Eastwood, arms around each other on the movie set in the foothills of my home-town. I mean, these guys did it! They went after what they wanted. They fought for it, and they stayed true to who they were. Roy didn't speak much, like most cowboys, but when he did, he was a deadpan comic with perfect timing and wit without cursing. The Mastelottos might have had an outlaw streak, but they were raised old school and didn't use profan-ity. Reminds me of the Corleone men in the mob movie *The Godfather.*

Every year we would head to the coast to camp and dive with the Brandts and Mastelottos. Every year we would end up sitting around the campfire talking and enjoying the aba-lone and pasta cooked by Roy. There would be old-school Willie Nelson playing on the transistor radio that someone hung on the redwood tree next to the campfire; the older cowboys like Bobby and Grandpa Brandt would tell nostalgic hunting and sports stories. Food and wine generously shared by each family covered the classic red and white checkered tablecloth. Italian pasta salads, salami, cheeses, olives…it was a timeless scene. The exact snapshot with the same families could've been taken one hundred years earlier. Camping, hunting, fishing, and diving in the ocean was something we did as families, similar to what humans did for the majority of their history, until recently.

I remember sitting at the fire as a young boy, desperately wanting to be part of the conversation and trying to emulate the men I looked up to in how they walked, talked, and made a living. All young boys look to male figures, regardless if they were present or not. I was extremely fortunate to have multiple men in my life who took care of their families, worked hard, and possessed enough self-confidence to encourage young boys to become good men. These men treated me with tough love, encouragement, and as the next man in line. They gave me the tools to strive and live outside and beyond the strict confines of my middle-class upbringing. These guys built businesses and sometimes challenged people—and the law. They weren't scared of anyone, and I admired that. I would quietly listen and observe my cowboy heroes talking and laughing around the campfire, wanting so badly to say or do something significant enough to make them take notice.

J. Lee Roy shouts out an order: "Chris Rockwell, come get this abalone hot off the grill!"

Bobby Mastelotto shouts to his brother, "J. Lee Roy, give that boy extra servings! We need to get him ready for football! How's it look for this season, Chris?"

I was always nervous around these men because I looked up to them so much.

"Pretty good, Bobby. I think we have a shot at the title."

Bobby Mastelotto and J. Lee Roy were high school star athletes, and Bobby went on to play fullback at the University of Utah. Bobby was the most polished and fierce businessman out of the brothers and built a successful chain of gas stations and convenience stores along with speculating on Nevada real estate.

Bobby looked over to Grandpa Brandt, the patriarch of the men in the group,

"Mr. B, remember in '52 when our Pop Warner team beat Red Bluff for the title?"

I always thought it was cool that these big bad men I looked up to addressed Clarence Brandt as Mr. B. Their nickname for him was a loving and respectful title that Clarence rightfully earned guiding those boys from their days before the road was paved on Canyon Highlands as next-door neighbors, through youth baseball, Pop Warner football, and on family hunting and fishing trips until he died.

"Why, sure I do. You and Roy kept tackling that running back until he quit. That's what it takes."

Roy continued the play by play. "Sonny was the star, though. He had three touchdown passes..."

Bobby joins Roy in the ribbing follow-up, "And two interceptions!"

Sonny smiles modestly as loving laughter fills the air.

Stories are told and retold into the night. Me, Matt, my younger brother Nick, Tyler Sharp, and Tyler Fuller hung out in the giant Redwood stumps sneaking beer and chew and hiding from the adults. I was still thirteen and discovering all the forbidden fruits of being a teenager: beer, tobacco, girls, and taking stupid chances to prove my toughness.

Tyler Fuller, a friend we grew up playing Little League with on Grandpa Brandt's team, was watching Matt pull out a new can of Copenhagen.

"Where'd you score the can?!"

"Stole it from the store in Clear Lake when we were gettin' gas."

Watching Matt put a chew in was just cool. He mastered the art of dippin' Copenhagen by age six from watching his older brothers and his Dodger heroes. He started with checking the date on the bottom of the can, validating its freshness. Then he would take his knife and cut the label to separate the brand-stamped tin lid from the traditional wax protected cardboard container. He would hold the closed can in one hand and tap it against the palm of his other hand to make the fine-grain tobacco condense, so it's easier to pinch a solid dip. Holding the can in his left hand, he opened the tin top with his right hand, somehow propped it open with his left, and with one masterful move out of a chewing tobacco TV commercial, he would drop the chew into his lower lip, pack it down with his tongue, and spit. He rubbed his hands together to get the grains and tobacco juice off his fingers. To us, it looked so fucking cool.

Tyler took the can when Matt offered it. "That's what Lenny Dykstra chews...well, Nick said he chews plug and Copenhagen at the same time. "

Matt checked Tyler, ensuring he was the source of that cool story of his big brother. "I told you that, Meat!"

We all took a dip and listened to Matt's stories.

Nick Brandt and Lenny Dykstra were roommates on the Mets for spring ball in Florida, and they partied with teammates Doc Gooden and Daryl Strawberry almost every night. Nick said Lenny was half fucking crazy. Matt recounted a story he told us months earlier.

"Lenny would dress up in a tight white disco outfit and walk around with his dick hanging out of the zipper waiting to either get into a fight or land some drunk chick. He pulled more pussy that way. He would piss on the bar, throw up on the floor, and still get the hottest chick in the place. He didn't give a fuck!"

Young boys honor crazy and fearlessness above all else because they are scared and insecure with most things. Matt had mastered the art form of storytelling, trying to keep up with his older brothers. I tried to emulate everything Matt did, even the way he talked. It was NorCal Stoner Surfer Athlete dialect; I still speak it today. Nick and Tyler tried contributing to the conversation with cliché responses that would alert the cool older kids that they didn't know what they were talking about. It was out of my realm, too; the difference is that I had been hanging and learning from Matt for a little longer and knew how to fake it better.

Matt was always on center stage for campfire stories.

"My brother Russ made me take my first chew when I was five. I puked my guts up."

"Serious? Whoa..."

Continuing the stage performance to his captivated fans, Matt transitioned from the topic of drugs to sex as a climax to his performance. "Hey, did you hear about Darcy Hill getting finger banged by Jesse Halter at Renee Buckly's party?"

Tyler adds to the story, like they hadn't talked about it the entire four-hour drive over in the back of Sonny's truck.

"I felt Darcy's tits behind the dugout last month. She's got a perfect rack."

Dang, I guess the dugout was her location of choice for giving us young guns our first thrill…and for breaking hearts. I didn't let on that Darcy brought me to the dugout only a few months earlier.

Trying to regain the spotlight, Matt jumps back into the conversation with another random but exciting junior high sex story.

"I heard Bobby Docker fucked Star at Renee's party."

Star was in eighth grade, and Bobby Docker was a junior in high school. He was a wannabe bodybuilder who never grew past 5'6" and continued his reign over young girls at high school parties for a decade after he dropped out at eighteen without earning his diploma.

Tyler upped the ante with, "I heard she fucked Darren Weinhard that same night."

"I know Adrian Liston fucked her two weeks ago."

Star was the oldest hippie granddaughter of the woman who lived next door. She and her mom would stop by and sometimes live there for extended periods of time between life transitions. We had a childhood bond growing up next door, playing together naked in the sprinklers and the creek that ran through our property. We would walk down the creek, stopping off to explore the beds of clover and flowers that we would eat and play in. As we got into elementary school, Star moved away when her mom started dating the keyboard player for Iron Maiden. They had just recently returned to town.

I worked up the courage to speak up and tell my story. "I kissed her."

Matt, being the big brother, said, "Yeah, when you were three!"

"No, it was at the junior high dance a month ago," I said, trying to recall the exact date but failing to back my story with confident certainty.

I just remember the song playing on the shitty gym speakers was Ratt's "Round & Round" when Star walked in drunk but in charge of the low-lit room. She was like Madonna: dirty and stylish, but prettier and sweeter. The music changed, and the Scorpions ballad "Still Lovin' You" flooded the makeshift dance hall. She led me in a slow dance, mesmerizing me and scaring the hell out of me at the same time. Only a few weeks ago, she was sending me to the dugout with her friend Darcy; now she was taking me for a totally different ride. I kept trying to imagine what the fuck I'd do if we left the dance and she took me to the dark side of the night beyond the innocence of lights and chaperones.

And with that, beer and Marlboro Reds flooded my taste buds as Star kissed me with her tongue and intense gypsy spirit. Everything went into slow motion, and I forgot where I was. Like a lightning bolt, it was over. She was off into the night, a marauder traveling the world, conquering boys' desires, while she desperately searched for her own song. She was a burst of life who burned out fast. But for a few moments, she was that rocker chick they all dreamed of being. She just never believed it and crashed to Earth not long after high school was over, overdosing in the Hollywood Hills at one of those famous rock and roll parties.

"She was my first love."

"Awww...shut the fuck up, fag!" This was the common form of adolescent affection between our crew. Negative humor and punching each other meant they cared...apparently a lot.

I started to spin from the chew as I tried to climb down out of the ten-foot-high old-growth redwood stump. I missed a step and hit the ground with a thud. My fall was quieted by the duff of redwood needles creating a soft bed covering the entire forest floor, but nevertheless, a fall like that knocked the wind and sense out of me.

Nick and I have always had a typical sibling rivalry, but we would step up to defend each other when shit got real bad.

"Chris! Are you okay?!"

"Yeah. Damn, my head is spinning."

My brother put his hand on my shoulder and made me feel better. "You'll be okay, man." We had that bond, no matter how much we butted heads as siblings.

I was staring down into nothing, on my hands and knees, spinning with a string of drool touching the ground.

"Yeah... Oh, fuck..."

With that, I started puking my guts up. I remember wanting to die at least twice during my life-altering experience. This was my first experience feeling the life leave me... or so I thought. The guys kind of checked to see if I was okay, then they started laughing, but out of self-preservation tried to keep it quiet from the adults.

Matt kept the party rolling. "Shhhh... Way to go, Meat! Hey, let's steal some beer and sneak over to Nick's camp."

I did my best to straighten up and get to my feet with the help of my brother, but I was fucked up and still spinning. Matt led us over to the ice chests in the shadows by camp, and we grabbed as many beers as we could carry without making it too noticeable. We navigated by campfire light and a faint echo of someone telling a story and people laughing about the Montana hunting trip back in '71 when they got trapped in a snowstorm and had to take shelter in a mountain lion cave. The cowboys had an acoustic guitar out, and a harmonica, and were all singing, "Candy Rock Mountain," led by Grandpa Brandt. As we neared Nicks' camp, we stopped in the pitch-black to pound a couple of beers between the five of us. I felt like an outlaw and I loved it.

Nick Brandt was the party. He could tell the best stories, get the girls, party like Ozzy Osbourne, and sign a major league baseball contract with the Atlanta Braves at 17 years

94

old. I grew up idolizing his every move. Hanging out in his camp was like entering a private den of decadence. The camp was situated on the edge of the soft sandbank of the Navarro River. It had the feel of the lantern-lit riverbanks in Mark Twain's *Tom Sawyer.* It was entering a different world. The prehistorically oversized ferns and lush tree foliage created the appearance of a giant cave illuminated by dancing firelight against the impenetrable darkness of the giant redwood canopy rising hundreds of feet above our heads, blocking light from the closest stars. Hell, even the full moon had its light force sucked out. You could hear the Navarro River just down the embankment from the edge of the campsite, gently rolling towards her destiny of the Pacific Ocean just eight miles away.

We listened to stories and drank from the jug of Carlo Rossi being passed around the campfire, just another coming-of-age ritual that I was more than ready to be a part of. I didn't pass on anything that was offered up that night. I was all in until I was out. Next thing I know, I'm waking up to complete darkness, freezing temperatures, eerie silence, and not quite knowing where I was. After a few terrifying seconds, I remembered that I had passed out around the campfire hanging out with Matt's big bros Nick and Russ and the older guys. The last thing I remember was watching Russ light a fart in front of his girlfriend, Sue. I was embarrassed and impressed.

Pitch-black silence was everywhere. My eyes, ears, and heart were lost in the darkness. I literally could not adjust my eyes to pick up any light. My ears could only hear my carotid artery pumping gallons of blood through my neck. It was so loud that I thought it was going to explode and drain out right there. I felt myself shivering uncontrollably from the damp cold and the shot of adrenaline coursing through my veins. The depth of darkness was incomprehensible to my mind. I felt claustrophobic and scared. I struggled every step, not knowing where I was going, but relying on my instinctive memory of the campground I had played in since I was a baby. I gathered my nerves and started heading in the direction I believed my sleeping bag and family were. I ventured into the darkness in search of warmth because I had faith that it was there. I stumbled and smashed my shin into a two-foot redwood parking post that nearly dropped me. I stopped to catch my breath from the vicious pain that ripped open my leg, oozing warm blood down my invisible limb. I stopped to use the agonizing moment to think about where that post was in relation to my campsite.

As I started to gather myself, the silence was torn into a new dimension with a howling moan that shook my soul to its core. I have never, to this day, heard anything so foreign and terrifying. I grew up in the wild and was accustomed to all the common nocturnal howls, from coyotes to owls, but this was a primal sound from a different, larger, and unknown creature. I felt my heart explode like a ritualistic tribal drumbeat signaling death by the hands of the Great Spirit, who wails in the night. It sent bristled chills down my back and neck. I knew what it was instantly, even though I had never heard it before. Terrified...frozen...alone in the pitch black cold. I was so scared I didn't know if my heart was going to stop from fear alone. I thought I might actually get scared to death! Being thirteen years old, I felt this horrible shame come over me for being so scared. I grew up with men of great courage and fortitude; I felt like the weak link and was already planning to banish myself from the clan for being such a pussy. But then I started to think about it and realized what I just heard in the middle of the night would scare the piss out of anyone, except maybe Clint Eastwood.

The howl echoed and penetrated through the trees like thick coastal fog. Then silence fell into the black. All I could hear was my heart pounding in my throat and ears, so loud I was afraid the monster might hear it and find me. My breathing was as if I had just finished running a sprint, even though I was motionless. The adrenaline shooting through my body put me in "fight-or-get-the-fuck-out" mode. I took a couple of deep breaths and pushed on into the unforgiving night. This was one of those defining moments for me—to man up or curl up and call out for my mom and dad. I got quiet and listened for the slightest sounds that would point me in the right direction. I thought of my dad's native tracking lesson from bowhunting. I started to make it a challenge to focus and keep Yeti off my mind. After a few more shin gashes and two face-plants, I made it to my sleeping bag and was never so happy to be sleeping next to my parents as a teenager.

FRIDAY NIGHT LIGHTS & BIG SHARON WAKOWSKI

Alcohol was my euphoric obsession from that first night I drank it around the campfire. Fast forward to 15 years old and a perfect fall evening at Amy Arlington's party that had me running from the cops, abandoned by my friends, picked up by a stranger, and passed out on my front lawn. I ended the night by puking in my parents' bathroom and then waking up the next day, knowing that the worst part of it was disappointing my dad. But none of those negative experiences could even touch the feeling, the rush, and the peace I felt when I drank. I drank until I blacked out. Looking back, it was a signal of a very long road ahead of me. It took many years, and even more heartache, to realize how powerful the mental obsession for alcohol is. I had no idea. Who does until it's too late?

Because my dad grew up in a poor, alcoholic home and didn't drink because it scared the shit out of him, the next morning, he demanded that there would be no drinking in our house. He gave me two aspirin and an orange juice on a TV tray as I sat on the couch. I looked over at my brothers and saw a unified disappointment of what I'd done. My dad must've been scared and upset.

That was the last real discussion we had about alcohol until I became an adult and started getting into serious trouble. But it was just the beginning, and it was all-consuming and exciting. Every experience was like it was my very first time, but it was really just a variation of the Friday night before. Either way, I didn't care what we did, as long as I could drink and feel free, listen to loud music, and maybe kiss a girl or two along the way. Little did I know what I was in for.

Matt Brandt, my big brother in every way but blood, was sitting out the first few games of his sophomore season of football after being suspended for getting caught chewing Copenhagen on campus...fucking ridiculous rules when kids are going to school high and drunk and not doing shit. Matt and I grew up together, and I still looked up to him and his brothers when I got to high school because they were scrappy star athletes. They were crazy and wild, always pushing the envelope to the next level. That was very attractive to me. So, I followed their path, slowly finding my own voice and direction.

I was a freshman in high school and loving what this new world presented to me. A few weeks after my first debacle, I was finally allowed to go out again. I was hanging out with my teammates to watch the varsity do damage to our cross-town rival Las Plumas. After the game, I was ready for a night of debauchery. I met Matt at the locker room entrance as all the sweaty players strutted out triumphantly, kind of showered and drenched in cheap cologne that saturated the cool smoky autumn evening. It was Friday night in my small northern California town, and I was high on adrenaline and anticipation of a wild night of drinking and whatever else we got into. I was still a novice at drinking and parties, but I was like a moth to a flame.

Matt and I headed to the parking lot after saying goodbye to our parents, guardedly hugging us with a look of worry and borderline disapproval. Without any form of evidence besides the fifteen years of our lives together, they had a pretty good idea that their night would be sleepless. Just then, Todd Rucks rolled up in an old Bronco to pick us up. He was a former high school athlete, and the fact that he was out of high school made things start out different from anything I'd done before. It was a little like the young Mitch Kramer when he hangs out with high school grad David Wooderson in *Dazed and Confused.* I felt cool but wary and finally resigned myself to the fact that I was with Matt, and I was safe. He was tough and always looked after me, especially in crazy situations. As I assumed my backseat rookie position, I peered between the two silhouetted heads in front of me and wondered where and how the night would end.

We left the familiar feel of the football stadium and stopped off at Town & Country Liquor to pick up some Miller Genuine Draft for the night. Todd had the physique of a big strapping athlete, but his big coke bottle glasses and brown curly hair gave him the look of a Jewish Napoleon Dynamite on steroids. We drove up to "the top of the world"—Foster's Hill—which overlooked downtown Oroville. The face of the overlook was a steep and nearly impassable mountain of river rock and dirt. Young guys had risked truck and life to four-wheel drive up the legendary hill for generations. The minute we stopped, Matt was grabbing cold bottles of beer and handing them to Todd and me.

I felt like I really was on top of the world and starting to fly high with a beer buzz on an empty stomach after watching a football game. I sat back, taking it all in, listening to Todd and Matt recap the game and the state of the Dodgers for next year. I was in and out of their conversation because I was soaring over the lights of my small town and dreaming of big things far away. Todd's stock FM radio was set to 93.9, the classic rock station out of Chico. I remember hearing "Black Betty" and Boston's "Don't Look Back" and singing the songs under my breath while I watched the front seat sports talk show hosted by Matt Brandt.

The engine started up and snapped me out of my musical dream, and we were headed out to our next unknown destination. I didn't care where we went. I was feeling great and up for anything. We chirped out onto the blacktop and headed into the night, looking for action. Since I was new to drinking and going out, I didn't know what it looked like. Todd mentioned something about stopping by his place, and next thing I know, we pull up right behind the high school, and he jumps out into the dark entrance of his front door that faces Mr. McCutchen's library. The proximity to the school had my nerves on edge, thinking about my dad and feeling a twinge of guilt before washing it away with another beer. Matt and I sat there in the dark, quietly talking about the game and some chick he was gonna nail. Mainly I just listened to all the new things I was hearing and seeing all around me. I was exactly where I wanted to be.

"Hey, keep your beer down! Cops are on the lookout."

I tucked the bottle between my legs between chugs and kept scanning the street for police, never losing my thought of my next drink and how I was going to get more. Suddenly, the silhouette of a mustang appeared out of the dark, and I quickly lowered my beer from my lips, spilling half the drink on my shirt. The car crept closer until it was right up to the bronco sitting under the streetlight. We both sighed, realizing that it wasn't a cop. It was girls! They pulled up to the driver's side and started yelling excitedly at Matt, making small talk about where the parties were at and if that was Chris Rockwell in the back seat. Not even knowing what was happening, I found myself in the back seat of their car.

I was a freshman, a new kid on campus, and the older girls liked preying on the fresh meat coming from junior high. I didn't know these older girls; shit, I didn't even know their names until Monday at school. It didn't matter. I felt like a star with alcohol and the attention of older girls. Next thing I know, I was making out with two chicks in the back seat of a brand-new Mustang. Great tunes were blaring on the stereo, the warm autumn wind swirling around us. The air was filled with sweet perfume and girls showering me with flirtatious talk, giggles, and kisses.

At the peak of this euphoric experience, cruising down the main strip, the world stopped. Without warning, I exploded puke all over the back seat and front console of the Mustang. Did I mention that this was a brand-new car? Her parents had just bought the car two weeks before. The girl driving almost swerved into oncoming traffic like she was having an epileptic seizure, and pulled into the car wash across the street from Burger King, the social connection spot to get the scoop on parties, fights, and grub on a Friday night. We screeched into one of the wash bays, and the girls ejected out of the car like they were on fire, screaming and crying. The front passenger was the only one laughing because she didn't suffer a direct hit. The poor driver, Sharon, got hit on her right hand resting on the console, and a little shrapnel hit her big '80s brown hair cascading over the back of her brand-new black leather seat.

I squirmed my way to the front door and fell out with puke all over me, and now wet from falling in the leftover water from a day of motorcycle mud and engine gunk being deposited onto the concrete of the wash bay. I remember feeling bad, but I was wasted drunk. In fact, throwing up made me feel like a hundred dollars, and I figured I was ready for the next round. I looked at the driver and told her I was sorry and would "fix" the problem.

I smiled confidently at them, but they were still in shock at what had just happened. I strutted past them, dropped four quarters *into* the box, grabbed the wand and casually walked over to the car, and fired the pressure washer into the back seat! The girls flipped out and nearly tackled me while the driver grabbed the weapon from my hand. At that point, things started to get hazy. I was crashing fast.

My next recollection was pulling into the driveway at a house I didn't know. I had no idea where I was and who these girls were, except for the fact that they were nice and were trying to help me out of the car, draping me over their shoulders and staggering under my dead weight. They got me into the house and up some stairs. They laid me down on my back, and that was all I remembered until I felt my shoes being untied and pulled off, along with my socks. I was semi-conscious but physically paralyzed from the booze and spins. I remember being thankful my shoes were off. Then I felt hands unbuttoning my tight-ass 501 jeans. I don't think it scared me, but it was a surprise, especially as the shadowy figure popped the last button on my pants and jerked them off. The room was dark, and I was in and out of consciousness at this point. My body was dead. I felt like I had been shot in the neck with a tranquilizer—like Will Farrell in *Old School*. As I faded in and out of consciousness, I felt a weight on my body that was significant, especially with the see-saw motion above me. I suddenly realized this chick was fucking me!

Now for all you folks saying, "How can you have sex and not know it?" ... I was fifteen and drunk, that's how! The breeze could blow north, and I could be dead asleep but at full granite salute; it didn't matter. So back to the story. By all accounts, this was not a consensual consummation. Hell, I didn't even know who the girl was! All I did know was that some chick stripped me and fucked me while I was nearly passed out. Next thing I know, the morning sunlight was filling the upstairs loft coming in from the skylight directly above me. My memory was sketchy from right after the car wash. I had a flood of regret about puking in that chick's car. I didn't know where I was, and I was supposed to be staying at Matt's house. All of this was racing through my mind while I was still on my back and trying to open my eyes.

I rolled over to my left to get the hell out of there and realized that my arm was stuck under a big naked girl! Holy fucking shit! I panicked for a second. I had never been in this situation before. When I got older and heard the term "Coyote Ugly," I remembered that morning and knew exactly what it meant. I gently, holding my breath, begging not to wake the sleeping giant, slid my arm out from underneath her boulder-sized head, and scanned the room for my clothes. I dressed in silence and quietly crawled down the stairs and made my way into the soft Saturday morning lit kitchen to call Matt for a ride. I saw a Ding Dong on the counter, looked around, unwrapped it, and took a bite to get rid of the alcohol vomit taste in my parched mouth. I lifted the phone receiver and started dialing. To my horror, Matt's mom answered the phone.

"Hello?"

"Uhh, hi...Jackie? It's Chris Rockwell. Is Matt there?"

"Hi Christopher, I'll see if he'll wake up."

I could hear Jackie walk into Matt's room and say, "Matthew...Matt! Chris is on the phone." Then I heard nothing except Jackie dropping the phone next to his snoring face.

"Matt!" I quietly pleaded. "I need a ride out of here." Silence. "Matt!"

"Hello?" Heavy breathing.

"Matt!"

"Heyyy..." Silence.

"Matt, I need a ride. I'm stuck at some girl's house up by the high school. Can you get me?"

"Heyyy Meat..." then snoring. Fuck! I was stuck and needed to get home. So, with Matt being passed out, I called my parents for a ride. Mom picked me up. I remember getting home and eating cold Canadian bacon pizza from Shakey's and sitting in the living room with my family watching college football on TV and having a casual conversation like nothing had happened. Meanwhile, I looked like I had been ridden hard and put away wet, complete with puke-stained pants and a shirt smelling like the floor after a keg party. As I watched the game and put some food in my stomach, all I could think about was that I made out in the back seat with two upper-level students, I puked in a brand-new car, attempted to wash the black leather interior with a power washer, and got raped by big Sharon Wakowski. My freshman year in high school was shaping up to be a wild ride.

SOUTHSIDE BASKETBALL COURTS & DRINKING OLD ENGLISH

Kevin and I were fifteen when I first told him about my crazy idea of starting a record label. I remember the day; it was a hot summer evening, and we were hanging out down at the basketball courts in Southside. We were trying to earn our game stripes against the veteran pickup basketball teams, usually made up of older and rougher street guys and former high school and college standouts and dropouts. Typically, we would get a quick elimination and return defeated to the sidelines and resume hanging out with the kids our age, sipping on Old English malt liquor, and laughing at the comedic heckling coming from our young ragtag crew.

The sun was starting to lay low, giving a soft, warm summertime light. Kevin, me, and the crew were sitting on the bench talking, patiently waiting to get back on the court to challenge the winners. Some guy's '64 was parked on the other side of the chain-link fence bumpin' Too Short. A small crowd of kids and girls were hanging around, joining in on the trash talk on and off the court. Rodd Welch ridiculed one of the big goofy guys out on the court,

"Punkin!! Do you know how sorry you are? Did none of yo friends ever tell you the truth?! They all been lying, Punkin! They lying!! You better not tell people you play with us!"

Punkin turns his sweaty fat head towards Rodd as he's chugging down the court. "Ffffuh…" Heavy breathing. "Fuck you…"

Without hesitation, Rodd turned to his next victim, Consuela, and the couple of girls standing to each side. "Whoooooo! You girls looking like Salt-N-Pepa's hood cousins from Oakland!"

Everyone fell out laughing.

Consuela hit Rodd with her Oakland counterpunch street talk. "Fuck you, Rodd Welch! Yo ass so big you be lookin' like a dump truck with legs!"

The girls all laughed along with the rest of the sideline crew. Rodd looked down in momentary defeat but gave an unfazed smirk to bandage his wounded ego, as the girls savored the moment, smiling and high-fiving with a new sense of confidence and swagger. Rodd countered like a boxer who should've tapped out. "I know you shame, girl! Big doesn't describe your purple African plate lips. Or that nappy hair. Is that your real hair? I heard you wore a wig. Is that true?"

Rodd shifted his eyes to Consuela's younger homegirl. "Hey, La Rhonda! Girl…you looking right."

La Rhonda cracks a shy smile. Consuela looks at La Rhonda disapprovingly like a big sister and punches her in the shoulder.

Everyone started screaming and yelling with the crash of the steel net shaking the court. Carl White, still the town's king of city league, ended the game by dunking on some serious street baller. As teams switched, the smoke and drink came out, and the music got louder. I was sitting on the side of the court with Rodd, Todd, and a few guys around 19 or 20 years old, drinking 40s, talking about the Tyson vs. Buster Douglas heavyweight fight.

"All I'm saying is that Tyson took the fall against Buster Douglas! I saw him look to the camera right before he went down. I bet the government figured that Tyson was getting too popular; the CIA was in on an assassination attempt on Bob Marley."

Kevin and I look at each other with a unified, *There goes Rodd again* look.

"Shut up, Rodd!"

Rodd's twin brother and comedic big boy, Todd, waddled over and, in his best Southern black preacher voice, said, "What my brother is trying to tell us is that the white man is trying to keep the black man down! Can I get an amen! White people like Rockwell. You know his great-grandfather had a bunch of slaves working his property down in the South. Masa Rockwell! Masa Rockwell! Can I get you anything!?"

Everyone around us, all black, started laughing. I joined in on the laugh with an unconvincing and self-effacing chuckle, "Forget you, Todd," I fired back with reserve like I wasn't fazed with the talk of racism and my family owning slaves—surrounded by ALL black people. Kevin came to my rescue and broke the uncomfortable moment by kick-starting our original discussion.

"Rodd! Buster Douglas whooped up on Tyson because he was better that day, and he wasn't scared of him. Tyson got his ass knocked out officially."

Our stuttering, sweet oaf Boo Boo tried joining in. "BuBuBuBu…Buster DDDDouglas is a WWWWWone hit wwww-waander!"

Todd Welch immediately checks Boo Boo, like they've been doing since they were four years old growing up on Elgin Street. "Boo Boo! I heard you and Consuela was caught fucking in the bathroom in the park. Is that true?"

Everyone laughed. Boo Boo, noticeably frustrated, yelled back in his best Fat Albert speech-impeded character, "Shshshshsh-Shut up, Todd!"

Consuela chimed in, still stinging from the first insults, "Fuck both you Hamp nigga twins!"

Todd reveled in the comic debate, "Consuela, I can just see you screaming out, 'Ohh Boo Boo! Oh, you know how I like it, Boo Boo! Get all this big thigh muscle!'" as Todd mimicked an awkward side pose of Boo Boo trying to get it on with Consuela. Everybody laughed hysterically, except Boo Boo and Consuela.

Suddenly a fight broke out on the court between Kelly Kimble and some other tough-looking dude from out of town. It quickly escalated.

"What the fuck, nigga! You keep foulin' me!" Kevin's older brother, Kelly, shouted to the guy guarding him.

The big man stepped in and pushed Kelly. "Fuck you nigga!"

Kelly responded with an all-out war mantra. "I can end this with one shot to yo cap, nigga!"

The big dude quickly realized he was in the crosshairs of a Piru Blood gangster with big boy stripes from the street. "Why it gotta go there?"

With a cold subdued stare from years of violence, Kelly responded, "It's always there."

The big dude nodded and looked at Kelly, handed him the ball, and said, "Your ball."

The game continued like nothing happened. Unfazed, like he had just watched a Saturday morning cartoon TV commercial for Kellogg's Frosted Flakes, Kevin shifted the mood and focus. "I'm telling you, Raiders looking good with Bo Jackson. But he still won't be like my man, Marcus Allen. He's the best."

Rodd immediately joined in on the sports debate. "Hold up, Chow! Come on! We all know my man Hershel Walker of the greatest team in the NFL is supreme. Did you know he does 1,000 pushups, pull-ups, and sit-ups a day?"

Boo Boo interrupted the flow with, "Yo Cowboys is sorry! My Giants be on they mark."

Kevin, somewhat patiently, said, "No running back ever had the game on and off the field like Marcus Allen. That man is a G! And he get all the fine girls of LA! I hear him and Magic Johnson be running on famous ladies in high places. Like judges, politicians, and Hollywood actresses. I heard Janet Jackson and Marcus hooked up."

About that time, I was feeling pretty buzzed from the forty I was drinking. "Serious? Man..."

Kevin smiled. "Ladies love looks and skill," he said, admiring himself. "That's gonna be me. I'm gonna have all the famous ladies in my pad."

I joined in with my dream and said, "I want to make music and movies, to start a record label and have a badass helicopter. We could produce rock and rap music. We'll fly to LA, New York, Miami. Anywhere, anytime."

Sitting back with a smile on his face, Kevin continued the dream with, "Yeah, you could get some Sac and Oakland underground artists and put out some real legit music, like Too Short stuff. Hey, Run-D.M.C. and Beastie Boys are at Sacramento in May. You wanna go? The Beastie Boys are this new rap group touring with Run-D.M.C. They're all white. But they fresh, man. Check 'em out. I like what they doing!"

"Yeah. That sounds cool!"

Todd Welch crashed the moment with a half-serious stand-up comedy prediction. "No white boy rapper will ever be any good. It's like white people trying to play sports. No offense, Rockwell. It's not their fault. For real. Just like we black folk are naturally better at music, dancin', and fuckin'. White people are just naturally sorry at all of 'em."

"Shut up, Clown!" I said with a laugh.

ELECTRIC WAVES AT 15 MY FIRST LIVE CONCERTS: IRON MAIDEN AND BEASTIE BOYS

Rock stars and their soundtrack lives have captured my imagination and heart since I was a little boy.

Flash forward a few years. I'm at Kevin's family's house in Sacramento, the "Dark Side," before the Run-D.M.C. concert. It was my first time in a tough black neighborhood outside my small town. Kevin, his cousin Cory, and I were drinking in Lil Marty's bedroom, Kevin's other cousin. Before we cracked our cans of Colt 45 malt liquor, Cory was already instigatin' me. It's just in his nature. He looks like a wiry six-foot spider monkey with energy to match, but his heart is huge, and he would back family 'til the end.

"Rockwell, you drinking like you scared! Haaaa!"

I immediately laughed and shot back, like I'd been drinking 40s and slingin' down at the park for years, "Fuck that! Let's drink!"

I started pounding the malt liquor, trying to get fucked up. I really was. I loved drinking a lot more than they ever would. Instantly, I looked at Kevin to step his game up and start chugging with me. We started challenging each other to

111

take the next big gulp of the copper-stained nasty shit until we were all laughing and giggling like kids watching an ABC after-school special. Kevin's big Uncle Marty nearly knocked the door down to let us know it was time to go, in Samuel L. Jackson style, "Let's go nigga!"

Kevin walked through the doorway and asked his older cousin if he would take us so that we could drink on the way. He looked back at me and then at Kevin with a cautious approval. We rolled out in the back seat of a classic scraper. The windows were down, and the wind was hot, even as the sun hung low through the hood. We were high and right, rolling out to a historic concert. It was a perfect moment. The song playing on KSFM 102.5 was "No Sleep Till Brooklyn" from the Beastie Boys.

We reached the amphitheater, and Kevin's cousin kicked us out of the car near the ticket booth with a permanent scowl of hoodism. Young people were walking around outside the show wearing big chains and Adidas. I was about to see two New York rap groups on a perfect summer night with my best friend.

The energy was crazy. I'd never seen so many black people and so few white people in one place in my life. It was the first time I felt intimidated being white. But that soon faded as we rolled into the amphitheater. Kev led us to the front to get as close as possible, requiring me to push past tough black guys and big drunk black women drenched in hair oil, cocoa butter lotion, and perfume. Just as we got to the front, the show started with the Beastie Boys performing. They had twenty cases of Budweiser and Old English on the stage. I ended up between two hot black girls while one of the few white girls was rubbing up on Kev. I remember Kev and me smiling at each other across a sea of fans. Life was good.

Lying on the floor, trying to go to sleep after the concert back at Kevin's family's house on the dark side, I reminded Kevin of my dream.

"Kev, we're gonna be on stage someday."

"Yeah Rock, we gonna do it big!"

Kevin's cousin Cory chimed in, "Rockwell, you crazy!! Whatchu know 'bout rap music?"

"Dude, it's all the same. Music is music. We saw a show tonight that proved color and sound have no boundaries. Trippy… People are people, man…and music is universal, dude."

"Rockwell, you a fool, man!"

Cory started laughing, and then everybody started laughing as we faded off to sleep.

When I first met Kevin, we both recognized that we believed and led in similar ways. We came from totally different worlds, and intuitively understood that collaborating and unifying just made sense and was more interesting. We talked about shit most people weren't talking about. The reality of race and the world and how people perceive things that aren't necessarily what they are. The Run-D.M.C. and Beastie Boys combo of white and black rap groups touring for the first time changed the game forever. Duce and I witnessed it live and reaffirmed that we were living that. We didn't give a fuck about color, even though we knew very well how powerful it was. We didn't want people to fight over it because there were bigger issues to grapple with, like teaching kids how to become good men in a crazy world. We knew it, and we talked about it up through the last night we hung out.

That first concert experience was legendary and opened me up to new worlds and musical influences and possibilities. But my first live rock show featuring Guns N' Roses opening for Iron Maiden was a religious experience.

Every concert I went to had a nostalgic party scene, beginning with the drive to Sac, listening to the bands on 98.5 KZAP with the windows down, and the hot summer air blasting us with the feeling of immortality, freedom, and the anticipation of rock star dreams. Pulling into the field that had been converted into parking grounds was always an intimidating but exciting experience, watching people hanging out drinking beer and bottles of whiskey, smoking, laughing, and music from the upcoming bands filling the air from old Chevy Camaros and stepside trucks across the newly formed village of rock and rollers. It was a timeless display of young people showing up for a unified allegiance to their favorite rock groups. It was all about the music and the comradery of that moment, being unified and one—no matter the color of our skin, what car you drove, or the amount of money in your bank account.

Guys wore cut-off or full length and tight Levi's, white high tops, and either a white t-shirt with random beer, whiskey, and tobacco brands or a black well-worn rock concert t-shirt with the tour schedule laid out on the back and the sleeves cut off. These blue-collar warriors would strut the parking lot with their buddies, trolling for girls as the evening summer sun danced with the dust and smoke in the air to create a dusky haze of yellows and oranges.

The chicks were ready to roll, with bright red lipstick, big fucking hair, and little shorts and tops that made them look like Daisy Duke's slutty hot rocker cousin from Northern California. Chicks are flashing tits for the howling guys, and everyone is ramping up on booze, drugs, adrenaline, and the anticipation of what was behind the fortress walls of the amphitheater a couple hundred yards away. I could hear a heavy as fuck sound from a band I didn't recognize. It ended up being Corrosion of Conformity playing "Seven Days" from the album *Deliverance*.

I saw a healthy dose of rock bands spanning '70s classic rock like Bad Company to '80s groups like our hometown heroes Tesla to my all-time heavy rock band Pantera, who ruled the heavy rock world of the '90s. My brother Nick and I saw Van Halen at the LA Forum. Every concert had opening lineups either from future greats or fucking horrible end-of-the-trend big hair bands like Faster Pussycat opening for Motley Crue. Each and every live show added fuel to my passion. The night we were in Sac for the hometown platinum band, Tesla, was electric. Watching a successful band play their hometown amps the experience up to "11." It's the same with sports. Playing for thousands of screaming hometown fans gets your blood flowing.

The music and the scene at live shows always pulled me in and led me down a path of chaos and mystery that I not only longed for but needed. I was able to feel a release from the expectations of everyday society and family that shackled the real me.

FIRST KISS

It was summer, and Mom was cutting my hair on our front porch steps. The sun was hanging below the huge magnolia tree, silhouetting its ornate white flowers while the sunlight flowed through the branches only revealed when the dark green leaves would flicker in the gentle breeze. The smell of jasmine in our yard and fresh-cut grass filled the evening air. My cousin Brandi stopped by to say hi, and during our conversation, she mentioned that she knew a girl she thought I would like. They played softball together, and Brandi said she was not the only one who thought I should date Becky.

Becky. I hadn't seen her since junior high, and back then we were friends but never really hung out. I remembered that she was cute, but she was a tomboy and would rather ride quads and play softball than date. And after my crash course in older, faster girls, I was feeling a little unsure about what dating even meant. I was currently "dating" a senior, and it wasn't working. It was kind of a forced situation and wasn't feeling right either. Brandi could sense my apprehension and curiosity. She told me a little bit more about Becky. She said in the past few years since junior high, Becky had changed a little; she had dated a few guys, and everyone liked her, no matter who they were or what clique they belonged to. She said she was just a genuine and good person. I remembered that about her, too.

"We—I mean, I—think you two would be good together. She's not dating anyone right now. She just broke up with Kevin."

I was still dating Lena; her best friend Cathy Quest, the doppelganger of the loud, failed redhead comedian Kathy Griffin pretty much convinced us to be together. It wasn't really going anywhere with her, and we both knew it.

Brandi was not my favorite person because she was pretty much out for herself. She was only concerned with looking good to the outside world, the kind of girl that would over-exaggerate her accomplishments and short arm a ground ball in softball to avoid an "error" instead of diving for the ball to make a play for the team. She stabbed people in the back as she smiled and hugged them. I wondered what she was up to. As she drove off, I sat there, wondering. Mom finished cutting my hair as I stared at the sunset being painted over the coastal mountains.

There was a baseball game on the TV as I cleaned up after my haircut, and we ate dinner as a family. The phone rang just as we were cleaning up from our meal. It was Thomas, my childhood buddy, who lived just down the street. He wanted to know if I was up for hanging out with him and meeting up with his girlfriend, Donna, and her friend Becky. I smiled, realizing what was going on; lifelong girlfriends and softball teammates, along with my buddy, were all in on the setup. Thomas, Donna, and Becky all went to the other high school in town; they hung out more often, and everyone thought we would be a good match. Thomas assured me it wasn't a date. I was sixteen, but Becky was only fifteen and not allowed to date yet. We were just going to grab some beers and meet up with the girls, nothing serious. That was all Thomas would say, and it sounded like a good plan to me.

Not more than fifteen minutes later, Thomas pulled up in his 1976 Stepside Chevy truck. It had a modified engine with dual glass pack exhaust and oversized BF Goodrich tires, the classic era rims with heavy clean aluminum and six oval cut-outs. The cream-tan color paint job gave it a modest look that kept in under the radar, most of the time. After Dad and Thomas talked about Chevy engines, trucks, and heavy equipment, we jumped in and headed out. My dad and Thomas connected on the level of cars and guy talk about engines and tools. Mom and Dad waved and told us to have fun and be safe. We were off into the perfect summer evening.

Our first stop, of course, was the liquor store. Pigg's Liquor was in Southside, and we were able to pay an older guy out front to buy our beer. He gouged us, expecting a five-dollar tip for a six-dollar twelve pack. We couldn't really complain; we just wanted the beer, and we were underage.

Thomas took us through Southside and into our old junior high school campus, Central School. He pulled into the darkened corner of the parking lot up next to the multi-purpose room that was once our gym, dance hall, theater, and cafeteria. It was dark, and there was no one else in sight. Thomas promised the girls would be meeting us there. Just then, Donna pulled up with Becky in the passenger seat. I almost didn't recognize her; she had grown up a lot. She was hot!

The car didn't stop, and it appeared that they were going to head off, but she was just messing with us and pulled her car in front of the truck. It was dark and we were in Southside, but we didn't feel threatened in our small town on a summer evening. We were kids hanging out at our old junior high campus to meet up and see where things went.

Since I was the "outsider" who went to the other high school and felt nervous about talking to Becky, I followed Thomas's lead as he jumped out of the truck and casually walked towards the girls' car. He was relaxed because he had been dating Donna for a while and they hung out with Becky all the time. They all grew up riding ATVs at Oly Hill as kids, and all three of them had dads that owned small businesses in town in lumber, asphalt, and mining equipment. They were from the same tribe. I felt like a total intruder, although I also felt like I belonged.

The girls opened their car doors, giggling about a joke that Thomas and I were not in on. It helped take the edge off the awkward teenage moment.

Thomas prodded, "What's so funny?"

Becky shot back at her childhood friend, "Nothing, Thomas. We're just talking about the softball game."

Thomas and I cracked our beers and we all just hung out. There was never a formal introduction since we had known each other in junior high. It was just four teenagers hanging out, talking, reminiscing, and joking lightly and innocently with one another. It was nice, and I felt pretty okay about it... but nervous, excited, and happy all mixed in.

Thomas and Donna had locked up against her car for a hug since they were already dating. Becky and I caught the cue to let them have some time alone and we went for a walk. I grabbed a couple Coors Light cans out of our stash in the truck, and we walked towards the gym, in between classrooms that formed the square where everyone would hang out at break, lunch, and after school waiting for the busses. We disappeared into the dark and walked south past the basketball courts, off the blacktop courts, and into the fresh-cut grass where kids played pickup games of soccer and tag football. We started feeling okay making small talk about our time as students at Central, reminiscing about the "old days," and we started to relax and enjoy the moment. Just then, the sprinklers opened fire on us! We were able to avoid a direct hit and made it to a dry zone on the edge of the blacktop courts. We laughed and celebrated our escape. The smell of the wet grass and the blooming summer flowers from Marcy Smith's yard down the street completed the feel for the moment. I'm not sure I had even drunk one of the beers I grabbed yet; I was simply captivated by her.

We talked about how we loved the sounds and smells of sprinklers in the summertime. I ran out into the "killing field" of ranch-sized sprinklers and got close enough to one to drench my head like I did when I was a little kid. When I stood up, water was dripping down my face, and we were both laughing. I had forgotten about the roundabout spray of water, and it hit my legs as I stumbled back to her. I was getting hit from behind multiple times before I made it to safety. She laughed at my stunt, and I smiled and laughed with her. It was something I had done a thousand times in our front yard as a kid growing up.

We stood there a few more minutes, watching the sprinklers, and then slowly walked back towards the gym and our friends. It was dark and we were alone. Suddenly we saw lights and heard walkie-talkie radios... COPS! We figured they must have pulled up on Thomas and Donna, just on the other side of the gym from where we were. I had two beers still on me and made a quick decision to jump up and place them on the door overhang at the gym exit. Beck and I huddled near each other as we heard the cops leave, then we came around the gym to meet up with Thomas and Donna. No one got busted; the police just wanted to check in and make sure everyone was safe. They knew we were just some kids trying to find some time alone.

I think we cruised Oro Dam Blvd a few times, stopping off at Burger King to say hi to a few mutual friends, and then we followed Donna's car to drop Becky off at her house. She had a 10 pm curfew. I remember nervously getting out of Thomas's truck at the bottom of her driveway to walk her up to the garage door, where the front door and porch light were out of view. As we said goodbye, we kissed. Innocent and real. We both turned and walked away, then looked back to smile and wave. I got to the truck and I was floating. I jumped in the passenger seat with a love dazed look and smiled at Thomas. "We kissed! I like her!"

ME & BECK—HIGH SCHOOL DAYS

T he rest of that summer, we all hung out and would meet up cruisin' Oro Dam Blvd or at parties at mutual friends' houses. We would find places to hang out like some random field or paved cul-de-sac in a future development we called the "Executive." Beck and I became exclusive by the end of summer, but we didn't take it as seriously as some high school couples did; we were independent, confident, and had our own lives and circle of friends beyond just the two of us. We also went to opposite high schools in town, so lunchtime became a big deal for us. Before mobile phones and the internet, we had to talk on our home phones the night before or plan the next day's destination during the ten or fifteen minutes we got to see each other at lunch.

Becky and I were both athletes, and that kept us pretty busy during the year, but starting the end of summer 1987, just before our sophomore year, we hung out together with friends. We spent lots of nights up on the dam hanging out; sometimes we'd take a swim or just play and joke around as we looked out over the lights of our little town and wonder and dream about the world beyond. Becky and I shared an unspoken energy that called us beyond our own city limits and connected us. We both came from parents who gave

121

us unusually focused, consistent love, guidance, and security. We had high self-esteem with big dreams but a grounded view of the world in many important ways. Family and hard work were the foundation. All unspoken, but similarities that bound us together.

One thing about Becky that set her apart from others was her fashion. I was instantly taken by her fearlessness when it came to fashion, especially in a conservative blue-collar town. She had no interest in some pre-designed outfit sold by the latest trend brand or pop star. She had a funky fashion that was all her own. She wore a bold and creative mix of clothes and accessories from Bay Area secondhand stores or the fashion forward shops of L.A. and or some sentimental pieces of vintage fashion jewelry from her grandma. She was edgy and always crafting looks that were inspired by people and styles she admired or just liked. Becky's fashion eye and her frugal shopping habits allowed her to put amazing outfits together for a fraction of the cost that girls were paying to look like just the mannequin in the storefront window. Her affinity for shoes was her main fashion cornerstone and obsession. The running joke with me and my buddies was guessing what crazy thing Beck was going to be wearing that day at lunch.

Beck was a tough girl who was the best softball player on her team, the team captain and All-League in her conference. She was naturally beautiful with big blonde hair and green eyes. She was smart, vivacious, and friendly to everyone she met. She volunteered to work with special needs kids at Sierra Del Oro before ever meeting my little sister, Nicole. Because of her confidence and kindness without arrogance, Becky was absolutely loved by everyone she met. The truth about her was obvious to me when I first saw her at the lake, then when I met her at the softball fields, and even more so as I got to really know her. Becky was different. She actually focused on the right things and was able to rise above so much of the nonsense teenagers misinterpret through a selfish lens. Becky truly and genuinely cared about other people.

Some girls were jealous of her and talked shit, falsely claiming she was snotty and conceited, but Beck was okay with herself in a way that made high school teenaged girls' shit talk impenetrable to her self-esteem and self-worth. I admired her sense of self. I watched her wear her hair and fashion so authentically and take criticism from haters and friends alike. Even her so-called best friends would mock her for her bold outfits because they were too scared to step out of the jeans, t-shirt, and high-top sneaker phase. Eventually, they would adopt some of her styles, but deny they were emulating her. Becky was always a trendsetter because she wasn't trying to be.

Our junior year in high school was fun! Starting in the fall was varsity football. I stepped in and earned starting positions as tight end and middle linebacker. I was off to a great couple of games. Becky turned sixteen on the first of October and got a red T-Top Trans Am with tinted windows and a powerful engine—and we were allowed to go on our first official date. Her parents made a deal with her that they got to pick out the type of used car she would get, meaning it could take a hit and not constantly break down, and promised that it would fit her personality. Becky would be responsible for paying half of the cost, and her parents held her to working and paying her part. Despite being a year-round athlete, Beck worked multiple jobs babysitting, cleaning houses, and working at Dave's shoes. She loves her shoes! I was working side jobs on weekends off and on to earn some money to buy Beck a Black Hills Gold ring from our local jewelry store. I didn't have a clue what I was supposed to do, really. I just wanted to show her that I liked her...a lot. I had no training on how to court a girl. I grew up in a house full of boys. No clue.

On the evening of our first date, I drove my dad's truck over to Becky's house, about three miles away from my house. I was about to meet her parents for the first time since I was at her thirteenth birthday party. Back then, Thomas and I showed up together, me in my knee brace and crutches from tearing my ACL during my second year in Pop Warner football. Thomas and I proceeded to cause a scene roughhousing and setting off firecrackers outside to show off. I danced using my crutches and was a typical loud and crazy 14-year-old kid. In the end, it was all innocent, but I didn't want her dad, Del, to think that was the kid I still was.

I pulled up and pulled off the road nearly into the neighbor's front yard. I nervously made my way up to the house, the very same house I toilet papered with Paul Wilson back in junior high. I noticed there were quite a few cars in her long driveway, and my stomach turned. I had anxiety about making this impression a good one. All the cars made me feel more nervous. Who all would be there for me to meet? There was no one outside, so I proceeded up the gravel driveway and onto the concrete walkway that cut through the front lawn and up to the front door. I knocked on the door about as hard as a moth hitting a porch light...pathetic. I knocked again, this time with respectful force. I was already overanalyzing my door knock performance, worried about how they would perceive me if I knocked either too soft or too loud. The door opened to a woman wearing a huge smile on her face.

"You must be Chris! Come in! I'm Aunt Berta!"

Before she could fully introduce herself, I was surrounded by a pack of happy giggling little kids.

"I was friends with your Aunt Terry in high school after they moved up here from LA."

Berta was a black-haired Mexican beauty with a gypsy's soul. One of the kids was her daughter Tracy, and the rest were cousins from other aunts and uncles related to Becky's mom Connie. I looked around to see if I could find Becky, but I inadvertently locked eyes with her dad as he peered around the partition wall dividing the small living room from the entryway. There were bunches of people, some I still hadn't met swarming around. Del looked at me over his reading glasses and, without a crack of a smile, looked me up and down, stopping at my mullet and Iron Maiden t-shirt. He nodded his head and spat Copenhagen chew into an old Pepsi can, and said, "Hi Chris." Then he turned back around towards the TV show he was watching; I think it was drag racing, and the volume was up pretty high to drown out all the family conversation and little kids.

By this point, the kids wanted my full attention, and I had yet to see Becky. I wasn't even sure she was there. People were saying hello, the TV was loud, and the kids were giggling and running around. Above all the chaos, I heard two women having an argument in the kitchen. I realized that it was Becky and her mom. I couldn't believe it. It freaked me out because we never did that at our house, especially when we had company. We just kept it in and rarely dealt with it. I figured that was the end before it started. As their volume increased, I was waiting for a family disaster to happen, where people blow up at each other and then don't talk for decades or simply pretend nothing ever happened and continue with a superficial relationship, cordially interacting during the holidays or at funerals. Instead, as quickly as the argument had escalated, it mellowed, and they ended up talking it through and didn't miss a beat with the food prep they were doing together. I was amazed by the scene, all of it. Unconditional love. I don't think I consciously recognized it then, but I knew it felt right.

We ended up staying there for a bit to have dinner with her very large family. They welcomed me like I had been a part of the family for ages. We went for a drive after dinner and got ice cream. We went up to the dam, and I gave her the ring I had been saving up for. After meeting her family that night and seeing the way they interacted—they were real and honest and felt safe together—I knew that I wanted her to be in my life and I wanted to be in hers, forever.

A few weeks later, she pulled up to the school to pick me up for lunch on my seventeenth birthday. I was standing on the southside of campus outside the gym and locker room with my teammates and buddies after fourth-period

PE. Becky's big blonde hair, black sunglasses, and magnetic smile, while cruising up in her red Trans Am, made everyone within view stop and stare. She was the best thing in my life. The best birthday present ever.

MARIJUANA MAVERICK

I grew up hiking the foothills of the Sierra Nevada Mountains and the Feather River Canyon, swimming the creeks and rivers of the high country and exploring with my brothers and buddies. Cory and Ron were always up for an adventure. They were hippie brothers who grew up mining for gold with their grandpa and growing organic fruits, vegetables, and weed...some of the best weed around in the mid-'80s. We decided one summer to plant some clones out in the wilderness to see how they would do. We chose a secluded and hard-to-get-to area, made the treacherous hike, and then left it up to nature.

It was the beginning of my senior year in high school when we went back up to see if there was anything to harvest. Hoping for the best, expecting the worst, we headed up the canyon in Cory's white Ford Expedition. Cory had already been busted once for growing on federal land, so we were on high alert, but I lived for this type of risky shit and the adrenaline rush it gave me. Marijuana was illegal, and the state and Feds were still handing out long prison sentences for distributing and selling even just a pound.

Ron was younger than Cory and me, and he was quiet and introspective but was always ready to share one of his conspiracy theories about the government or aliens when we got high. He was like a wizard full of knowledge that seemed foreign and strange to me back then but made for great stony conversation. We would spend afternoons in their backyard under the camphor tree smoking, tending to the "crops" and discussing all sorts of random and interesting things. I learned how to grow from the organic masters way before organic was cool.

Growing up together and spending so much time in the wild gave us a deep and trusting bond. These guys pretty much kept to themselves and didn't share much about their home life with just anyone, but they knew they could trust me and my brothers. We all grew up a little different from most, so we shared that connection too.

The canyon was the perfect destination for a hot fall day. The temperature was still blazing, and the cool water of the river and creeks was a refreshing break from the heat. Even if the deer had eaten our wilderness grow, we would have a hike and a swim to look forward to. When we arrived at the trailhead, Cory parked the truck, and we loaded our packs with tools for our hopeful harvest, a bag of weed, and some drinking water. We may have had a sack of trail mix or some crackers, but I doubt it; we were kids and never packed what we needed.

We looked almost straight up, took a deep breath, and started in on the treacherous hike once again. It was a risk and an adventure just to get to our destination, on purpose. The harder it is to get to, the less likely anyone else would try or even know it existed. Ron was like a wiry mountain warlock and could climb and scale rocks and cliffs like a Tibetan Billy Goat. He was the quickest of all of us and, within a few minutes, was already out of sight. Cory and I were slowly ascending the near-vertical climb, mindful that each step would either be successful or lead to a fall that would, at the very least, mangle our bodies. We were focused and determined to make it to the top unscathed. I think each one of us had some minor scrapes and bruises from the first time we made the climb to plant the seedlings. Panting from pushing ourselves and nearing mental exhaustion from focusing on each step up the slick granite, we made our way closer to the top. The waterfall was roaring, muting out all other sounds, and spraying the rocks, making each step even more dangerous.

The final obstacle was an almost impassable sheer granite cliff. We ducked under thick brush following an old deer trail on the north side of the falls, grasping vines and vegetation to help us scale the wall. A slip now would not be good. Without words, Cory and I instinctively reached out a hand to help one another when needed. The sun was beaming down, and sweat was dripping off us. We were tired but young, strong, and excited about the possibilities that lie ahead. As we made it to the top, it was like we entered another world. The sheer exposed granite that had challenged our bodies was now gone, and we stood inside a thick canopied forest full of life. Lush green foliage enveloped the meandering creek that fed the raging falls we had just scrambled up. Ferns and wildflowers painted the landscape as birds sang and swooped to catch the insects buzzing near the surface of the water. The bubbling and gently flowing water replaced the crashing waters of the falls, and the forest creatures scampered about without a care that we had just intruded on their little wonderland. It was a refreshing and much-needed break from our climb.

Just as we started to feel a sense of relaxation, we heard Ron yell out with an unsure "Whooooop!" Cory and I looked at each other, not knowing if it was a "whoop" of celebration or a call for help. The adrenaline kicked in instantly, and with goosebumps of uncertainty, we quickly headed in the direction of the yell. We hit another small waterfall surrounded by exposed granite and climbed up with precision and conviction, knowing that we needed to get to Ron. The stream narrowed, and the forest thickened, making it darker and harder to traverse. Cory took a nosedive into a patch of jagged rocks but popped up, almost ignoring the bloodied knee and hand he suffered from the fall. He was an athlete and had navigated these hills his whole life; he knew how to take a fall that would disable the average hiker. Plus, that was his little brother who had called out. He was more worried about Ron than a little blood.

We were both urged on by the same need to get to him. I was imagining the worst: a bear, a mountain lion, law enforcement, or a deranged gold miner. Just then, we rounded a corner where the forest opened to a bend in the creek where the sun shone down on a small island sitting amid the meandering water. And there, on that little island, were eight of the most beautiful pot plants I had ever seen dancing in the breeze and sunlight. Ron popped out from behind the emerald forest of bud with a huge smile of excitement and pride and let out another "Whooooop!" We all started whooping and celebrating the most amazing crop in the most picturesque setting I could dream up. We struck gold!

Cory broke out the trimming scissors and we set out to harvest our bounty. Ron rolled a celebratory joint. We shook our heads in disbelief at what Mother Nature had just bestowed us with. Eight plants, about eight feet tall, and just loaded with bud simply cultivated by the earth, sun, and water.

We trimmed and loaded our backpacks and headed back down the steep trail to the truck. Silently, we calculated each step down the slope to ensure our safe arrival with the reward for our journey and trust in Mother Nature. It was peaceful, even though strenuous and intense. We were stoked on our haul and made it to the truck just at dusk. As we crossed the highway to the truck, we noticed another vehicle nearby. It was a newer looking white SUV with tinted windows. Our stomachs dropped. Had we been followed? We casually continued to approach our truck, unloaded our packs, got in, and drove back down the canyon.

The other truck hit their lights and began following us. I knew we were toast; it was either undercover cops or someone who wanted what we had. My paranoia can take over and imagine the worst scenarios. The cab of our truck was silent. Cory scanned the rearview mirror to see what the white

SUV's next move would be. As we hit a rare straightaway, they accelerated and approached us, and then passed us. We were left alone in the quiet tranquility of the Feather River Canyon—childhood friends, brothers—living an adventure we would never forget. We would often reminisce about that day as we got older, one of our many growing adventures.

CUTTHROAT SALOON

I f it wasn't a live concert, it was the great outdoors that set me free.

We were heading back to camp after a long soak in natural hot springs that bubbled up in the meadow cradled by massive granite mountains outside of Markleeville. There was a manmade four-foot-deep hot spring pool, a yellow, green-tinted soup of minerals and bodies mingling with the cool and clean high sierra air. It was as if you were transported to the Swiss Alps. It's a breathtaking natural experience that revitalizes the spirit. And the cold pool, built next to the hot pool one hundred and fifty years after miners first discovered the soothing hot mineral water bubbling out of the meadow, refreshes the skin and mind, making the body yearn for the heat and tingle of the hot springs. We spent days hunting and hiking the old silver mine mountains in search of a blood trail or obsidian arrowhead left behind by the natives who made the area their home during the summer when the valley on the east side of the Sierra Nevada Mountains got too hot and the deer headed to higher ground. Our annual pilgrimage followed this timeless migration of Mother Nature's creations to the High Sierras.

Bathing in hot springs and ice-cold mountain streams were part of the memories and traditions of a forgotten past covered up with modern-day amenities and conveniences that numb the senses and mind to the true struggle and joy of our place in nature. Our annual return was a primal calling of simpler times, a reconnection to the mountains and our place among the world of timeless beauty and history, a reconnection to the truth. As a child, it was like being in a western movie with adventure and action in a setting that was surely a backdrop at one time for old western films. We camped and hunted on mountains covered with scars and old buildings and relics from the silver mining boom. Mark Twain was out west bumming around and hiking those same hills when his brother was appointed Secretary of State for the Nevada territory and busy settling Carson. I was surrounded by Wild West pioneering history, and it made the experience like an old western movie. And like those films, I discovered there that it doesn't always have a happy ending.

I remember the adult men reveled in the opportunity to escape their clean-cut upstanding-man-in-the-community responsibilities and image and return to the old west as hunters with an outlaw attitude. Bowhunting made me feel like we were part of the native hunters who hiked the same hills and harvested deer in a similar way. It was like being in a world far far away from the modern world. I have a never-ending supply of memories of fishing Poison Creek as kids and hiking through aspen and pine trees, cussing, spitting, and laughing all the way down to the beaver ponds. Despite all the wild bear and mountain lion, we never had an adult with us. We were venturing into wild territory equipped with buck knives on our belts and our fishing poles. It was fun and scary, and made us all more self-confident. I am grateful for my parents giving me independent thought and freedom at an early age.

My dad and Sonny Brandt loved the idea of living back in the pioneer days. I get it now, more than ever. They grew up in that disappearing world and felt a calling, deep down, to reconnect to their pioneering roots and the hardworking, blue-collar men they came from. They took great pride in being family men, and they camped with intent to hunt and feed the family, despite the ice-cold beer and tri-tip Grandpa Brandt brought for the first night's meal. Our families set up camp traditionally down the dirt road where Poison Creek meets the lush aspen grove, about six fence posts north of the spring we got our water from. My dad was more like Clint Eastwood versus John Wayne. He was a renaissance man, conscious of the world around him, and wanted to appreciate, preserve, and respect nature and the hunt.

He talked to us about his philosophical struggles with killing an animal and the primal instincts that drive us to hunt and compete, pitting man against prey in a fair challenge, with bows and arrows, stalking them on foot. I remember riding out of camp early in the morning in the back of the truck with my bow by my side and my hat on backward, leaning into the cold and dark before the sunrise, in search of prey, always hoping I would kill my first buck and share in the celebration back at camp. I looked up to men who were every bit tough men yet refined as fathers and figures in their community.

I was one of the lucky ones; my dad was every bit that man, and I appreciate it more every day I get older, and life gets more challenging. Sure, we were on a "hunting trip," but really, we were on our annual family camping trip. I was seventeen and in prime shape from working in the lumberyards and lifting weights all summer for my senior football season and dreaming of big college football scholarships by the end of the year. Anything was possible; I was invincible. We had been hunting here since I was a baby, and this was the trip when I was finally one of the "big boys" who got to stand up in the back of the pickup with the older warriors like my dad and Sonny.

After a great day of hunting and a long soak in the hot springs, Nick Brandt asked Matt and me if we wanted to stop off at the Cutthroat Saloon for a beer and a shot of "Crown" before we headed back up to camp before nightfall.

"Hell Yeah!"

I was all in despite my reservations about my parents' concern about me drinking and the fact that I was going to try and pass for 21 when I was a baby-faced 17-year-old kid. Fortunately, the old UCLA Football t-shirt I was wearing and my long unwashed hair gave me the appearance of just possibly being out of my teens. Even so, I was more worried about disappointing my parents than getting caught underage. Nick parked his old Chevy truck under the giant cottonwood across from the bar. A row of motorcycles lined the street in front of the bar. As we got out of the truck and started walking across the street, I felt my anxiety spark. In the back of my mind were flashes of disappointing my parents or getting kicked out and having to sit in the truck while the other guys sat in the bar to have a "couple drinks" and some laughs. I was a little intimidated by the Cutthroat Saloon's raucous history along with the large number of motorcycles in the front—enough to constitute a biker gang.

As we walked across the road, I imagined what it must be like inside the saloon. Ever since I was a kid driving past it when we went to town or the Hot Springs, I dreamed of what went on in there. I'm not sure I even imagined anything in particular, just good times, music, women, and whiskey; images from all the western movies I grew up watching with my dad. I had a couple years of weekend binge drinking and parties under my belt, so I was ready for my first drink in a real bar, and this was not just another bar. This was the legendary Cutthroat Saloon, originally located on Silver Hill during the boom, then relocated to Markleeville. The Cutthroat was an icon in outlaw folklore, celebrating the many brawls and shoot-outs during the boom days of silver mania that swept the hills of Markleeville back in 1858.

As we neared the front door, the faded neon Budweiser sign blinked and glitched; I was ready for whatever was waiting for me inside that bar. Nick confidently swung open the door, and we made our way into the dark saloon. Old pine walls were littered with poorly framed black and white photos and artifacts from "the good old days." Pictures of locals with their trophy bucks, logging and mining images, and some old rusted railroad spikes, a few old mining lanterns, and antique bottles—everything from the original Coca-Cola to some sort of heroin opium-based medicinal elixir. There were some aged and dusty taxidermied deer and bear mounted behind the bar. An old potbelly fireplace sat in the center of the room, and an antique record-playing jukebox sat on the north side, where a narrow stairway led up to the old brothel rooms.

But the big surprise was the ceiling covered with bras. Every kind and size imaginable. To a 17-year-old boy hopped up on testosterone and the anticipation of whiskey, that was a cool addition that only made it a more historic place and moment. Despite the stares by the bikers and bartender, Nick made his way to the open barstools in the middle of the long wooden bar that ran the length of the east and south walls. Matt and I instinctively followed big bro's lead and knew what to do. Act like you know what you're doing and act like you belong there. So, we pulled up a stool to the right and left of Nick. I sat to Nick's right, for no particular reason, other than the fact that the old-timer bartender was to Nick's left, and I wanted to dodge his judging eye. I knew it really made no difference, but I still wanted to give myself a fighting chance.

With no ID and an obviously never shaven face, the bartender gave us the curmudgeonly peer over his glasses to determine the situation. He took what seemed like hours to decide our fate. I remember casually looking around and seeing women laughing and wearing leather and bright red lipstick. I could hear Lynyrd Skynyrd's "That Smell" on the jukebox as the bartender asked Nick, "What'll it be?" I couldn't believe it. Nick ordered up three shots of Crown Royal and Coors bottles and quickly handed the old man the money, including a hefty tip to keep the drinks coming...despite two of us being clearly underage. The smells of old tobacco smoke, perfume, and whiskey filled the air as I tipped back my shot and set my glass quietly down like a true amateur, and someone underage trying to be discreet. The whiskey hit my stomach like fire lighting gasoline. I felt the surging urge to throw it up, but I kept it down as my eyes watered, and my face turned pale. For a moment, I even felt like passing out.

After picking my balls up off the old wooden floor, I grabbed for my beer and took a couple of good chugs to dilute the poison I just dumped into my body. Within a minute or two, I felt the warm sensation of the whiskey running through my veins. Time stopped, and I never wanted it to end. It felt like I had just been touched by the spirit in the sky. Little did I know it was the grim reaper in disguise. I felt amazing. I was drinking whiskey with my idols in the Cutthroat Saloon. I had arrived at manhood. As I finished my first beer, Nick was ordering up another round and told us to pay up for it. Matt and I happily reached into our dirty Levi's for all the loose dollar bills we had. We brought the cash, hoping to score some booze for our fishing trip we planned to take down from camp to the beaver ponds. Instead, we were buying shots at the Cutthroat Saloon and feeling like real outlaw cowboys, dodging the authorities, which were literally across the street next door to the general store.

I felt like I was floating and could hardly contain my drunk, giddy excitement as I took my second shot with the ease of a hardened drinker. Scanning the room to take in the wild activity of all the people in the bar enjoying themselves, I noticed that the guys with the leather-clad women were real bikers, not the weekend warrior lawyer types. Nick was in pure form and already capturing the attention of the biker chicks on the other side of the fireplace. He gave them a cool smile and then casually glanced at the bartender to set us up with a third round. As the shots were being poured, one of the bikers stood up and said to Nick, "You staring at something, buddy?"

Matt sighed as if he had been through this scenario a thousand times with his big brother. "Here we go…" he muttered as he took his shot and grabbed a chaser with the second beer he was nursing.

Nick calmly reached for his shot and knocked it back with a crooked smile at the guy and replied with, "Yeah, your chick." With that, I swallowed my third shot and got up, expecting my first Wild West bar brawl.

The bartender cut the tension with "No fightin' in my bar or you're gone, and the cops are next door." Then the old-timer said, "I think it's time you guys left." We walked away from our unfinished beers and headed to the door. As Nick was reaching for the door, the biker yelled out, "Figured you'd run!" Nick snapped and ordered the overweight bearded ex-con out for a good ol' street fight. The place stood up as we walked through the door. Matt somehow was able to push Nick outside with me trailing behind, looking back at a saloon full of pissed-off bikers. We made our way across the street to the truck and headed back up the hill towards camp. As we crossed the bridge over the East Carson at the edge of town, Nick stopped the truck in the middle of the road, flipped a bitch and headed back with an intense focus. I looked at Matt, waiting for him to stop him, anticipating what we were headed back for.

Nick pulled right up to the sheriff's station, slammed on his brakes, jumped out, and walked next door into the general store. A few minutes later, he returned with a paper bag cradled in his left arm and a pack of Camel Lights in his right hand, trying to unpeel the plastic wrapping with his teeth like a wolf ripping into a carcass to get at the life source inside. I glanced at Matt to see a big smile on his face, knowing what was inside the bag. Nick was still fired up and in his own world, trying to let go of something he wanted to finish his way. He would deal with the consequences if and when they arrived. Nick lived intensely in the now. As he closed his door and lit up his cigarette, he kept staring across the street at the Cutthroat with an intensity that could be seen and heard in every drag he took. Without taking his eye off the bar, he reached into the bag and handed me and Matt each a can of Coors and brandished a fifth of Jim Beam with a half-smile, making him momentarily forget about his war with the bikers, and within himself.

Nick cracked his beer between his legs with his left hand while the cigarette smoldered between his lips using his right hand, turning on his stereo to play his worn-out cassette tape of Neal Young's Greatest Hits. He squinted from the smoke, sun, and warfare in the bar. A sheriff was pulling out from the office next door and gave us a look before moving on to his previous thought, probably about getting home to crack a beer like us. We tore out and headed up the hill like bandits running out of town after raising hell. The evening sun and alpine surroundings and smells created the perfect backdrop to bring us down out of the intensity and back into the rhythm with nature for our cruise back up the mountain to camp. None of us were in a hurry to get back. We had just enough daylight left, we had booze, and we had freedom! Then Nick spoke up with a plan. "Let's sneak into Heenan Lake and fish it!" Matt and I replied simultaneously with, "Fuck Yeah!"

The Indian summer sun was dipping behind the endless peaks of granite to the west as we drove up the canyon with the East Carson to our left. The temperature instantly and noticeably dropped as the sun sank from sight, with cool shadows and campfires replacing it. With every blind turn, we inched closer to our fishing destination, a youthful drunk high, fueling endless optimism. The music, beer, and whiskey made us feel like outlaws. I had never fished Heenan, a high mountain lake where they raise native Lahontan cutthroat trout, but I did witness Sonny, Dad, and Russ shoot a couple with their bows after a long hunt on Silver Hill. Fishing is restricted, with the exception of a few days a year. And even then, you have to use exclusively single barbless hooks for catch and release. With no strings attached to the arrow, the guys had to strike with laser accuracy, then strip down and wade out to retrieve both.

We were sneaking in on a day you couldn't fish, armed with Rooster Tails and Cast Masters with barbed treble hooks. We knew from hunting the area our whole life that the lake was full of very large fish and was a major watering and feeding ground for black bears and lions. The sunlight was disappearing with each turn up the mountain. We stopped a few miles below the lake to smoke a joint and enjoy the moment. After another beer, a couple swigs from the Jim Beam bottle, and a few stories about past adventures in the hills surrounding us, we jumped back in the truck and made it to the lake just as the light vanished over the western peaks of the Sierra Nevada Mountains. We stumbled out of the truck, trying to be quiet but failing miserably at it. Cans and an old Crown bottle fell out of the passenger side, prompting a harsh tongue lashing from Nick towards his sidekick little brother as we all laughed and stumbled around drunk, blind in the moonless darkness and more interested in fucking around than fishing. Nick made his way to the back of his truck, using only the light of his Zippo. He opened the camper door to grab his fishing poles, tackle, and a couple of beers for each of us.

By this time, the temperature had dropped significantly from the afternoon high. We were at 8,000 feet, in shorts and t-shirts, but we were too full of booze and youthful stupidity to realize that we were ill-equipped for the adventure. We didn't care. We laughed it off and headed towards the lakeshore in total and infinite darkness. Not a moon to speak of. The entire area was covered in volcanic rocks and could cause some serious face-plants and scarred shins and knees, even in the kindness of the midday sun. We made it to the shore bloodied, yet undeterred.

We tossed our lures out and started reeling in the pitch-black only to discover that we were casting into a forest of lake vegetation covering every inch of shallow water. When we weren't talking and laughing at each other for falling and maiming ourselves, the quiet was deafening and full of threatening anticipation. My heart pounded in stoned paranoia and was getting the best of me when Nick fell hard, and Matt started laughing at his painful expense. "Way to go, Larry!" Nick responded with a groan of real pain and a faint, "Fuck you, Meat!"

"I broke my pole!"

I made my way towards the voice, so I could find safety among the chaos. We hobbled our broken bodies back to the truck, finished our last beers, and headed for camp. Little did I know what the next day had in store for all of us: In less than 24 hours, our brother would be dead.

DEATH OF A BROTHER

The next morning started even before the sun was up. My head was heavy, and my mouth parched. I had to take a piss two hours into my mummy sleeping bag, but the frigid darkness kept me from leaving the safety of my cocoon. My solo tent was set up across the creek from my parents' camp trailer and the firepit, where we all gathered for meals and stories. It gave me some independence while maintaining the safety net of my parents, but it also alerted them to my every clumsy intoxicated move.

My dad woke me up early by unzipping my tent and was blasted with the stench of stale alcohol. It was his unspoken way of letting me know he wasn't happy that I had been drinking with Nick and Matt the night before. I hated disappointing him, especially knowing that he feared what drinking could do to me. We struggled to communicate about it, but I could tell it was taboo. He came from an alcoholic father who took his low self-worth out on my dad, his oldest son. I figured that I was old enough, and seeing that I was achieving big things with football, I had an arrogant attitude towards my dad's biggest fear; I figured I was man enough to do whatever I wanted.

Matt and I were already learning how to get up and go hunting hungover with little to no sleep. We'd drink a cup of black coffee at Sonny's camp and figure out our plan before daylight. We jumped into the back of the trucks with our bows and arrows and the adrenaline of the hunt brewing like the coffee grains I was still chewing on. Our hats flipped backward, kneeling on the rusted and frozen metal truck bed, we scanned for deer. Matt pulled his can of Copenhagen out of the back pocket of his faded 501s, snapped the can, and opened up the lid to take the first dip of the morning.

One of the passages of my youth into manhood was enduring pain in the form of heat, cold, and grueling work. The early mornings heading out of camp in the back of the truck was what we dreamed of doing as little kids, but actually experiencing it was hardcore freezing and bumpy! That's what a man is: someone that can endure pain and succeed. I'm okay with that definition at this stage of my life. Regardless of the discomfort, the sting of the early morning hunts produced some of the most memorable and breathtaking outdoor experiences of my life. The sunrises touching the velvet on the antlers of bucks in rut on top of Silver Mountain is timeless beauty from a simpler time. Those hard-earned moments helped me frame the meaning of life in a majestic and purposeful way.

I was hungover and trying not to throw up or pass out. Fortunately, a big buck followed a doe out from behind a ponderosa pine about eighty-five yards up the hill from our truck. Sonny and my dad got out to slink up the hill to get a better assessment of the situation. We anxiously waited for their signal and plan of attack. Both men approached hunting like they played competitive sports—with the intent to use strategy and teamwork to achieve victory.

The buck caught wind of us and stopped in his tracks long enough for Dad and Sonny to sling their arrows sixty-five yards up the hill, one flying over the back of the beast and the other hitting the sagebrush just inches below his chest. Both deer darted for cover at the top of the hill, hopping almost like kangaroos over sage and buckbrush to the top and eventually disappearing out of sight to their safe domain in the aspen quakies covering the top side of the hill. Dad and Sonny kept focused on the deer and continued hiking up the hill towards them. The older Brandt boys—Wayne, Russ, and Nick—were out of the truck and quietly starting up the hill as well. I stood in the back of the truck with my bow, wondering if I should jump out or if it was a lost cause at this point. Dad and Sonny were in the pine trees and out of sight. I wasn't sure if we were going to begin a big hike over the mountain and chase after these deer for the rest of the morning, or if we were going to get to Silver Hill before the big bucks moved out for their morning drink. Sonny popped out of the trees with my dad laughing and talking as they hiked back down to the truck. Silver Hill it was.

We split up to cover the hillside tucked into the giant Sierra Nevada mountains, and the rest of the morning was a memory of making our way up to the top of Silver Hill as the rays of sunlight peeked up and over the furthest eastern peaks and Heenan Lake at the base of the hill. The patch of pink, orange, and purple clouds gave the water surface a beautiful deep Pantone of color that seemed as if the famous artist Remington had painted the summer sky and Wild West landscape dream.

I was by myself, positioned downslope from Matt on the east side of the hill, waiting for any bucks that Dad and Sonny might push our way as they worked the thick buckbrush and manzanita on the ridge. The sun had not yet crested the tall mountains, and we were shrouded by the early morning light of dusk. I caught myself daydreaming about football practice the next week and college football looming in big lights on ABC Sports on Saturday mornings after my Friday night football games. I had passing thoughts of my girlfriend Becky and wondering what would happen after we graduated. I remembered the heart with our initials that I had carved in an Aspen tree in camp earlier in the week: CR + BF. But my focus was about earning a college football scholarship and finishing my final year out with a bang. I really didn't have a worry in the world, and limitless possibilities were in front of me. Here I was, in the great outdoors, with men I looked up to and respected, men I emulated, pitting myself against nature and claiming my place as a man.

I grew up with the Brandts and Mastelottos dominating Oroville High School football, basketball, and baseball. Hunting and sports defined so much of our connection and identity that, as the first Rockwell boy, I was bound and determined to make my family name proud, especially my dad. I was on a mission that didn't allow for much time to ponder and enjoy relaxing thoughts. So, at that moment, I was trying to take in everything I could and not future trip on the daunting season of football and expectations ahead of me. I had been waking up to succeed—to *dominate*—since I was a young child. That was my normal. It was framed as a healthy approach to life.

The warming sun was finally cresting over the eastern peaks and reached my face and the side of the hill I was standing on. I could still see my breath from the deep chill in the air. The stillness and cold had helped to clear my foggy head. Within a matter of minutes, all the animals that call Silver Hill home seemed to spring to life. The ground squirrels, sage hens, and birds of all kinds, including a bald eagle, were suddenly appearing from everywhere, hunting for their first meal and living for the day, not lamenting yesterday's mistakes or current insecurities. I remember feeling jealous that the animals around me seemed certain of their purpose and reason for getting up in the morning. I felt confusing pressure to succeed in things that I was trying to make sense of, in terms of their relevance to living with purpose and happiness. I assumed that I was doing what I was born to do. But as fast as the thought appeared, I would begin deconstructing its components, trying to relate it to my finite earthly existence and proper use of that time.

I was already becoming a little disillusioned with the sports achievement thing since it required so much time and dedication to the negligible reward and joy I was getting out of it. The rewards, in my opinion, were not adding up to the way I saw myself in the world, how I valued my existence, my time. I was watching nature at its purest; many of the animals around me had never seen a human before. They were not scared, simply going about their day with absolute certainty. I didn't observe them wasting much time questioning their decisions or self-destructing because of it. They woke up to eat and reproduce. As confident and certain as I felt at seventeen, I was also feeling lots of encroaching confusion. The more I observed many adults in contrast to the natural world, the motion and intent were very different.

My mind continued to wander as my hangover began to wear off. What would my future look like after I graduated high school? Music was my passion far beyond sports, but I was raised by solid, hardworking men, and that good fortune required meeting up to the expectations of that tribe. Since I was physically built to compete, it was assumed the next steps were to continue to achieve in that framework, which to me meant succeeding as an entrepreneur, like the Mastelottos, after I finished my sports career. I was starting to really believe that college football was my destiny. I felt a warm moment of pride, knowing I was carrying the torch of the great men and big brothers that laid the foundation for me to rise even higher than thought possible. At least, that's how I saw it.

Snap! I heard a stick crack underfoot as Matt and our dads walked towards each other in otherwise near silence but continuing to gain volume as they got closer to each other. Realizing the hunt was over for that morning, I felt a weight of expectation lifted. I heard a few muffled words of serious intent, and then laughter filled the clean mountain air with good vibes and a moment to celebrate the effort and experience of hunting on top of old Silver Hill with the guys I grew up idolizing. I felt my chest and vertical frame expand with a deep pride and confidence. I looked over the eastern landscape one more time and then turned up the hill and hiked to where the guys were congregated and talking about the bucks Sonny and Dad got into.

As I neared the guys, I continued to pick up my pace because of the gravitational pull of men and the measurements of that included being around to tell the stories of the experience and comparing notes from the hunt. It was a special moment that always seemed to be one of the moments that defined the reason we hunted and camped together every year. It was to connect to nature, ourselves, and our families. That was a part of the natural order of things. It felt right to me when many other things simply did not. Breathing in the intense natural smells of fresh pine, sage, and dirt filled my lungs, mind, and soul with the legacy of millennia that transported me forward with purpose and spirit. I felt strong and alive, like I was where I was supposed to be.

It's kind of trippy to look back and think about the mindset of immortality that summer after lifting weights and working out hard preparing for football. That morning and the adventure the day before at the Cutthroat Saloon with Nick and Matt had me feeling like I was becoming a man and wanted to test every fiber of my being. I guess I possessed enough ignorant ambition and optimism to actually believe it at fleeting moments. Life has a strange way of showing up and challenging our sense of what is real. Up until then, my path and outlook were pretty solid for a seventeen-year-old kid. I actually kinda had a plan for life after high school, and I was set on making it a big step. I would figure out the details later.

For now, I was feeling like a pioneer from the old days when miners built a town on top of that mountain and lived and died by her. I felt it through my bones. After we all congregated and recapped the chase, we made our way back up the ridge on the old road. The hike back to the truck was not far, but it was steep. It seemed like there was always one more hill to climb.

We took a breather at the truck, drank water from our canteens, and grabbed a handful of trail mix to quiet the gnawing hunger from hiking and hunting all morning. We sat on the back railing of my dad's old 66 Chevy long-bed truck and made our way down the mountain, back up Monitor Pass, and down into camp for breakfast. The other kids and I were intent on heading off to go fishing downstream to the beaver ponds or the Carson River. We got word from the Federal game trapper camping near us that Fish & Game were planting cutthroat trout that weekend.

Grandpa Brandt had the griddle over the fire and poured hot cake batter next to the sizzling bacon he had piled high. As I waited patiently for my breakfast, I gazed over at the fire and saw my baby brother Dan and the Brandt kids chowing away on pancakes like dirty, happy heathens. Camp was active, and the sun was shining. The smoke from the fire and cooking gave the camp a smell of timeless western pioneering Americana. I grew up around that campfire for all my seventeen years, every fall for deer hunting season. I knew nothing different in the middle of August until football made its way into my life. I resented that it took deer hunting and camping away from me for years. I had to cut my trips absurdly brief and even missed some trips altogether. They were two opposite but totally connected worlds—football and hunting. Football was a part of the passage that I felt I had to forge to be part of the legacy on top of Silver Hill, and those hunters I respected more than any man in my life.

Deep down, I knew it would be a long journey before I would be able to return to those mountains as an older man to relax and truly enjoy my days there again, like I did as a child. I was convinced that I would set out to achieve fame and fortune and set up my cabin in the mountains, listen to Lynyrd Skynyrd, and drink beer and play music. Minus the booze, that dream really hasn't changed much. And the road back has taken much longer than I ever imagined.

I remember feeling excited to head down to the river and try my luck at catching some fish and swim off the dirt covering my body, giving me a shade darker tan than I really had. I grabbed my fishing pole, swimming trunks, and Copenhagen and loaded up for a ride with Matt and Nick Brandt. They came out of his tent half-cocked from a few beers and a couple shots of Crown each and were raring to go. As we headed out, I remember watching Nick cracking a Budweiser and thinking how I would drink one if my dad weren't there. I was still kind of hungover and a little tired. I knew a beer would put me right. I figured I'd sneak one or two down at the river.

We headed out, and my parents gave me the concerned look like they always did when I was hanging around the Brandt boys, especially now that I was seventeen years old and coming into my own. The minute we were out of site from camp, Matt handed me a beer, and we drank all the way down the hill and started fishing and swimming for the rest of the afternoon with both families catching up with us over the next hour or so. I ended up not needing to chase the booze and was just happy to be hanging out at the Carson River with my family and closest friends. It was a great day.

As the sun began dropping behind the western hills, we packed up and started heading back up to camp for the evening. I remember not being in the mood to hunt and was glad to hear Nick and Matt weren't either. We climbed into Nick's old white Chevy truck with a camper shell and started back up the hill. The long stretch just before the Monitor Pass monument is a big open expanse that allows you to see straight down the road for a couple miles, making high-speed driving and passing a fun opportunity. We passed Rusty and Sue in their red Mitsubishi truck and Wayne in his truck. I remember passing by and all three of us making faces at Russ and Sue and them smiling back with a mellow, content look. They were nearing the monument when we passed them and headed off to camp.

We pulled into camp and were enjoying the smell of dinner cooking and the evening light starting to set in. I felt good but hungry. Suddenly, Sue's red Mitsubishi truck driven by Wayne Brandt, the oldest son, came flying into camp, followed by heavy skidding and a dust cloud looming just behind. The door flew open, and Wayne nearly fell out of the truck as if he were drunk and about ready to pass out. He uttered the words that would change our lives forever.

"I shot Russ, and it doesn't look good."

"What?!" a gasping reaction shot out of Sonny's guts.

All hell broke loose, and people started to run around in chaos, shattered by the information that we were trying to process. It didn't compute, but it did. I remember standing near Matt, and I instinctively followed his lead. I knew we were heading out, and I knew Matt would get there fast. His uncle David was already pulling his Ford truck out, and Matt started running for it as it was moving. I reacted and jumped into the back with him, and we headed out.

Matt and I were the first ones to the scene after we jumped out of David's truck and ran through the aspen quakies directly behind the Monitor Pass monument. We came out of the clearing to see Sue crying uncontrollably. Matt and I got to Russ, and I remember standing over my big brother's body and noticing the blood oozing out of his abdomen, and his body was lifeless. I was in shock and didn't know what to do. Matt was vigilantly trying to save his brother by applying pressure to the wound, while CPR was given to him.

I looked over at Sue, crumpled up on the ground, and made my way to her to hold her. My mind was processing the situation with as much pragmatism as I could. I was stunned and in denial that Russ was gravely injured. We knew he was, but we held on to the hope that we could get him down the hill and fix him up. He was Rusty Brandt, the toughest and gentlest man we knew. He was a man among boys in so many ways. I couldn't convince my mind that this was something more than a crazy story that Russ would tell when he was old and gray.

By this time, I heard other people as they began to appear out of the quakies carrying a stretcher. An off-duty nurse and an EMT stopped off to help along with some other concerned folks. My last recollection was helping load Rusty up and carrying him off the hill and onto the ambulance. From there, we headed back to camp to await what to do next. During the mayhem, some of the Brandts and Masetlottos headed down the back side of Monitor to Lake Topaz, thinking they took him there.

After sitting in camp and feeling the world coming apart as the moans of mothers and family filled the air with the eternal pain of loss, I heard Sonny cry loudly as my dad hugged him in Grandpa Brandt's camper. I remember watching Dan using little broken sticks to write his name by the creek where Russ would take us fishing. We were waiting for news—*any* news—but hopefully good news so we could get back to life as we knew it.

The sun had set, and my dad and Sonny decided to pack up the families and drive down to Russ. We were about two hundred yards out of camp when a set of headlights were flying down the dirt road at a clip. As it got right up on us, it hit the brakes, and a figure staggered out of the truck. It was Nick Brandt, and he could barely get it out. He staggered a few steps towards our caravan and spilled the words, "Russ is gone..."

I remember sitting in my dad's truck squished between my parents and brothers, and we just started crying and telling each other we loved each other. We exited the cab of the truck, and I found Matt and went to hug him as he staggered out to the moonlit sagebrush and dropped to his knees and looked to the sky.

I promised myself that night that I would live my life out to the fullest and not let death rule my life like I saw so many adults do.

Rusty Brandt was twenty-eight when he died that day on top of Monitor Pass. His whole life was ahead of him. I hate it when people say that. It's not true, otherwise it would've been. His life was an example of how to live and treat people. He wasn't perfect, but Russ was good deep in his bones. He was not a big man, probably 5'9". But his rock-solid physique and lion of a heart was no match for his bigger brothers or any tough guy on the football field or in the streets. Rusty was known for being a nice guy, but a beast if provoked. In football, Russ earned All-League as a defensive lineman weighing less than 150 pounds!

Russ was gentle and kind to us younger kids. In fact, he even babysat us a few times as a big bad high school football player. No shit! Russ was a quiet, cool soul looking for more than being popular and good at sports. He had a quiet searching in his eyes. There are countless pictures of Russ playing with me and my brothers, talking to us, listening to us. He was a good soul who protected our innocence with big brotherly care. It was just part of who he was.

At the hot springs, he would play with us younger kids, tossing us around and play-tackling us in the shallow end of the pool. The older I get and look back on how he treated me and my brothers, I see him as very paternal. I didn't know Russ in other ways because I was so much younger and not old enough when he was wilder. Over time, Matt and I would spend many drunken and tearful nights sharing nostalgic stories of Russ. Matt loved his big brothers so much; he said Russ was special and always looked after him in a unique way. I don't know if he had an enemy. I bet even his enemies respected him. It's just the way Russ was.

We packed up and went home in a quiet and solemn mood. We had lost a great man, an important man to our family, and a hero to me. But no one really talked about it after that. It was time to get back to football, school, and "life." Russ's death became a rarely referenced topic at home even though I needed to talk about it—the loss, the pain, the almost intolerable sadness. It was all brushed under a rug, and we were expected to just move forward. I look back and realize that my parents had a special needs child to manage, and I closed off my emotions and communication and drank to escape. My brain didn't know how to deal with it all. I was seventeen. Just a kid. Becky listened. She cried with me and was there for me, but she was just a kid, too. I was expected to move on, let it go, and perform. So, I did. But my heart and my head were broken.

RECRUITED TO PLAY
COLLEGE FOOTBALL

Despite struggling with the death of Russ and the pressure to perform, I had a great football season on defense as a senior and was heavily recruited. I had the opportunity to fly out to a few different schools that I thought would be good prospects and turned down even more offers to schools I had no interest in. I was going to play for a winning team. Period. Even if that meant saying no to a lot of great prospects. San Diego State was interested in me early and even flew up a few times to recruit me. They had a full ride offer on the table and a flight set up so I could go down and drink in the beautiful opportunity they were offering me. In my dad's counseling office, the recruiter asked me flat out where they stood, and I arrogantly told them they were way below Washington State, who had also shown serious interest. It was the lure of the Pac-10 that had me negotiating like the child I was. They flew me up to check out the program, the campus, and the life of a Cougar football player.

The minute I landed in Moscow and was driven to Pullman to meet the coaches and some of the veteran players, I was paired up with a giant black defensive lineman from Compton. He was easily over 300 pounds and hood black. I was a recruit from California, and his job was to show me a good time and look after me. That's how recruiting goes. Since I had never been on a recruiting trip before, I figured everything was business as usual. I remember it was freezing cold as we drove by campus dorms and empty snow-covered streets. It reminded me of the classic brick buildings of the Chico State campus, which made it a little familiar. We pulled into a liquor store in his old Chevy blazer, walked in together, and he grabbed a case of beer and casually walked out. Kind of shocked, I just followed his lead and strutted out awkwardly, like Gene Wilder in *Stir Crazy,* the classic black and white comedy he did with Richard Pryor.

Next thing I know, we're at a house party, and the place is full of Pac-10 college football players and girls, and they were excited to meet the new recruits. It was like a blast of energy and desire unlike anything I had known, even as a small-town football star. I felt like I had arrived, and I was loving every beer, smile, giggle, and hug. I was hooked with the college football drug. It was like out of a movie. The 1988 movie, *Johnny Be Good,* is about college recruiting a small-town football star in a comedy format. The state of Washington and Seattle would be part of my story. It was already happening!

When I got back home, out of the blue, we got a call from Fresno State. My recruiting tape had inadvertently been lost by a recruiting assistant and then found again. They had taken a look at my recruiting tape, meticulously put together by my dad before digital photography and recruiting sites existed, and called with significant interest. They were sincere and excited about my spirit. Located in the middle of the hot and dry eastern edge of Central California, I initially felt this was a downfall, but they were winning, and winning big. They offered me a full-ride scholarship, and I took it. It was a hard decision because so many great opportunities were being thrown at me, like Southern California and Pac-10, but it was absolutely the best choice. As it turned out, Washington State went with another player, and San Diego State moved on because they assumed I was going to choose Pac-10. I was meant to play at Fresno State. Taking the opportunity to play for Coach Jim Sweeney became one of the best and most significant decisions I made as a young man, and in my life up to this point.

I spent the remainder of my senior year celebrating the celebrity life that was about to become mine. I partied hard, worked out, got stronger and bigger in body and mind, and because of it, I nearly died that year. I spent a lot of time partying in Chico, the number one college party school in America at the time, according to *Playboy Magazine.* I was hanging out with college football players and wild students who were there specifically for the party. The alcohol turned it all into a blur of one nonstop debaucherous adventure. But the power, seduction, social pressure, and influence were just too great for my insecure and inquisitive mind to stand a chance.

I was hanging out with my buddy Kyle and his Cal football friends who were home for Christmas break, and we were pounding "Rattlesnake Bites." Jake, one of the Cal players from Quincy, brought elk steaks to grill from a recent Colorado hunt. We barbequed and drank the night away. Kyle's older brother Mark shared the Chico State apartment with two other guys from Oroville. They built a full bar with a Kegerator and had beer available to us at all times. On this particular night, things went from great to worse. I passed out on my back in Mark's room. Sometime during the early morning, I left and made my way back to my parents' house. I got a phone call from Mark when I got home. He had been out of town and returned home to a bed and room covered in vomit. The scariest part, which was funny to me at the time, was that I literally had no idea that I had even puked! His screaming in the phone was the first I knew anything about destroying his room. I honestly didn't know what the fuck happened that night. The last thing I remember was pounding shots with the college football players. Thankfully, I had my head tilted when I blacked out and sprayed Yukon Jack and beer all over Mark's comforter, floor, desk, and TV; otherwise, I would've been just another statistic.

I felt really hungover and was trying to put on a good face for my dad when I drove up that morning to help him get some work done. He gave me a disappointed look; he knew I had been up to no good... probably by the fucking earring one of the Cal football D-lineman punched through my ear after he found the stud buried in a dirty tray of change on top of the fridge.

Walking off the baseball field after a win against a solid Pleasant Valley team, I was approached by the head baseball coach at Butte College, our local junior college that is nationally respected for their sports programs. The head coach was originally from my hometown and grew up with the Brandts and Mastelottos, and he was leading a winning program at Butte. My parents and grandpa politely waited off to the side, outside the baseball field, for me to handle my discussion with Coach Lowman. I had to own my decision at that point and be straight with him, so I didn't lead him on or waste his time. I loved baseball and was also being scouted by the MLB and recruited by colleges, including Fresno State.

After he made his last pitch to get me to play for him, I respectfully explained to him that I was headed down to Fresno State on a football recruiting trip that evening. My grandpa was going to fly me down on his plane, a little Cessna 172. I remember the sun was setting low, and the dust from the baseball field was in the air giving the appearance of a classic baseball movie scene portraying old-time Americana. He appreciated my direct honesty, shook my hand, and wished me the best.

After saying goodbye to my parents, my grandpa and I headed out to board his plane. He had me fly part of the way, including takeoff, because he was teaching me how to fly. At the end of the day, after a few flight school classes, I realized that it wasn't for me. Although he would always tell me that, statistically, there were fewer crashes flying than driving a car,

I reminded him that there were very few "fender-benders" in plane crashes.

At that time, the Fresno airport was a very small agricultural airport, and upon landing, I felt a little unimpressed. I was nervous but excited. The airport was a part of a small town and farmland, and it smelled like it. My grandpa taxied me up to the drop-off, and we said our goodbyes. He left as I stood in Fresno for the first time. Alone, I watched him fly away.

I made my way to the arrivals gate and was greeted by Fresno State football linebacker coach Willie Robinson, a Type A Plus overachieving undersized linebacker, but a solid and extremely loyal former walk-on player. Coach Rob had been to my house with his father to visit me and my parents for an in-house recruiting visit earlier that year, so we knew each other at least from that experience as well as a few phone calls and a visit to my high school to meet with me and my dad. He was a straight shooter; I knew that for sure. But I couldn't tell if he ever laughed. Nevertheless, he took me to my hotel at the Piccadilly Inn, a nice hotel owned by an Alum and Booster to the football program. I was sharing a room with another Northern California recruit, a quarterback from Aptos named Trent Dilfer.

After I dropped my bag in my room, we drove over to the Fresno State Sports facilities next to the university. On the drive over to the stadium and sports and training facilities, Coach Rob started to relax a little bit and talk to me about what to expect for the weekend. My itinerary was planned out meticulously. I would be chaperoned by a veteran player who would be my host. He was from Northern California, a middle linebacker named Chris Peters. Chris and I played against each other in a high school championship game when he played for Shasta, and I played for Oroville. They won. They were tough, and a very hard-hitting team made up of guys from a similar logging town like mine.

After visiting the facilities and meeting some of the coaches, I got to see the weight room and then the football stadium for the first time. We made our way over to the baseball stadium with a game in the fifth inning, and we met up with Chris Peters and a few other veteran players sitting up in the stands heckling the opposing team. Coach Rob walked me up the bleachers and introduced me to Chris. As he said his goodbyes and walked away, he turned back to remind Chris to keep us out of trouble. With a mischievous grin and laugh, Chris said, "Yeah, no problem, coach, haha."

We hung out and watched the baseball team play San Luis Obispo. The following day I was scheduled to do a campus visit to see the business school.

Chris was cool, and he reminded me of the Brandts. He was a hard-drinking, hard-partying, and hard-hitting middle linebacker who was a starter for the Fresno State football team as a sophomore. That was impressive, especially to a kid from the hills in Northern California like me. We had a lot in common, and it reminded me of hanging out with Matt Brandt, so it just kind of clicked. Next thing I know, we're heading off to a party. There we met all the other recruits, including Trent, my roommate, who was already drunk and acting like a giddy schoolboy. Chris and the defensive players laughed and made a comment about lightweight quarterbacks. We all laughed.

The night was a blur, but I do remember that the fun was still going on after the party because I was escorted back to my hotel room by two "sweet" country girls from the party wearing tight Wranglers. They took me into my hotel room and hung out with me for a while. As the night wore on, one of the girls pulled out a can of Copenhagen, snapped it, and threw in a dip! She threw the can to her friend! Sweet and Country for sure!

It was late when Trent came busting in the door, slobbering drunk, and proceeded to pass out on his bed. The girls left. Trent ended up puking all over his bed and fell asleep in it. But as he was fading off to sleep, I remember him mumbling out to me, "Hey, Rock...are you going to sign here? I think we should...we can win here..." Then came the snoring.

The next morning, we were picked up separately. We had meetings to meet coaches and do the university campus visit. The first stop for me was Lions Restaurant, where I would be meeting the head coach, the legendary Jim Sweeney. When we arrived, I walked into the restaurant with Coach Rob. In the far corner of the open floorplan restaurant was a white-haired older man with his arms draped around two black athletes, one on each side of him. He was telling a story, and the kids were laughing. The aura of this guy was special, and that was a moment I won't forget. Coach Rob walked me over to the table and introduced me to Coach Sweeney. As we got close to the table, I started to get nervous but realized I was on a recruiting trip; *they* were recruiting *me*. Coach Sweeney looked up at me with a sincere look in his eyes and had me sit down. Without missing a beat, he kept telling the story but now included me in the group. It was an awesome experience to see how this man commanded not only the table but the entire room. I knew right then and there that I was going to play for that man.

After breakfast, I did the business school tour with another recruit, Ron Rivers, one of the top running backs in the country. Ron would go on to play in the NFL and play alongside the legendary Barry Sanders, alternating between plays at running back. I was fortunate enough to watch him play against the Chicago Bears when I was in Chicago at Soldier Field one year on business. During our walk through the business department, Ron asked me if I was going to sign to play at Fresno. I told him I was. He said he was going to sign too and that he'd heard that the quarterback was going to sign as well. I was feeling really good about my decision and where things were headed.

The next morning my grandpa and my friend, Thomas Rogers, flew down in my grandpa's plane to pick me up.

Thomas was getting his pilot's license and was clocking hours flying with my grandpa. I had just determined my future and was ready to start living it. Like Mr. Magoo, my grandpa taxied onto the runway. He didn't realize that on this small, very low-security airport in central California back in 1990, he was taxiing out in front of two military F-16s ready for takeoff!

Grandpa was immediately flagged down by multiple federal and military agents and reprimanded profusely by the radio control. Grandpa flashed his police and WW2 cred (as if that could justify his slapstick taxi move at an airport!), and they showed him just enough respect by not throwing us all in federal prison! After violating the military airspace at an airport, our plane was cross-checked, and we were allowed to fly home. The weather was perfect, and we enjoyed the flight home. I was floating above the clouds with the idea that I would be playing college football for Fresno State in the fall.

NORCAL LUMBER

I spent my final summer at home, working long hours in the lumberyard and hanging with Becky and our close friends. Her uncle had a lumber company in a town 45 minutes from home. We started work at 6 am, so I was up by 4:30 six days a week. When big orders for trusses and packaged lumber to construct a custom home were coming in, which was all summer long, we were hustling 12-hour days, sometimes seven days a week. I couldn't wait to get to football camp after working in 110-degree heat running an old band saw with an open-tooth blade.

My job was resawing twenty-foot beams on all four sides to give it a rough-cut look for visual purposes. We were on a tight deadline for a huge order, and I was trying to keep up. The problem was the band saw was old and dangerous as hell with its open-face blade and diesel engine spitting fuel and fumes in my face while I was trying to guide a twenty-foot green Doug fir beam with finesse to shave just a few millimeters off the surface of the finished cut lumber. Back then, they didn't even issue me a mask or earplugs despite sawing into chemically treated timbers; it was totally dangerous to inhale the burning chemical-soaked wood, not to mention, illegal. It was definitely old school. My saw had no automated guides, or any guides for that matter, except for a roller stand to support the three-hundred-pound beam while I manhandled it through a ten-foot band saw. Without guides, the teeth of the saw could grab the beam and literally pull me and the beam into its jaws if I didn't hold it steady against its massive strength and aggression. I ruined a few beams along the way and was always waiting for something to go wrong.

Every day I battled the "Steel Dragon," as I called her, resawing 6x14x20 pressure-treated beams. Finally, it happened. I was moving the beams through at a fast pace to keep up with the orders for the day when the band-saw blade snapped like an alien dragon, flinging the flying steel teeth in my direction. Imagine a twenty-foot band-saw blade, with two-inch razor-sharp teeth, spinning on two big wheels. When it broke on me, it made a crack like a Glock 9mm and screamed like Godzilla. It made the hardest criminals working on the truss line duck for cover. It was like a drive-by from the sky.

No one was injured in the accident, and it was just another day working at NorCal Lumber. I was almost decapitated for $7 an hour. I wasn't there much longer after that because I had to report for rookie camp at Fresno State the day after my high school all-star football game in mid-July. I left town while the rest of my workmates would continue working in the yard until the business closed from the great recession, or they wound up back in the yard at San Quentin or Folsom Prison just down the street.

Although I managed to survive a summer working on the "Steel Dragon," I ended up heading down to Fresno with nine stitches in my thumb from tackling the fullback and ripping it open on his helmet snap during the Senior All-Star game. Life was changing at light speed, and I was saying goodbye to everyone and everything I loved to go make my way into the great wide open.

4

COLLEGE FOOTBALL
Underdog Champions

College Football

WELCOME TO COLLEGE FOOTBALL, KID!

The day after my high school all-star football game, I had my thumb stitched back together, and we packed up and headed off to Fresno, a place I had only been to on my recruiting trip even though it was only four hours south of my little NorCal town. I honestly wasn't even sure where it was. I remember sitting in the back of my parents' station wagon that they had recently traded their old VW bus for, and I felt a sinking feeling in my gut. I was leaving my girlfriend and everything I knew to live in a foreign land and compete against some of the biggest, baddest college football athletes on the planet. I wanted to turn around and just go home. God, did I want to go home. But I knew I was on a mission that had to be completed for every reason under the sun. Deep down, I knew I was supposed to be doing what I was doing. It felt right in so many fundamental ways, but my heart was ripping into shreds with each passing mile southbound on Highway 99.

Staring out the window, I saw and smelled the rancid reality of industrial cattle and chicken slaughterhouses and the smell of onions, garlic, and manure. Pure hot ugliness. I was asking myself what the fuck was I thinking. All I really wanted to do was launch my music career, but something deep down told me that I would not make it out alive. I had no other option; I had been raised with the idea that college was the natural next pragmatic step after high school. I was not stoked about it, but I had convinced myself that this was where I needed to be. I was from California, and I had experienced the majesty of her natural beauty at home and all around the state, from the coast to the mountains. But it was mid-July, and Central California smelled and looked like a rotting third-world town in Mexico or Iraq.

I remember we exited onto a road in what seemed like Tijuana, complete with a Mexican ice cream cart. With each mile closer to my destination, my nose, eyes, and guts all singed from the putrid hot air, and the heat waves on the streets dancing like a bad acid trip. We pulled onto Shaw, the main strip that led from Highway 99 to the eastern side of the Sierras, cutting through the heart of the newer north side of town where the university was built. Old Fresno was south of town and was a shithole of industrial waste and street violence. We settled into our motel room near campus that night and didn't leave the place except to grab a quick drive-through dinner. I couldn't think about anything but what the next day was going to be like.

I was trying to come to terms that this foreign land was going to be my home for at least four and a half years. The coaches had decided to redshirt me to get me bulked up and trained on the defense and speed of the game at that level. I woke up before the sun and felt paralyzed in my cheap hotel bed, wondering how this adventure was going to turn out. I was scared and maybe a little excited...but mostly fucking terrified. I knew I was entering a world of violent giants, a world that was beyond anything I could understand. Deep down, I was just ready for the adventure to start.

My dad and I jumped in the station wagon, grabbed a quick breakfast at the Denny's down the street, then headed to the incoming freshman rookie camp sign in. The first two guys I saw were Dee Edwards and Kenny Hall. They were going back and forth on the most random topics. Both were quietly heckling and impersonating everyone they could snare with their eyes. Dee Edwards was a California standout with bad grades from East Palo Alto, but he looked like a 22-year-old lifer from San Quinten prison. He was a big, good-looking Mulatto thug with a deep laugh. He was built like an NFL nose guard, and pure comedy at all times. But he could get street-tough real fast and just as quickly return to cuddly, funny Dee. Kenny was a giant Eurcle with glasses and a goofy smile. Kenny's uncle was an all-pro defensive end for the Green Bay Packers. The difference was clear. Kenny had the 6'5", 300-pound physique of an all-pro, but his soft momma's boy temperament and goofy, almost nerdy disposition told me he was harmless and someone I might like.

"Dude, it's so hot here I heard some little nigga from Watts got hit in practice and never woke up. True story!"

"Ah, Shut up, nigga!"

Kenny defended his source. "For real! I put that on my mom!"

"Oh, For real?" Dee submitted.

As I would soon discover, "putting it on your mom" is like saying it's a scientifically proven fact. "Putting it on your mom" is an absolute certain guarantee of truth if you're black, or even 25% black. I would hear, "I'll put that on my mom" over fifty thousand times before I finished playing college ball. I think I even heard a white guy say it once…but generally, we "swear to God." I'm not sure which one is more of a test of the truth. But they're both pretty big chips to bet.

Coach Hysell, the hardened Montana Cowboy, mustered up the energy from his hungover state of mind to spit out his frustrated thought, along with wet grains of Copenhagen. "Are you gonna dick around all day, or are you gonna sign your papers?"

Hysell was my defensive coordinator at Fresno State and recruited me out of high school. He was a smart, tough country boy who grew up drinking Jack Daniels and fist fighting the toughest men in the mining bars in Bozeman. His stories are legendary. I will never forget the day he walked into my dad's counselor's office on my high school campus wearing a cowboy hat, rattlesnake skin cowboy boots, chewing Copenhagen, and walking like John Wayne. He and my dad hit it off immediately and began talking about deer hunting and their run-ins with rattlesnakes.

Coach Hysell was on a mission to find out if I was the "bad kid" that he'd heard rumors about; that rumor was spreading from, of all people, my high school basketball coach Dennis Burnham. People that were supposed to be in my corner from my little hometown were actively trying to sabotage something special that I earned with lots of sweat, blood, and effort. I had envious adult male teachers and coaches hating on my success; it made no sense to me. I was getting a sour taste of bitter boys and men underperforming in sports and life. I came to find out that this is how many people operate. Sad.

Coach Sweeney recruited Hysell to play football for him at Montana State, where he eventually returned to finish his career as a head coach. Coach Hysell knew tough, knew winning, and understood how to turn kids into men.

Reminiscent of Bill Murray in Stripes, Kenny mocked his authority. "Uh, uh...yes, sir."

Coach Hysell continued to drive the point home, so he didn't have to speak again and agitate his pounding head. "Does anyone else have an attitude problem?"

"No, sir," Dee responded in over-the-top soldier fashion.

This was my new world. I was intimidated but intrigued by the scene.

We started first thing the next morning with a 6 am wake-up, mandatory breakfast, meetings, and practice—and repeated it all again in the suffocating Fresno summer afternoon. We were getting ready to join the ranks with the veteran warriors when they arrived.

We experienced basic training wake-ups every morning for the next few weeks to air horns, clanging trashcan lids, and insults. Anything loud and obnoxious enough to make sure we knew our place, which was at the bottom of the rung of our new militaristic reality. It was make or break, do or die, every play. It was hell. No matter how hard it was, they couldn't break me. I was shocked by the number of loud talking full-scholarship rookies that went out the first week. Some had gotten huge Fresno State Bulldog Football tattoos that covered their arm or leg to show their commitment, only to quit a week or two later. I stayed focused on why I was there; to start and to win. Once the veterans joined us, the team leaders rooted out the weak and the posers. It was exciting and terrifying. Only the strong survived.

The big double metal doors flew open, like in the old western saloons, smashing into the walls leaving noticeable scars to add to the countless assaults it had sustained by testosterone-raged young men and coaches surging recklessly in and out like the violent rise and fall of the arctic tides. The entire team is coming in from the first practice of the day after being together for two solid weeks. The guys are starting to gel and become pretty tight. The banter is going on everywhere. From my locker, I had the perfect vantage point that allowed me to observe everything happening around the room.

I sat next to Billy Scott, the hillbilly J.C. transfer from Oklahoma who looked like he was thirty, some Asian black dude named Sal, and an Oakland drug dealer we called Foster. Billy started the conversation theme off; its predictably some random fact that he didn't know the details about. His speech impediment and fucked-up trailer-trash teeth made it hard to believe anything he said. Ironically, he was smart but sounded like a hillbilly version of Cliff Clavin, the know-it-all mailman from the legendary TV sitcom *Cheers*.

"Hey, man (in a whispered Oklahoma drawl). I heard one of the D-linemen was shot last week. My buddy said it was a deal gone bad, and he took a deer rifle to the chest and lived for three days."

Sal immediately countered, "Shut the fuck up, Oklahoma! He died the next day!"

Sal was a smart dude from the Bay Area who had just transferred from the Air Force Academy. He got popped for selling weed and fucking a chick soldier on the campus square one night while a captain was roaming the area after returning from church across campus.

Billy was trying to keep his story together, unlike the chew spit flying out of his mangled railing of teeth. "Well... it could be true..."

Over at the locker section across from me was the loud comedic team of Dee Edwards, Kenny Hall, and their super quiet and super black friend Stacey. Dee was imitating Sonny Evans, the pretty brother with a Smokey Robinson voice and soft R&B demeanor. As I was sitting at my locker, slowly trying to get my pads and cleats off my broken body, I took moments to breathe and watch the Dee and Kenny show impersonating Sonny.

"Ahh Dog, my hands require special lotions to keep this Mulatto complexion consistent. It's all about being consistent, my nigga. Do you feel me?"

Everyone was fucking dying laughing.

Sonny tried to make a limp stand, directing his comment towards Sal, the recent Air Force transfer sporting a big, wet Jheri curl. "Ah, fuck you, niggaaa... Whatchu laughing at, with that oil-drenched afro curl?"

The locker room was a place of team, camaraderie, and a lot of shit talk, but sometimes it felt totally silent and empty. Because of my old-school training, I would show up to the locker room early. I was terrified of being late or unprepared. Many times, I was the first one in, and I enjoyed the quiet calm. Plus, I got to know Tony, the equipment manager. The distant sound of the Beach Boys classic "California Girls" playing in the background on an old locker room radio softened the silence. Tony would hum the song while he washed and dried our gear from practice the night before and reminisce about the 1960s when the song was a hit, and he was a young, carefree man before leaving for Vietnam. He would return to raise his family and enjoy the rest of his life in the Central Valley of California. Tony had thick salt and pepper hair and a perfect tan and skin that only a man originating from the rich fishing heritage of the Mediterranean could possess. He stayed in shape simply by being on the move constantly and keeping a positive outlook on the world, despite the horrible things he saw men do to each other during wartime. He reminded me of my dad in look, energy, and attitude.

I admired that Tony seemed to find the glass half full, singing Old Portuguese fishing village songs and smiling, always smiling, and willing to lend a friendly word of encouragement after a tough practice or loss. My locker was next to the equipment room, so I had the good fortune of befriending him. With all that he'd survived, his life seemed so simple and underplayed to me. I recall on more than one occasion that I envied his simple job and life. I envied it while I was disappointed by it at the same time.

I now know that I was thinking from the perspective of an 18-year-old boy who knew nothing of what true success and living were. But at the same time, I was playing Division 1 college football, an all-or-nothing competitive platform that demanded and measured our daily worth by success or failure, winning and losing. I failed to understand that he played on a field of real life-and-death competition and survived to come home, earning the "simple" life I saw him enjoy.

PLAYING FOR LEGENDARY HEAD COACH JIM SWEENEY

If you've ever watched the Mel Gibson movie *Braveheart,* where he portrays the life of William Wallace, a late 13th-century Scottish warrior and dedicated leader, you might get a sense of the personality of Coach Jim Sweeney. He was a fiery, sometimes controversial, college football coach who led with his heart and possessed a drive and charisma that awoke a sleepy little town in California and brought it a nationally ranked college football program. I am very lucky to have played college football for him during his long and final stretch of championships before retiring. Next to the primary male influences of my dad and grandpa, I certainly would not be who I am without the influence of Coach Sweeney.

James Sweeney was forged from humble and hardworking Irish-Catholic roots in a small mining town in Montana, where his father worked tirelessly and died young as a hard rock miner. Coming from those circumstances forced Sweeney to grow up tough and fight for what he believed in. I vividly remember his heartfelt stories of struggle and perseverance at the end of practice or just before a big game, with tears running down his face. It was impossible not to be inspired. In this age of bailouts and complacent personal accountability, Coach Sweeney taught us to be responsible men who had to "fight the good fight, never back down from what we believed in, and make no excuses." This wasn't "feel good" political rhetoric. He led by example and expected us to do the same.

I like to say Coach was an old-school progressive. He had street smarts and an understanding that earned trust and respect from all kinds of people—black athletes coming out of tough inner-city neighborhoods in South Central Los Angeles, small-town country boys like me, and an entire community of fans and alumni. And we won—a lot. It's not hard to understand how that experience had a major impact on my life and my vision for uniting and leading people.

I have so many memorable stories about Coach. There was the Utah brawl with me ending up engulfed by Ute defenders on their sideline and Coach ripping his shirt off to protest holding, and then he called the head coach out for a fistfight after the game. There was the Aloha Bowl night Sweeney was returning liquored up from a media dinner and proceeded to lead the entire hotel, mostly players but also a few scared Japanese tourists, in a "no dogs down" chant, finished by him getting so fired up he threw chairs into the pool before jumping in with his clothes, wallet, and brand-new hearing aids. His wife June, a fellow Irish spirit and former athlete and coach, went ballistic. These were comedic moments that showed Coach's inspiring and colorful side. I could totally relate to his spirit and heart. He was real! Always.

Most days after practice, Coach would throw the double swinging doors open and march into the locker room. He was always noticeably tired and frustrated after decades of fight and struggle to compete as a man and a college football head coach, judged only by his last championship or loss.

"Hey, looook! Billy Scott!" came the thunder of Coach Sweeney's roar.

Coach was scanning the locker room from left to right in a slow turn of his head and body, looking around for him. Billy was sitting on the same bench and set of lockers as me.

Sweeney turned around and appeared to be marching directly towards me.

Holy shit. *Dear Jesus, please don't make eye contact,* I'm thinking to myself as he gets closer.

I don't want to become part of the Crucifixion of Billy Scott. The scene gets tense, like the buildup of a heavy Black Sabbath song. There are fearful glances by the young men as Coach Sweeney goes down the bench like General Patton eyeing a row of men lined up at attention, taking in their faces until he came to Billy's.

As he stopped in front of me and turned to his left, his arms were folded, but his right arm was bent at 90 degrees, pointing his index finger to the sky. When he got really fired up, his arms unfolded and his stout freckled white limbs pumped as he turned red with furry and exploded, "Billy Scott!"

"Yes, sir!"

"What the fuck were you thinking out there today?!" He was almost crying over Billy's bad practice. "Why can't you remember to pull hard LEFT?! Jesus Christ!!"

"Sorry, Coach..." Billy whimpered out respectfully.

"What the hell does 'sorry' do when your quarterback is put out of the game? Shut the hell up with you're sorry!" Coach started getting fired up as he walked away and spun around like a general staring Billy down with a street fighter's glare and tears in his eyes. Coach would trail off with a thought and then come back with an unexpected uppercut of an emotional volcanic eruption that only came from a manic mind that abhorred and combatted daily the mediocrity trying to stop his destiny. Coach was starting to get tearful about the struggle, triumphs, and tragedy from that place and time.

"Fuck sorry!"

He faded off somewhere in his youth and began telling a story that had a relevant lesson from his street-fighting days in Montana.

"My dad went into those mines every day, risking his life and filling his lungs with deadly particles that eventually killed him before he was fifty. Miners consumption ... (filled with tears and tender anger) ...*that's* sorry. You must sacrifice everything for this team."

"Rockwell...Jesus and Mother Mary...you look light a deer caught in the headlights! Get mean!"

"Hey!" He yelled to the rest of the players in the room. "Hey, looook! Wake the hell up!!!"

The whole locker room had gone deadly silent, and the players waited for Coach to make his move. He started back down the aisle of players and locked up with Tony Brown, the most thug of any player from South Central. Tony walked slow and erect with cornrows and had a thousand-yard stare from taking and losing life in the streets since he was thirteen. Tony and I were in the same recruiting class, and he was cool with me. I learned from him that saying less is more. Sweeney's face lit up, and he started telling Tony a joke that his BYU Mormon head coach buddy Lavelle Edwards shared with him. They would trade drunk Irish and Mormon jokes all the time on the phone. It was a testament to both men and how they shared the similar ideology of uniting people beyond the shallow confines of mainstream political correctness. They were bold men. The locker room eased from its tense silence as everyone felt Coach turn jovial and reminiscent.

To be a great college football head coach, you must be able to establish trust with the spectrum of races, especially inner-city black kids. That's progressive. I laugh when people try and minimize the power of sports and the "dumb jock" stereotype. We were 100 years ahead of the '90s—or even today's idea and practice of multiculturalism and black and white relations that were proving to be dismal failures. Coach Sweeney was taking worst-case 18-year-old alpha males from extreme backgrounds and successfully uniting and teaching us to work together as a family.

Coach put his hand gently on Tony's shoulder for a moment and began telling him a joke about Blacks, Mormons, and an Irish priest. Sweeney was a natural politician but was certainly not politically correct. I found it honest and refreshing. He answered to the Irish-Catholic upbringing and didn't care what authority said. He lived for God, his family, and his players. He pointed out the differences and put them on the table without judgment. He was a rebel against the establishment but kept them in favor since they helped keep him in office.

"Tony, you looked great today."

"Thanks, Coach."

"How is your mother doing?"

"Oh, she's good, Coach. She's good. Thanks for askin'."

"I still remember the pie she made when I visited your house. That's the best key lime pie I ever had."

"She made that special for you, Coach."

"I love your mother. She's a great woman."

Tony cracked a smile that I had never seen from him. It was a smile from a young boy who was appreciating a grown man in power showing love and respect to him, something he had only glimpses of from an occasional uncle or big brother in the gang he was affiliated with. He never knew his dad. But Tony smiled warmly, thawing the nineteen winters that had turned his soul into a hundred years of pain.

Coach walked up on Judd and Melvin laughing it up about something that was probably illegal and really fucking funny. Judd was a crazy steroid and drug-fueled redneck with a flat-top from Santa Rosa. He "accidentally" shot one of his buddies when he was home during the summer, running around their ranch shooting off his shotgun and freaking people out just for the fun of it. He was the leader of our defensive line and one of the leaders of our team. He and Melvin were best friends from opposite sides of the ball, and the planet. But there was a love and brotherhood that transcended color and culture. Sports promotes this better than any other organized group, with the exception of military brotherhood in actual battle.

"Hey Coach, where are we staying in Hawaii?" Melvin mischievously asked with his classic high-pitched voice and big grin. Melvin is referring to the all-star game in Hawaii.

"Melvin, my son! Anywhere you want." Coach put his arm on Melvin's massive black shoulder and peered down at the cigarette burns blotching the length of Judd's suntanned Popeye forearm. Coach was perplexed and shaking his head like a disappointed father after studying what would be life-long scars.

"Judd Foel, are you goofy?? What the hell is wrong with you??"

With a crazed look of pride, Judd blared out, "Hey Coach, I beat Ruggeroli except for one time!" He was referring to their cigarette forearm burning competitions.

"Shut the fuck up, Judd!" Ruggeroli fired back with Italian force and a Las Vegas mafia grin.

"You are two of the goofiest bastards I know!"

Coach was shaking his head about to laugh, but perplexed at the absurdity, trying to figure out what the hell was wrong with his hell-raised surrogate children. With a glimmer in his eyes, something primal surged in him to beat them at their crazy game and win! His spirit burned as brightly as it did during a street fight outside the saloon in Bozeman, Montana, in the middle of winter when he played football for Montana State. He could feel the youthful energy surrounding him, and he thrived on it. He needed it like a heroin junkie needs a fix to live. The energy was raw, wild, and could move mountains and destroy them just as quickly. But that was college football. And it provided the platform for boys and men to live the adrenaline-fueled highs and the black and blue lows of gladiatorship.

"No pain, no gain. Right, Coach?" Judd said to the white-haired Irish coach with a crazy but adoring smile.

Coach walked on, shaking his head and smiling with confusion. His next stop was our star fullback Lorenzo Neal, the son of a preacher and a standout freak of a fullback who would go on to an NFL Hall of Fame career. He could've been a comedian or in film. He's now an NFL analyst for Comcast Bay Area, covering the 49ers and the Raiders. On this day, though, he was giving a sermon, naked with one foot up on the locker room bench, displaying a side shot of his bulging muscular physique like a statue of a black Greek God. He was preaching about how they must be healthy in body and mind, slightly tongue-in-cheek, based on some passage he knew from the Bible.

Coach was attracted to the energy and listened as Lorenzo tried to keep up his cocky swagger and continue his performance in front of his fearless leader. I could see that Coach fed off the energy, probably more than anyone. It was visible. He would start shaking and shouting crazy shit. He was the Irish Ozzy Osbourne of college football. He was the exact leader I needed in my life.

Lorenzo continued, "Brothers! We must unite and march through the forest of darkness to reach that city of gold and victory! Can I get an amen! I said, can I get an amen!"

Everybody said it, including, and most enthusiastically, Coach Sweeney, who then grabbed the reins and commanded his spotlight. "Light 'em up!" Coach screamed as he lost his mind over the collective energy of his soldiers gathered together after a brutal practice, preparing for a big game against Colorado. When he went manic high, he could make a stadium of fans run through a brick wall.

"Light 'em up!"

"No Dogs Down!!" Coach demanded.

"No Dogs Down!!" the team sounded off like a gunshot blast in a canyon.

"Monday..." he continued, the tribal bonding through chanting together.

"Tuesday, Wednesday, Thursday, Friday, Dog Day, Dog Day, Dog Day!!!"

The team and coach finished the words with mounting force.

"Hip hip..."

At this point, like any addictive person, Coach couldn't stop his cheers because he didn't want the live performance to end. It felt too good, too connecting, and too powerful. Like a lead singer at a live rock concert, Coach could unite and direct and build the crowd energy like a real rock star. He had it. You could feel his heart pulsing off his chest while tears rolled down his unabashed face because the fire in his eyes let you know they were tears of explosive energy and heart.

"Hooray!!"

"Hip hip..."

"Hooray!!"

"Hip hip!"

"Hooraaaaay!!!!"

Everyone finished the finale strong like the cannons firing at the end of a rock concert, including the position coaches who were brain dead and exhausted from the constant pressure of Coach's demands to get better and figure out a way to win against very bad odds.

The players go back to doing what they were doing before Coach pulled will call on them with the cheers. It was his way of always keeping us on our toes and not letting us get complacent. A few locker rows down, my D-line coach Jethro Franklin was walking out, and he noticed Sonny Evan's feminine style sticking out like he should be selling clothes at a fashion store for urban men.

"Damn! You got mo perfumes and lotions than my girl, Sonny!"

"They're not all mine, Coach," Sonny answered, embarrassed, and tried to play it off.

Someone from the other side of the locker aisle yelled out, "It's true, Coach. Some of these lotions are gifts from his boyfriend."

Everyone laughed, except Sonny.

"Fuck you!" Sonny said in a half-elevated voice, trying to show a tough exterior of sheen that everyone could always see through. Sonny only signed his full-ride scholarship to get girls and try and hang with the big boys. He was naturally talented but too soft and pretty to want to be good at football or anything in life that required deep conviction and work. Sonny was used to being a girl favorite and wasn't interested in much else except being famous. But then life crept up, and he realized he was a bodyguard for famous people. Crazy how life goes if we're not paying attention.

"Sonny Evans!" Coach Sweeney yelled out.

"Yes, Coach!" came the response, with a tremble of fear and respect.

"Good effort on scout team this week."

As Coach Sweeney was walking by Sonny's open locker, he saw all the lotions and colognes and stops to make sense of what he was looking at inside a men's football locker. Coach was in his sixties, old school, and could never understand some of the metro guy shit that football players were doing at the time.

"For Christ's sake, how many fucking bottles of perfume and lotion do you need!"

The entire room erupted with laughter as Sonny had a laugh at his own expense, and Coach disappeared behind the doors to his office.

D-LINE PRACTICE WITH COACH JETHRO FRANKLIN & DOMINOES AT JUDD'S

My first D-line coach was Steve McLish, an older bald white guy with thick darkened glasses that made him appear more like a college computer engineer professor than a football coach. His social graces amounted to wiping the dried white spit from the corners of his mouth, usually after he was finished talking or screaming six inches from my face. I kinda felt sorry for Coach McLish when I wasn't angry with him for making my first August out of high school a living nightmare. I could tell that he was a good guy, the kind of good guy that did right by his parents as a kid and broke his back for his boss no matter the sacrifice or self-deprecation it required. I swore I wouldn't end up like that. I couldn't understand what motivated him to get up in the morning.

Coach McLish feared our head coach like everyone, but McLish would act over-the-top serious and intense any time Sweeney was in his presence. It was like watching a kiss-up sales guy in a middle management position, like Steve Carell in *The Office*. He would create this dramatic scowl on his face, including a left eyebrow he could raise higher to give him the look and feel of a deranged serial killer or Dracula's bald and less charming older brother. The guy really laid it on thick, even yelling out absurd lines like the classic, "Rip out their jugular!!" The irony is Coach McLish didn't mean it. He actually never hurt anyone in his life. It was all a sad act of desperation to connect, to be liked, and to hang on to his soon-to-be-lost job.

The organizational experience of college football was very similar to the hierarchical structure in any company I've worked in. There's the head coach (CEO), his handpicked assistant coaches (senior executives), supporting staff (middle management), and the athletes who grind in the trenches for scraps (employees).

To say our organization was an intense place to work would be an understatement. Coach Sweeney led with heart and thunder. I watched grown men shake and stutter with the fear that Coach might target their performance for brutal ridicule if they weren't getting it done. I paid close attention to the dynamics between Coach and his coaches. Their connection to Coach determined how he interacted with them. His original guys from Montana State, where he played and began his career, had a noticeably elevated status. To be clear, it wasn't an elevated status that protected them from having their ass handed to them in front of the team if they weren't handling their job, but Sweeney had deep roots with those Montana State men, like Coach Hysell. It was a bond that kept them together through decades of grueling days.

The coaches took the punishing leadership from Sweeney because he actually cared, and they knew it. When Coach Hysell's wife and a couple other coaches' wives were in a deadly car crash on the way to a game, Coach Sweeney went out of his way to be a rock for those families—forever. I saw it up close and personal when Coach gave Nick a full-ride scholarship out of junior college. He took it to a higher level when he not only honored my brother's scholarship after he injured his back, requiring surgery and ending his Fresno

State football days prematurely, but Coach even paid for his master's degree.

Coach Sweeney was a lion and a saint, and that's why people—particularly his coaches, staff, and players—wanted to follow him. We knew his intentions were right, and he was all in to fight the good fight. For people who didn't "get" that, Sweeney represented a loudmouth bully. I remember listening to people bitch and complain about Coach; never in front of him, of course. I bitched about him at times too! The man was hardcore, and I was a soft young boy who needed someone to call me out and hold me accountable to my dreams and commitment to the team.

Every practice, we would warm up as a team. During a well-organized stretching routine, Coach would let us know what was on his mind and what he expected that day and week. We had a team chant, then we would immediately break into our groups led by our position coaches.

In my case, the D-line would run drills with Coach Jethro Franklin, who had replaced the worn-out McLish. When he became frustrated at the guys' lack of effort, he would go into a mini tirade, blowing his whistle, like he was trying to use it as a blowgun with poison-tipped darts.

Jethro Franklin was a former standout defensive–end for the Bulldogs and played in the pros for a few years. He was in his first year of coaching after the NFL. He was a cool young black guy from San Jose who came from good folks who taught him manners and a serious work ethic. I looked up to him and feared him. He possessed a big infectious smile and a heart of gold. He was truly a good human, and we were lucky to have him guiding us.

As I became a veteran on the team, Jethro and I would sometimes battle on strategy and plays. He was a great player and an inspirational coach who led by example, but he was a rookie college coach. I would challenge him and push his buttons. I look back now with the utmost love and respect for that man. Thanks to Coach Sweeney seeing Jethro's potential despite zero experience, he went on to be one of the great D-line coaches and recruiters in college and the NFL. As I write this, Jethro is coaching D-line for the Seattle Seahawks after a long stint with the Oakland Raiders. We still keep in touch; he's like a big brother to me.

"Hold up! Tuputala! Look! Do you even want to be here?! You look like you're gonna have a heart attack! You need to lay off that poi, or whatever you Hawaiians call that nasty, no-tasting purple paste. Are you gonna stop dragging your ass? Or do we need to start working on our endurance?"

Breathing like a stuck pig, Tuputala sincerely cried out, "Sorry, Coach! I'll try harder."

Sonny was giggling with some slap-dick walk-on transfer next to him. Both of them would never see much time in a game. I knew I was not going to be them. I was out to win a starting position from the first day I got there.

Coach Franklin narrowed his laser-pissed eyes and growled with clenched teeth, "Sonny Evans! What could you possibly think is funny at this moment?"

"Sorry, Coach. Nothing's funny."

"Too late. Now you have my attention. And it better be funny! Or we're doing up-downs for the rest of our session!"

Sonny conceded. "Damn. Okay, Coach. I was saying, every time Tuputala hits the sled, he squeals like a bitch."

Tuputala goes islander, in talk and stance. "Fuck you, Sonny! Everybody knows you a fag!"

Everyone laughs, including Coach Franklin, while Sonny and Tuputala start to wrestle around attempting to hurt each other in full pads on a blazing hot day. Jethro let them go for a minute and then snapped the practice back on track like the drill sergeant his father was. At that moment, I was in the back of the line standing next to Judd. The offensive line ran by, and Melvin Johnson grinned at Judd.

"Judd Foel. Dominoes tonight."

"Melly Mel! Hell yeah! Meet you at the water jug in thirty!"

Judd was a certifiably fucking crazy country boy from Santa Rosa, looking back now. But at the time, he was the senior warrior I looked up to. He was cool to me but also kept the distance a veteran does with a rookie.

"Hey Rockwell, dominos at my place tonight. Come through."

Trying to contain my Christmas morning excitement, I said, "Yeah, man... I'm there!"

This was the invitation I had been waiting for. I was just a freshman and was getting called up to the big leagues with the two leaders representing the offensive and defensive line. They also represented the South-Central gangs and the NorCal country boys.

Dominoes at Judd's

It's a perfect day, and I remember riding over to Judd's on my mountain bike, drinking a 24-ounce Coors. The Steve Miller Band's "Joker" was playing in my mind. I showed up and knocked on the front door. A loud voice yelled, "Door's open!" I entered to see Judd, Melvin Johnson, Joey Ruggeroli, and Judd's old man smoking a big cigar. You could instantly see the resemblance and bond between Judd and his dad.

Judd was high as fuck, smoking a blunt with his Olympia hat on backward and grinning. "Melly Mel! I hate to do this to you. I know a white country boy shouldn't disrespect a brother from Lynwood like this, but—"

Bam!!! Judd threw the bones hard onto the table, and Melvin gave Judd a mean and solemn stare.

"Judd, I respect that move. But you know, you just fucked up."

Melvin exploded with laughter, and Judd and Ruggeroli fell in line and gasped, realizing it was funny and not gonna get them shot.

The guys looked up at me like all veterans look at rookies; it's a look of *What the fuck do you want?* Joey Ruggeroli, our other senior D-lineman, is from a connected Italian family generations deep in Vegas. Dr. Ruggeroli was also on the World Boxing Federation's board. He annoyingly puffed up and said, "Who the fuck invited Rockwell? Hey man, are you cool?"

He was mainly concerned with me snitching on them for smoking weed. Ironically, a few months later, I was his exclusive pot dealer!

Judd calmed Ruggeroli down. "Rockwell's cool."

Immediately following that near crucifixion, Big Melvin Johnson started in on me. "You need to chill the fuck out on scout team, Rockwell! Trying to be All-American and shit... you need to pace yo'self." He said it smoothly but sternly, coaching me so I'd take it easy on him and his line...or he'd have to check me.

I shook my head in acknowledgment and made a horrible attempt at a cool laugh, but I was visibly nervous. Without expression, Melvin pointed next to his chair for me to sit down. Looking back, he reminded me a lot of Biggie Smalls in body, quick wit, and charisma. Melvin was the most gangster and fierce college football player on our team and a strong third-round NFL draft pick. He was built like an out-of-shape tank, but in reality, he was an offensive guard that could pull like a jaguar and hit opponents without remorse.

I experienced what it was like to get hit by Melvin when he pulled to block a defensive end. He knocked me out! I woke up to dirt and grass in my eyes and a ringing in my ears and head. I had to go against Melvin in one-on-one drills nearly every day. He made me much tougher, and he made me more streetwise to the world. Not to mention, he respected me because he knew I would battle him in practice every day. He validated me both on and off the field.

Out of respect to the winner, he nodded to Judd to grab his dominoes first out of the pile, then it went around the room finishing with me. Judd directed me to catch up and not be a liability. "Grab your bones, Rock!"

They were passing a blunt around with light conversation about the team and the upcoming game, and some fat white bitch Melvin and Judd hit after the Hawaii game last year. Melvin handed me the blunt, and I took a hit, praying I didn't cough like a punk, but I knew my asthma might let me down. As we started a new game of dominoes, I felt like I was just made in the Scorsese mob film *Good Fellas*, joining the ranks of the veterans on the team. I never wanted that day to end.

SHARK ATTACK IN THE RED TRIANGLE

I t was the first spring of my college career, and I was momentarily back where I belonged, where I fit. I was nineteen, and we were diving the "spot" at Navarro. The day was perfect. The sun was warm, and the water was flat. Everyone was in a happy mood. Drinking a beer with his right hand and his fishing rod in his left, Nick Brandt grinned at his younger brother Matt, awkwardly trying to get up on the rock out of the water and kelp.

"Hey Meat, you look like a seal in distress!"

Nick was already lit up and dressed to hang out on the rocks and casually fish. He drank cans of Coors, smoked Camel Lights, and looked like a 70s pro athlete meets Carl from *Caddyshack*. His getup was cut-off long shorts, some old high-top boots, dirty white socks, an old man bucket hat, and a faded Budweiser t-shirt with the sleeves cut off to expose his Irish white pitching arm and a scar from a fight he got into a few nights back in a biker bar in town. He was casting out funny observations and one-liners about anything and everyone. Besides being one of the greatest baseball players from my hometown ever, Nick Brandt was also ridiculously hilarious and tough as nails. Nick could've been a stand-up comic or a hitman. He operated on instinct and could take it as far as it needed to go.

"You look like Captain Kangaroo with that hat!" Matt spat out the funny comeback as everyone laughed.

"Did you see Sonny?"

I always thought it was interesting that they called their dad by his first name. I tried to imagine calling my dad by his first name and winced for such disrespectful thoughts. Nick pointed past me, out towards the rock island where Sonny and Dad were fishing. Everyone scanned the rock island for humans, but we saw nothing except a lone seagull protecting its nest on top of the worn peak.

"No. I thought they were already back here with you guys."

"They're probably headed towards the rock outcropping beyond the island."

With a Jack Nicholson creepy trademark grin and squinted eyes from a late night of partying, he said, "I've never seen so many abalone as the time I was diving right out there with Scott Mastelotto when I was just out of high school. I remember how open the water felt... like there was something there. Me, Scott, and Guy had just smoked a joint and downed a gallon of Carlo Rossi. Scott came staggering up to us to say he saw a big shadow over his head as he was heading to the surface after picking an ab at the bottom. Me and Guy started laughing and thought he was full of shit. We just figured he was probably paranoid from the weed!"

"What did Scott think the shadow was?" My little brother asked innocently as he sat next to me on the rocks after finishing our dive.

"I can bet you it wasn't a fuckin' sea perch!" Matt answered with his usual shit-talking little-brother anecdote.

We all laughed, but the mood grew concerned for Dad and Sonny. The reality was that our type of lived adventure involved very real life and death risk. We had lost Rusty just a year and a half earlier, and everyone was still cautiously on edge.

"I'm sure they're on the other side of the rock," I spoke up to convince the crowd, and myself, that things were under control. I was the oldest of four and always had that instinct to look after the younger ones, and my parents. Diving with my dad was crazy because he could hold his breath up to two minutes in his prime, and he could disappear underwater for such a long time that it would really worry me. But he was also very athletic and smart, so I knew he most likely had it handled. I still worried.

"Yeah, I bet you're right, Chris." Matt and I were the same age and inseparable. He was a lot more experienced and street-savvy than me, but we were trying to figure it out together.

"I think I saw them go around earlier to fish the point," My younger brother Nick said optimistically to make everything okay. Diving and hunting over the years and dealing with our own tragedies had made us vigilant. "Hey, Chris... did you see that?" Nick hit my arm and had a very serious and confused look like he had just seen a spaceship fly out of the water.

"What!" I was talking and laughing with Matt about the chew they stole from the Curriers grocery store.

"Did you see the water out there? It looked different. I thought I saw a big splash," my brother continued.

I was annoyed for being interrupted but looked just in case.

Suddenly, the water became chaotic right where we had just decided Dad and Sonny were diving and fishing. A quiet panic set in, then quickly escalated from the frozen silence.

"Oh, God!! Shark!!"

Everyone yelled out, "Shark!!!"

"Jesus Christ!! Dad...Dan!!! Get out of the water!!!" I screamed as only a terrified big brother can at his baby brother in danger. I felt my mind and body illogically trying to make me jump in the water to save him. Dan was only 14 years old. He was still diving in the water close to the rocks, spearfishing, unaware of the danger. He had a stringer of bloody fish he speared hanging off his weight belt; he was practically chumming the bloodthirsty beast. He was oblivious to the danger until we all started shouting louder. My little brother finally heard the warnings and looked up to see us yelling at him like we just saw Jaws! He knew it, almost instinctively. At that point, he knew he was bait and started swimming for the safety of the rocks we were standing on. He was kicking his jet fins so hard that he was almost elevated above the water like a zodiac dive raft skipping across the surface.

"Swim, Dan!! Swim motherfucker!!"

My brother Nick and I were yelling like head coaches demanding he save his life.

"Swim!!!"

The ancient death machine exploded out of the water like a subsurface nuclear warhead, except this eighteen-foot serpent had a full-grown seal in its jaws. As fast as it appeared, it disappeared into the black and bloody water, only to return and battle another giant great white shark competing for the carnage. The sharks took turns striking and shredding the corpse so brutally that parts of the seal were flying in the air, attracting every seagull in a five-mile radius. It looked like the bloody second coming of the devil. I could feel my adrenaline pulsing through my body. We all knew we were experiencing a once-in-a-lifetime moment worthy of a National Geographic special.

Dad and Sonny were still nowhere to be found. As the group continued to scan the horizon, our nerves overloading on visual and mental sensory, the patriarchs peaked out from around the corner with their spearguns and fishing poles, standing on the edge of the rock with an enviable vantage point. It was a surreal and powerful moment of Mother Nature wielding its truth about life and death. We bowed to her command and watched in awe.

AFRICAN AMERICAN STUDIES AND CLOYD THE WHITE SUPREMACIST

I was forced to attend African American studies as a mandatory part of my college education. I wasn't forced by gunpoint, but I was signed up for the course by our black athletic academic advisor, a Billy Dee Williams lookalike who hated white people. I couldn't remember his name if I had to. He was riding the wave of political correctness on campus and swung his affirmative action bat with a swagger and arrogance that would make Rick James look Amish.

Fortunately, I was in the class with my buddies from the football team, guys like Dee Edwards, Kenny Hall, Ron Collins, and Stacey. I knew Dee and Ron would make the class intense and entertaining for sure. They weren't militant; they just grew up in Berkeley and East Palo Alto. They weren't angry, just intent on stirring the pot. Besides, these guys had teammates—brothers—who were redneck white guys like me. As football players, we dealt with intense race conflict and resolution almost daily. We were true brothers who came from totally different planets. But Coach Sweeney helped us address and then drop the race thing and focus on the team as more important. He meant it. And we ended up working well as a mixed-up bunch of misfits, better than any other example offered by the racially "sensitive" rhetoric spewed by the liberal party and liberal education.

I always found it odd that we were forced to attend a class by an obviously anti-white agenda professor and a predominantly white university faculty that were adhering to the extreme political correctness of the early 1990s. It had nothing to do with "educating" us on the current struggles of the black man. It was divisive social engineering allowed by a bunch of scared, gutless pussies willing to accept condemnation for being white, and dancing the dance to not rock the boat and maintain their pathetic tenured job, hiding from the reality going on outside the university and media fantasyland. I witnessed the distorted interpretation of "modern American society" supposedly representing the merging of the cultures and best practices that elevate societies. Instead, I saw the hypocrisy of affirmative action and similar laws that were creating inequality and divide, while race was becoming less of a factor in the real world thanks to technology and the general sense of color and gender no longer being a real divider socially and economically.

Back in the classroom, affirmative action was in high gear, and white male athletes—actually, white males in general—were demonized and somehow owed the world an apology. I found that to be ignorant, simplistic, and extremely racist. In very specific terms, Dr. Mack was telling our class that white men were responsible for slavery and the world's ills as if it were a scientific and historical fact.

I find it ironic that black people are complete victims of slavery. But I knew this professor was too stubborn and ignorant—and validated by the politically correct climate—to understand or acknowledge the dark truth. Entitlement was clearly the only viable reason this guy had a job at a university.

"Dr. Mack. So, you're saying it's a conspiracy against the black man?" Heidi was a mild Christian conservative who grew up wealthy because her family owned vineyards and almonds throughout the valley. But she grew up with the expectations of hard work, being grateful, and being charitable. She was at Fresno State on an equine scholarship, riding horses competitively. She seemed to be grounded and asked logical questions while trying to understand the point of why she was forced to learn this information when the university would never allow a class on campus that pushed her Christian way of life. The reality is that Heidi came across as more objective, educated, and less prejudiced than anyone else in the class.

Her calm and organized thoughts and pointed questions only made the professor more defensive and argumentative with Ebonic flair and spit flying from his over-toothed mouth with stale alcoholic breath and body odor that permeated the classroom. Looking back, he reminded me of a black Bukowski with the same pockmarked complexion, vile manners, and limited depth of knowledge of history due to his belligerent fear, biases, arrogance, and ignorance. I sat in that class and didn't say a thing all semester, not because I was scared to say something in fear of offending my black classmates and teacher, but because I knew that the arguments were not even based on facts. It was senseless, hostile emotion based on preconceived hate that was brewing in California like a meth lab about to explode.

All I observed the entire time I was in class was the black students and teacher yelling at any white person who raised a question about anything—literally *anything*. It was a joke of a class and made me feel like it was one big political and socially engineered form of psychological racial warfare. As I got older, I realized that politicians on the far-left, primarily rich and white, created the senseless divide by branding white men as evil. And universities and the entire academic system, starting at kindergarten, are funded and controlled by the powerful teachers' union who are puppets to rich and power-crazy elites like the Rockefellers, Gates, Soros, and are known to push academic agendas into the classroom that keep the entire system out of sync with the times. Purposely designed *not* to create thinkers, just repeaters, droids, and cogs.

It's easier to control the paying union members if they aren't fighting the system but tied to its survival. My California State University experience was proving to be more of the same.

I didn't learn anything new about Africa or "African Americans" in that class. I didn't even learn a thing about slavery in America. I did learn that the racial divide is a perpetuated ideology pushed by the most powerful to divide and conquer the masses. The liberal politicians pander to the black vote in what I consider to be a sadly outdated protest against the old white system. Some black people, most of my class that semester, felt like victims in the system as we're sitting in a college class they were not paying for. Why not Jewish studies? Why don't we talk about the strife and oppression of the Irish Americans who were also slaves in America? We don't because they united during really fucked up times and succeeded, together. Blacks still haven't.

Dr. Mack replied to Heidi with the hope that he had just recruited a new white disciple. "That's exactly what I'm saying, young lady."

Then a young man's voice with a twang said, "That don't make sense! There would be a lot less complaining if they just worked hard and quit blaming all the hardworking white people."

Cody was a white country boy who was clearly frustrated and impervious to the usual black-on-white intimidation. He grew up without a father thanks to a bad batch of heroin from Bakersfield and watched his mom struggle like the rest of the single parents on the poor side of town where race was nearly irrelevant. Survival was a racial equalizer for the working poor. The room reactively winced at someone questioning Dr. Mack's mantra about the white man keeping the black man down.

"Ooohhh!"

Cody's comment ignited a passionate division between him and much of the class. My hybrid teammate, Ron, jumped in, apparently feeling very black, even though it represented less than 25% of his racial DNA. He was more of a giant Pacific Island-American mutt—a bigger, louder, and less attractive version of the Rock. They could be brothers or cousins for sure. Ron had a loud, offsetting sense of humor, but his heart was pure gold. There was nothing bad in the guy, but he was very passionate and intense. Most of the guys I played with had this similar makeup. You have to have passion and a burning desire to strap on a helmet and crash into an opposing player. We were kindred brothers. But for this guy to claim black was a big stretch.

"You did not just say that!"

Cody continued, "The hell I didn't! I'm talking from fact, not prejudice. I believe that black people, in general, don't have the work ethic of, say, the Mexicans, Jews, or Asians. I'm a poor white kid who was raised by a single mother in a trailer park in Coalinga. I grew up with less than most of the black kids I knew. This ain't about race no more. It's about money. Some people expect to earn it, and some expect it given to them. Life ain't fair, and handouts are something rich politicians invented so the poor would vote for them. Just like us being forced to take this class."

Hothead Ron reacted, but with nothing to refute the argument except a flood of testosterone and his own prejudiced view pushing a reactionary, strike-first angry black response.

"Fuck that!"

Ironically, Ron was never institutionalized or even busted for anything except a bad grade or maybe for talking too much in class. He was taught this behavior growing up in the Bay Area, a place that still thinks it's in the 1965 Civil Rights Movement where you have free speech unless you're a Conservative. Ron and I are like brothers. Still are. We battled in the trenches every day on the field, we partied together, prayed together, and shared our homes like a real family. You should've seen the time Ron, Stacey, Sonny, and Kenny all came up and stayed at my parents' house, sleeping in our childhood bunk beds. A sight to see for sure. But you get into a race discussion, and all of a sudden, that doesn't exist, and we are thrown back into the Civil Rights Movement. Give me a break. (I'm hoping to dispel some of that in this book.)

Dr. Mack condescendingly responded, "No, this is good! Wait! We need to talk about this, even as ridiculous as this white boy sounds."

The professor's words were about as smug and racist as you can get. He lived in a moment in time that had flipped the script, and he was reveling in it—where affirmative action (aka entitlement starting in the 1960s, reaching its PC zenith during the 1990s). The class was at full pitch and volume when the black girl sitting next to me tapped me on the arm and smiled; she rolled her eyes at the debate that was going on around us.

"Hey, Chris Rockwell. You look good. I'm Ricky."

Ricky was a dark black girl with mild features and a big, beautiful smile. She was tall and had a nice athletic ass on her. She looked like she was straight from Nigeria but spoke like a total valley girl. It was kind of a trip, and I dug her immediately. She was cool.

"We should hang out sometime."

Then Ricky dropped into a sexy whisper and almost mocked the ridiculousness of the emotional racial debate that was surrounding us. "You ever been with a black girl?" We smiled and laughed.

A chair crashed to the ground with some books, and Ron jumped up and challenged Cody to a fight. Some of the kids were holding Ron back. Cody wasn't even flinching, even though he couldn't have weighed 150 pounds to Ron's 300 pounds. My other teammate, the crowd rouser, Dee Edwards, was coaxing a fight with a sly grin. Dee could start a riot or a party with his gravitational aura, looks, thug swagger, and humor. He had an uncanny sense of people, timing, and humor. Fucking hilarious.

"Aww, dog! He called us out!"

Meanwhile, I was thinking about Ricky and her invitation, considering I was sitting in African American studies class being lectured about how bad white people are. I saw more prejudice and hate in that one class than anything I had ever seen on the streets. She and I were the perfect example of reality, connected regardless of our skin color. Like most people, we didn't need a college class to understand our humanness, love, and understanding other people...not "African Americans." The PC culture had created a different set of confusing and conflicting rules

This is a good time to illustrate how race relations should function in the most extreme case study. This is where politically correct sensitivity training breaks down, and my philosophy of race relations steps in and works. This really happened. I put that on my mom and God!

There was a white supremacist named Cloyd that I worked with in the lumberyards, and he always wanted to hang out. I sometimes obliged because he was a happy, harmless kind of guy, willing to offer a stranger of any color a big sincere smile with rosy cheeks and dimples. I know...how does that make sense? Anyway, he was your classic penitentiary White Pride gang-affiliated dude, except he looked anything but hard. He looked like a soft, blond, curly mop top with a thick heavy body and a happy-go-lucky personality.... when he wasn't jonesing for smack. He was tatted up with *White Pride* on his arms and calves, along with a full quota of spiderwebs, naked chicks, and skulls. He was a walking contradiction, like most people. He kinda reminds me of the Dave Chappelle's white supremacist character Clayton Bigsby, a blind Southern black guy who led his KKK chapter. It's that ridiculous and funny.

Cloyd liked everyone. He worked side by side with a fellow heroin junkie named Sylvester, an old black man who still chased the dragon, despite losing everything and slowly dying of liver failure from Hep C. They all lived and died by the sword—either the gun, knife, or the needle. I worked with Cloyd and Sylvester on a daily basis, building lumber packages for the truss and wall orders heading to the east bay. These two guys would lovingly joke about race, but it was never even cutting. It was like a Fat Albert episode. It always struck me as strangely progressive. Talking about it defused any tension that naturally built up through hard workdays, 110-degree summer heat, and a dust-filled yard that choked out the oxygen and caked everyone's face and lungs with a thick layer of silt by the end of each day.

The one thing I have always noticed in the poor working segments was rough-cut honesty. On the lumberyard, as on the football field, guys said what they felt about a guy and his race, and that was it. There were no lawsuits or fear of job loss for racial discrimination by saying something that may be offensive. It was honest talk that allowed men to say it out loud and defuse the real but inconsequential differences of race and culture as they worked together as a team, a family, to achieve a goal. And coming from a very liberal white-glove approach to race relations, I found this refreshing and very healthy to moving forward as a team and not getting hung up on the little things that don't really mean what they did. The ruling elite has truly fucked up the natural assimilation that was happening post-Industrial Revolution. Race should be mocked and respected. It is NOT the foundation of who we are as a human or as a soul. It is an irrelevant factor in today's global economy and social community, and as a nation.

Staying hung up on race, and worse, trying to pass laws and regulations to "equal" the racial quota in today's world is crazy. I'm serious. I can't believe I even have to write a book to discuss this. But that's my point, folks. We are thinking about our global and local human relationships with an expanding fragmentation brought on by Far-Left and minority groups thinking they can't succeed in America because of race.

It takes common sense and balls to deal with race, not a fucking college degree and perfect politically correct language consisting of soft words and a matching tone of a mellow hippie. I'm not saying it doesn't make it not exist. In fact, it rears its ugly head as prejudice towards white men like me. I've worked in the hardest blue-collar jobs and in the billion-dollar technology empires of Silicon Valley. Hands down, the white elite, especially Silicon Valley Sleestacks, are more prejudiced and fucked up over race than anyone. They just intellectually live in a false utopia justified and denied and reconstructed in their convenient elevated view of mankind and themselves but distanced from the working hands of reality. They deny it and say they love everyone…except their actions are completely impersonal, disconnected, and counter to their haiku.

Fast forward to a couple of years later, after a football game on a perfect fall night. We had just won a big game and were ready for a raucous post-game party. Cloyd unexpectedly showed up at that game and waited outside the locker rooms to greet me after our victory. My mouth dropped. Remember, my football team was made up of about 75% black guys. More importantly, many of them were serious gangsters from South-Central LA and Oakland. The crack epidemic certified these crazy stats. Especially the South-Central kids. They were packing guns when we would go out at night.

I got caught up in a black club one night when haters started hatin' on some of the players I was with, simply because they were actually doing something with their lives! Guns started poppin', and 175 people ran for the door. I remember running down the sidewalk with two of the guys I was with. One of them had a gun pulled and was checking his shoulder as he sprinted for the car down the street. Our third friend came flying over the brick wall and crashed into the bushes next to the car and basically rolled into the back seat as we sped off into the night, escaping one more disaster for being in the wrong place at the wrong time. Nothing good happens at closing time in bars and clubs, ever.

And here stood Cloyd, a walking billboard for white supremacy. I wasn't quite sure what to do with him as I was headed to our victory party. So, I invited him to the party, warning him about the setting. The night went off without a hitch… until we were leaving. I wish I were making this up, but this can be certified by my teammates who were standing there when it happened.

So Cloyd followed me out of the party, and as I was saying my goodbyes to guys in the front yard, Cloyd stepped up on the all-black crew and thanked them for the great time. The guys actually seemed to get a kick out of him. And then it happened.

"You guys are the coolest niggers I ever met!"

The proverbial needle scratched the record, and everything went silent.

"Whaoooooo……!" was the collective response from the guys Cloyd was "complimenting."

I felt my heart literally go, *what the fuck?*

"Rock, is this dude with you?" asked one of the black guys, still totally in shock that a cotton-top mud rat of a white supremacist could openly say nigger to a bunch of street thug black guys as if he was the black comedic godfather, Richard Pryor. His comment followed silence and heavy stares from a bunch of street legit black guys after a testosterone-laden night of football and partying, complete with the usual condiments of booze and drug supplying hangers-on and groupies who trailed the college football parties to get and give something to be part of the crazy roadshow of adrenaline and decadence. We were all on the same ride…except for Cloyd. With one word, my buzz and prospects for the night were snuffed out. I had images of telling the guys to pop him so we could all just go back to having a great time.

"What the fuck, dude?!" I shot back, hoping the offended guys would realize that Cloyd and I had different views.

"Yeah man, what the fuck's wrong with you?! This ain't a white pride party mothafucka! You better back it down!"

I felt like Steve Carrell in *40-Year-Old Virgin* when he gets caught up in the South-Central beef between his black coworker and a wannabe gangster hothead played by Kevin

Hart. I looked to the right of the guy talking and noticed his friend was ready to kill him for being so stupid. And I decided I would help them bury his fat ass for putting me in this fucked up situation in the first place! Fuckin' Cloyd!

"You lucky you know Rockwell. Just sayin'. It's time for you to go." And with that, Cloyd walked off into the night.

The guys handled it totally cool because they understood the context and dealt with it accordingly. This lived experience proved a lot to everyone involved. And I think it elevated everyone's perspective on race and people in general. We are *all* judged unfairly. Deal with it. How we work through those preconceived prejudices and skewed perspectives with others is what matters. After it was all over, I was proud to be part of that moment. It reinforced my convictions about race and people.

Out of nowhere, as I am writing this book, I got a message on Facebook from the man himself. He's cleaned up and living a new life helping other addicts find the light. I'm glad he made it out. I wonder if he still calls black guys niggers to their faces…

BIG MELVIN IS MURDERED

It was Christmas break, and I was back home for a few weeks seeing family and my girlfriend Becky, who was going to the junior college back in our hometown. I spent my Christmas break working in the lumberyard again for her uncle to earn a couple of bucks for the spring semester since our full scholarship didn't cover extra stuff, and the NCAA didn't allow me to work except in summer. I remember it being a bone-chilling December, and the fog was so thick and creeping damp-cold that warmth wasn't a known concept. My task that morning in the dark was to remove the steel cables from the units of lumber, usually 2x4 and 2x6, which makes up the majority of truss and wall construction in California.

Mike Brittain was walking up to me with the look of a tired gold miner forcing his face and body to fight through the pain of being up so early working, hallucinating for a warm bed and sleep. He was a rough-and-tumble thirty-something dude, who wore a rebel flag bandana, surfer sandy-blond thinning long hair, and a ZZ Top beard like mostly all the white bikers I worked with in the yard. Most of these guys were in revolving doors with the drug and prison system. A lot of them had done time in a real prison like San Quentin for anything from drugs to violent crimes. Many had drug addiction struggles, and prison was the byproduct of it. I would personally learn twenty-five years later that we shared more similarities than I could've known back then at nineteen years old.

"Hey Chris! Chris! You have someone on the phone that says it's important!"

Getting a call from someone during work hours at the lumberyard only meant bad news. As I stood on the open-train lumber car with the grey fog closing in on my worst thoughts of what the call was about, I tried to think positively, but I have always been too pragmatic, despite being a dreamer, to know when to prepare for something unexpected and life-changing. All of a sudden, I discovered a new enthusiasm for working with cold steel cables in the freezing fog outside.

I wanted to stay there until dark, until I couldn't keep my eyes open or process a thought of anything but the task of unloading lumber from the train. After chasing that dream away from the reality of news I wasn't looking forward to, I gathered my thoughts and looked down at Mike with a nod and jumped off the train car and hit the gravel tracks with a force that sent shock waves up the icy brittle leg bones supporting my suddenly feeble body from the cold and news I was reluctantly walking towards, as if I was walking myself to the gallows.

I entered the warm and quiet office, and Beth said to use the phone in the vacant office, the boss's office. Sparky was gone on business that day. I remember feeling strange being in the boss's office without him there. I picked up the phone, hit the line with the red flashing light, and heard my mom's voice.

"Chris, Melvin Johnson was killed last night. He was shot, and so was his girlfriend. I'm so sorry, Chris. I know how much he meant to you. "

I was numb. I wasn't sure if it was the tingling heat from the office heater trying to resuscitate my cold body or if it was that my nerves had just detached from my sensory center. Everything seemed to stop and shift gears into a new and heavier reality. It felt like the weather I had been working in. My body felt like the cold fog of creeping death had worked its way deep into my bones and somehow infiltrated my soul with its eternal night. My friend was murdered.

The door swung open, and I walked back outside to the yard and train cars in a trance. Giant forklifts were flying around and lumber trucks jockeying in for position to get their load of trusses and head to the Bay Area to meet the deadline we promised. We had about 150 guys working in the yard, either building trusses, cutting lumber, or building lumber packages to go with the truss orders. It was a cold, dusty operation that spat out profits and created a lot of decent-paying jobs for a poor town full of nearly unemployable but hardworking men. I walked through the yard, oblivious to the craziness all around me. Prior to the call, I always thought the lumberyard and the guys in it weren't really part of me. But suddenly it was.

All the older guys knew I was passing through, but they also respected me because I worked as hard as anyone. And I would party with the craziest of them on Friday nights after working all week. We drank Budweiser, shots of tequila, and polished it off with a dirty glass pipe of meth and kept the train rollin' until Sunday morning, when I would dive off the Nelson Bridge as the sun was coming up to wake up my tweaked-out soul. I was young and bulletproof, so it was just a big adventure on the edge with the toughest and scariest guys I knew existed. But now, I felt a piece of that distance slip away, inching me closer to the men in the yard who toiled endlessly to nowhere to deny their demons and their reprieve from prison. I felt the darkness of thought and hope shutter like an earthquake, the kind that makes your body feel out of control and nauseous.

I slowly climbed back onto the railcar and continued robotically unfastening steel cables from the tied down lumber as if to set them free or send them to their final destination after death. I heard the thousands of snow geese and ducks surrounding our island, camped out on the six-inch lakes of water covering square miles of rice fields that ran along the highway frontage and behind us, extending east for miles towards the Sierra Nevada Mountains. I just wanted to float with the sounds of the birds and slowly drift away into the fog and disappear. I couldn't cry yet. Too soon to process that emotion. I was in shock. Plus, I was in the lumberyard with a bunch of tough men. No fucking way! So, I just kept moving to stay warm, masking the hot sword piercing my guts from the loss, and reminding myself that I was alive, and it would be okay another day...but not today.

On Thursday, January 2, 1992: "Melvin Johnson, the Fresno State football standout and his girlfriend were gunned down tonight. Sources say it might be the connected to his girlfriend's ex-boyfriends little 14-year-old brother. The killer used a sawed-off shotgun and shot him from behind as he tried fleeing the scene. The football star was scheduled to fly out to Hawaii for the Hula Bowl, the senior college all-star game. The Oakland Raiders were scouting Melvin as a pulling offensive guard."

The news report didn't mention the cold-blooded fact that the killer let the girl plead for her life in the street before blowing her head off.

Melvin reminded me a lot of Warren Sapp, with his happy-go-lucky but don't-fucking-cross me 21-year-old that had seen enough murder and gangster shit to make a whole Dr. Dre and Snoop album. The most memorable story I have of Melvin is when he got arrested coming out of breakfast at the college food cafeteria one morning. That morning I happened to be sitting at the same table as Melvin and Coach Sweeney. It was one of the best mandatory 7 am team breakfasts I recall because Melvin and Coach were in rare form, cutting it up and laughing. Next thing we know, Melvin walked out of the dining hall humming "Gin and Juice" when the cops hold him at gunpoint as more cops throw the giant black bear to the ground and handcuff his paws behind his back, accusing him of stealing a red escort GT and carrying a concealed weapon. The cops were right, but Melvin got off as usual. People either loved or feared Melvin Johnson. I loved him *and* feared him. But mainly I respected and really liked Melvin. He made me smile and laugh.

SPRING FOOTBALL PARTY

A big Samoan in tribal tattoos rose up with his intimidating look set on the black guy across the table from him. Everyone went silent.

"Twenty-four, you African bitches!!"

The crowd went insane as the game-winning domino was slammed onto the table: "AAAAAWWWWWWWW!!!"

The reggae beat dropped, and everybody started laughing, socializing, drinking, or smoking the joint being passed around. Everyone was feeling right.

My roommate Jason, some of the Samoans, and one black dude were shotgunning beers by the barbeque and smoking a joint. The weed and the barbeque created a thick cloud of smoke to set the backdrop of the laughter that filled the air. This wasn't a typical weekend party at our place; it was the annual celebration of the end of spring football. That meant football for the entire spring semester was over, and classes were about finished for summer break. Since August of the prior year, we had been practicing and playing a grueling schedule while trying to manage the secondary focus of our academic responsibilities.

When you play big-time college football, you realize very quickly that you have graduated past college education to learn the harsh and complicated maze of winning and losing in the adult business world. The real world, not theory.

Grades from tenured college professors were not believable or credible to me, based on what we were experiencing every day out on the practice field and in games, learning to work as a team through pain and adversity to achieve victory. There is no tenure in real competition, so a college professor held little weight with me. They couldn't get fired for doing a half-ass job. That countered everything we were learning. And the statistics prove my point. College athletes, by percentage or any other measurement you want to dig up, do better in their work life than the average college graduate. I will also say college athletes are battle-tested, while kids living the fraternity and sorority life tend to run from the scary search to discover their own voice. They learn to network, say the right things, wear the right clothes, but rarely develop a backbone that comes from knowing who you are and standing up for what *you* believe in.

Jason James was our 300-pound starting center, and my roommate and closest friend on the team. We were similar in many ways and loved hanging with people. He was yelling at me from across the back-yard patio, waving a joint, with a mischievous smile on his face.

"Rock! Rock, come get this!"

We made eye contact, and I quickly moved towards him following the huge plume of barbeque and pot smoke billowing up. Our place was cheap, and we didn't care if we destroyed it, which we did by the second party. It became known as the go-to after-game party or the anytime party place. We would do bad things and really funny and stupid shit there, all at the same time. Jason and I were the crazy white boy ring leaders constantly trying to take the party up one more notch.

Jason continued, "This is gonna be ridiculous tonight!"

I replied nonchalantly with a cool smile while I handed Jason some psychedelic mushrooms. We stared at the dried-up sticks and caps with childlike anticipation. Scared and excited, we looked at each other and threw them in our mouths and started chewing fast in order to get the nasty shit down before we started gagging. Then we shotgunned a beer and prepared for the evening ride. The sun was starting to hang low as the people started rolling in, and the energy was full of possibility.

As I started floating with a smile, I made my way to the living room, where there were some black teammates playing Madden football. Dr. Dre/Snoop's "Gin and Juice" was on, and the guys were going back and forth about which high school football team from South-Central was the best, and which conference was the toughest. Then it would shift to gangster talk about whose street was the toughest, or which set was the hardest. They were talking shit nonstop, and it was pure comedy.

As usual, Ron Collins was dropping a competitive insult to Sonny. "Did I do that? Did I just do that?!"

Sonny tries to make a lame excuse like he usually did when he would get rolled up in practice.

"Man, my controller got stuck!"

"Stuck like that dick in your ass!"

Everyone laughed at Sonny. He frowned and said, "Ahh, shut up nigga," which faded into a whisper.

Sonny tried to turn the attention to Stacey like a kid on an elementary playground who just got punked. "Wutchu laughing at, Blackness?"

Stacey was a really nice, quiet, and very black friend of ours who played defensive back. "I'm just saying, Sonny, you a feminine man. You pretty!"

Everybody laughed.

It was always a big celebration at the end of the season. But the end of spring ball was the ultimate. The weather and end-of-school freedom was a perfect formula for a party, and I never wanted it to stop. It wasn't long before the walls started melting, and Ron Collins looked like a live totem pole.

COCAINE, GUNS,
& GROUPIES

W alking on campus as a college football athlete was a pretty cool experience. It's a fleeting moment, and a delusionally inflated reality in terms of how the students and fans interact with the college athletes, particularly when the football and basketball programs are nationally ranked like when I was there. Our coaches were rough-cut winners, and that made them controversial. The basketball team had the "Shark" Jerry Tarkanian, NCAA's poster boy of corruption and victories. He was a cool dude; in fact, he and Coach Sweeney both possessed a charming, almost nostalgic throwback old-school approach to the game, the players, and the media. Not politically correct. They were loyal to their players, not the media, and they honestly didn't waste time caring about what some slap dick fan or sports journalist had to say negatively about them, but they would strike back when they attacked one of their players. They weren't afraid. Then the journalists and media, being the liberal pussies they are, called them dumb, outdated, and corrupt.

I swear, journalists, of any category in media are some of the most passive-aggressive, weak, wannabe bitches I've ever met. They have a disdain for stars of any kind; sports, politics, entertainment, and business. They are the wannabe hardcore obsessive fans that turn to a suppressive life of covering a subject they have a true love-hate for. Be careful what you believe based on what some clown fuck from the Columbia school of journalism wrote in an article. I consider the mainstream media irrelevant, especially the "critics." You wanna talk about some sick twisted fucked-up people! These people are the ones who can't but wanted to really badly. And now they are on the sidelines, and their only power is to throw rocks into the creative process and try and destroy it and the human doing it. In the process, they feel like they have equalized the star they couldn't be. Nice attitude.

Back on campus after spring break, the attention from college girls was in endless supply. Then there were the guys who wanted to hang out with me, providing me with all the alcohol, drugs, and false praise I could consume. I obliged and gave them what they wanted, although I constantly struggled with guilt. I knew that people were in awe of the gladiator symbolism of the college football player. I knew it wasn't me, it was Chris Rockwell, the gladiator, just a fraction of me, and I was always aware of that. It started way back as a kid playing sports and navigating a social life of attention and scrutiny to achieve. They didn't know who I was. I recognized it was a game, but I also enjoyed the high my ego felt from it. College football was a wonderful Molotov cocktail. But at some point, you crash, and the damage can be ugly.

One night I was in a club called Willikers that the football and basketball players frequented across the street from campus. We drank for free and basically did whatever we wanted. We ran that place with an iron fist and championship bowl rings. Ironically, my big bro D-line teammate Judd got stabbed in the parking lot the year before I got to Fresno. I was approached by Brad, who I called Oklahoma, the walk-on rich, freckle-faced juiced-up white fullback who was cooking crack and was caught up bad with cocaine and the dealers because he fell behind on payments. I had been partying with my white-trash friends on the team, the other tough country boys, but I was looking for something new and a little less predictable.

"Hey Rockwell!!" Oklahoma grabbed me and got up in my face wanting to connect. "Do you wanna do some blow?"

"Of course!" I was like a moth to a flame when it came to cocaine after drinking half a bottle of Jack to warm up the night. He smiled with a crazy stare that went right through me. I didn't give a fuck because I didn't really care about him either. We were junkies standing at the altar of the cocaine gods, ready to sacrifice our souls for a burst of life fire that feels so good that it becomes a chase for the oasis that never arrives. It's a sick feeling even when you're chasing it. You know deep down it's gonna end badly. And that night would be no different. Not many guys were into coke on the team, but the ones who did were my running partners.

He led me over to his table. Sitting there was Daryl, a shady-looking black drug dealer, and a couple of coked-out white girls. One of the chicks could've been a brunette hoodrat with a couple of baby daddies locked up for gang shit on the west side of town. It's like a fucking third world across the tracks. I was so out there living the alcohol and drug-fueled college football warrior experience that I constantly pushed the edge. I reveled in crazy.

Fresno in the early '90s was nothing nice. In fact, it was heinous. Every day was riddled with murders. It was the convergence of a low socioeconomic demographic with a criminal element that made for Chicago shooting stats, especially during an economic downturn and the race riot meltdown in LA It totally warped my sense of safety and security and gave me a front-row view in the Coliseum of Hell. I'm not exaggerating; it was a statistical reality that was light-years from my Mayberry small-town upbringing.

Brad and I approached the girls and Daryl. "Hey D, this is Rockwell."

"What's up." We shook hands.

"Ladies, this is Rockwell." D offers the hands of his coke bitches.

"Heeeyyy Rockwell..." These chicks were giving heavy fuck eyes like vipers out for blood.

"We're hitting D's place for an after-party in a few. Are you in?"

I glanced at the girls looking at me, smiling, and turned to Oklahoma after giving D a quick look, questioning his intentions but not letting on.

"We think you should come," said the coke bitches, one biting her bottom lip in anticipation of what the night might bring. I knew she was D's trick, and she was "gifted" to me for the night. Although I appreciated the gesture, all I could think about was the "white rhino"...cocaine.

"I'm in. Let's do this."

We left the club, and I jumped in the back seat with the chicks.

"Hey, we need to stop off on the west side for something real quick."

He turned back to look at me and was acting sketchy. I remember thinking, *This could end in a shallow grave.* You can never trust a drug dealer, especially one high on his own product... and *especially* if it's cocaine. That violates the golden rule of successful drug sales and distribution protocol. It's one thing if you own a drive-through coffee shop and drink cup after cup of your coffee. It's difficult to bankrupt a business that way. But it's another thing to be addicted to your product if it's blow. It's real easy to snort up all the profits plus the money owed to the dealer within a week or less. At that point, you pray for bankruptcy instead of the inevitable bullet to the face.

I was already feeling good from the whiskey and ego strokes from the club full of bottom feeders. We pulled up to a South-Central-looking hood house adorned with art deco bars across the windows. D got out and went into the house. It was dark, and I heard him pop the trunk. Within a couple of minutes, he came back out and looked back like something bad just went down. Nonetheless, he casually got back in the car, and we rolled on down the road. I didn't care or want to know what went down at the house in the hood.

Once we got to D's house, we started drinking Jack Daniels while D opened his silver bowl of blow. He poured it onto the glass coffee table into a mountain like in *Scarface*. Next to the coke were two big handguns and some cash. D chopped up off the mountain of snow on his black glass table and offered me the first line. I obliged by snorting a giant rail and rubbing another pinch between my cheek and gums. I sat up straight from the electric shock of sunshine and took another big shot of whiskey to set me straight. I didn't care what happened next. I just wanted more of all of it.

I remember showing up to my finals the next morning still awake, dressed in my night-before black leather jacket and whisky stained shirt, and covered in the smell of sin. I was living the dream...

CHRISTMAS ON CRENSHAW

It was two minutes till midnight. Christmas Day was coming to an end, and my plane was landing in LAX. I was coming off a one-day visit home to surprise my parents and my girlfriend. My brother Nick made it happen by picking me up in a fogged-in Sacramento Airport on Christmas Eve. I was homesick, and I needed to see Beck. My parents were so excited. It was the family bond rejuvenation I needed to finish up the task of playing USC in the Freedom Bowl in Anaheim Stadium. After my brief homecoming, I landed in LA and walked past the baggage claim, scoffing at the exhausted travelers waiting like zombies for their unidentifiable black bags. I strolled past them with my backpack, decked out in my new Freedom Bowl sweatsuit, and out onto the sidewalk, feeling the warm ocean air putting me in an LA vibe.

This old cutlass pulled up with music from the cheap woofer speakers bumping and rattling the whole car. The guys inside were totally loaded, and very hood black. The fear was palpable from the few people waiting for their friends and family to pick them up; they wanted nothing to do with our reunion, and you could see them stealthily move away from it, not wanting to be noticed or outwardly offend anyone.

James Fuller, the taller version of Eazy E from NWA, yelled out of the car to me, "Rock! Rock!!"

I jumped in the back seat behind him. I was so excited to see my teammates! This was their neighborhood. They carried guns and would use them. What I didn't think about at the time was that brandishing a gun and the mindset behind it makes a person a deadly weapon, especially if you're raised in the hyper-violent South-Central setting of the late 1980s. The crack cocaine epidemic hit, and by the time I got to college, the world was in a new chaotic chapter. Riots and racial divide were rampant. These guys were as close to me as country cousins I'd known for my entire life. But instead, they were black kids from South-Central who were just as confused and friendly as me. We were a band, a team, a family. Nothing could touch us, not even race.

The guys swooped me up, and we rolled down the highway with downtown Los Angeles as our backdrop. We had to be back to our hotel near Anaheim Stadium, where we would be playing against USC in a few days in the nationally televised Freedom Bowl. We jumped onto the 405. The first thing I noticed when they picked me up was their demeanor compared to how they were when we were in Fresno. They were back on their home turf and felt a new type of confidence. It was street confidence, and it was totally different. It also meant they knew how fleeting life was in their hometown. The guys picking me up were all from South-Central LA during one of the most violent times in the city's history.

It was 1992, and the LA Riots had just exploded the city into black and white fragments. I was riding in a suicide machine. So, like many times before, I took a deep breath, exhaled, and made the decision to jump on the bull for another wild ride into the unknown. These guys had seen violence that I could not fathom—losing friends and family members and quite possibly taking lives, all before signing their college football scholarship. Now I truly appreciated rap icon Ice Cube's line "None of my friends got killed in South-Central today."

"Shep" lit a blunt as we rolled down the freeway listening to Dr. Dre's *Chronic* tape. We exited onto Crenshaw.

"Hey Fuller, don't forget to get gas," Ben spoke in his choppy Uganda meets Compton dialect but with better manners than all of us. I remember looking back to notice the back window was gone, replaced by a funky plastic and duct-taped job.

"Hey Ben, what happened to Fuller's back window?" I asked naively.

"It got shot out last night at a party. Crazy people, man. Crazy people, ya know?"

Smiling, we pulled into the gas station on Crenshaw Avenue. "Hey Rock, stay in the car. And lay low." I knew that I was on borrowed time sitting on Crenshaw Avenue at 12 am on Christmas night. But it was pure excitement.

Thank the devil for alcohol to calm me from this world of tragic death and intense daily battle in a hyper-competitive environment with gangsters and super athletes. I was mentally struggling to crash course the brutal reality my friends experienced growing up. It was also very telling of the times we were living in. Los Angeles was a war zone. As we flew down an eerily empty 405 Highway through LA, the warm ocean air filled the inside of the '67 Chevy Slantback with the familiar aroma of playing in the ocean down the road at Huntington Beach during the O.P. surf classic as a kid visiting my grandparents. Then I started wondering what memories were associated with the same smells for my friends. Was it killing a kid in a drive-by? Was it a first kiss? Was it watching their twelve-year-old sibling being gunned down as they rode their bike through the neighborhood streets?

I felt my world and paradigm shift like the earth rotated upside down and started spinning backward, whispering a message of destruction and sadness for an entire generation of young men, and all the innocent folks of all colors getting terrorized and killed in the process of the insanity. I knew at that moment that those childhood memories connected to those smells would be altered for the rest of my life. And then I realized that those smells would connect me to this night for eternity. It was my new reality of SoCal. It's still as vivid as if it were last year. Driving down a desolate LA highway Christmas night and pulling onto Crenshaw Avenue to get gas is laser cut into my memory bank. We were a band of brothers on top of the world for a brief moment in time.

As we flew down the highway, I remember taking in the moment. The guys in the car were in my class, except for Ben. He didn't have a birth certificate, so no one was sure how old he was. We always fucked with him about being thirty years old. He seemed it, probably because he came from a war-torn Ebola and AIDS hot zone in Africa. Ben was a pretty good athlete, good enough to earn a full ride from Compton. But he was awkward, like football and America was still a foreign concept, kinda like his choppy gang slang English mixed with a polite disposition from his upbringing and language. His English dialect was classic. The black guys from the hood always fucked with Ben about it, in a brotherly way.

Ben was a sweet soul from a brutal region of Africa and transplanted in South-Central. To Ben, it was like moving to Hawaii. He was so thankful to be living in South-Central during the crack epidemic and fucking riots! He said it was a lot less violent than the day-to-day in Uganda. Talk about perspective. He was thankful! Ben was just different. The gangsters took it easy on him because they knew he was a good dude and hella smart but dangerously naïve to the little nuances separating brutal gang warfare in Uganda and South-Central. He went on to become an education administrator and lives in Malibu with a beautiful family.

The story of the four of us was a microcosm of what would become of our team after college football was over. A few would have their run at playing in the NFL, some would die from bullets, one ended up doing life in prison, but most would return to the life they knew before college. Many of the guys either remained in Fresno or went back home to get a job and settle down with a family. Deep down, I knew I wasn't going out like that. I had been altered through the college football ride, and I knew I wasn't going to be able to go back to my small town to work in the lumberyard. I had shit to explore and build. I wasn't sure what it was exactly, but deep in my soul, I knew it was going to be a creative continuation from college football and the people I met and were influenced by. I had a life-and-death drive to explore and experiment at full speed and test my limits, like flying down Highway 405 at midnight, headed to play a game on national TV. Full speed. It was how I always lived, long before I played college football. This was just a wild chapter in a life full of constant adventure and discovery.

We were preparing to play USC in the Freedom Bowl. Every sportswriter, the USC players, and their coaches figured that Fresno State didn't have a chance. It was the classic underdog story—small-town kids versus the mighty Trojans of USC; David and Goliath. How could a small-town football program possibly beat the elite program of USC? Coach Sweeney took this personal; we all did. He gave us a pregame speech that still gives me chills. He walked into the locker room with an intensity that was palpable. The room was silent and full of uncertainty. His silent energy could be scary.

"Men, we are in a street fight! Our family has been disrespected. This is a test of your heart and resolve. You can either accept what everyone is saying about you, or you can stand up, face the challenge, and prove that we are champions. You owe it to your bloodlines and all the players that came before you. How do you want to be remembered? How bad do you want it? Let's march out there and hit these guys with everything you've got. Light 'em up!"

The locker room erupted, and we ran out onto the field and beat USC that night. The feeling was unbelievable! What we didn't realize at the time was that Coach wasn't talking about football. The lesson was that in life, we must rise to the occasion, especially when times are tough, and you feel like everything and everyone is against you. We all have the choice to fight or lie down and let our circumstances defeat us. There are *no* excuses. Coach Sweeney challenged us to stand tall and fight the good fight, especially through tough times.

AFTER THE STADIUM
LIGHTS GO OUT

I was a D-lineman, basically one of the unsung heroes in the trenches, smashing and grinding for position against the massive offensive line. I was never a star, but I earned some recognition from my coaches as well as the media and other conference coaches. I was highlighted in magazines and on some covers, had plenty of decent write-ups, and received awards that legitimized me as a Bulldog.

I spent my first two years in obscurity. I started my college football career as a redshirt freshman. Every day I had to go head-to-head against the starting offensive team running the opposing team's defense. It was brutal. It was Darwinian, eliminating many full-ride freshmen sentenced to their first year of hard labor. I gave my all in every play and was awarded the Red Shirt Scout Team Award. It's one of my most cherished awards and accomplishments.

I saw limited play during the beginning of my sophomore year, but as we were heading into the final stretch of games, I began to see some time on the field. I ended up filling in for an injured starter, Earl Oliver, during our game against USC in the Freedom Bowl. I did my job, filled gaps, and even made a couple tackles against some seriously talented veteran players. Our underdog victory paralleled my personal victory of playing well in one of my first big college football games, which earned me a starting position for the following year.

In my junior year, I was out to prove I belonged on the field as a starter and leader on our defense. I had to really concentrate, but once I had the confidence and general understanding of my craft, I started to play with instinct and intuition. The only way you can lead is if you make plays—big plays in big victories—and I did. That year I played against great players and teams. I had the privilege of playing with and against multiple Heisman trophy winners, NCAA record breakers, and future NFL Hall of Famers. I considered myself an overachieving blue-collar worker who showed up, worked hard every day for the team, and did my job respectably. I led the defense in solo-tackles that season. I am proud of my career and the humility, wisdom, and accolades it gave me, and the camaraderie with my teammates was pure gold.

There are some games I look back on with pride, like our BYU victory at Provo Utah and the Jeep Aloha Bowl in Hawaii. I remember playing in Utah in front of a crowd of 70,000 screaming Mormons. Their screams ironically included many racial slurs to our black players. I was awarded Defensive Player of the Game by Coach Sweeney and the media. It was a great feeling, especially because Becky flew out to watch the game with our childhood friend, Teri Bisson, and some other Mormon friends who were attending BYU.

We finished the season receiving the selection to play in the Jeep Aloha Bowl in Hawaii against a very talented University of Colorado. Their quarterback was Kordell Stewart, and their star running back was Heisman Trophy winner Rashaan Salaam. The tight end I was lined up against all game, Christian Fauria, had just been selected to the All-American team, and he still holds the Big Eight Conference record for pass receptions by a tight end. We lost to a good team. It was close, defense played well, offense uncharacteristically turned over the ball, and Colorado responded with the necessary points to win the game.

My senior year playing at Fresno State was anticlimactic compared to my junior season, mainly due to the mass exodus of starting talent that had either graduated or left for the NFL. The biggest blow was our quarterback Trent Dilfer foregoing his senior year to enter the draft. Trent was a high first-round draft pick projection after his junior year. His name had been seriously tossed around as a Heisman candidate. Our defense was dealing with a similar situation, albeit not as devastating as the end of the offense that broke many NCAA records.

I had some memorable moments on the field with my team during my senior year. I dealt with some humbling losses and injuries, but the overall year was solid. Nonetheless, I was ready to move on

The best part of my senior year was playing against Ohio State in the Disneyland Pigskin Kickoff Classic. Nick was coming up as a free safety, recognized for his stealthy, close, and brutal strikes to the opposing receivers. We were having fun being back on the same team; it had been since little league on Grandpa Brandt's Triple-A Indians. Our dad was our assistant coach back then, and we were a dangerous duo. Nick would catch when I pitched, taking down batters, giving me savvy calls while hiding his signs with his oversized glove.

Having Nick play at Fresno State while I was there was special for me. We were able to hang out and experience the ride together for a moment. The Disneyland Pigskin Classic was a televised game in the same Anaheim Stadium where we played and beat USC a couple of years earlier. This time the field would be prepped as a football field on the existing Angels baseball field that had a dirt infield that felt like gravel when I would tackle someone and hit the ground. The best part of the bowl game experience was spending the day at Disneyland as a team. The media gave me and a few other players, including Nick, video cameras to capture the moment. Imagine two college football teams lumbering around Disneyland like gangs of tribal warriors getting front row access to all the rides our Disney hostesses escorted us to.

Me, Nick, and the rest of the guys were like crazy giant kids ransacking and taking over the Happiest Place on Earth!

We finished the event with a big evening celebration, which included a huge float showcasing the head coaches and players they chose to represent each team parading down Main Street. Coach selected me to stand next to him at the front while Ohio State's coach had offensive lineman Korey Stringer, the All-American and eventual first pick in the NFL draft. He was a large black man. I literally felt like an underweight kicker next to him. The coaches introduced us before we started the parade and took our places. I had been training all summer with this guy's picture in our weight room, and after shaking his hand, I felt like all those days were a total waste of time. This guy was a fucking giant!

As we were standing around in the backstage loading area where the Disney floats and characters prepare for the nightly parade and events, we heard a scream from our head coach. He had been backed over by a float. Worse yet, he was recovering from back surgery. The Disney folks freaked out, and paramedics were there immediately. As Coach made it back to his feet, the Disney legal team was on site. They were prepared to head into a potentially massive lawsuit due to their negligence. In a moment of heart and genius, Coach told them to give all his grandbabies lifetime passes and it was all good. It was a done deal, and we boarded the float and proceeded to cruise through Disneyland and watch curious and excited onlookers and fans cheering at the celebration of gladiators fighting on behalf of Disney.

My game against Ohio State was marked with humbling moments of being physically dominated by the two All-Americans I faced. Tight-End Ricky Dudley who was selected by the Oakland Raiders in the first round of the 1996 NFL Draft and went on to have a solid NFL career, and the massive Korey Stringer. I had never played against such a dominant offensive tackle. I mean, the guy was well over 300 pounds, but he could move quicker than my 240, and his strength was ridiculous! I always joked that Korey would roll me up in the Anaheim field dirt like he was battering fish to fry. Each time he helped me up after dominating me, he would say "good play." He was truly a nice guy. Korey tragically died overheating during pre-season practice playing for the Minnesota Vikings.

I did get a few tackles against Heisman Trophy-winning Eddie George. He was a special player and tough to bring down. Class act guys at Ohio State. USC was the opposite.

I remember my 21st birthday when we were playing in Hawaii. Becky was there, and I snuck over to her hotel even though we were not allowed to leave ours after the game. I had a concussion from our tough 47-45 loss and just wanted to see my girlfriend. As I came into the lobby of her hotel, a small crowd of Fresno State fans and Boosters recognized me. One Booster, a successful businessman in Fresno named Johnny, slapped me on the back and bought me a Corona and wished me a happy 21st birthday. Becky walked into the lobby to see me drinking beers with fans and Boosters, and she could only shake her head, she knew the draw I had to the party. But this time it didn't take long to slip away and I got to hang out with Beck for the rest of the evening.

I know how people can hype their stats and accomplishments. I have no intent on overdramatizing my college football career. I put a lot of blood, sweat, and tears into earning a starting position, and I performed well enough to earn some team and conference awards. Those grades, more than my academic grades, are the ones that mattered then—and now.

Defining self-worth...hell, defining *self* after the last college football game was played was definitely a mindfuck. What was I supposed to do after that? The experience of making a big play in front of thousands of screaming fans and the millions of TV viewers elevated my concept of what was possible. Since the time I stepped onto a soccer field as a seven-year-old to play the first year of youth soccer in my town,

I have always been considered an accomplished athlete, and I lived for the thrill of victory at center stage.

I excelled in football and baseball all the way through high school, and our winning record was impressive, credit to our town's old yet forgotten tradition of tough teams and winning. My high school football career was marked with four conference championship seasons, and I was the first kid in my town to sign a full-ride scholarship to a legitimate Division 1 college football program in 25 years. I was conditioned for the accolades. I was conditioned to have the attention of the coaches, the fans, and the girls. People wanted to be around me; they saw me as a winner. And I was.

Even though I was aware that I was living a fleeting moment, no matter how long it lasted, I was not fully aware of the trap a gladiator sets for himself; it had always been all-or-nothing for me. Big victories brought big spoils, but I couldn't fathom how the losses and ending would bring devastating anonymity. Although I was burned out with the grueling regiment, injuries, and mental toil, I was certainly not excited about starting all over. Life at the top of college football was amazing. It was a magnificent, decadent, and adrenaline rush high of being "on go" at all times, accelerating to the top, and I wasn't ready to let that part go.

The game was over, and suddenly, I'm supposed to assimilate into a normal nine-to-five. Impossible. It was like my experience leaving the ranch to head to preschool. This time the idea of settling into a predictable, secure job, family, and social routine just seemed almost unbearable after what I had experienced. Rock stardom at the level I was at was truly an addictive lifestyle that is as powerful as any drug I have ever taken. I was blind to how programmed and addicted to it all I was.

When the stadium lights went out, darkness set into my life. I didn't fully understand how to live at a different level. If it wasn't center stage with thousands of screaming fans, parties, and accolades, it wasn't a level I was interested in playing at. I was born to perform and lead, not follow. I couldn't understand why so many guys settled after such a big achievement. I couldn't grasp that a loyal and loving relationship bound by trust and commitment *was* a huge accomplishment. In my quest for continued greatness, I failed to appreciate those closest to me, those who truly loved me.

My dedicated girlfriend and future wife, Becky, worked at Dave's Shoes and the local hospital in Oroville as a low-paid CNA doing hard work. She spent every hard-earned dime to drive and fly to most of my games. She was there, win or lose, cheers or boos, highs and lows. As always, she gave everything and sacrificed a lot just to see that I had the support and the stadium lights I needed. Just as in the summer before my senior year in high school, she was there to take care of me when it was all gone, and I was lost.

I was so consumed with the all-or-nothing intensity of my path that I lost perspective. I found myself psychologically caught in the middle of what was important. I knew intellectually that relationships and human bonds—family—was most important, but that's not what I saw rewarded in the circle of athletes or business elite, and I needed to excel in that world. All or nothing. Win at all costs. I was chasing gold like a crazy miner who leaves his family behind for adventure, money, and fame. Gladiatorship cost me this precious love twenty years later.

"Chris Rockwell... is a modern-day Ironman."

My football career was over.

"Senior Chris Rockwell led the Bulldogs in solo-tackles last year despite suffering a serious neck injury."

I was finishing up my last semester, and I was having coffee with Coach Sweeney. It was early morning at the training hall, just him and me in the players' dining room, when he offered for me to join his staff. He told me I had the makeup to be one of the best if I dedicated myself to coaching the game the same way I did to playing it. I would train under the master head coach and eventually run my own program.

> *"The Bulldogs have an outstanding individual amongst its talented defensive unit by the name of Chris Rockwell."*

It's challenging to put into words how pivotal a moment this was in my life. I had a respect for and healthy fear of my head coach, and this was a crossroads I had to face that required me to override my shy nature, especially around my mentor. But, thanks to him and the strength he had summoned out of and driven into me over the years, I was able to assert my conviction and not be dissuaded.

"I don't want to coach football..."

After momentarily feeling a slight sting of pride and competition, he said, "What the hell is wrong with you?!" He nodded graciously, looked to his right out of the window into the oncoming winter rain, and the wind whipping the leaves into a frenzy of coordinated chaos that made sense to us.

> *"Rockwell's toughness rubs off on Fresno State's defense."*
> – *Daily Collegian* (Fresno State School Newspaper), Sportswriter Dennis R Claborn

I mastered the courage to tell a lion of a man, and my general, that I did not want to coach because I wanted to build businesses like he built football programs. He gave me an Irish grin and a twinkle in his eye, sensing I was as crazy and ambitious as his younger self.

"Well, what are you going to do?"

"I don't know exactly, Coach. You taught me how to lead and win against the best; that's the hard part. But I need to learn how to *build* businesses. So, I plan to work for other people first to learn." Coach was quiet for a brief contemplative moment. He talked about jobs and opportunities that he passed on to raise his kids in Pullman, suffering many hardfought losing seasons in the Pac-8, but also winning conference coach of the year and the love and loyalty of the Wazzu fanbase. I listened to his memories of lost moments and will never forget the wisdom in the lessons he was sharing.

I completed my college degree in December 1994. Four and a half years, a laughable 2.1 GPA, and a signed graduation certificate from a university president I had no respect for. It was laminated on a wooden plaque that has never left my storage box of artifacts from that era. I didn't need it where I was headed. I was already very aware that my college football credentials carried far more perceived and real value for any job I might be interested in.

I was ready to go home for Christmas to relax for a moment and then contemplate the rest of my life. I had no concrete idea of where I was going to start next. The idea of traveling just to travel or do something not relevant to my destiny made no sense to me. I had already turned down many good starting offers from the fraternity of fans and former players in the Bulldog business community before graduating. I was hungry to get started, and something inside me told me to go see Dan Sweeney, Coach Sweeney's son, and a man I trusted and looked up to. Dan was a lumber broker, and that was familiar with all the lumberyard work so much of my family and I had done in the industry. I figured it was a great place to start, not to mention that he would be a great mentor to learn from.

I walked into his office and stood before him. He was seated behind his desk like an old-school broker.

"I'm not hiring."

I stood there, stinging from his blunt and direct style and answer.

"I don't have the budget or plans for another broker."

Deep down, I knew this was where I needed to be so I could learn; to be with someone I trusted and respected. Not knowing what else to say, I spoke from the heart and expressed what I felt.

"That's okay. I want to work and learn from you. I will work for free until I earn my way."

He looked at me with a cocked head and a curious squint bordering on a scowl. Then, after what seemed an eternity, he started laughing and said, "Are you crazy? Look... We'll work something out. Go home for Christmas, and then you can start with me after the new year."

So, I did just that. I showed up for my first day on the job wearing an old three-piece dress suit and alligator dress shoes, compliments of Coach Jethro Franklin's closet of old digs he wore back in the 80s when he played for the Seahawks and had a Jheri curl. I looked like a sad attempt at a redneck pimp from the middle of nowhere.

The minute I walked through the door, I heard Dan's voice, along with another, lower and full of non-filter hacks, laughing and asking, "What the hell are you dressed up like that for?!"

I realized that Dan was very casually dressed, wearing shorts, a golf shirt, and white sports shoes. I felt so stupid I wanted to run away and send him an apology for being such an idiot. While my pride was trying to recover an uppercut, the baritone smoker's voice reminding me of Wolfman Jack piped in, "You look like a Miami dealer trying to sell us penny stocks or cocaine!"

With the tag team hazing, I started to laugh at myself and realize that it was okay; I had a long way to go. Nonetheless, I was excited to get started. After meeting Dan's partner, Ross, I sat in a chair in front of Dan's desk and asked him what he wanted me to do. He looked dazed at the question, preoccupied with a deal he was working on. It was then that I realized he had not thought about me working for him since the day he told me to come back after the new year. My anxiety was setting in. I started to feel like I was flailing. Suddenly, Dan focused on the situation at hand and looked around. He glanced at Ross's desk, then opened and closed a couple of drawers. Upon locating what he was looking for, he revealed and dropped on his desk what seemed like a ten-pound *Yellow Pages* phone book. It contained the contact information for every business in the Central Valley.

"Start calling businesses that will buy lumber."

Meeting self after the stadium lights have turned off for the final time, and no one knows your name or where you fit or why you're even here; that's a dark, lonely, and humbling place. And it's where the greatest growth comes from. Learning to not need the fans and lights, to not need gold and fame. I learned that when it was too late.

5

PIONEERING INSIDE THE INTERNET & MEDIA REVOLUTION

Pioneering Inside the Internet & Media Revolution

1995: WINTECH.COM – STARTING MY FIRST INTERNET COMPANY

The Internet hit the scene as I was finishing college with Netscape giving mainstream people access to the Internet in 1994. I left convention behind again, knowing that my next challenge would be bigger than anything I'd done. But I had no idea. I became obsessed with the concept of the Internet and becoming the next twenty-something millionaire overnight. That's all I read and watched in the business news from the time I was a senior in high school. I think many young people in my generation felt an overwhelming sense of urgency and a feeling of being way behind, unlike any time in human history. Things were ramping up at light speed, and shit was about to get crazy.

Looking back on my defining crossroads of walking away from suburban gold career jobs to build an Internet business from conceptual scratch was pretty out there, especially in the Bulldog football society I was part of. Guys like me had mainstream career opportunities offered to us as we stepped off the stage of D1 football and graduation ceremonies. But at the same time, that bold and fearless society gave me the competitive skills and leadership to successfully accomplish my vision, if it made fundamental sense.

I didn't have a brilliant Internet idea the day I graduated from college; I just knew I was going to be an entrepreneur. So, I decided that a sales and business mentor was a good place to start. I loved Dan Sweeney like my big brother during my years playing, so I asked to work for him even though he didn't have a position for me. He was a generous big brother, business, and life mentor right out of college. I appreciate that more every day. Dan also knew I was a restless kid, and he was supportive of me, despite my short stay with him, so I could get closer to home and launch what would become WinTech.

I was totally geeked out on the idea of connecting everyone together and the collaborative possibilities and breakthroughs that could be achieved from it. I had my idea. I launched the first sports recruiting service on the Internet and named it WinTech, connecting college coaches and high school athletes. I was naïve, ambitious, and too early to market—and underfunded. But I was all in and knew I was on to something big that fundamentally made sense. Unfortunately, I no longer own the domain name wintech.com, and the name is used for many businesses today. But I was the first.

Back then, my idea to utilize the Internet to connect high school athletes to college coaches, especially helping small-town kids like me get better visibility to college football programs, was new and innovative. Until then, high school "scouting services" were mostly shady mail order scams that convinced vulnerable and gullible parents and athletes to spend hundreds, if not thousands of dollars, to have them send college sports programs a profile and sometimes VHS video of game footage. Rip-offs. I was one of those suckers.

My WinTech concept consisted of a combined test custom designed to measure key physical data and have it standardized and approved by top college, NFL, and Olympic coaches to certify the data. No one was doing anything like this except for the NFL and the Olympics.

Trying to figure out how to test and standardize all these physical data was a very daunting task. I called up my good friend Steve Sobonya, Fresno State's head strength and conditioning coach, and his private client roster of pro and Olympic athletes helped to streamline and validate my plan. We became close over the years as he worked the hell out of us in the weight room and on the practice fields with grueling and challenging workouts, including jump rope, plyometrics, and pushing trucks in the middle of summer across the football practice field. In addition to that, we had just hiked Yosemite's Half Dome together. We were similar hardworking country-boy athletes, and we were both loyal to Coach Sweeney and loved to drink beer and compete with passion and heart.

At the turn of 1995 in Fresno, finding a software engineer was challenging because there was about three total in the entire valley. But seriously, it was a new world that the agriculturally rich valley was not on the cutting edge of. Silicon Valley was literally due west just over the hill about 160 miles, but it might as well have been a million miles away.

Bob and John Reber came from Silicon Valley, and they believed in me, so they backed WinTech and me. Thanks to the *Yellow Pages* business listings, I found a small software developer in town doing mostly basic database development for "Ag" businesses to track their grapes. Eric was my age, maybe a couple of years older. He was a pasty Scandinavian with a soft demeanor that made me wonder if he still lived with his mom, nice enough engineer type with limited personality. To his credit, he was open to taking on my unheard-of project. After months of back and forth and thousands of dollars, we had an actual working prototype that generated revenue with Fresno area athletes. I would test them and input the data to our WinTech database, and it would provide the athlete and parents a certified report of the athlete's stats and how they compare to similar athletes. It wasn't sexy, but it worked. It was an exciting start. And then I was out of money.

I set out to write my first business plan and financial forecast in order to bring in more investors. They were rudimentary at best, and my least favorite part of the deal, but it forced me to do it. I met with businessmen and women and coaches that I respected, some mocked and some mentored me through some of the processes. I had endless ideas and questions, and they could see my passion and drive. It was exciting for some of them, too, but most just thought I was out there.

As I got a little further down the developmental road, I asked Coach Sweeney if he would endorse WinTech in a promo video I wanted to put together. He agreed and told me to have my camera crew at his house located on the Sunnyside Country Club Golf Course One. To have Coach support my vision with enthusiasm meant so much. I was humbled by his belief in me, but Coach had confidence that I would work my ass off until I met success. He bet on me because I gave him everything for his dream. A crossroad moment was the morning we sat in the dining hall drinking coffee as I turned down his offer to coach for him and telling him of my calling to lead and build my own businesses. Without deep conviction about where I was going, I might be coaching college football today.

I drove the I-5 corridor meeting with head coaches from USC to Stanford, Cal to Oregon, to Washington to meet with the Seattle Seahawks. I received endorsements from Pac-10 Coach of the Year Mike Belloti of Oregon but had a rude welcoming from Stanford's then-head coach Tyrone Willingham, the overhyped black coach of D1 football, who refused to meet with me. He walked into the lobby to ask his assistant a question, not realizing that I was still there. He looked at me without a smile and told me he had no interest in what I was doing and walked away without even shaking my hand. So much for affirmative action and its wondrous benefits. He fizzled out after unprecedented opportunities at Notre Dame and Washington. He got paid big money, lost a lot, and then got fired—then sued the program claiming racial discrimination.

Down the street from Stanford University campus was the infamous "Wall Street" of Silicon Valley money, Sand Hill. I had my first meetings with venture capital firms that took me about as seriously as the Stanford football coach. I was shocked and let down that the "smart investors" couldn't see it, although, in retrospect, I'm sure my pitch was very rough and confusing.

Through those tough experiences, I also earned the first endorsements of its kind, in writing, by Pac-10 head football coaches as well as professional and Olympic gold medal coaches and athletes. The experience was a good lesson about the bleeding edge of innovation. I spent every penny I had, including a few thousand dollars from a couple of older mentors and Trent Dilfer, my former teammate and Superbowl-winning quarterback. I appreciate their belief in me, especially back then. They knew the odds and what they were risking, but they invested in ME, and that's what they told me. At the time, I thought they meant my brilliant business idea, but they meant they wanted to see me grow as an entrepreneur and that making them money if it all worked out would be the proverbial icing on the cake.

I look back and smile with gratitude for all the support friends, my brother Nick, and Becky gave me. She helped me with testing, and as always, she happily supported me and my crazy idea. She was one hundred percent by my side and supportive. She knew I was developing something unique and extraordinary, and she accepted that I needed to leave my job and dedicate everything to WinTech. She went to many high school and college softball tournaments to help me gather the data I needed to continue to pursue my goal. On top of all that, Becky worked ten-hour shifts in the oncology ward at Fresno's St. Agnes Hospital, taking care of terminally ill patients. She was exceptional at developing relationships with patients to ensure that they felt as comfortable as possible. She was dedicated to a job and people that were challenging both physically and emotionally, and it could be very draining; she was also responsible for toe tagging and cleaning up patients who had passed away. Nonetheless, she worked her ass off and supported both of us after the small savings I had pulled together eventually ran out; she was dedicated to me and our collective future as a team. Having her by my side made all the difference in the world.

I was paying for hard knock wisdom, just like I got from playing college football. Practice, practice, practice. The start-up experience was hard on me emotionally and mentally, not to mention a backward road financially. I had no frame of reference, so I'm sure I made very simple things extremely difficult. But I also look back in amazement at how many measurable milestones we accomplished developing WinTech. We developed an operational subscription service with a custom database, built standard test fields (the WinTech Test), and had paid customers with a successful beta testing.

In an odd twist, I wasn't getting much support from additional investors or the new head football coach at Fresno State, a handlebar-mustached clown named Pat Hill, who was finally fired after losing for over a decade and disparaging Coach Sweeney and his winning ways. Becky was a standout high school softball player and told me that I should consider women's sports in general, starting with softball. That talk gave me the idea to go try my luck with the Fresno State Women's Softball coach, Margie Wright. At the time, Margie had just won the national championship and was heading to Beijing to coach the Olympic softball team. Her reputation was that she was a fiery-tempered Irish woman who butted heads with the fiery Irish Coach Sweeney and the entire football program. I knew I was facing a huge uphill battle to actually get her to see past the Fresno State football practically tattooed on my forehead.

I remember literally sweating as I sat down to introduce myself to her in her shabby little office that looked more like the history professor's office than a national championship head coach's office. Instantly, I understood why she had a bad relationship with the football and basketball program. She outperformed them and got treated like the redheaded stepchild. That changed towards the end of her illustrious career when she became the all-time winningest Division One head college softball coach.

I am drawn to softball girls for their passion, toughness, competitive spirit, and work ethic. Margie Wright has a career without flaw. Pure class. She held herself and her team to unbelievably high standards of character, preparation, and execution. I mean, if my knucklehead football teammates and I had to live up to the standards Margie set for her softball players, nearly every player would be kicked off the team! She was a stone-cold field general who competed with a spirit like Joan of Arc. Margie could command performance that was impressive to watch. There's a reason she went on to coach in the Olympics and won a gold medal and national championship. She out-prepared, out-disciplined, and outclassed her opponents. She was ruthless in her preparation and expectation for laying everything out on the field for the team.

As I spent time talking and developing my WinTech athlete testing program with her college and Olympic players, I could see a totally different side of Margie. I had the great fortune to see her in action on and off the field. Margie had charisma and sensitivity that was unveiled to me like a flower opens in the morning sun. Her instincts with people were spot-on after forty-plus years of coaching and recruiting top talent. She sensed my sincerity, probably bordering on shy anxiety.

It was my friend, Shelly Stokes, former Bulldog and US Olympic team catcher, who worked out with my friend and conditioning coach Steve Sobonya, who told Margie that I was creating something special that could be a huge benefit for women's softball. I really appreciated the support and enthusiasm from Margie, Shelly, the Berg twins, and many others that I met and hung out with during that time. Dot Richardson, Lisa Sanchez…great athletes and solid humans.

I will never forget the risk Margie Wright took on WinTech and me. She used her influence and respect to recruit the best softball players on the planet to help me run drills and develop a new concept that is now the foundation of so many drills and tests for recruiting services and media.

Looking back at my experience building WinTech, I now recognize how innovative and courageous I was for trying to create and build a groundbreaking sports technology company from scratch—at the dawn of the Internet revolution. As naïve and blindly ambitious and optimistic as I was, I absolutely knew I had a great idea that made sense. WinTech was just a continuation of my life, and it was at a defining moment where I needed to decide my path as an adult. I had to choose between going for it and leaving nothing to regret or building my "successfully safe" suburban life. I listened to my heart and trusted my life vision, walked away from easy money, comfort, and praise as a name in the Fresno Football Alum community, owning businesses in the Valley and calling everyone Buddy or Homie, while I flipped another widget to a fellow alum in real estate or insurance. Just shoot me!

WinTech didn't show me success in the conventional framework of sales, revenue, and profitability, but the experience confirmed in me that I had what it took to compete in the bleeding edge of innovation and build truly great companies and products that people wanted. I may have wasted time and money trying to be too formal, but at least I was doing it out loud. Those experiences were crucial to my development. Failure wasn't how I looked at WinTech or anything that wasn't "profitable" in dollars.

WinTech was the most important step I ever dared in my entrepreneurial path. I had supreme confidence, great vision, and lots of blind spots due to my lack of experience. Not only did I want to build a great company and team, but I wanted it to be revolutionary. It was. I can't say exactly why I intuitively felt or believed I would or could create greatness, but I assume each step towards that vision was based on my spirit and early gifts of parental love, support, encouragement, and confidence.

I enjoyed the process of trial and error, figuring something out through a scientific approach, basically running experiments until a result is reached, continue, or stop. There really isn't much difference with how I develop ideas today. I just have more experience and resources to be more effective, with fewer errors and more success. I figured out how to ride my proverbial bike twenty-plus years after WinTech. I'm just a typical "overnight" success!

1999: BUILDING RIVALS. COM DURING THE GREAT INTERNET GOLD RUSH, MOVING TO SEATTLE AND HALLOWEEN WITCH TRIPPERS,&DOT-COMXMAS

WinTech was out of money, so I took a break to coach high school football with my old teammates Jason James and Shawn Murray. Buchanan was a local high school with a brand-new college-styled sports program and facilities. We coached their first varsity team and won. I had started and dropped out of the MBA program with a few classes left because it was too slow for my ambition and experience after college sports and my first start-up.

My Silicon Valley investor and mentor, Bob Reber, a veteran in the semi-conductor era coming out west from Fairchild with Intel founders like former CEO Andy Grove, told me I should go to work for a company he was on the board of. So, I went home to work for the outdoor travel gear company Kiva Designs. They were known in the emerging outdoor travel gear category as a team of exceptionally talented designers and engineers from Apple and the North Face. Kiva was a domestic manufacturer of their own brand of travel gear and a private label side (North Face, Patagonia, Japanese brands) providing design and manufacture both domestic (NorCal) or offshore. I headed up sales and learned more than I realized at the time.

Looking back now, I recognize that I was placed in a situation where I learned how to develop a vertically integrated brand; create a brand and product, manufacture, market, and proceed to sales. Within months, I was schlepping luggage and driving a worn-out silver Ford Aerostar van full of bags up and down the West Coast, stopping off at luggage and travel gear stores in strip malls from San Diego to Seattle. I was also flying around the country for big trade shows and meetings with new and existing clients.

During that time, I couldn't let the WinTech idea go. In my ongoing research, I stumbled upon a Seattle-based company that was light-years ahead of where I was with my business. After a day of getting no sales and a bruised ego at a chain store in Seattle ran by a guy named Mort, I got in my van, and instead of screaming in angered frustration, I sat there and gathered myself. I was determined to refocus my confidence and make one last stop in the city.

I went down First Avenue downtown until I reached Paulson Avenue, part of the famous waterfront "Skid Row"; no, not the 80s hair band. It was 1999, and the area was now a hotbed for the emerging Internet start-up companies. They were renovating old warehouses and offices into contemporary industrial expressions capturing the hubris and exposed hundred-year-old timbers, brick, and steel construction. Accented modern redesigns focused on open rooms of working pods, paint colors to give a feel of sophistication, relaxing yet inspiring, but a little daring at the same time. It felt smart.

After a personal pep talk, followed by a few excuses for why I should come back tomorrow or maybe just drive back to California, I got out and walked up the steps of the building. I felt my heart race and my confidence rattle. I had to remind myself that I was good enough to compete with these people, and I wasn't leaving until I walked through their doors and pitched myself and WinTech to them. Coming from a blue-collar town and upbringing, I battled the invisible but very real social class mentality that tugged at my confidence and belief that I belonged with the best minds in the Internet Revolution. I had to pump myself up by flashing back to college football, a moment where I was facing an imposing athlete and how I mustered the courage to compete head-to-head with the best and come out victorious. After I ran through that visualization of facing adversity and challenge, I smiled and knew I'd be okay. I confidently walked up to the front of the building and was met with the stiff, unyielding wall of locked doors. I was devastated.

I stood there dejected and watching my hope pounding me on the head with every drop of rain. My peripheral eye caught the water painting of a woman dressed in black, waving a security key fob in front of a sensor smoothly opening the door. I reacted like I was chasing down a running back and snatched the door away from closing with inches to spare. My "break-in," as some would say, proved to create a small scene among the four people just entering the lobby and shaking off their dripping umbrellas. As I heard the door close behind me, I realized I was in a new world of Internet start-up executives and engineers, and there was no turning back.

No one smiled. They barely looked my way after the initial glance-over, except for the mystery woman in black who inadvertently opened the door for me. She turned towards me when she heard the door shut as she was walking towards the elevator and gave me a cautious smile. I smiled back and started following her. She was dressed in a black dress, black shoes, and a black London Fog-style raincoat. She looked like a banker from New York. Three silent men were also waiting for the elevator. One guy was wearing an old-school *Star Wars* Yoda t-shirt, jeans, and fucked-up Converse shoes. Another was wearing Elvis Costello glasses and a cynical attitude. The third musketeer was wearing a button-up dress shirt, no tie, two top buttons undone, white t-shirt slightly exposed, tucked into jeans with a thin belt. He had an Iron Man watch and Nike running shoes, and a simple gold wedding band like my dad wore.

Elvis Costello waved his security key to the invisible security guard. I knew this game was serious, but I wasn't sure what that meant. I had no clue what to expect. I had never been inside a high-tech start-up company before. When the elevator doors opened, we all shuffled in. When the doors closed, so did my escape route back to the pathetic safety of my beat-to-shit work van.

I stared at the steel doors when Runner Guy enthusiastically asked, "What floor can I get you?"

Fuck! I didn't even know what floor the office was on!

"I have a meeting with... Rivals.com." I felt like a twelve-year-old trying to steal a pack of gum from the neighborhood corner store.

He pressed the button for the fourth floor—the top floor—and looked back to acknowledge his friendly gesture with a smile. At that point, I was ready for him to start twenty questions with me about who I was there to see and who I knew, but he didn't. He respected my space, and that made me smile back, basically thanking him for not blowing my cover. The elevator dropped off Costello and Yoda boy on the second floor, and we continued up. I noticed that the fourth floor was the remaining number lit up as the doors closed, and I felt my heart drop. Not so much from the pullies yanking us upward, but because I realized that the remaining three of us were all going to the same place. Are you fucking kidding me?!

I knew they were on to me. I was torching holes into the floor with my eyes, hoping no one would acknowledge me. I felt like an undercover character posing as an Internet executive, and I felt like they all knew. But I stayed in character because deep down, I knew I belonged. This was no façade. As the elevator inched two floors up and finally released me from the silent interrogation, I shadowed the movement of the man and woman exiting in front of me, trying to act like I was part of the pod. As we entered the main entrance, I felt a blast of intense light and energy. There were young people on the phone, moving and flying around the open space. Boxes, wires, and paper were everywhere…it was the epitome of controlled chaos. I was entranced, nervous, and excited.

"Welcome to Rivals.com. Do you have an appointment?"

I was at the next video game level of my entrepreneurial quest and had to try and play this moment cool to advance to score a meeting with someone influential. I literally didn't know any names, so I gathered myself like I was at any other sales call, pitching myself and my product.

"Hi, don't worry, I'm not trying to sell you anything. I'm in town interviewing with Microsoft and Real (I knew from CNBC coverage that no one called them "Real Networks," especially in Seattle for Christ's sake). I found you guys on the Internet and wanted to see if there might be a fit."

I didn't even know where the hell those two companies were located in the area. The young receptionist, likely a business major at the University of Washington, and absolutely a sorority girl, gave me a quick scan to see if I was worth talking to. In her defense, businesses get hit up every day unsolicited. So, I was starting to think I overcame my fear and summoned my courage for nothing.

"Okay. I'll call to see if they are willing to talk to you."

The snot-nosed sorority gatekeeper picked up the phone and gave a put-out sigh that would impress crotch rot "comedians" like Chelsea Handler and her equally vial sister, Sarah Silverman. She owned her moment of power, kinda like David Spade's character Russell Dunbar-Patel, the inept employee and shit-talking womanizing receptionist in the comedy TV series, *Rules of Engagement*. My pride and ego were trained for idiots like this from years of cold calling and schlepping luggage around, including negotiating with Hasidic Jews, the guys with the black suits and long curly sideburns speaking Yiddish in the garment industry of New York. This chick was definitely a little Jewish princess. They're the worst!

"There's someone here interested in an interview." She rolled her eyes and sounded overwhelmed with my request.

As if this bitch was doing me a favor! She said a few more things, her hand covering the mouthpiece as she looked at everything but me. My pessimism was kicking in and creating these bubble-filled conversations above my head of what Miss Delta Gamma Jew was telling the person on the other end of the line. I decided to let the chips fall where they may. But part of me was already telling her off as I headed for the door, feeling the rejection starting to infect my dream.

I kicked back into game time with a tap to the right side of my thigh, a trigger to help me break my fear. I had a bad college football neck injury that nearly left me paralyzed during a goal-line stop against Oregon State. I struggled to get back and play full speed. Coach Sweeney sent me to a psychiatrist, and he gave me this little positive visualization trick used commonly for athletes trying to return from a devastating injury or slump.

After what seemed like an eternity, this big guy dressed in a golf shirt, jeans, and casual dress shoes walked directly towards me with intent.

"Hi there, partner! I'm Scott Pelluer, Director of Network Development."

I enthusiastically shook Scott's hand and made sure I looked him in the eyes and didn't mess up his name. I've always been bad with names, numbers...basically, more than three or more steps with anything I'm asked to do, I forget.

"Pleased to meet you, Scott. I'm Chris Rockwell."

He shook my hand with a strong, friendly handshake but not annoyingly over the top break my hand 'cuz I'm trying to show you that I'm stronger than you' handshake. I matched his grip strength, but he had a bear paw of a hand and the old-growth strength from years of hard work. I could instantly sense that Scott seemed nice and willing to meet and talk for a few.

"Well, come on back, and I'll show you what Rivals.com is about."

We were walking into the heart of the operation, past people oblivious to us with all the activity coming in and out of the building every day. Scott was high-fiving and giving shout-outs as we wound through the new colony of ants busily constructing their new temporary home.

Scott led me to a cool Space Age-looking conference room with glass walls, a modern conference table, and all the latest tech gadgets to produce modern start-up presentations or a music video. The chairs were black and built of what looked like Kevlar mesh and carbon, and steel for ergonomic perfection. We sat down. Bottles of water were ready on the table for the next of many daily meetings. I was officially in awe of the sophistication and amount of money being spent as Scott settled into his chair and started in with a loosely scripted background on himself and the company. He sipped his water casually, not arrogantly.

Scott played for the New Orleans Saints at the same time as the legendary quarterback Archie Manning, father of Peyton and Eli Manning. He had a standout college career at Wazzu and had been recruited to Rivals.com by the founder and CEO. He was now a middle-aged dad and former college linebacker coach for the Washington Huskies. Scott's younger brother was the local legend, a star quarterback at UDub and went on to a successful NFL career, even playing a few years for his hometown Seahawks. Everyone loved the Pelluers. Sons of a legendary high school football coach who adopted them from a rough situation after their father died unexpectedly.

"So, what made you want to check out Rivals.com?"

"I found you on the Internet one day when I was searching for sports-related Internet start-ups. You guys seem to be pretty far along. Who's the founder?"

"Slim Dickman is the founder and CEO of Rivals.com. He was in college when my brother played for the Huskies. He ran a college recruiting magazine called *Sports Washington* and basically created a network of college magazine publishers and took it to the Internet. The result was traffic that grew and surpassed CBS Sportsline literally overnight. Rivals.com is the largest sports network in the world as of last month. He's a visionary for sure. I'll introduce you to him at the end of the tour. So, tell me about you."

"Well, after playing football and graduating from Fresno State, I went to work as a lumber broker before my current job working as sales manager for a travel products design house in California called Kiva Designs. We do custom design and domestic manufacturing for brands like the North Face, Eddie Bauer, and Patagonia. I've opened up over one hundred retail accounts and signed five private-label deals in two years—"

Scott cut me off and said, "Wait, you played football for Fresno State?"

"Yes, I played defensive-end from 1990 to '94."

"Who was your coach?"

"Jim Sweeney."

"Trent Dilfer was your quarterback, right?"

"Yeah, we roomed together on our recruiting trip. He puked all over our room after a recruiting party with the defense. Lightweight QBs!"

Dead silence. Scott got out of his chair with a serious look and came towards me. He stuck his hand out and gave me the Coach Jim Sweeney "Bulldog" handshake, which included a snap at the end. I couldn't believe it! We literally hugged after the handshake knowing we were connected at the college football defensive player level.

"I'll never forget the Sweeney handshake! He spoke at our pregame practice one year before we played Fresno State.

He told us Wazzu was where he raised his family and coached longer than any other place. He is an Original!"

He called me brother and hugged me. I was feeling pretty good about where things were headed.

"D-end? Wow! I figured receiver or tight end." We both laughed at my expense. Scott was giving me shit for my slim build for a typical D-lineman, as he slapped me on the shoulder with a big-brother thud.

"No problem. Junior Seau thought I was the kicker during warmups at the San Diego State game at the Murph." We both laughed, and then Scott explained what was next. My mind was elevated and trying to grasp what was happening, but I didn't have time to think about it except to stay focused and see where the ride would take me.

"Let's walk around, and I'll show you the rest of the team."

Scott led me out of the door and went up a ramp and into an open main room full of people; Scott's network development team was busy signing deals with sports publishers. The guys were in four deep rows of desk cubicles with young ex-jocks with headsets selling a dream of the largest sports network in the world. Two guys in opposite cubicles were playing catch with a football. Another one was standing up with a headset and swinging a wooden bat as he explained the benefits of partnering with Rivals.com instead of remaining independent. A girl played with a tennis ball and talked sexy to a male sports publisher on the phone. The young guy sitting across from her grabbed two balls and played with his imaginary tits, trying to break her concentration. She smiled and tried to keep her momentum and focus while enjoying the flirtation.

The energy was young and full of exciting and world-changing possibilities. The dot com revolution had begun, and I had just walked into one of the rocket ships that would change sports media and the media model forever.

"All right, settle down. I want to introduce Chris Rockwell from California. He played defensive end for Fresno State. He's here to see if he might want to join our team."

Scott was used to associating a person to their sports achievement in the jock or business circles he ran in. And since Rivals.com was a sports media company, I had some high-ranking credentials. I received a warm welcome from a crew that held college and pro athletes in high regard like the Romans idolized their gladiators. It was surreal. Just minutes before, I was a total outsider full of insecurity and fear. Suddenly, I was glowing in the center of people who openly celebrated me from that minute on. It was a very special moment for me.

The guy holding the baseball bat stepped towards me to shake my hand like the senior ambassador of the young former athletes and coaches, all my age.

"What's up, man? I'm Jeremy Briggs. Nice to meet you."

He was not a big dude and probably was an average baseball player at best. But he was the smart, overachieving kid that rode pine and ended up coaching it better than most. He was an interesting combination of Ferris Bueller and Jerry McGuire with David Spade's cutting wit. Briggs was a happy, funny, local Scandinavian, like a large percentage of folks who settled Seattle. Apparently, he was an intern for UDub baseball for two years and was also coaching the Mercer High baseball team. Jeremy continued to sell me on his coaching resume and strategy, just like he had been trying to do to impress his father over the course of his life.

"My JVs...we're five and seven. I know that's not good. We lost the last three games by a total of three points. Can you believe that? But we have our top pitcher back in the lineup next week."

As Jeremy continued talking, there were grumblings in the ranks about him talking too much.

Finally, someone said in a tomboy octave, "Shut up Briggs, you'll scare Rockwell off! Hi, I'm Lisa."

Lisa looked like a twenty-five-year-old Brittney Spears, years before Brittney made it cool for white girls to have an ass and dance like black chicks. Lisa was like a lioness unabashedly out to hunt men like she was on the great African Serengeti. She was fast, and I liked her honesty. She wasn't snooty like many in the educated elite tech start-up scene. She likely grew up either totally rich and spoiled, like some tech founder offspring can sometimes be, but my bet was that she came from Tacoma and a blue-collar upbringing.

"Hey, nice to meet you, Lisa."

I was telling myself not to stare at her giant fake tits, but she and I both knew that was the point. That's why she had them, thanks to her last boyfriend, a sorry ass tight-end named Williams, who played on the Seahawks squad for a few years. He ended up getting traded after a gun incident at the Showbox in downtown Seattle at a rap concert.

"You should work here."

Briggs, feeling his spotlight slipping fast, jumped back in with a corporate dork cock-block.

"Leave Chris alone. YOU'LL scare him off. Chris, my advanced apologies for Lisa's harassment. What can I say, she is a former Seattle Seahawks cheerleader."

Everyone laughed, and Scott cracked the whip with his presence, even though I would never consider him fierce in any way, except on the football field where he took out his grief of losing his father at a young age. I would not want to let him down. I could sense that in his team, and it confirmed my gut. Scott was a good man.

"Alright, alright...back to work, knuckleheads. Come on Rock, let me introduce you to the rest of the team." Did he just call me Rock? I smiled and felt my confidence rising and part of something special.

We continued our walk by the technology team, and Scott introduced me to the chief technology officer and the director of publishers.

"Phil, this is Chris Rockwell. Chris, this is Phil Borington, our chief technology officer and co-founder. Chris played football at Fresno State."

Phil was this big goofy Microsoft millionaire originally from North Dakota but did his undergrad at Iowa and his master's at UCLA while playing in the marching band and probably playing *Dungeons and Dragons* at night with his computer science counterparts. Phil looked like an ogre with bad breath, bad demeanor, and zero social graces below his façade of money and status within the new Internet tech world. Phil had a sarcastic and argumentative verbal style like his mentor and former, Bill Gates.

"Fresno State, eh? You guys did well in the Freedom Bowl defeating my nemesis, USC. I am a Bruin, so I enjoyed that game. Hello, Chris Rockwell. Did you learn anything at Fresno State? They're not known for their academic prowess."

"That's pretty accurate." I was trying not to act defensively or offended. I was used to socially inept dorks from elite colleges viewing me as a dumb jock. Goes all the way back to elementary school—hell, preschool. This helped them compensate for never pulling a hot chick or being invited to a party. The irony is that I was never a bully or a dumb jock. But I learned to let these social dorks feel cool for once in their lives while I played chess with their arrogance and blind spots. This guy was the epitome of revenge of the nerds. He looked like the hunchback from Notre Dame and had the worst attitude of any human I think I've ever met. He was repulsive in a way I couldn't quite put my finger on. Then it dawned on me; his heart and soul were diseased with a blind arrogance from his Microsoft millions and a hot wife he bought along with his new house. The guy was pathetic, and I knew I could play him like a fucking yo-yo.

"Well, do you think you are cut out for an Internet start-up? This is a different league."

"It's all a game to me. Good to meet you, Phil."

I wanted to tell Phil how inferior he was, other than his bank account and new Porsche. The problem with the tech revolution is that it gave dork boys God complexes, like the generation of mamas' boys I grew up competing against. These computer engineers developed a false sense of self and success based on a one-dimensional prism of society's making. They just happened to be born into a time where their particular skill was of value. I saw this experience as a fun challenge.

I mean, think about it. I infiltrate this company, with basically no knowledge of the business and end up inside the belly of the beast, interviewing for a job I didn't even want. I just wanted to see if I could put together a strategic deal for WinTech. Serious. Nevertheless, I knew I could play at this level and excel, like anything else I attempted. It was absolutely not about money to me, yet the thought of being a twenty-something millionaire had a nice ring. I was there to form a partnership.

Our next stop on the dork train was an even stranger character. He reminded me of a quirky speckled and salt-and-peppery-haired finance professor type with zero emotional expression or ability to read emotional cues. If you have watched the Netflix fantasy football sitcom *The League*, Rodney Ruxin could be this guy.

"Chris, this is Darin Schmirnoff. He's a Senior VP here at Rivals."

Darin Schmirnoff was like this weird little sports statistic junkie that rarely spoke. And when he did, he sounded like a cross between the autistic genius Rain Man and the physicist Stephen Hawkings speaking with his computer-generated voice. This dude was wound tight. He had a lot of built-up tension and a clear love-hate with his obsession with sports. He looked at me deadpan and spoke like a fucking robot, each word disconnected from the other. It was a trip. I started wondering if I was talking to a cyborg.

These guys excelled in this new world. They were techie rock stars. Imagine. They had no interpersonal skills but were deadly good at writing code to develop new applications for content and data management online. I was always impressed and fascinated with that side of the business. That's the main reason I was there. I wanted to understand the mechanics of building an Internet company from scratch. I knew this place offered me that, even if I was going to have to coexist with guys who had a clear love-hate (actually, resentment) of what I represented to them back in high school and college. Until they got to know me, they assumed I was just another clueless jock. You couldn't have a more extreme contrast of people under one roof. Jocks and nerds. And I was both.

"What brings you to Seattle?"

"I was in the neighborhood interviewing with Microsoft and a few others."

"Really? What division of Microsoft?"

I had a feeling this fucking guy was going to give me trouble. But I knew I could pass his test. I've learned to counterpunch the arrogant mistake geeks make about casting me as a simple jock. They are totally unaware of the social and interpersonal cues around them, and they create a superhero image of themselves through warped narcissism, isolation-living at mom's house playing plenty of video games, while the other boys were out testing their abilities against real kids in an uncontrolled social setting. Seriously, if you talked like these idiots to regular kids, you would get knocked the fuck out—not by a guy, but probably by a chick!

I smiled to myself and was ready to finish snowing this clown.

"Sales."

"Who are you meeting with there? I know some of the recruiters."

"I met with some guy named Dave, I think."

At that point, I was starting to think my cover was blown.

"Hmmm. What do you think you can add to Rivals. com?"

"I'm a team player, and I have a strong track record in sales. I think I work well with people." I tossed him a cliché' sound-bite response just to stay under his radar.

He was silently staring at me like he was going to pull the fire alarm to call my bluff. Scott broke the silence to move the dork train down the road to meet one of the lead engineers.

"And this is Ben."

"Hey Chris! Cool to meet you!"

Ben was this crazy smart computer whiz kid, probably 18 years old at best. He was idealistic and searching for the meaning of life and lived in wormholes of philosophical books, code, and the ancient Chinese chess-style game *Go*. He was cool and super good at what he did. Ben was socially half retarded and just awkward in most other ways, but I liked his depth, curiosity, and kindness. He was different than the other engineers. He would eventually be someone I hung out with, eating mushrooms and tripping on life.

"Hey man, good to meet you!"

Scott walked by the big glass offices with views of the Puget Sound. The CEO was in his office with his back to Scott and me. He was meeting with a big black guy in a suit, clearly a pro football player. They finished and shook hands, and the big black guy left the office and walked right past us, dwarfing my six-foot-four height and confidence.

As Scott was talking to me, I faded off in amazement at the General running this company. In my mind, the scene went into slow motion with Soundgarden music representing the wild, crazy Seattle Internet scene, the musical flashpoints of Hendrix, Heart, and Alice in Chains rounding out the bands that captured my idea of what Seattle was artistically and creatively. I knew I had arrived somewhere that promoted new and bold people and ideas.

I was star-struck and intimidated by what this guy was doing. I wanted to be him but also knew I wasn't in his league, yet. I knew I would be someday, but I also knew that I had a lot to learn.

"Slim, this is Chris Rockwell. He played defensive end for Fresno State and was in town interviewing with Microsoft for a sales position. He thought we may be a better fit, so he stopped in to check us out."

"Good to meet you, Chris. Did you recognize that guy? That's Lincoln Kennedy, the Minnesota Vikings star offensive lineman and a former Husky. Come on in and sit down. Thanks, Scott."

Slim sat quietly for a second, gathering his thoughts. He was noticeably under heavy pressure, but I could tell there was something about it that he loved and fed off.

I broke the silence and said, "Your office and company are amazing."

"Thanks." He apparently wanted to quickly pass on pleasantries to keep his linear progress on hyperspeed. "So, you played for Fresno State. That's great. That was the Trent Dilfer era, right?"

"Yes, that's right."

Slim began repeating the Rivals.com story that he pitched 100 times a day. I heard most of it from Scott already, but I acted like it was the first time out of respect. Plus, the way he pitched it was like watching a great guitarist perform a solo that captured the adventure of man. He gathered himself with a quiet moment, started by a deep breath, closed his eyes for a couple of seconds, followed by a calm speaking style that made you feel instantly comfortable. I knew he was a serious player; I was nervous and intimidated but excited.

"Well, I started Rivals from scratch after running a sports magazine called *Sports Washington* and successfully running magazines for Ted Turner's Goodwill Games and the NFL. I started Rivals.com because I saw the Internet emerging, and I envisioned a network of team sports sites providing the most in-depth, up-to-date information on their favorite team. I was able to get a group of sports publishers to join together and launched a year ago. In our fifth week, our servers melted down, and we crushed CBS Sportline and ESPN overnight. We became the number one sports network in traffic and stickiness overnight. I've raised over $20 million from Hummer-Winblad, Intel, and Softbank (their investors include Bill Gates, Warren Buffet, and Michael Dell). I raised $10 million from Intel and Hummer Winblad, without a business plan!"

Slim continued, picking up momentum.

"It's like the battle of Scipio Africanus. Scipio the Great was a general in the Second Punic War and statesman of the Roman Republic. He was best known for defeating Hannibal at the final battle of the Second Punic War at Zama, a feat that earned him the agnomen Africanus, the nickname "the Roman Hannibal." Or like Guns N' Roses. After *Appetite* (referring to GnR's breakout debut, *Appetite for Destruction*), the attitude changed; they did too many drugs, Duff McKagen is my next-door neighbor and good friend. Anyway, they defeated themselves. The Beatles experienced a similar melting period. All innovation has that rise and fall period. It's about being in the upswing of any innovation. And the Internet is the way of the future."

I was speechless. This was only stuff I had read about in *Fortune* magazine and the *Wall Street Journal*. It was like being in a dream.

"Wow. That's amazing, man. Look, I have a similar business I started called WinTech. I'm just not as far along as you guys. It's a complimentary concept because it gives athletes a statistical perspective on how they match up to other kids their size, height, and age versus rivals.com's focus on content for the fan. I have Pac-10 and Olympic endorsements."

Slim paused, smiled, and looked at me like a big brother does when he's about to give some good advice to his little brother.

"Look, come help me build Rivals.com. You've got a great concept, you're young, and you can get paid to learn.

I spent my twenties poor and stressed out, trying to run my own businesses. I'll teach you how to build your own empire. And you can help me build mine."

That was a life-changing moment. I had met my entrepreneurial mentor.

Moving to Seattle and Halloween Witch Trippers

Two months later, my brand-new wife, Becky, and I packed a U-Haul and drove to Seattle. There was a hurricane-level storm of wind and rain the night we arrived. We were hauling furniture into our Ballard apartment in the black of night on a very busy street just outside of the city. Becky was crying, and I was thinking we just got ourselves in over our heads. We were both unsure and already homesick. We carried our stuff up a flight of stairs and finished the soaking wet and cold night eating pizza and drinking a few beers in silence.

The next day, I started working at the fast-paced and energized office and was already having fun. Rivals recruited Becky, and then she helped launch a Hollywood start-up digital fashion studio just down the street and found her own thing. We were rocking it in Seattle during the Internet boom. Anything was possible. We were young, newly married, and excited about our new adventure in a world away from our small town, family, and friends.

It wasn't long before I had developed friendships with a few of the engineers and journalist types. Many of the sales and executive types rarely communicated with them, but I quickly grew bored with the sports talk and senseless debates. I found some of the engineers to be not only interesting company, but they introduced me to some good times and places. They reminded me of some of the kids I grew up with. I would drink and even jam a little in a studio with some of my new buddies. Ben and Jason were my guys.

I was invited to the engineers' Halloween party hosted by Jason Allen. Halloween in Seattle during the Internet boom was a memorable one for sure. The energy of the city during the boom was electric, especially being in my late twenties. We ended up eating a bunch of mushrooms and walked around dressed as the grim reaper, accompanied by the devil and Jesus. I couldn't make this shit up. We found Jesus…I mean Ben's brother, Damian, at their house in the basement—naked and trippin' his ass off on mushrooms. His long hair and beard gave him the real appearance of J.C. himself, especially since we were frying our asses off at this point. We threw some Jesus clothes on Damian and hit the road to nowhere. We had no idea where we were going in the rain, but we knew we had to get the fuck out of the house. I was starting to feel the walls closing in, and Damian was already gone after trippin' alone in a basement bedroom.

After we smoked a few bong loads to really amp our paranoia, we headed out in search of other aliens that were speaking our language. It was Seattle on Halloween, so we knew it wouldn't be long until we crossed paths with Witch Trippers or Fallen Angels dancing on fire. Seattle at midnight on Halloween, walking around the rolling neighborhood hills rising to the east of the city, gave the backdrop of our walk a shimmering emerald city of lights. It was a haunting and alluring feel that made my drug high even trippier. I think we were all floating, and I saw the colorful neon lights drip like thick rain and disappear as if they were engulfed by the blacktop on the iridescent avenues.

Dot-com Christmas

Next thing I knew, we were attending my company's big Christmas party at Microsoft co-founder Paul Allen's newly built Experience Music Project museum, complete with a Jimi Hendrix section and the Fender guitar he played at Woodstock. This was next-level shit only billionaires could fathom spending money on. My idea of what was possible was exploding and expanding at light speed.

Slim Dickman walked by smiling, looking like the creepy reptilian founder Jack Dorsey of Twitter, while his eyes darted around to see who was seeing him at all times.

"Aren't you glad you moved here now?"

"Slim, this is my wife, Becky."

"Nice to meet you, Becky." His eyes locked on her, taking in her beauty and innocence and trying to suck her into his disturbing magnetism. "Your husband's doing a great job. Sorry we keep him away from you so much."

"That's what he likes. That's why we're here. I think it's all exciting and unknown."

"Exactly. Well, enjoy the party." Slim slunk away, holding his gaze on her for a few more unnerving seconds.

Becky turned to me. "I don't know what to think of him. One thing is for sure; he will either be huge or crash to the ground."

"That's why I think he will be great."

"At what expense? This all seems too fast and irrational. I mean, how can all this money come in from investors and the dot-coms don't make any money?"

"You just don't understand."

"Okay Chris, I think I am starting to understand."

Becky looked across the room at the little floozies hanging on the newly paper-rich bachelor Internet stars. There was definitely the feeling of decadence, like the scene in the Scorsese and DiCaprio film *Aviator*, about the visionary entrepreneur Howard Hughes, at the Coconut Grove in Hollywood. People were dancing, drinking, and listening to a live band—oblivious of the crash that was lurking in the shadows.

2000: SEATTLE EXPERIENCE MUSIC PROJECT

A big part of my musical education would happen in Seattle. Home to some of the greatest musicians of all time, I was destined to end up there for one reason or another. But mainly, I was pulled there by the sludgy sounds creeping out of the dark raining emerald city of the northwest.

My first experience was ten years earlier, flying into SeaTac airport as an eighteen-year-old on a college football recruiting trip to Washington State. I was on my way to Pullman, Washington, by way of Moscow, Idaho. Wazzu, as the insiders call it, had very cool coaches, students, and a chill party vibe with some country attitude. But all I could think of were the sounds that I could see emanating off the shimmering towers of downtown Seattle. The ripples of the city's color-filled reflection on the Puget Sound it touched to her western edge.

A decade later, when I moved to Seattle to join Rivals. com, I was bound and determined to join or build a rock band and learn as much as I possibly could. I began pouring through local free music magazines and hitting every bar and club that had live music. I worked downtown in the old "Skid Row" section of Seattle on the water's edge. I was a couple of blocks from Pioneer Square and a handful of bars with all kinds of live music—blues, jazz, rock, cover-band performances. I would spend hours after work just cruising all over Seattle in search of anything connected to the rock music scene. That's what drew me to Seattle in the first place.

Starting out, I felt like a total outside musical novice in the cathedral of sound. Seattle is home to titans of music, legends like Jimi Hendrix, Quincy Jones, Heart, and the 1990s "grunge" cultural explosion that made the 1980s hair bands of LA go extinct overnight. Seattle became the sound machine of my college years, represented by the bands I respected.

Although Pearl Jam was the biggest commercial success of the Seattle movement, they were my least favorite because I could tell lead singer Eddie Vedder was a wannabe who teamed up with the right lily white boys from Seattle who were into Jimi Hendrix and jam bands. They were perfect for the social issue bullshit Bono era of MTV. Pearl Jam is a joke, like Creed. The only difference is that Pearl Jam comes from a cool city, and they rode the politically correct wave perfectly, retaining their allegiance of aging Gen X pussy-whipped husbands and unhappy wives missing their wasted risk-averse youth. Pearl Jam fans are U2 fans. Gay wannabe music fans, approved by the mainstream vanilla factory that also produced the Metro Man's pop band of emasculation, Coldplay.

I first met the band I ended up joining when they were playing a gig at the Firehouse in Ballard, down the street from where Becky and I lived. They were losing their drummer and looking for a replacement. I remember going there by myself after work and digging their heavy sound. They were very much in the direction of Josh Holmes's early band Kyuss. The singer was a burned-out drugged-out guy who worked at the boat docks like his drunk old man did. He was good, but his addictions ruled his life and marginalized his talent and singing aspirations. Funny how I thought I was different than him at the time because I was younger and making good money building a sports media company during the boom of the Internet Revolution. I felt like I could pretty much do anything. I sensed that he had lost his core confidence and burning desire.

The band was called 9.Fifteen, a reference that I didn't understand until I looked it up. It made sense based on the lead guitarist's interests and work in the wireless space. 915 MHz is part of the industrial, scientific, and medical (ISM) portion of the electromagnetic spectrum. Kevin, the guitarist, was a big *Star Wars* fan and was all about space and futuristic technology. He was a working-class stiff, making shit pay as an electrical technician guy in Northgate. I worked with guys just like him with just a touch more confidence and a lot more arrogance, but they were making five times as much working with me at Rivals.com as computer engineers. Kevin ended up being a nice guy and musical friend to me. We would spend hours jamming together and working out parts to new songs we were developing for the new album that I would be playing drums on. We had a natural connection musically, and it allowed us to create structured pieces like Maiden would, but then we could just jam effortlessly and fearlessly, finding sounds that fit the influences we were inspired and led by.

I met the guys after a show and then reconnected the following night at Kevin's house, where he had a practice and recording room built out of his garage. It was advanced for a garage that still had an old wooden garage door that would swing open during practice if it weren't locked. Besides that, the rest of the room was covered with acoustic padding, electrical wires, Christmas lights, and lava lamps to set the mood right. It was perfect. It was a band practice space in a Seattle garage. I was on my way. But first, I had to actually try out for the gig.

I forgot to mention that the only band I was ever in was never. I mean it. I grew up jamming with my brothers at times and played my guitar alone in my room during college, but I never had time to play in a band. I didn't have time to commit to building a touring band set on world domination.

I had never been a drummer in a band, and I had never performed live. I knew my chances weren't great, and I also knew there were many solid drummers around town who wanted to join the established local act. Two weeks earlier, I had made a total fool of myself trying out for a speed metal band that required double pedal kick drumbeats throughout nearly every song. Beck and I bought the drum kit at Guitar Center that night, proceeded to lock our keys in the Explorer, and I was late to the tryout.

For this tryout, I met the band at Kevin's house on a Thursday night, and it was raining. It was always dark and raining, which helped me understand the mood of the music coming out of the Northwest. The house was in a working-class neighborhood that had seen better days. Kevin grew up in the house with his mom and younger sister and ended up staying there when his mom remarried and moved to Texas.

I nervously knocked. Kevin opened the door and greeted me with a cigarette and a cool smile. "Hey Chris, come in."

As I entered, I could feel the warmth of the house, smell old cigarette smoke, and beechwood incense. There was a big *Star Wars* poster pinned up on the right wall over the TV. The two other guys welcomed me with handshakes and darting eyes, preferring to keep their distance. Besides Kevin, the singer was the only guy I remember. Funny how bass players often are camouflaged into the group and sound even though they carry a big ax. This bass player didn't have any of it. He was an argumentative science geek guy who couldn't seem to hold a job or girlfriend long enough to expound his endless diatribe on computers, phones, or engineering boards. You name it, he was the expert. I smiled to myself because I was working with a bunch of guys just like him. It didn't bother me like it bothered everyone else, probably because I had only spent five minutes with the guy.

I was feeling very fucking nervous as we stood around in the living room. The door into the garage was open, and I could see the drums and a bunch of cords and recording equipment. My nerves had me wanting to run out of the house but knew I had to face this challenge. As we were making small talk and drinking our beers to loosen the tension of a new guy being in the room, the singer, Mick, blurts out in his brain-hazed slur from too many years of alcohol and inhaling sanded fiberglass working in the shipyard, "Well, are we gonna play some fucking music? Ha!"

The bass player, and only non-drinker in the room, sighed with exasperation due to his wearing patience with Mick's half-assed alcoholic approach to life.

I sat down at the drum kit as Kevin and the bass player strapped on their guitars and began playing what they were practicing before I showed up. I could tell they were having a disagreement on direction, but I could also tell that they both could play pretty well. I was sure they would find me out and tell me to get the fuck out of their legitimate band's practice space. As they started realigning their rhythm and sounds, Kevin looked over at me with a nod to start drumming. I almost passed out from fear; I'm not kidding. I took a huge drink of my Coors tallboy and dropped the drumstick onto the top hat, and kicked the bass into gear. With that, we were off and jamming our way through a few minutes of a song they were working on.

I saw Kevin smile at my rhythm and instantly locked into my zone. It was as if I was back in my jam room at my parents' house as a kid, which was precisely the last time I had a drum kit to play out loud. I relied on my innate rhythm and visualization from air drumming every day of my life. I don't just air drum with my hands, I always make sure I'm staying in rhythm with the bass kicks as well. Sounds crazy, but I can see and feel it. So, when I sat down to the drum kit in that Seattle garage that night, my brain produced the performance that I always felt, even without drums. I didn't know if it was good enough to make the band, but at least I wasn't feeling like a fucking joke.

After a few songs with Mick belting out some solid gravelly sounds, the guys all stepped into the living room to take a break and discuss my performance and fate. I stood up and drank another beer and gazed off at all the musical cliché that I worshipped. I began chalking it up to a great experience and a big step in the right direction. I had only been in Seattle for a few months and felt like I was finding my way, but also realized how far I had to go.

The door swung open with Kevin and Mick walking in with a serious look.

"You got the gig…welcome to the band, dude!"

That moment was, by far, more fulfilling and exciting than my number one successes in college football or the business world. I had been validated as a rock musician in Seattle! I couldn't believe it. I was on a high that set a part of my soul free. No other way to put it. That part of me—my truth—had been locked up, and the key had been tossed in the locker during my all-consuming athletic career spanning the past two decades. I had found my people, my music, my home. I remember driving back to my apartment and threw open the door, excited to share my greatest success ever. Beck knew what it meant to me and genuinely celebrated that moment with me as if I had just had an album go platinum.

I wouldn't be in Seattle much longer after that. But I managed to develop a new album with the guitarist, Kevin, and a new singer who was a Layne Staley protégé, a homeless Irish dude dealing with some serious anger and addiction issues. I even let this guy stay at our place a couple of nights. It was pretty cool of my wife to let the homeless heroin junkie lead singer of my Seattle rock band sleep in our living room. It was all one big crazy adventure that I wasn't about to half-ass. I was finally starting to dive all in with the music aspect of my life

It intensified as I realized I was living in the Seattle Internet psycho culture of working all the time to build something that will be obsolete in weeks. I was losing passion for that race and becoming totally obsessed with my creative space, leveraging the start-up scalability framework that the world taught me. I now realize that I was being given the education I needed to set out and create my own sound and vision of what rock music meant to me. I didn't have the fortune of spending years touring with my young bandmates, learning the business the old-fashioned way. I was playing catch up and was not interested in simply being in a band. I wanted to compose, record, and produce rock music with the best. That approach gave me the peace with my past regrets of starting late and the road map that would allow me to make music a part of my life forever, in a way that fulfills and inspires me. I wanted to make great music. It's that simple.

2001: INTERNET
BUBBLE BURSTS

The first bubble bursting recession I lived through was when I was 29 years old, living and working in the eye of the storm of the Internet start-up world. Becky and I made the move to Seattle to join the Internet revolution right after getting married. Fortunately, we were young, and I knew we could move back home and find work if things didn't work out. We were in it for the adventure. The dreams of millions from our stock options fed by the mania around us was intoxicating and something I would do all over again. We arrived with no money, made a few bucks, and spent a lot on rent and eating out with friends after work, taking trips, and enjoying the experience thoroughly.

The Internet explosion and subsequent crash back down to Earth is a normal human mania phenomenon displayed throughout recorded history. Capitalism isn't necessarily a neat and clean process when innovation is happening. There's plenty of excitement and fast-paced living, and plenty of collateral damage along the way, too. Lots of cash changing hands, new concepts becoming a reality, and new millionaires. But even more, dead start-ups, failed CEOs, and big losses by early-stage investors. I have lived in the belly of that creative beast the majority of my adult working life. It can be a love-hate because of the constant change and never-ending fight to stay on top. I can understand why most people are not equipped to weather the crazy highs and crashing lows of building a new business from scratch. It's a beast that has no mercy on the weak.

I have always understood that building businesses from scratch in the Internet space was literally the Wild West, the new Industrial Revolution. The Internet captivated me back in college in the early 1990s. That's why, within a few years after graduating, I launched my first Internet recruiting database business WinTech. I saw this new Internet thing happening and made an early attempt at building a business off its platform. I had the constant belief that the idea was good and could be huge. That's what makes entrepreneurs wake up and want to take on the day-to-day grind—building something new and exciting. I walked away from my first business start-up with no money, but an amazing adventure that taught me things about myself and business that enabled me to try again and again and again, until I finally had enough experience, wisdom, and urgency to create a profitable global business from scratch.

Starting a business is so much more difficult than the media and liberal politicians will have you believe. We are in a global economy with lots of young people with access to smartphones and information to disrupt markets and build the next billion-dollar business; innovation doesn't care if you are rich or dirt fucking poor. Nonetheless, it's nearly impossible, based on statistics, to get a business from idea to profitability. Getting knocked down from an economic collapse is humbling. I remember the day they were doing the first massive layoff rounds at Rivals.com. I wasn't impacted personally by the cuts, but I instantly began preparing; my exit would be on my terms.

Anyway, the company was dysfunctional. The entire dot-com bubble was about ready to explode and decimate the first wave of the Internet era, kinda like when the dinosaurs were wiped out.

Beck and I went down to the boat docks that evening where we would sit and dream, saying goodbye to a place and time that would be forever in our memories.

"I can't believe it's over. Remember how excited we were that first night in the hotel when they flew us up to recruit you? We sat on the bed dreaming about what we'd do with the money from cashing out our stock from the successful IPO. We were going to buy our parents and siblings things they only dreamed of. It was the best and worst of mankind. I saw a lot of greedy people who lost sight of creating something special and becoming obsessed with the dollar."

"Yeah…innovation is not pretty. It's primal, survival of the fittest. It's no different than being on the football field. You have to pick your teammates very carefully and execute a solid game plan effectively. A team cannot succeed unless it has a good idea and leader that attracts and inspires great talent. If you can do that and stay true to that along the way, you can create anything. Someday I'm going to build something great that inspires people, Bubble. "

"I know you will, Bubba. I love you. Just listen to your heart, and don't try too hard. This will pass."

We sat there holding hands, looking out to the horizon watching the sunset, both of us thinking about our path going forward. But we were young and confident, and we knew we would be okay. We had each other. We packed up and headed home broke. I decided to go to the ocean and work with my grandpa for a while and get things figured out…and to fish.

Emerald Triangle

The smell of brewing coffee and sizzling bacon lit the morning campfire in my mind. Images of a perfect day of fishing with my grandpa made me smile in anticipation. The coastal tri-level house he designed and built wasn't fancy, but it was spacious and welcoming, designed to accommodate lots of family. The house was usually full of light coming in from the massive windows opening the living room to expansive views of the Pacific Ocean and the Lost Coast Mountains that anchored the north and south rim of our quaint fishing cove like insurmountable kingdom walls of the Jurassic gods. Shelter Cove was built by a lava flow, creating a beautiful strip of land and a protected cove with some of the best fishing in the world.

Each morning I would look at the ocean and make my determination on whether it was going to be a good day of fishing or not. Men take pride in learning the indicators that make them skilled at the kill. My grandpa could tell within seconds. It was uncanny. I grew up around it and had a good feel. Ultimately, every day at Shelter Cove was a good day. Each morning began with black coffee and the overwhelming optimism of catching monster fish. I loved hanging with grandpa. Drinking a beer out on the boat or on the deck and talking about building stuff, my sports career, or fishing. He was a living example that tough times arrive, and we have to figure out how to walk through it. That's what being a man is all about. G-pa didn't have to say much to make a life-impacting statement. He lived it.

"It's about working hard, standing for what you believe in, and helping others. That's pretty much it."

Then he ended with a pause to think about leaving his home in Dodge City, Kansas, to work on a ranch in Colorado at eleven years old during the Great Depression. I think he got teary-eyed behind his sunglasses for a moment. Grandpa came from sturdy German stock, directly from the Pennsylvania Amish country, immigrating from Oldenburg, Germany. They lived right, worked hard from dusk 'til dawn, and never complained. They just dealt with the circumstances and persevered. Like most parents dealing with high mortality rates in an agriculturally-driven region of America at the turn of the 20th century, the Lance family had eleven children.

His little brother, Junior, was killed by a milk delivery truck when he was just about five years old when crossing the street with G-pa and some of the other siblings. My grandpa kept a little newspaper clipping about the tragedy; despite it not being his fault, he never forgave himself for Junior's death, and it affected him profoundly. Their dad, Chaney Lance, and his six-foot-tall German beauty, Rose, raised a vibrant family that valued hard work. They challenged and encouraged one another using the teachings from the Bible. They were good, intelligent people who worked hard and appreciated simple but quality living and nature.

My Grandpa Lee was a classic World War II veteran who fought bravely in the North Atlantic against Hitler's Nazis after being transferred from the USS Arizona just weeks before it was sunk at Pearl Harbor by the Japanese. He lost most of his buddies on that one earth-shaking day. He made the most of a life he knew was fleeting. Grandpa traveled, flew planes, built houses, invented things, and had an adventurous spirit. He was never financially wealthy, but he lived beyond the worldly accumulation of gold.

We spent evenings on the deck as the sun kissed the blue waters of the Pacific. One evening, as Grandpa was gazing off into the setting sun, he turned to me and confided feeling the burning guilt of surviving without explanation. He explained that weeks prior to the bombing of Pearl Harbor, the top brass at the Pentagon got a tip that the North Atlantic Ocean was going to be the flashpoint where the allies and the Nazi U-boats were going to collide for historic battles. What wasn't expected was Pearl Harbor being attacked.

My grandpa possessed an inventive mind and happened to be a skilled diesel mechanic. He attended the Navy's elite diesel engineering school in Cleveland, Ohio, where he met my grandmother Ethel Anne, the daughter of Bryan 'Groco' Downey, former boxing middleweight champion of the world. As soon as the Pentagon received their tip about the increase in activity in the North Atlantic, he was shipped off to an allied Dutch fighter ship there. The fighting and north seas turned out to be as rough as expected. He vividly described working in the smoke-filled bowels of a warship, maintaining the massive diesel engines, the beating heart of the ship, while depth-charged bombs were pounding and bending the steel hull around him like it was tin foil. Grandpa continued the imagery of a North Seas ocean so violent that there were footprints up and down the walls from the extreme side-to-side motion caused by the monstrous forty-foot swells.

Grandpa told the story like it was in a movie. He didn't lie or add dramatic flair. He just lived an adventurous life and had some great stories to pass down and live up to. He told his accounts in a matter-of-fact way but also knowing they were part of the highlight reel of his life experiences. I could tell that those horrific moments of war and the great economic depression in his life didn't shake or scare him in ways it did most men. He had a deep sense of conviction, much of it grounded in his Catholic faith and old-school humble beginnings. He also had an adventurous spirit that passed on to me. Fishing in particular, and his personal adventures on the sea, the Great Depression and World War II were handed to me as a parting gift of wisdom that I could take pride in and build from.

"Chris, you are either going to be a millionaire or end up in jail." He said it as if it was a known fact. I'm sure he wouldn't be surprised I managed to do both! It was my all-or-nothing personality. He admired, although sometimes questioned, how I lived my life, but mostly he loved spending time with me and sharing our lived adventures. I wouldn't flinch when we'd head out fishing on the rough north coast of Shelter Cove in a small aluminum boat in high swells and great white shark-infested waters, not to mention the pilot whales that would surround the boat, surfacing to let us know that they could flip or eat our little boat for fun. I loved the thrill of those experiences and taking them back to shore. We would often return with salmon or lingcod, and a story or two related to encounters with the beasts of the sea. I would arrive back to shore feeling seasick, usually trying not to fall over as I stepped ashore like a drunken sailor.

As my grandpa was nearing the sunset of life, he started sharing his edgier stories. The best story was a page right out of Captain Cook's discovery of the Hawaiian Islands and their beautiful, gracious, and naked native women. You have to picture Oahu in 1946. It was still pristine, and the locals commonly covered their perfectly tanned bodies with little to no clothing. With a beer and a sly smile coming from a memory sixty years ago on an island far, far away, G-pa told me about the time he was a young 19-year-old sailor aboard the USS Arizona. They had just arrived at port after traveling thousands of miles through the massive expanse of the Pacific Ocean. Upon docking into Pearl Harbor, the soldiers were given a 24-hour leave from the ship. The captain warned them to return before the deadline or they would be left, and court marshaled.

The herd of testosterone-fueled and sexually repressed boys headed straight for the bars and broads to get the party started. Grandpa and two buddies grabbed a bottle of rum and met up with a few native girls. The girls led the boys to an unspoiled waterfall pool where they drank until everyone was celebrating naked and diving off cliffs to impress the native beauties. G-pa said it was about the only time he could recall getting drunk. He meant it, which made the story even more special. They knew it was a once-in-a-lifetime moment they would retell a million times in their mind before they died as possibly the greatest day of their young lives. As they staggered back to the ship, they were only halfway down out of the lush forest of palms when they heard the final steam horn to board ship. These young sailors, drunk on lust and rum, staggered out of the trees carrying their buddy, Tom McLemore, on their shoulders like he had been ambushed by island warriors. Apparently, he passed out drunk at the waterfalls and was just starting to come to as they boarded ship.

G-Pa continued his reminiscent thoughts. "They should put old guys like me at the front lines in Iraq!" The Iraq War was in full tilt. We took a drink of our beer to lighten the heavy words and thoughts still hanging on the salty air sweeping against our faces from the waves smashing the black lava cliffs a few hundred feet away. I knew this was a special moment with my grandpa. The setting sun over the ocean united our spirits beyond this world, beyond this time and dimension. I savored that moment because I knew I was experiencing a timeless and nostalgic memory I wanted to recall forever, until I was like him looking west toward my passage to the new world, wherever and whatever it will be. I saw it in his eyes. He was ready and at peace, as at peace as any man can be knowing his work is done on this earth, and he's heading on an unknown eternal journey.

"Or they should just let us old fisherman float out to sea ..."

It wasn't long before I was back in my hometown with my wife and working again for KIVA Designs when the phone rang...

2002: BUILDING SCOUT. COM & THE CEO'S SWINGERS CLUB IN VEGAS

I t was the beginning of Scout.com, Slim Dickman's answer to his being kicked out of Rivals. He was out to build and overtake his former company. I worked side by side with him from the beginning. I quit my job at KIVA once again and jumped on a plane the next day, slept in his basement, and worked day and night by his side to help him re-recruit the sports publishers he had royally pissed off at rivals.com, resulting in a massive lawsuit against him and rivals.com for false promises. Despite all this, in less than three years, we had recruited most of the top sports publishers back, and he and his investors sold Scout for $58 million.

The entire fledgling company was mostly white men, with the exception of a gay-mannered Asian white guy who was a former writer for the *Seattle Times*. Glen was Columbia educated and the effeminate poster boy of women's rights and resented the men he secretly craved. Our CEO's whore Asian freckled assistant, Tina, was our other diversity quota hire. She was slow upstairs and would do anything for money and to be near men with money, fame, and power. I always kinda felt bad for her because she wanted to be a nice girl, deep down, but she was an idiot with no vision outside her shallow and fading complexion and body.

Moni was the other female at the office; she was an engineer and a thick Scandinavian with blonde hair and blue eyes. I used to drink with her up the street from our first office on Polson Street. We would ransack the Irish Pub Tiernanogs (Tír na nÓg, Irish legend of the underworld), with my musician and engineer buddies. Moni was one of the guys and could take a sexist comment and dish it without a whimper or sexual harassment lawsuit. She was fun and quietly smart. We could talk shop and drink beer with the guys until the lights went out. In fact, she was probably the toughest engineer out of all the meek urbanized metro geeks on staff.

There were a few guys I ended up becoming good friends with, but most of them were like my CEO—undersized, pissed-off guys who lived competitively obsessed with size athleticism and trophies because they didn't have it. Most of the publishers have this strange love-hate relationship with guys like me. They love to hang out and associate with my past sports successes, then their eyes change from admiration to jealousy and resentment and sometimes even hate after just a few beers. I've seen it my entire life. It's just a human condition, to hate on the guy who's on top. I can go there too, but envy is a bad emotion that makes me feel like a shitty person. I have to remind myself to just focus on my path and try and not to compare. Sometimes that can be a daily challenge when I am feeling like a loser next to dorks I shouldn't even think about. Money is such a mindfuck. It can make a good man feel like nothing, and bad men feel like gods.

Dickman held a recruiting convention in Sin City, trying to lure the publishers back into his lair. We arrived in Vegas with about one hundred of the top college football and basketball team publishers from across the country.

I realized I was around lots of career, money, and power-obsessed people with strange social insecurities that make geeks act even more awkward. Then it dawned on me that these were the kids who played D & D and all the fantasy goofball video games instead of taking a chance on asking a girl out on a date or going up her shirt in the dugout. But somehow, these guys thought that a few bucks and a little status in a circle jerk club like the college sports publisher's association would transcend them into the arms and beds of real women looking for real men. With each shot of whiskey, these guys got more ridiculous, bragging about "bagging chicks" and "hosing bitches." I just smiled, acted impressed, and gladly accepted the shots they were buying me.

I wanted to disappear, and so I did a nosedive straight down to the bottom of a bottle of Jack. Then I headed to the craps tables with Brian Kosar, the financial whiz kid brother of the Cleveland Browns legendary quarterback Bernie Kosar. Brian kept feeding me chips to keep me at the table and keep him company. He was always cool to me and showed me that some of these guys were good guys, but not many. I can say the ratio holds true in any group of people, rich or poor. While we were in Vegas, I got a call from my mom that she had a brain tumor. I was riding down the elevator with my wife and Kosar that morning. He could tell I was wrecked and asked what was up. No sooner did I tell him, he was on his cell phone with his brother and putting my mom on the priority list at the Cleveland Clinic Brain Center. She was on a plane and getting VIP care by the top doctor in the country within the week. His big brother was a hometown NFL hero for the Browns, and he happened to be on the board of the Cleveland Clinic, arguably the top specialty clinic in the country. Just like that. That's Brian Kosar. I owe him for life and have great admiration for his example in a sea of selfish, arrogant morons.

At the afternoon presentation, Dickman gave his usual marathon speech, selling us on his accomplishments and greatness, leading us to the promised land. It always looked contrived and awkward. But he knew he didn't have to have style points. He didn't know how to dress until he made his millions and started running with the LA and New York media scene where fashion matters. In Seattle, it's cool to dress like a bum waiting for a bus in the rain. I remember standing in the back, thinking to myself, *Pretty sure I'm done with this sick charade!* Pretending to want to hang out with a bunch of sports-obsessed dorks with horrible personalities that reminded me of Mike Judge's awesome parody movie *Office Space* had become intolerable and just childish to me.

It was a surreal moment because I felt my time learning and succeeding in the sports media Internet space and dealing with the culture had run its course. I lived in this strange land for over a decade, working closely with engineers and all kinds of ambitious new business Internet start-up adrenaline junkies like me. It was a great drug for a lot of years. Don't get me wrong. I kept going back to the opium dens of Silicon Valley, Seattle, and Hollywood to get the rush I was used to. But the problem was that the drug stopped working, and my soul and mind knew I had to cut the dragon's head off and make a clean break. It was rotting me from the inside out, like an invasive cancer that I've seen so many friends and family die from. I knew it felt futile, but I was stuck on the hamster wheel from my sports training, where you grin and bear it until you feel the thrill of victory, the ultimate high of any drug. That's why everyone was in the Internet start-up game. That's why entrepreneurs do what they do; it's for the thrill. Some do it for the discovery, cash for others, fame for others. For me, I am passionate about creating, building, and learning. The rest of that shit, money, and fame, are simply byproducts of doing good work. They just cause distractions and can easily corrupt a person's creative and moral compass.

I knew I was done with it and going to sail on to explore new worlds after this tour. With that decision, I felt myself relax and focus on the task of smiling and recruiting the top publishers in the country to build the number one college sports network in the world—for a second time.

Our CEO's presentation included a few fiery questions from pissed-off publishers that Dickman fucked over with our first company rivals.com. No matter how bad things could get, he could get them back to the table and convince them to join him again for another round. I've never seen anything like it. And I helped him recruit these idiots. It was good cop/bad cop...more like big evil bro and innocent and naïve kid brother that the publishers could trust. I was damage control and ambassador to a possible psychopath. I was blinded by his worldly business achievements and balls. I really admired his vision and fearlessness. He made me better and tougher in a world that was a continuation of college football. It was intense, and all or nothing every play. It's a lifestyle that will eliminate anything and anyone in the way of its appetite for flesh, blood, and blind ambition. We may have been playing the same game but by different rules of conduct.

The bottom line is that the publishers and employees would bitch and complain, call him El Diablo behind his back, but ultimately fall in line and do what he told them to do. The ones who complained the loudest were the highest-paid to play for him. It was a very fucked-up group of codependents addicted to Dickman's web of chaos and promises of riches. I was all in and drinking the blood from his hand. I wanted what he wanted, easily as bad. But he was doing it on a level I could only dream of at the time. I knew I was going to learn from the master and achieve greatness! I can't believe how screwed up my vision was! I looked up to a guy that was borderline psychotic. I was just as fucked up as him but justifying it by being a student of the game.

Dickman was a visionary but suffered from human minutia of team building, and he had an out-of-control need to be liked, feared, and followed. I was watching a man barely keeping all the balls in the air at this point, and I didn't want to end up like him. He was divorced and struggled to function normally in society. By this time, he had developed physical ticks that were becoming noticeable and odd. At the time, I thought I was very different and not going to make the same reckless mistakes. After we wrapped the meeting, Dickman's dumb slut assistant directed the guys to the Coyote Ugly bar across the walkway inside New York, New York. I contemplated quitting right then and there and escaping into the setting sun and red desert to freedom. It was so close, yet so far away.

I felt like I was at the Mustang Ranch's attempt at a family hotel, like everyone was trying to do on the Vegas strip back then. It turned into a perverse Disney freak show that turned off adults and the kids. It was a strategic disaster because every guy and chick wanted to go to Vegas without their spouse, and especially without their obnoxious drama clown kids fucking up their one moment to feel like a dirty whore before returning to the slit-your-wrist daily grind of schlepping the kids around in the family van and making sure your grass is cut like Jan's next door. We arrived at the bar with Coyote bitches lined up, clearly paid extra, to make these fat smelly slobs feel like rock stars for one night. And then we would sign them to five-year contracts, which they would regret in the morning.

Be careful how bad you want something. That's my takeaway from that experience. I didn't have to lie or force these guys to sign anything because they wanted the pot of gold coming out of Dickman's ass. Slim's business model and vision were solid in my mind. His execution was hyper-speed, sloppy, and ego reckless. These guys would accept a small up-front signing bonus and the promise of revenue sharing profits that would far exceed anything they could do on their own, in almost every case. But the alternative wasn't a great option either. The publishers knew they had to pull a card from a rigged deck cut by Dickman. But he was able to convince them. Like I've always said, in theory, and if executed properly with suitable leadership, Slim Dickman's businesses penciled out and made good sense for the whole group. But in reality, he steamrolled the fundamentals required to make the business and people successful due to impatience, greed, and ambition to get to the top faster and with more cash.

I was always up for a party, but what I saw in that bar made me want to try and get sober…again. Imagine watching three fat, smelly, disheveled men laying on their backs getting fed shots by hot young Coyote Ugly barmaids. I was struck by the false reality we were paying for. As disgusted as I was, I jumped like one of Pavlov's addicted dogs.

"ROCK!! Come get a shot from Tammy Sue!!"

Jesus Christ. Tammy fucking Sue? I wanted the drink bad, so bad that I was ready to grab the bottle from the friendly little country girl feeding drinks to Stan Hemstock, the publisher for the South Carolina site. So, I took a deep breath and put my fun party face on and dove in headfirst to get my fix. Three shots of tequila later, we all headed out to meet our wives and girlfriends. Others wandered onto the gambling floor or bar right next door. The single guys, and some of the married ones, headed off to the strip clubs. But the CEO and his crew, including the top publishers and a few select team guys that would help him recruit the publishers, were off to the next adventure at the Rio Hotel. There was a VIP party at the top of the hotel outside on the deck overlooking the entire city. That's where Dickman and all the investors and senior executives were staying and meeting backdoor to make sure they ended up on top when the shit got ugly. They were smart, because eventually, like always, the publishers formed a group and tried to strong-arm Slim in a way that was not good for anyone.

At this point, I was finally starting to feel okay. Beck and the CEO's new wife, Tori, were hanging out and having a blast; dancing, having some drinks, and laughing like two giddy high school girls. Everything was going so well, I figured that I'd be a millionaire by night's end. The live DJ had the celebrity crowd rocking the roof party late into the night. I felt so alive and on top of the world! After we did our rounds at the party, we went back inside to find our wives, dance a little, and head up to Slim's suite to eat, drink, and hang out. As we staggered and swayed our way to the room, we were all laughing and joking around like we had been friends for years.

As we entered the suite, Beck and I looked at each other, smiling like kids, with the anticipation of bubbling champagne, chill music, and good times floating around us. The suite was huge, complete with a full bar and hot tub. Dickman jumped on the room phone next to the bed and started ordering everything that sounded like the most expensive shit you could order at 3 am. I was pretty well drunk at this point and was craving a burger and more beer—always more beer—until the lights would go out. As we waited for the party to arrive, we would soon learn we were the only guests invited. While Slim was talking to the room service lady on the phone, his drunk wife was taking off her blouse, and stripped down to her Garanimals undies. Swear to God, she was wearing Garanimals undies. I should've known I was dealing with Juliette Lewis's drug-spun trailer-trash cousin from the Pacific Northwest.

Coming from old-school Mexican family values in word and practice, Beck was of the belief that exposing one's body was exposing vulnerability and liability of one's class and composure. Apart from family, she didn't preach it or expect other girls to adhere to her old-school values, but Beck wasn't going to bend for anyone or anything. She was always the same person, no wavering on weak moments to be liked or accepted by a person or group like the rest of us in that room. Stardom and celebrity didn't faze her. She saw it as seductively destructive. She isn't a downer, she just sees through the mirage of gold and lights to the core of a person's truth, their soul.

Becky is naturally high, clear, and alive, and always ready to drop a funny anecdote about her observations of people, places, or things. As conservative as Beck is in some ways, she is adventurous and was always up for my next crazy idea. She's all in, even though it was worlds away from what we both grew up knowing. She holds her beliefs close to her heart and doesn't feel the need to preach because she is so closely tied to her family that outside judgment influences can't sway her like most of us searching to be recognized, loved, and admired. She has all of that, including the healthy mindset of keeping family first, so she doesn't judge herself based on what outside people think as much as me and most others I've met. She is the best person I know.

So, here was this modest Mexican girl and her drunk, gold-crazy husband in a hotel suite with the boss and his wife inviting us to get naked in their hot tub! Tori unsnapped her bra to unleash her post-baby momma milk jugs that looked like two buoys splashing down onto the water, trolling for a young executive sitting next to her in his underwear...I knew I should've worn black underwear! I couldn't believe what I was witnessing. I looked at Beck to check her demeanor, trying to gauge how she was feeling. She had rolled up her white summer pants to just below her knee and had her feet in the water, sitting with her back leaning up against the wall looking down on Tori and me in the hot tub. Slim stripped down to his underwear, finishing up the order, and was ready to join in on the fun.

"Right on Chris! Come on Becky! Take it off and join the fun!"

Slim was trying to coax Beck to strip down and get in, and his drunk naked wife was joining in on Beck to try and persuade her to take off her clothes and jump in. Unmoved, Becky looked at me for my reaction. At this point, I had already stripped down to my underwear and jumped in the hot tub next to Tori, facing my wife still sitting on the edge elevated above the evil brew boiling below. I was oblivious. I wasn't thinking the bigger picture through. She shook her head at me with an uncomfortable smile and then looked at Tori and Slim to tell them no. It dawned on me at that moment, very late in the game, that they were swingers, and we were their prey!

Dickman was undeterred and set on getting my wife naked in the hot tub and then in bed to swing like monkeys in the city of sin. Dickman was not taking Becky's no as final. I smiled, knowing this guy had met his negotiating match, except Becky was better. Always the dealmaker that couldn't take no, it was his Achilles heel. Slim started to press her, standing there in his tighty whiteys. Beck was firmly standing her ground as he continued to try to get her to do what he was starting to demand.

Beck gave my boss a final, "No, Slim!"

He proceeded to pull his dick out in front of us, as if to close Becky with his package, but to no avail. With that crushing blow of sexual denial, Slim turned around to face the bed and fell face-first onto the bed and passed out. One second later, the doorbell rang. I tipped the guy $50 on Slim's AMEX Platinum card, grabbed two Heinekens, and got the fuck out of swinger hell. We walked down the hall in a silent daze, not speaking and feeling dirty and violated as the sun was cracking light on the red rock desert outside. It's so disconnected from the fundamentals of peace, happiness, and love. We crawled into bed, snuggling away the strange world we had just experienced and were so happy to be back in our simple little room in the cheap old section of the hotel. My relationship with Slim Dickman would never be the same.

2004: CO-FOUNDING WATERHOUSE FUNDING, REAL ESTATE CRASH

He snowed me just like all the "haters" I defended him against. I was so naive and blind. It wasn't enough that Dickman totally fucked me over with our selling of Scout to Fox, but for fuck's sake, $39,000...when he made north of $10 million!? What a dick. I'm okay with the founders and investors getting the king's share of the spoils, but seriously, I worked side by side with that little Napoleon wannabe, busting my ass for shit pay and the promise of a big payout. It's not like I was just another cog in the company's business. Slim brought me in as his wingman of salesmanship and integrity to re-recruit the biggest sports publishers that hated him. He needed someone like me. I was totally loyal, innocent, and the publishers could respect and relate to me. Slim was smart, surrounding himself with many good and talented people. He was smart that way. It was also calculated. He knew he could run his team with an iron fist and a smile.

I never negotiated my pay with him. He knew I was painfully shy about money and business-related topics, especially related to me. He could look into my eyes and know I admired him and struggled to discuss it with him, so he took as much of me as he could get, for as little as he could possibly give. I recruited and built the team of publishers that made up the value of the $58 million company. He made millions and built a mansion on one of the islands just off the shore of the Puget Sound. He gave me a stock check for $39,000. I was devastated. I paid off my used car and bought a new roof and central air for my little fixer-upper house.

When I returned home from my latest stint with Dickman, real estate was warming up. I grew up building houses with my grandpa, and he helped me understand real estate as well. Eventually, he found an opportunity for me and Beck to buy two lots in Shelter Cove. They didn't cost a lot, but they were the corner and adjacent lots with an ocean view from atop the cliffs. It was exciting and inspiring to own oceanfront property, to dream about building a home, and watching the sunset from the deck every night.

Needless to say, I had an affinity for the business and decided to partner up with a family friend and a fellow Silicon Valley veteran. Jeremy was the analytical yin to my outgoing social yang. We had very similar tech start-up experiences and the hunger and ambition to start our own company from scratch and to do things the right way, at least in our mind. We both had baby sisters with similar disabilities and similarly competitive dads who worked in education, and I think that made us more connected and more aware of people's differences.

We launched Waterhouse Funding and became the top producing firm in my home county, specializing in distressed properties. We would go the extra mile to work with homeowners to find their next place to live or pay bills out of their profits up front and even purchase RVs, cars, trailers, houses—you name it, we did it. It took extra work and creative thinking, but taking care of people stuck in a desperate spot comes back around. We didn't have to fuck people over. We were the only investor group doing things the way we did. We told people the hard truth from the start and helped them with a reasonable solution based on the situation they found themselves in. We helped a lot of people out of some pretty bad situations rendering them unable to make payments and putting them face-to-face with foreclosure.

I saw some crazy shit, including meth heads living like animals, a crazy Vietnam vet who took me out in his back forty in the hills, dressed in fatigues, acting weird, and questioning my intentions like he was going to kill me for trespassing. He ended up having a heart attack on me. No shit. I had to help him take his nitroglycerin pills from his top left fatigue pocket. I had another woman die of a heart attack the day before finalizing the Deed of Trust paperwork, sending the deal into a six-month probate with the courts, ultimately winning the decision because her kids told the judge that their mom trusted me. That's gold to me! She lived next door to Gary Burghoff, the guy who played Radar on *M*A*S*H*. Radar called me after we got the house through probate because a water line had broken and flooded his property. But the worst shit I saw is what the banks, in cahoots with the federal government, were doing with outrageous interest rates and penalties. The homeowners lapped it up without thinking twice because they needed, or wanted, the money. Either way, what the banks did is predatory lending, and that's why Bank of America and Chase had to settle multi-billion-dollar fraud charges after the real estate crash.

"Hey Babe! Just helped a couple save their credit from foreclosure! Everyone's happy!"

I walked through the door, excited and proud. Becky was in the front room, reading, and looked up, smiling.

"That's great, babe!"

"It's amazing. Many of these folks I'm working with are in foreclosure because of home loans with 20% interest and higher! I've seen despicable lending practices by the most reputable banks in America."

"Isn't that illegal?"

"Yeah. Banks are basically putting people in loans that they know they won't be able to repay on time. Foreclosure is part of the plan!"

Beck countered by holding all parties responsible for the mess. "Yeah, but people taking out the loan also sold their soul to get it. Slow and steady will return a generous bounty."

My mind drifted away from the topic; I was most excited about sharing my idea with her. "Babe, I want to start a record label. I like real estate. But I want to follow my passion."

"Sounds cool."

"I want to create a brand that speaks to the youth through music and film."

"How about a helicopter?" She smiled with encouragement. I picked her up and squeezed her with a loving smile of appreciation.

Real Estate Crash of 2008

I was very proud to be able to stand tall in my hometown after the great real estate crash, knowing my business partner and I treated people with respect and fair business practices and improved properties in my community. Win-win. I still run into some of those folks occasionally, and they smile with sincere thanks. One tweaker bitch I knew in high school sued, accusing us of predatory bullshit. She was in a heap of trouble, and we tried to help her, but she was a pathetic monster created by the welfare state and always demanded more, no matter who it hurt. But in most cases, we met homeowners who either bit off too much debt during the boom years or got caught with not enough cash to pay the bills. More often than not, there were sad situations like health issues, job loss, death, divorce, or alcohol/drug legal problems. We built the top business in my county and earned a reputation for honesty and doing good business for everyone involved.

During our run, my business partner suggested that it might be smart to rent out some of our properties. We were bombarded with broke people who qualified for federal funding called the Section 8 voucher program. In Section 8 housing, the federal government covers all rent cost that is above 30% of the renter's income. For example, if the renter has a monthly income of $2,000, Section 8 will cover all rent costs over $600, which is 30% of $2,000. What we ran into, though, was totally different; folks making $2,000 per month would have been a godsend. Our research on the statistics showed that most participants didn't end up paying their small portion of the rent, and they destroyed the property while they were at it. Call me racist, and I'll call you ignorant and oblivious to the glaring negative realities in our country's system. We reward criminal behavior, people, and a government who steal and extort hardworking people's money.

We decided to shit-can the whole subsidized renters' option because we felt that it was not in line with our philosophy. And we certainly weren't impressed with the way these falsely entitled people treated us; like we owed them the place for free or they would cause shit. It was a revealing experience to show how far our society had spiraled into a liberal black hole of unchecked spending, entitlement, and criminality... anti-Americanism. So, we decided to let someone else put up with people that are destroying our country through laziness, greed, and a total lack of empathy for themselves and those around them. It was a huge eye-opener and showed how fundamentally disconnected we are with the different groups in our country.

Michael Lewis's book and movie, *The Big Short*, starring Christian Bale, was a left-leaning but fairly accurate portrayal of how the housing bubble came to be and how a guy with Asperger's drilled down into the mortgages being sold and began to realize that the entire thing was overinflated and catastrophically overvalued. Wall Street created credit default swaps and some other creative mortgage products that allowed them to repackage shit into pretty bundles with a new rating, then sell them off to the next sucker who would hold it for a second and flip the shit down the street. In 2008 the entire Ponzi scheme crumbled. That's exactly what it was, a huge fraudulent investment scheme that had government approval. Of course, they denied it while Obama and the Left sold the story that Wall Street was the sinister antagonist of this dramatic real estate crash. The government was totally complicit, and the consumers were more than happy to snort up the coke-white lies of overvalued home equity by spending lavishly on new boats, parties, and swimming pools.

Just as our real estate business was finally hitting stride, we saw the tidal wave coming and proactively closed shop October of 2007 prior to the bubble bursting December 30, 2008. We paid off our investors with their agreed return, took a couple of hits with a few special circumstance properties (just land, or bad neighborhood) we couldn't sell in time, and took the loss personally. I walked away, literally penniless. We chose not to file for bankruptcy, unlike most of our competitors and affiliates in the real estate business. I'm proud of that. But the experience was surreal and a huge lesson.

One of the mistakes I made was investing most of my free cash into my next venture, King Duce Records and clothing brand. I was young, very confident coming off a few big business wins, and leveraged the cash on a start-up that faced huge risk in a regular economy, let alone the great recession that was about to flip my life upside down. Over the next couple of years, I watched those two industries get hit by the inevitable shock-wave tsunami that swept it all away. Brutal times.

I literally ended up schlepping copy machines for guys I went to high school with who never liked me. My drinking accelerated during this time as I tried to escape from problems I didn't know how to solve.

2005: MY DRUG OVERDOSE AWAKENING THAT IGNITED KING DUCE RECORDS

I thought of Becky and my sister, Nicole. I felt so bad for fucking up and dying. I was lost but not suicidal…at least I thought that then. I was about to die of an overdose. I couldn't believe it. I called Beck at 4am from the waiting room of the ER. Something was wrong and I was dying, I just wanted to hear her voice and have her bring me back from the edge, I told her I was sorry…. I was in and out, and then silence…. Everything went black.

What the fuck? The nurse and doctor came speed-walking back into my room after reading my EKG. I knew something was wrong. My heart was all over the place, and I was scared that it was gonna explode at any moment. Life passed before my eyes. The doctors and nurses all looked worried. It wasn't some paranoid kid trippin', I was actually in danger of the lights going out for good, and I didn't want to die. My body was not working right, like a computer flashing warning lights nearing a fatal shutdown. As I was apologizing to my family and unfinished dreams, the EKG went off with a high-pitched ring that sent a shock wave through me, reminding me that my heart was fighting to survive the punishment I dealt it earlier that night. I wasn't sure if it could withstand the plate of blow I snorted up like an insane Tony Montana in *Scarface*.

My breathing was getting shallower and faster; my body was on fire from the nitroglycerin they had just pumped me with to keep my artery open and my heart functioning. Suddenly, an imposing but safe hand grabbed my left arm. It was a big male nurse who looked like a guy's guy; I assumed a former Iraq vet medic or something... He looked me in the eyes and said, "Just relax, brother. It's going to be okay. You just need to relax!" Then he gave me a shot of Valium and flipped my gurney bed 45 degrees upside down. The blood, fire, Valium all rushed straight to my head and heart, and I started to go out...and I wasn't sure if I was passing out or dying.

At a follow-up visit, the cardiologist told me how lucky I truly was.

"You should be dead. Have you ever heard of Len Bias, the Celtics number one pick that overdosed on cocaine the night he signed? Well, his artery went into a spasm and eventually collapsed, and he died. Your same artery was spasming just like Len Bias's except your artery stayed open, and you lived. Your heart is a tank, and I attribute it to your genes and athletic conditioning growing up. If you do it again, though... you will die."

I was back in the hospital 90 days later from another overdose.

Something seriously had to change, or I was another sad statistic of something I didn't understand at the time. I was making more money than I had ever made; I had built a successful real estate and construction business, and was buying toys for the first time in my life. I had it all: the beautiful wife, the diving trips to Maui, the BMW, a bass boat, campers, travel. But something was missing, and I knew exactly what it was. It was getting louder every day and haunting me at night. Music. I spent so much time denying and avoiding my passion out of fear bordering on terror. I grew up quietly creating art, away from my jock redneck buddies who thought that shit was for "faggots," and I kept my dream of making a life of music to myself because sports was a wave I was riding straight into a full-ride scholarship. At that point, around 17, I decided my dream of hitting the road with a band would have to wait. I spent years regretting my decision. But over time, I realized I probably would've been dead by my second tour.

I was lucky to walk away from the crazy alcohol and drug-fueled party of college football that created lots of casualties. But something told me that I would not have been able to moderate my full-throttle personality around the intensity and high of rock and roll every night.

After my Seattle band, I continued recording my songs on a Korg mixer in my home office. I was dedicated to learning and appreciating the depth of what it takes to compose and record a great song from start to finish. It's technical and time-consuming. My ear knew enough at that point to know the difference between good engineering and my rough-cut conceptual work. I needed to find a pro. But after leaving Seattle and my band, it seemed almost untouchable and too far out from my domestic life of a wife and a mortgage and a business. After my overdose, I sat in bed for three days recovering and reading Johnny Cash's biography. I knew what I had to do next; otherwise, I was dead. It may sound dramatic to many readers, but music and my creative fire had been forced down inside me, building pressure until explosion. King Duce was born from the ashes of where I had been and where I wanted to go from now on. The next stage of my musical life journey was about to begin.

It wasn't a few months before the devil himself rang with my next opportunity. With King Duce in its infancy, I was off to Silicon Valley to do the dance one last time...or so I thought.

SILICON VALLEY
SLEESTACKS & METRO MAN

"You can be unethical and still legal;
that's the way I live my life."
- Mark Zuckerberg, co-founder/CEO
Facebook, May 2019 *Vanity Fair* **Interview**

Despite my resentment from my last experience, I found myself back with Dickman on yet another Internet start-up adventure. This time we built out zazzle.com and artzprojekt.com. He convinced me that this time would be different. It wasn't. Today I view it as one of the great lessons in my life. I choose wisdom over bitterness and resentment…most of the time. I've learned that letting go and moving forward in a positive direction pays and feels better.

Slim Dickman was so neurotic and almost robotic in a creepy way. He had beady and piercing eyes that could sense his prey's weaknesses and desires, almost as if he was a fucking cyborg, a reptilian. He was extremely analytical, like most guys in high tech, even on the sales side. And like most tech geeks, he was socially awkward. Knowing what I know now about autism and similar brain styles, I wouldn't be surprised if he was operating from a brain that struggled with social and people cues. Although crazy, in some weird way, he looked after me and gave me opportunities that I may not otherwise have had. And in a world of boring, Slim Dickman sold an adventure that could be very exciting, especially as low and desperate as I was. But this time, he was withholding key information about his character defects and flawed business strategy that would result in lots of unnecessary damage. I was in dire financial straits, so it wouldn't have mattered anyhow. I learned critical life lessons that made me better. It made me look in the mirror. At the end of the day, it was simply time for the student to leave the sick confines of the mentor and build my own dream.

How we choose to perceive our daily challenges determines the outcome. We choose. I chose to get out of my comfort zone and immerse myself into a world of brilliant minds creating innovative companies but void of sincere human emotion due to the unrealistic expectations of building a business and culture in light speed. No time to assimilate organically. No one has time to be real. It's a liability, and it fucked me up. The culture is so intense and seductive that it envelopes your soul and places it in a modern prison of glass, steel, dorky art, free food, and foosball to mask the fact that we are spending our life force working ourselves to death to develop another technology platform or app that has as much long term significance as the people making it...and they know it.

The workaholic fragmented family reality that is Silicon Valley and the start-up culture overcompensates their neurotic, around-the-clock quest to feel significant in a sea of cogs turning cranks in a modern industrial revolution factory. But instead of spitting out plumes of noxious smoke and pollution, Silicon Valley culture spits out a virtual reality of healthy and balanced people who profess to care about the earth and humanity. Coming from a blue-collar lumber town in NorCal, I was raised by educated and adventurous parents who worked hard but dedicated their time to their *children* and teaching us about real caring, for our bodies, for the environment, and for each other. They weren't making the typical Silicon Valley executives' plastic comment of "I care about everything so much…but I never really see my kids or the great outdoors that is just outside my office door." My parents taught us healthy from day one, and they actually enjoyed spending time with us. Just be honest about what you truly care about with action. Kids and adults all hate empty promises.

I laugh at the failed state of manhood in this androgynous PC world we live in today. I'm serious. Men, especially white men, have been beaten over the head with a feminist sledgehammer and castrated by the PC legion of minorities and pissed-off man-hating Far-Left, lesbians, and homosexuals. The bottom line, the Far-Left have done a really good job of selling a bag of shit to the masses that men, white men in particular, are enemies of the state. Serious?

When did it become customary for white men to apologize before entering a room? Shut the fuck up, you passive-aggressive effeminate boys and bitches who worship at the altar of the liberal all-women show *The View* and MSNBC's Rachel Maddow. Being a man is reserved for males that have heart and balls when times get tough. You want me to apologize that my dad and grandpa and ancestors risked their lives serving and defending this country? They stand up for their friends and family. And they don't lie to your face with a plastic smile and condemn people for their love and defense of American values.

This is the era of the smartphone idiot, or as I call them, the tune-out generation. I'm burned out on suburban white guys who are probably the most fucked-up pussies I've ever seen in my life. Nothing compares to watching someone you love get sucked into the vortex of the never-ending wants and irrationally selfish demands by a liberal Bay Area girl who will never be satisfied because she lives in a constant state of fear and narcissism masked as charity and everything else except her husband's needs. The modern family in suburbia is like a praying mantis where the man is only a sperm and money provider, forced to be vigilantly self-deprecating, and constantly on the go, striving to meet up to his wife's unrelenting to-do and I-want lists of insecurities and the inability to stand alone on her own merits.

I see too often, in real life and constantly portrayed in the media, men being subjected to their wife's ridicule and humiliation for screwing things up *again* in front of the kids and friends and in-laws. So, the wife becomes the brilliant one, and the guy gets stuck looking like the Sonny and Cher version of the dumb joke. It's not funny what is happening with the way media and liberal attitudes have diminished the value of a man and what a man stood for: hard work, integrity, willing to help a friend in need, tough when times are tough, and protects his family with his life.

That picture of a man has been replaced with a picture of Mark Zuckerberg. This guy is the embodiment of the modern man. They constantly talk about diversity to prove their open-mindedness to culture and enlightened thinking and the perception of a globally conscious man. Mark Zuckerberg is a spoiled, self-serving, anti-American elitist. He's the second coming of Lucifer's son George Soros.

Yahoo's former CEO, Marissa Mayer, is the cultural symbol of what I'm talking about. A workaholic freak who tells mothers that they can't work from home, while she can afford to pay nannies, teachers, stylists, chefs, and a fucking butler with some of her compensation package upwards of $50 million. Can someone remind me what she actually did to add value at Yahoo? Her play-it-safe, over-diversified, and risk-averse moves were fear-based and unimaginative. Was it her big, bold talk and prepackaged fashion? I'm going to give her a D- as a working mother simply because of how out of touch she is to tell hardworking mothers that they need to do it her way, which is to hand your baby off to a nanny and work all the time. Her failed attitude, strategy, and leadership are a direct result of the hyper selfish culture that breeds "stars" like Marissa. She's talented, but like many people who jump straight from elite schools to the high-tech start-up scene, they miss some world experience that would enable them to understand people, particularly related to racial and socioeconomic differences and truths they conveniently avoided.

These white geek CEOs are talking about equality and sensitivity like Silicon Valley is an exclusively white man's club. It's the exact opposite. Silicon Valley and the high-tech start-up environment are the most open playing field for immigrants and minorities in the history of mankind. *Anyone*, right now, can go there with a dream, a smartphone, and a crazy work ethic, and they can make it happen. For some reason, white CEOs in the Valley speak to the opposite of that. I believe it's because most grew up in a pampered, racially exclusive elite environment and don't know a fucking thing about the reality of race in the real world. I do because I lived it. Some pretend to care and feel guilty about the inequity of race in rhetoric, but their actions are all white-bread bullshit.

Most kids who grew up in Palo Alto never even crossed the highway to hang out in the predominantly black neighborhoods of East Palo Alto (EPA). One of my best friends and Fresno State football teammate, Dee Edwards, was born and raised there and was a straight hardcore, gang-affiliated black kid. We would joke about the divide between EPA and the Stanford Palo Alto most people imagine. So, it made me shake my head at these collectively frustrating and diametrically opposed principles and actions swirling around my mind all the time while I was building the next soon-to-be-obsolete technology, once again. It was getting very fucking old and monotonous.

Now, I'm not saying the people working in the Silicon Valley tech scene are inherently delusional or bad. Many are very intelligent, driven, and talented people who want to build something that hasn't been done before. It's a place that attracts dreamers, pioneers, entrepreneurs, but also some greedy fucking vultures. There are winners and losers. That's what I love about it. It's clear about who wins and who loses. Anyone who has ever worked in that world knows how fast success and failure can happen. It creates a sense of urgency, coke highs and lows, and zero security. That's something the middle-class world I came from does not understand.

Silicon Valley is too fast and all-consuming for family, relationships, and raising kids. You have to "lean in" 24/7 to keep up and be successful. And, like anything, when a machine and people live and operate in the red for too long, they crash and burn. So, they mask the frantic neurotic days with a façade showing the world how "healthy" they are; how small their carbon footprint is, protesting any and all social and environmental issue whether they truly understand them or not, as they sit in traffic for hours on Highway 101 and go home to a wood- and steel-built home. They talk incessantly about it, trying to one-up their friends about how NOT prejudice they are, and how much they care about diversity. As Tucker Carlson notes in his book *Ship of Fools*, "The marriage of market capitalism to progressive social values may be the most destructive combination in American economic history" (pg 37). Hypocrisy is too kind of a word for what I witnessed. I was fried from the inside out and couldn't take another day of fake toxic smiles and syrupy valley dialect that is reminiscent of the chick from *Romper Room*. Fake.

I saw good people like me get sucked into the vortex of the Silicon Valley machine. I fought with everything I had left to free myself of the soul-sucking tether of my inflated salary and stock options. After crashing my BMW blacked-out drunk in Dublin on the East Bay due to too many tequila shots with my graphic artist buddy D Strong, I got locked up in Santa Rita Jail near Oakland and missed a meeting with a client who had flown in from the East Coast to meet with my company and me. It was the beginning of the end.

I'll never forget the day I jumped in my Chevy Duramax Diesel ranch truck, the only one in the hybrid-dominated parking lot, and drove past the Tesla car company just down the street in its R&D infancy. I cracked a beer and jumped onto Northbound 101 and hit the Embarcadero Bridge with the cool ocean air filling up the cab of my truck and revitalizing my outlook. I remember the feeling of exhilarating freedom that I can't begin to describe. I reached the peak of the game. I crossed the bridge and headed on to a new adventure. I began by slowing down long enough to get to know myself for once and not the chameleon of faces I had to pretend to be to please people I didn't even care about. I had my own dreams that I needed to get back to. I left Silicon Valley with a middle finger to my old office building and some sincere thanks for the crazy, amazing experience. I was on to the next chapter.

6

KING DUCE RECORDS

MUSIC, MURDER, & THE GREAT RECESSION

King Duce Records – Music, Murder, & The Great Recession

STARTING KING
DUCE RECORDS

K evin opened the door of his apartment in Chico and greeted me with a big, welcoming smile.

"Hey Pat'na! Our Raiders just got the first pick in the draft! April is gonna bring us a black quarterback that's gonna be an all-pro!" Ironically, Kevin was talking about NFL bust JaMarcus Russell, a prototype giant black quarterback who promptly flopped and returned to living half-ass off his ridiculous talent and signing bonus. The dude was hella lazy and gifted…entitled.

"Right On! Gannon's been doing his thing, but his time is up. It's like watching Roger Staubach with less personality." Duce put his hands up to his mouth in mock disbelief, laughing at the cut I just hit Gannon with. Turns out Gannon's a really great guy.

"So, what's up Rock? Whad'ja wanna talk about?"

"Real Estate has been good to me the last couple years. I finally got caught up after Seattle and the Internet crash. I'm ready to start my record label."

"Record label?! Seriously?!"

I could tell Kevin wanted to believe me but was like a little kid hoping he wasn't going to get his hopes shot down.

"Just like I always said, Kev. I was going to start a record label someday. I've spent the last few years recording my own music, and now I want to step into the big leagues and launch a record label that produces world-class rap, rock, and reggae. But I want to start with rap. You know what sound and artists we need to recruit. Who should we sign first?"

"You're serious! Okay, okay...I feel you, Rock. Damn... you ain't playin'. You need to get Keak da Sneak. Yeah, Lil' Willie runs with him. I met him at a party about a year ago in Chico. He's cool. And his music is underground and hot."

"Let's set up a meeting right away!"

"You're serious..."

"I'm deadly serious. Kev. This is what we dreamed about when we were at the basketball courts drinking 40s and talking about making it big. This is our dream!"

With that, Kev was dialing his cell phone.

"Lil' Willie! It's Duce. Yeah, look, Rockwell is starting a record label. For Real. Damn, nigga! Be quiet! Rockwell wants to sign Keak da Sneak. What?! Nah, I ain't playin' witcha! Set up a meeting right away in Sac and hit me back! Yeah, I know. We gotchu! Just get shit set up with Sneak. Yeah, I'll be there, too. Make sure he knows Rock is real fam. I'll tell him...just lock a meeting!"

He hung up the phone with authority, knowing he had just closed a big deal. His ivory-white smile said everything I needed to know.

"It's good. Lil' Willie said he would set it up and let me know. Yeah, it's good!"

"Perfect! Dude, we'll be able to produce music like underground rap and heavy rock like Pantera at the same time as we're smoking a joint to some cool-ass reggae tracks. We'll build a following of people who share our love of the music and clothing that goes with it. This is global."

"It's gonna be big," Kevin said with a growing excitement and realization that this was actually happening. Duce rubbed his hands together like he did whenever he was contemplating something exciting. We shook hands and hugged to celebrate the forming of the label.

The very next day, we were in Sac to meet up with the guys. We were on time at 8 pm.

"Willie said they on they way up from Modesto."

"Modesto?! Damn!" I said incredulously. Little did I know how many nights I was going to be waiting hours for rap artists to show up on "hip hop" time. Growing up respecting other people's time was an important part of building my reputation and character. Funny how that is seen as the opposite value by insecure people using time to control their situation, to somehow enhance their value. I found it childish, foolish, and a pure waste of time and money. That would be like me showing up to the lumber yard at 8 am when we started at six. That concept is lost in a culture that doesn't value hard work or other people's time. That's a deeper symptom to a deeper problem.

"They should be here in about an hour. Let's just lay back," Duce assured me.

"Yeah, come on!" We went straight to the bar. "Two Jack and Cokes and a Coors."

"You bet. Coming right up," the bartender responded and looked at us like we were somebody. We could sense it and knew things were gonna change fast. And we were absolutely ready for all of it.

Two hours later, Duce answered his cell phone, slightly frustrated.

"Yeah, okay. They're right around the corner."

Keak da Sneak and G Will walk in loaded and smiling, soaking in the attention of the customers who were trying to figure out who the two obvious rap stars were. There were three young suburban white girls attending Sac State that recognized Keak da Sneak and asked for autographs and pictures as they neared our outside patio table in the cool winter night. Keak da Sneak was becoming a nationally recognized rap artist and leader of the Hyphy Movement.

"Hey Duce, this is Sneak."

Keak da Sneak and Duce slap hands and hug, familiar from the party a year ago.

"My homie… Wut it do?" he said in his trademark raspy voice and twitchy demeanor. He was an Oakland cat that came up in South Alabama with his mom, a soul and funk radio DJ who introduced him to the music and the gypsy life of a musician.

"You know, just trying to get this record label off the ground. This is my man, Chris Rockwell. He's real family."

Sneak was instinctively studying my whiteness and listening to Duce and G Will put their reputation on me. But I could tell he still needed convincing. He was shifty by nature and seemed kinda sketchy on me.

"What's up Chris. Good to meet you, man. G Will says you want to start a record label?"

"Hey man. Cool to meet you, too. Yeah, I need someone that can establish our brand in the rap world. Duce says you're the man."

"Thanks for the love. I try to hold the Bay and Sac down, yadamean?"

A cute young waitress excitedly recognized Keak da Sneak and told the other girls working there before she approached the table. They all showed up, readying themselves and their cameras for their fifteen seconds of fame, checking their overdone makeup and fake tits, with big smiles. These kinds of girls did everything they did for this exact moment. It was almost a choreographed recital for groupie bitches.

"Have you decided what you'd like to drink?"

"Yeah, I'll start with you and then have a shot of Henny and a Miller."

"Sure! I get off at 11."

"Yeah, gimme the same. Duce, you want the same?" said Will.

"Yeah."

"I'll have a Jack and Coke," I said. I was coming out of negotiating complex multimillion-dollar deals in the Internet start-up world, but this would prove to be my most challenging business deal ever.

"So, G Will says you played college football, Rockwell?" Sneak uncharacteristically asked a question. He wasn't much for conversation because of his self-medicating Molotov cocktail of coke, alcohol, blunts, and cigarettes. But when it came to music, he was spot on.

"Yeah, back in the day. I had a good time. It gave me the foundation to build businesses from scratch and now my dream of a record label. I have the plan and team to create a platform that can give a brand and its artists a stage that can reach millions of hungry music fans."

"Damn. You got a plan!" Looking and smiling at Duce, he said, "Let's finish our drinks and go to my Hummer to check out my new track."

Keak Da Sneak was surprised but enthusiastic because he could sense I was real. We went out to his black Hummer parked out front. Kev and I got in the back seat, while Sneak and G Will got in the front, started up the CD player, and lit up a blunt. The music started, and the blunt was passed around while we all bobbed to Sneak's, "That's My Word." Kevin and I looked at each other, knowing Keak da Sneak was the perfect fit for the label. We all felt it and started high-fiving and shaking hands during the song as if to consummate a deal. We were on our way. At that euphoric moment, I had no idea how much would be sacrificed for my dream.

LAST NIGHT WITH MY BEST FRIEND

A few nights later, I was hanging out at Kevin's apartment for a college football bowl game. There were a couple of other high school friends there chillin' and smoking a blunt. The game was good, and the guys were debating the usual stuff.

"That cornerback is weak!" M shouted. M, as we called him, had quick street smarts, humor, a big mouth, and no fear to back it up. He was a small Native American from the local Maidu tribe. He was loyal and would always be there for us when shit got bad. I don't know many guys like that.

I chimed in, "Hella slow!"

"Man! I would love to put the pads back on." Duce was excited and smiling and rubbing his hands together, feeling the fire to play again.

"It would be fun for a minute. But that shit would cause a lot of fucking pain!"

"Rockwell, you used to break fools off." M jumped in, recalling days we played together in high school. M was a little defensive back assassin that would smash unsuspecting receivers when he couldn't have been but 5'5" and a hundred pounds. But that dude had a killer instinct; he was our secret weapon. M represented his friends and family with a deep sense of honor, and Duce and I could always rely on him for it.

"Duce hit harder than me."

I remember the first time I had to go against him when I was a freshman. Kev and I had to go toe to toe. I remember my head hurting like I had just been hit by Lester Hayes, the famous Raider DB from John Madden's 1976 Superbowl champs.

"Kev, you helped make me tough and able to play against the big boys like NFL Hall of Fame running back, Marshall Faulk," I said, trying to get the attention off myself.

There was another guy there; I didn't know him. He was mostly quiet because he was stoned out of his mind, but all of a sudden, he had something to say, "Man, that running back is good. I don't know what you niggas is thankin'. My cousin Lil B ran with him."

Duce countered, "That don't mean that motherfucka's any good, nigga! Matter fact, yo cousin should be ashamed for running with this sorry-ass nigga! Slow niggas run with slow niggas!"

Everybody laughed, except for the black stoner.

"Whatchu laughing at M?! You fo' foot midget!"

"At least I don't live with my mom." M dealt the final blow to this dude.

The game ended, and after M and the black stoner left, me and Duce hung out, drank, smoked blunts, and told old stories all night. We were having such a good time that I didn't care if I missed my flight to Seattle in the morning to meet with my media mentor Patrick Crumb to get his input and guidance on this new endeavor.

I woke up on Kev's couch and staggered in the dark, almost stepping on some big black guy and his girl sleeping on the floor, finally making it to the bathroom down the hall. I peeked into Kevin's room to say goodbye. Not sure why I decided to wake him up to say goodbye and give him a hug, I just remember I tapped his shoulder and he woke up wearily but immediately. He was relieved when he realized it was me and gave me a big smile. We shook hands and hugged, promising each other that our record label was happening, and we were going to set out to start linking the right people up to the dream. We were stoked. I told him I loved him, and he smiled big and told me he loved me too. It would be the last time I would see him.

DUCE IS GUNNED DOWN - *February 25, 2006*

"Chris! Chris! It's okay...it's okay...it's just a bad dream." Becky gently wrestled me free from the claws of my nightmare. It had been a long day of travel and little sleep the days prior due to all the excitement surrounding the new record label we were launching. We were staying at our friend Larry's place in the Belltown district of Downtown Seattle. It was a small but very cool single-bedroom townhouse complete with a fireplace, modern colors and design, and a view of the Puget Sound. Beck hadn't been back to the Emerald City since we left after the great Internet crash of 2001. We met and worked with Larry at Rivals and Scout. He has a quiet, intelligent, and friendly way about him. He has an MBA in Finance from Pepperdine and is a native of Seattle by way of Canada. He is a diehard University of Washington Huskie's football fan and college alum. He takes UDub football very seriously. It's a religion to him, as with many of the native Scandinavians who grew up revering the university for generations.

After getting ready for the day, I decided to join Larry for a morning stroll down to the corner café for some fresh baked scones and coffee. Larry doesn't drink coffee. But like most intellectual dot-com folks, he works out and lives a life focusing on his work and charity. Larry has a kind heart and a skilled business mind that I value. He is a trusted, lifelong friend and business partner.

As we were leaving his townhouse and waiting for the elevator to take us down the six stories, I decided to check my voicemail. I was surprised to see that I had 12 messages. After a message from my real estate business partner about a deal we were closing, I got the voicemail that would change the course of my life. It was my dad saying in a shaky but certain tone, "Chris, Kevin Kimble is dead. I'm so sorry to have to tell you this." I remember listening to it as I was entering the elevator.

"Ahhhh…FUCK! FUCK! FUCK! Oh my God, Kevin's dead. I don't fucking believe this!" The elevator door closed on us, trapping me with the claustrophobic news I had just been dealt.

We made our way back to the house in a haze of disbelief, I broke the news to Becky, and we shared the moment. I was in total shock, and Becky was crying and hugging me.

"I'm so sorry, babe."

"I'm good." I was trying desperately to brush off the reality of what happened. "I'm numb right now. I can't believe it. Fuck! Why Kev?!"

"You guys had something that will never die." She grabbed my face to convince me that it will be okay.

"I love you, Beck. Until the day I die."

"That's gonna be a while, Bubba. We have a lot of life to live. And we'll continue to live passionately. Every day is a blessing."

Becky hugged me tightly to provide extra comfort from the tragedy. My life changed forever that day. That's when I realized that we were all playing for keeps, whether we knew it or not. My test was just beginning.

DUCE'S FUNERAL

I was at Duce's funeral and sitting by my side was his younger cousin G Will who had just introduced us to Keak da Sneak a few weeks earlier. I'd known Will since he was about five years old. Even back then, Will spouted any and all thoughts that entered his mind. But this day, he was motionless, completely devastated, and out of his mind. We were sitting in the front row with the rest of the stunned pallbearers after carrying Kevin's coffin out to the front of the packed church. My mind was drifting in and out of reality as I settled on a hollow stare at the new tattoo on the back of Will's hand in honor of Duce. Just two days before Kev was gunned down, we were hanging out at his place in Chico, watching football, playing dominos, laughing, and talking about the old days—like playing basketball in Southside, smashing fools on the football field, and going to the Run-D.M.C./Beastie Boys concert.

On our last night together, every discussion somehow made its way back to the focal point of our life, music, and our new record label. It seemed crazy that just weeks earlier, Duce had brought in G Will and Keak da Sneak. Will was a promising young rapper too; he joined the label. G Will brought in Lace Leno and the Unda Turf Family, as well as some other young street-tested rappers. After a couple hang-out sessions, Sneak was down with our passion and agreed to sign a record deal with our yet-to-be-named label. Everyone was hyped about the possibilities. I remember Kev smiling and rubbing his hands together like we had just discovered the secret formula. "It's gonna be real big, Rock!"

Earlier, me and Kevin's big brother, Kelly, were in the back room with the other pallbearers and close family. It was the same room where I, Kevin, and the other groomsmen dressed and toasted drinks before my wedding ceremony. It was totally different this time. People were talking quietly and whimpering with the unbelievable loss of their hope and future. They lost the true patriarch, heart and soul of the family with the single pull of a trigger down the street from where he grew up in South Side.

"Rockwell, why did they have to take Duce? Why, Rockwell? I should have been there to protect him!" lamented Kelly.

I hugged Kelly, and he broke down. "I'm sorry, Kelly."

"He loved you, Rockwell. Don't stop doing what you doing. Duce would want you to go on. He'd be saying, we doing it big! We doing it real big! He believed in you, Rockwell."

I walked up to Kevin's mom, Judy. She was sitting down and motionless. I stood before her and let her recognize me through her days of tears and hopelessness. I felt her look to me for an answer she knew I couldn't give—that everything is going to be alright.

"Oh, Chris. Why did they have to take my baby? Why?" Kev's mother was sobbing and broken.

"I'm sorry, Judy. I love you guys. I'm so sorry."

I moved over to Big Marty, Kevin's uncle, and the patriarch of Kevin's family. Marty was a reformed OG trying to stay straight, working construction and raising a son who was playing college football for Utah. I discovered a lot of fucked-up hidden shit after Kevin's death that would turn my world and perspective upside down and inside out. I had to write this book just to try and make sense of all the bullshit and lies we as a society of black and white live and pretend is reality. It all unravels and shows its ugly fucking truth the moment there is a murder.

Big Marty hugged me. "We love you, Rockwell. Duce loved you very much. You must go on without him. Don't stop. We know you can do it. We hurtin' right now, but we must press on. Duce is looking down on us, telling us to do it big. You feel me? He's sitting up there helping you, Rockwell. Just let it happen."

Then I approached Kevin's grandmother, dressed with pride despite being in a wheelchair. I've never met a woman with more beauty and grace.

"You gave so much to Kevin and our family. Kevin was a special child. He was a sensitive child with a smile that could capture the sunshine." She paused to reflect on his smile. "He loved you...we love you!" Kevin's grandma gripped my hand with a smile and passion that is from a life of struggle growing up as a black woman in the segregated South back before Martin Luther King was marching at Montgomery. She had experienced real racism and lynchings. She was like a Nubian Queen of wisdom and grace. She was different. She was a distinguished older woman with perfect ebony skin. She dressed like royalty and finished her look with perfectly placed gray hair. Just classy. She rarely spoke; she had no need to. Her presence moved the air in the room like the force of a Caribbean breeze that could lift your spirit and find hope when there was none to see. Her deep faith gave her a strength that I saw in her ebony eyes.

"I love you, too," I told her. She looked me in the eyes and grabbed my face lovingly. Then we cried together and hugged.

Not long after Kevin died, I reexperienced Kevin's death with her on her death bed. She was struggling to breathe; she could no longer speak due to a stroke, and I held her hand and talked to her, thanked her, and told her that everything was okay. She tried to talk, and I told her she didn't need to talk because I knew what she was saying with her eyes. Her aura and presence were from another world. We both started to cry, and she squeezed my hand. I felt a sense of peace and joy knowing her struggle on this earth was almost over, and she was finally able to find peace. It was an experience that has never left me. Miss Johnson is always with me. Kevin and his grandma were the same person in so many ways, especially in spirit. Good, beautiful, dynamic, loving spirits. I learned so much from them.

DRINKING WITH BLACK & THE HIT MAN

Have you ever had a hit man buy you a drink out of respect? I have. It was a fucking crazy mind twisting night of realizations about a dark cold world of death and deception that blew my mind like a Glock pistol point blank to the side of my head. After Duce was killed, I wanted to meet up with his friend 'Black', the guy I almost stepped on the last night I stayed at Kevin's place on the couch. Apparently Black had just got out of prison and he was sleeping on the floor with his girlfriend next to the couch I was passed out on. I wanted to get the true story of how things went down the night Kevin was murdered. The gossip in my hometown, where the murder happened, was buzzing with hearsay and dirty rumors that people we grew up with had harbored the killer. I learned the power of haters during this experience. Weak humans.

Black was meeting me at Tres Hombres, a nice Mexican restaurant and bar literally across the street from the Chico State campus. Needless to say, it made for a nice place for good food, scenery, and optimism from the energy of all the young college kids, although arrogant, tenured professors and environmentally conscious elitism is spewed at every other booth. The tables with the college kids ordering beers and eating chips and salsa for dinner preferred to keep their discussions to girls and what weed strain was better than "Girl Scout Cookies." The contrast made for good laughs while I waited for fish tacos and a refill of my water that never came. Must be something about conservation or a lame excuse to cut down on service and expenses. Either way, it was kind of an odd place for me to be hanging with a black gangster for drinks, but that was the contrast I lived. It's where I felt normal, at constant odds with the clashing behaviors and ideologies I grew up observing.

I was sitting at the center of the bar that runs nearly the length of the south wall, made of old brick and adorned with glass shelves and metal brackets for strength and appearance with equal balance in purpose and style. My eye always looks straight to the top right with everything, then darts around to consume the rest. In this case, it was a collage of alcohol brands and colors of whiskey and tequila of every kind. Believe me, folks, there is a major difference with the qualities, flavors and highs of tequila. Drinking Jose Cuervo Gold is like drinking Mexican piss on a hot day in TJ. It's evil shit going down and coming up. I fucking hated tequila for two decades from my indoctrination to what I would call a Mexican Golden Shower. It feels about that demeaning and disgusting—and stupid funny, if the hangover wasn't so fucked up, especially on a blazing hot summer morning when the temperature hits 100 degrees before noon.

As my wandering mind circled back to the young bartender standing in front of me, I smiled and ordered a top shelf tequila and quickly slammed the double shot without a sip of my Modelo Negro and lime. I'm not a brand loyalist or snob. I build brands, so I prefer exploring new ideas that intrigue me. What I care about is quality and sensations that please me. It doesn't matter if it's music, food, people, places, or ideas. To me it's all good if it's all good. I started to really think about it as the warmth of the tequila moved outward from my core, the loss of my best friend keeping my mind in a haze, but laser-focused now on life and purpose.

Life is short, but most people are scared shitless to lose what they think they own. News flash—we own nothing. It's an illusion and an excuse to live for self and justify weak performance. Running in a circle and going nowhere while watching ESPN has become the modern man's vicarious warrior outlet of passive existence. It's hard to watch business professionals and middle America slobs that walk around the arenas with their families attending sporting events like they're the Griswold's from National Lampoon's cult classic movie *Vacation*. Goofy suburban lemmings with fan-glazed eyes, a silly smile, and an unquenchable greed for vicarious thrills. They pay homage to their sports team through illogical spending on foam fingers, jerseys, and shitty snack bar food sold at exorbitant prices. The fans are oblivious since they are at the altar of their gods, and they are paying a small penance for the right to be in the church of gladiators. Be very fucking careful what you idolize.

My focus snapped back to the big screen above the bar with some scantily clad chick dancing in the stands, not even sure what sport I was watching. It's always been that way since I was a kid. I was always more interested in the production of the sporting event than the play by play of a game. I was interested in how the whole thing was put together to attract thousands of paying fans and millions of viewers. Even when I played college football, I would catch myself drifting off into the crowd, the big screen replays, or sideline dynamics as I was standing at the center of a stadium catching my breath before the next play in front of seventy thousand screaming fans.

"What's up, Rock!"

Black approached my left shoulder, and I stood up to hug him. We both looked a little haggard from Kevin's murder and its aftermath. I just wanted to get to the truth, and I knew Black would tell me, despite people telling me that he was somehow accountable for his death because he was with Duce that night. I felt differently because of how Kevin had talked about Black as family. I wasn't in the mood to smile or have a good time catching up or reminiscing about old times. I wanted some answers, so we got down to business.

"Hey, Black, good to see you. So, what the fuck happened? I'm hearing lots of mixed information and some disturbing stories of some people we know who harbored the killer. Just tell me what happened."

Black above anyone, had taken the most heat for Kevin's murder for a couple reasons. First, he was a known gangster from Compton and a transplant from Africa where his father was a soldier and political leader. Many people thought his erratic behavior caused a cloud of accidents and incidents that showed a trend for someone who was indoctrinated into violence. Black told me that violence in America is like child's play compared to the viciousness of what he witnessed growing up in Africa.

"Rock, they talkin' like I had something to do with it, man. Rock, you gotta believe me! Duce was my guy! He put me up at his place and picked me up from prison when I got out. I loved Duce, Rock! I can't believe he's gone. And people think I had something to do with it. Fuck, man! You gotta believe, Rock; I loved Duce like my big brother; you know that!"

"I believe you."

Talking about Kevin's death made me order four shots of Patron Silver and two beers for us. We were both shedding tears and lost in our own tragedy, oblivious to the fact that the crowd was darting looks at us, trying to figure out who in the hell these two big imposing guys were at the bar. With each shot, we were starting to smile a little more and even started laughing about some old stories of Kev. We had discussed the details of the night Kevin was killed, and I felt satisfied with it, so we decided to drink to Duce and celebrate him.

Before long, we were becoming too loud for the chill scene, so we headed over to The Normal Street Bar, a stand-up, old-school bar with enough room to order and start drinking. Before we could order our first drink, Black introduced me to Sam, an old, pock-faced, overweight, heavy breathing black dude with graying eyes like dying people have. He was polite and had a smooth charm to him that relaxed me despite his look. By this point, I was feeling pretty drunk. Sam left momentarily and returned with drinks for all of us.

"Mr. Rockwell, it's a pleasure to meet you. He shook my hand with kind respect. Black tells me you and Duce were best friends. I'm sorry for your loss. He was a good man and a brother."

And with that, he raised his drink in a ghetto toast to death.

"To Duce. May he rest in peace."

We crashed our whiskey glasses together with a burst of energy from our united bond in the tradition of drinking in honor of a fallen friend. We couldn't tip 40s, even though I knew Kev would be laughing at me for thinking about it, just because it was such a fucking gangster cliché to honor the dead. Kevin was frugal, almost a black Jew if I didn't know better. Serious. He could stretch a dollar or create a dollar out of wit and charm. And he was confident and bold enough that people simply believed. He had a similar charisma that reminds me of Magic Johnson, the legendary Los Angeles Lakers forward. Both had big white smiles and an encouraging but demanding expectation that was unshakable.

I didn't know the connection to Kev and this guy Sam, but Kevin seemed to know everyone in every city we would travel to. I remember we were in San Diego for a trip one time and Kev ran into at least three people he knew. It seemed like everyone loved Kevin, and the few that didn't—apparently really didn't.

Glass shattered on the floor next to us from the waitress getting bumped by "O Danny Boy', a fellow drunk Irishman who looked at us with an embarrassed goofy smile, as if to say, 'Sorry fellas, I'm just a harmless drunk looking for a good time.' His personality endeared him to us. We gave him a look of "all good, brother, we got you; enjoy making a total ass of yourself tonight."

Sam quietly excused himself at that moment of distraction to make his move to the restroom and refill his drink. The jukebox kicked back on with "Strutter," a 70s rock classic from Kiss. I love that testosterone-fueled anthem of young lust and invincibility. I was living it, and I figured it would be my theme song for the night. And I dug the idea that Black seemed to like rock music. Most black guys who are into rap music secretly love heavy rock songs. The energy and beats are the same.

I was starting to feel good about the night and was ready to rip it up, when Black dropped a bombshell on me with a quiet whisper to my ear among the crowded noise.

"Hey, Rock, Sam's a killer for hire. If you ever need someone handled, just let me know, and he'll take care of it for basically nothing. He usually charges around five grand, but he liked Duce."

My guts sank and everything changed color and sound into splintering pain and my body turned hot with rage and fear from the shock of the world that was being unveiled to me. I wanted to puke and just disappear. I walked out of the bar as fast as I could to find air and freedom from the darkness of death attacking me from every angle. I lost my cool in the middle of the intersection.

"Fuck! Fuck! Fuck! What the fuck, Black?! What the fuck is going on? I'm not from this world, man! This is fucking crazy, and I don't want to be part of this shit!"

I was shaking and in tears. Black was a killer, but he calmed me down, not really understanding why I was so upset since he had seen or participated in horrific murders since he was a little kid. I was having an out-of-body experience because I was touching and dancing with death. I knew I had to get my shit together and put my game face on. Black was cool about it. He helped get me back on track and finish up our drink with Sam the Hit Man. I wish I could say that we called it a night after that, but Black was all fired up from showing me his dark world and drinking in honor of Duce. He wanted to keep the party going. I guess I did, too.

We headed over to The Bear on the south end of the Chico State campus to change the scene up before the sun went down. Since it was a warm spring break at the end of March, the place was packed, and the outdoor seating area was alive with inspiring young college energy. Black and I did not fit the typical upper-middle-class Chico State student profile. We both towered around 6' 4" and 250 pounds. Add to the fact that I was a former college football player and Black was a gangster from Compton, and we were fucked up. We were out to live, and The Bear was like a trailer park in the wrong place at the wrong time. We were an F5 tornado ripping through its peaceful neighborhood, about to destroy everything in our path.

After Black tried talking politely to a young blonde college student, the security guards quickly interfered and told us to leave. Shit started rolling downhill fast from that point, and they were on the phone with the cops as we were trying to talk sensible. We split out the back door and headed to La Salle's, another well-known college bar on the strip. We didn't even make it to our second drink when I notice security pulling Black out of the girls' bathroom and escorting him out of the back door. The guards weren't stupid enough to rough him up like the usual drunk customer. They asked him, nicely, if we would leave. They even said please. It was pure comedy. Black was so spontaneous and out there when he got drunk, kinda like me, that anything could happen. But on the upside, anything *could* happen. We were actually good running mates, except I knew my night would come if I played that deck too long. There is just something about that crazy edge of life that calls to me.

We knew at this point, after our Chico blitzkrieg, that we had better split town. We walked out of the bar, crossed the street, and jumped into his old, white Impala. It was literally parked across the street from our last stop after we had been bar-hopping all over downtown Chico.

We jumped in his ride, and Black looked over at me with a look I wasn't sure about. It had been a crazy night, and I wasn't sure I was up for any more crazy shit. But I guess I was. I always was.

Black calmly and seriously said, "Let's go for a ride."

With that, I put my seat belt on, and I remember putting in a White Stripes CD. Of all the fucking things you would play with a gangster from Compton, right? We chirped out and headed down the highway listening to "Seven Nation Army" at full blast, both of us playing air guitar and drums. It was a once in a lifetime moment. Black shared my music like Duce did. We shared our worlds genuinely, and those moments of bridging worlds through music is other-worldly and a unifying experience that dismantles hate and prejudice. I didn't know where we were going, and I relished it at that moment. Flying down the highway, just like Duce and I did twenty years earlier heading down the same highway to the Beastie Boys and Run DMC concert in Sac that scorching summer evening. Black and I were celebrating Kevin that night; bonding over each other's music and telling old stories and ripping up the night and running from the cops one last time. We didn't want to let go of the crazy young and fun days with our friend Kevin. Black and I clung to him that night. We cried, laughed, and lived. But what happened next was out of a movie.

The high of the alcohol and music wore off as we headed south on Highway 70 towards Sacramento, about an hour and a half south of Chico. It was about 1:00 a.m. at this point, and I was starting to wonder where we were going and starting to worry if I was going somewhere I might not return from. Did I jump into Black's car too hastily without thinking about his past and what just happened with Duce getting murdered when they were hanging out? My mind started racing through all of the murder, lies and deceit.

"Where are we going, Black?"

He just looked over at me in the dark, the whites of his eyes looking like two full moons from a black voodoo doll. My head was fucking with me, and I was starting to get the feeling that something bad was in the air. But I learned through experience that once I get that far into a dangerous and foreign world, I literally say, "Fuck it" and prepare for the ride. I replace the fear with a gladiator's sword and fighting helmet and attitude. We exited off the highway and into the dark side. Fuck, I knew where we were. I knew what was going on at this point and realized I better get ready for anything. We slowly drove through a few dark blocks of ragged houses with barred windows and pit bulls. No lights. Creepy shit. As Black slowed down and pulled up next to a house lit up and crawling with young guys with no shirts, dreads, and acting wily, he looked over at me with intent.

"These are real killers, Rockwell. You're with me, we family, it's good."

With that, we pulled up ten yards from the front porch. I about pissed myself before looking at Black with a "Got it."

I followed his lead as we exited the car. I stood there trying to get my balance and bearings. The air smelled like spring flowers, burning trash, and blunts. I was in the hood. I was almost frozen outside my passenger door as I gently and quietly closed it so as not to cause attention from the natives. Black walked with purpose to the back of his car. My heart sank.

"Rock, come here!"

I swallowed, looked up at the yellow light on the porch eerily silhouetting the black urban soldiers looking at me with primal curiosity and skepticism as a few of them walked down the stairs and down the sidewalk until they surrounded me.

Black popped the trunk, grabbed something, and came around to the front of the car. He started tossing t-shirts with our brand new KD logo to the crowd as one after the other performed their free-style rap in hopes of signing with King Duce Records.

MTV TAKES KING
DUCE NATIONWIDE

Before I was willing to sign Sneak to a record deal, I invited him to reciprocate my visit to his turf for our first meeting and asked him to come to my home in Oroville. He and G Will rolled up from Sac and met Kevin and me at my place around 10:00 at night. Sneak was a little sketched out about hanging with a white country boy in my redneck town, despite the reality of a significant black population here. Within a half an hour, we were all having drinks, and Sneak's music was turned up on the stereo. We were picking up and riding the same wave we started the first night we met in Sac. That night, we solidified a brotherhood that would carry us through the murder of our friend Duce.

After locking the deal with Keak da Sneak, we did a test run to see how the street would take to King Duce logo and clothing. We rolled up to the E-40/Keak da Sneak concert at Memorial Auditorium in Sac in our full stretch, blacked out Hummer Limo. It was me, Becky, G Will, Lace, Robert, and Black along with a few King Duce Promo Girls, and 500 white KD logo t-shirts and stickers to give away to the crowds.

The Sheraton hotel was hoppin' as we pulled up with videographers and a cameraman; we had a crowd surrounding us instantly. They didn't know what was going on, but they knew something big was happening. I had my brother-in-law Butch, a Marine wrestler and cop, as my bodyguard and Robert, Black, and the girls handing out tees and stickers conspicuously from cool black Kiva duffel bags. Everyone knew King Duce was the real deal. The party moved into the lobby until the show.

Black and Will made their way up on stage during the show, repping KD logo shirts, and tossed tees and stickers to the crowd. The party continued in our suite after the show with champagne by the case and beer and food flowing all night. It was a success by any standard. King Duce was legit. Right then and there, I knew we had done it.

Our next step was our brand being repped in the newest music video with Keak da Sneak. The steps and time it took to reach this point required two years from the time I started the record label that would eventually become King Duce. In that time, I had gone from making the most money I had ever made with a limitless future to the murder of my best friend that I started the dream with and then the collapse of the economy and my income and real estate business. This music video represented a triumph of perseverance and a bond of brothers shining and rising together through all that life had thrown at us. Keak da Sneak repped the KD hats in his music video out of respect to what he was a part of and out of respect for our fallen friend. He even included Kevin's cousin G Will and friend Lace Leno in some clips in the video.

"Where's Sneak?"

I had just arrived in the parking lot of the East Bay United Way building to shoot a music video for Keak da Sneak's latest track, "That Go." He had agreed to rep the King Duce hats I had just dropped twenty-five grand of my own cash to get. It was a one time, very limited edition deal I worked out with New Era, the most respected hat in the urban fashion industry and music scene at the time. We designed six styles in three colors—white, black, and red. They were an instant hit and established King Duce as a serious brand. Having major influential rap artists rep the hats in a music video would instantly legitimize and launch King Duce as a record label and clothing brand nationwide.

Despite the irritating aspect of waiting for people to show up, I was electrified, spending hours in the green room as they filmed, soaking up the process, watching Keak da Sneak wearing different versions of King Duce hats as they filmed. When I saw the final version of the music video on MTV, I couldn't believe it! Not only was it street legit hot, but it connected King Duce to New York by featuring Prodigy of the Queensbridge crew Mobb Deep.

The 1990s was a tragic war of words and violence that ended the lives of ambassadors representing the West Coast and East Coast. Tupac, the Bay Area son of a Black Panther mom, was gunned down not long after New York's Biggie Smalls had been murdered in a rain of bullets. The more I've learned over the years, the more tragic and unnecessary these wars and losses are. And worse, much of the industry violence is perpetuated by the artists and record labels for greed and fame.

Looking back, King Duce Records positively united East Coast and West Coast rap music artists. Rival groups and enemies were connected, repping King Duce with the same level and pride and ownership of the brand and movement. King Duce attracted respected underground and mainstream rap artists in the game, from both sides of the map. Attraction, not paid promotion—huge difference. The key lesson to all the "experts" is you can't buy respect and loyalty with money and fame; it's about intentions and being real.

To be very clear, I never wanted King Duce to be a record label or clothing brand for everyone. Not even close. I believe in setting a very high bar and maintaining that through collaborating and associating with only the most talented people with heart. I wasn't out to win the biggest fan base; I was and continue to do it to create amazing work with other artists I respect.

Keak da Sneak had earned the respect from E-40 and Too Short to rep the Bay, and this respect became nationwide with E-40 and the "Hyphy" movement led by their collaboration "Tell Me When to Go," produced by Atlanta's "Crunk" movement ring leader Lil John, another early supporter of the King Duce movement when we met out in the Bay back in 2008. "Tell Me When to Go" was an instant radio hit and eventually reached fever-pitch rotation nationwide on MTV. This was all happening literally as King Duce Records signed Keak da Sneak.

King Duce had arrived onto the national scene within months of starting the record label. It happened so fast, like my experience in fast-growth media and Internet start-ups. The difference was that I had spent a fraction of the start-up money to establish street credibility and respect from some of the most powerful urban influencers for a record label and clothing brand. King Duce spoke to them. I didn't have to buy their endorsement, the power of the look and feel of King Duce...its DNA attracted them. Sure, I paid some cash for a record deal with Keak da Sneak, but he was dropping KD on tracks and owning it as family long before he was paid. That matters. Doesn't mean anyone should do something for free. Keak da Sneak, like so many artists and athletes, knew that associating with King Duce was good energy and ultimately good business. People could sense my intentions and passion and respected my success in college football and business. The King Duce logo, backstory, and early following of young artists attracted Keak da Sneak and E-40 early on to support the movement—without pay. That's powerful.

RIDE OR DIE – SPONSORING X-GAME ATHLETES – FROM HEROIN JUNKIES TO GOLD MEDAL STARS

"King Duce is an essential cross-section of California's music, art, and action sports scene. It's so rare to actually find a crew of people from seemingly different subcultures band together naturally without it feeling contrived or manufactured. But King Duce is the real deal, and it's a movement more than a brand. Inspired by the memory of fallen family, the voice of King Duce reverberates worldwide because of its authenticity. To see LA street and comic artists connect with hip hop heads and snowboarders, and to align with King Duce has been inspiring, and to be a part of it an honor. King Duce has home grown authenticity with global relevance and that combination is extremely powerful when communicating with the cutting-edge of popular culture."

- Andy Howell, founder of Element Skate Clothing brand, artist, and former pro skater.

After establishing the record label and street credibility from the underground rap music scene, I ventured into a world I was both familiar and comfortable with, sponsoring professional extreme athletes to promote the King Duce clothing and music brand to the X Game fans across the globe.

Pro-Snowboarder Travis Kennedy – TK – The Kid

My first move was to recruit emerging and high-profile extreme sports athletes. One of my video guys at the time also shot a lot of snowboarding films and suggested a couple of guys that might fit the King Duce vibe. Travis Kennedy was a rap-loving white boy from Alaska. He had just won Rookie of the Year by *Transworld Snowboarding* magazine and inked a sponsorship deal with Forum Snowboards to co-design his own line of snowboards and merchandise.

I met him one night in Sacramento on a Forum snowboard promo tour. It was my first experience at a snowboarding film viewing promo party. I remember rolling up to the parking lot of a snowboard shop in Sacramento and seeing a crowded parking lot and an older tour bus with the Forum snowboards logo slapped on the side of it. It was a rock & roll kinda party scene. I spent the first two decades of my life skiing and snowboarding in Squaw Valley Tahoe, so I was pretty familiar with the mountain version of the surf/skate culture.

As I made my way into the bright lights of the spacious warehouse-styled retail store, I looked over to my left and saw a mass of cool, young, good-looking guys and girls all dressed, acting and talking the lazy "I don't give a fuck" cool, aloof attitude that makes a stranger like me feel separate and not part of the inside crew. Whether they were aware of it or not, it was just as intended—to keep a warm blanket over the massive youthful insecurities swirling around each drink of beer and drag of their cigarette. Denying our vulnerabilities takes a lot of masking with drugs and alcohol. The room was exactly that.

I wasn't in my twenties like most of them were. I was in my early thirties, married, built multiple start-ups, survived a drug overdose, and my best friend had just been murdered. I was trying to be sober at the time, and I had just walked into the devil's lair. I wanted to dive in headfirst and join the party, get fucked up, and float away into the reckless lustful regret. But I was on a mission to find, meet, and sign a deal with Travis Kennedy, except I didn't know what he looked like!

Shoving aside my apprehension, I walked up to a young little stoner wearing a gay Neff beanie and a lanyard with the store logo on it and asked him if he could point Travis Kennedy out to me.

"Yeah...sure, dude. Wait, who?"

"Travis Kennedy," I repeated.

"Oh, TK! Yeah, dude! He's the one standing up in the middle of the crew sitting around next to the big screen."

The minute I saw him, I knew he was perfect. Everyone wanted to be around him. He was average height and build, not particularly good looking, but his electric ADD personality, humor, and love of rap music were obvious. There were bigger names on the Forum squad with more experience and wins, but I immediately knew this was right. Although this was all new to me, it was all familiar; rock star athletes being celebrated by brands, retailers, young aspiring snowboarder fans—and tons of snow-bunny groupies, working super hard to look cool and party like the guys. I smiled in my mind as I watched these kids getting to ride that fleeting moment of feeling alive, on top of the world, and bulletproof. The beers were flowing, and the scene was a party underway. Navigating a floor of young snowboarders sitting and hanging out talking and drinking and laughing, I almost tripped on a couple, but managed to end up face-to-face with "the Kid."

"Are you Travis Kennedy?"

"Yeah, dawg! TK!"

"I'm Chris Rockwell. I spoke to you on the phone about a possible sponsorship with my record label and clothing brand King Duce."

"Oh shit! Hell, yeah! Wutz crackin' on that!"

Travis was twitchy, bouncy, funny, and constantly looking for the next pop of action or interest. He was sidetracked by some girl who was trying to get his attention in a room full of people who wanted his attention, including me. I could tell that he was on top of the world. He quickly shot his attention back to me and extended a sincere look and handshake. His grip was firm. I like that. Too many guys these days, especially in Cali, have soft metro handshakes, so as not to offend with their evil masculinity. We had a solid connection that we both sized up and instinctively could sense that we were good. So, I moved the handshake introduction forward to planning a time we could talk and get down to business.

"Can we talk after the show for a few?"

TK was noticeably conscious of making sure he was showing respect with his attention to planning a time and place to talk, when, by his nature, he didn't naturally know how to plan details because someone else handled that. I'm the same way. But here were two spectrum brains coordinating a business meeting in the middle of a party celebrating him!

"Hell, yeah! Let me knock this out and maybe one of the girlies! Ha! And then we can meet out at the tour bus and hang out and talk. Cool?"

We smiled, and TK immediately started introducing me to his fans and friends. It all just felt right. He insisted that I sit with him and his homies. I looked down at the sea of snowboarders sitting on the floor and heard a girl's voice.

"Sit here! I'm Tanya!"

TK chimed in with a quick intro. "Hey T, this is Chris Rockwell of King Duce Records."

I sat down next to Tanya and her friends. She kinda reminded me of the groupie Penny Lane in Cameron Crowe's biopic *Almost Famous.* Tanya seemed at ease and knew all the riders, and they seemed cool with her. She was cute, but not hot or well built; she was the kid sister type with money out to "find herself." I soon learned that she was a writer for *Snowboard Magazine*, and a few months later, she would invite me to Squaw Valley for an interview.

TK gave a quick intro to the surrounding people as he headed to the front of the store to talk to a fellow snowboard bro who made the trip down the hill from Tahoe to see Travis and the rest of the Squaw Valley crew, transplants from all different places around the country. Snowboarding and mountain life were their connection and a few eight balls of blow and some ecstasy he drove over for the party.

I sat there with mixed feelings of belonging but also uncomfortably out of place. I was sober and working on a new phase of my life after my drug overdose and years of working and partying aimlessly and recklessly with people and places just like I was surrounded by. I was in a totally different mindset at that point. As much as I wanted to let go and jump headfirst to the bottom of a bottle of whiskey, I knew that it was not where I needed to be, especially the hell I had already put my wife through.

As I felt myself getting caught up in the euphoric atmosphere, I thought of Becky back home in our bed, trying to sleep and not worry about me heading out into the night to conquer another step in building something that had truly taken over our lives. The economy was shifting, and the great recession was looming in the near future. No one, including me, would realize it until it was too late.

Feeling my anxiety and desire to accomplish my mission, I stepped out of the party and walked outside into the warm October evening. The parking lot was full and quiet. I called Sac rap artist and lil bro G Will and told him to grab Yaberation and meet up and help me recruit Travis to the team. In rare form, they showed up in less than an hour. By that time, the Forum promo film was over, and Travis invited me out to the tour bus to hang with the Forum team and talk shop.

As Travis led me into the bus, I could see a few riders hanging out and drinking beers from the five cases stacked up on the front bench seat running the side of the bus. My stomach turned, and my mouth watered. I was nervous about meeting so many people sober. I felt out of place and didn't know how to live in my sober skin yet. Everyone around me was drunk and high. I loved and hated the feeling and suddenly wanted to just quit and go home and work on sobriety. But I knew that wasn't realistic. I still had some cash and excitement about what I was building, and the King Duce train was off and running. But the pressure to make it a hit was already starting to weigh on me.

Just about that time, G Will and Yaberation (we all called him Baber) rolled up to the tour bus, and some terrified middle-aged tour manager popped his head into the bus.

"Is there a Chris Rockwell in here?!"

"Yeah! Right here."

"Um…there are a couple of guys out here that are looking for you…" This dude looked scared for real. I smiled, knowing exactly what he feared. Two black gangster rappers, one standing 6' 4" and repping a white New Era King Duce hat. Will peeked his head in and flashed his big smile, and I jumped up to tell the manager to let them in. Still unsure, Travis told the dude it was cool. It was a classic way to introduce Travis to G Will and Baber.

After a round of introductions, G Will told TK to put the new King Duce CD on so we could listen to it on the bus while we hung out. The minute the music started hittin' on the blown-out speakers, everyone was bobbin' their heads and lighting up blunts and cracking beers. The music was like a flame to the snowboard bunnies and riders exiting out of the store. Before we knew it, the bus was full and rockin' and surrounded by fans. Everyone was amped and instantly on board with the King Duce family.

The feeling was pretty amazing. To see top pro snow-boarders and rap artists from the streets rockin' that bus with our music and gear was a special moment of validation. I knew we had a hit. Everyone there knew King Duce was a rocket ship. It was electric! There was no question in my mind. That night the King Duce engines had just fired another critical fuselage, extreme athletic sponsorship. And I had just received a verbal commitment from TK on the bus while G Will stood by. We all smiled, shook hands, and hugged.

As I was talking to a couple of riders, I noticed Will, Baber, and Travis were gone! As I scanned outside the tinted windows, I could see the guys towards the rear of the bus talking and exchanging real close to each other. Everywhere I looked, I was surrounded by drugs, alcohol, girls, road managers, and pro snowboarders celebrating all of it. I felt strangely removed from it all at the same time. After my experiences building two number-one sports media companies and playing big-time college football, I was focused on building and not playing around.

I had invested nearly all my cash and was feeling the weight of committing money, time, and effort to so many people in such extreme worlds. I just wanted to get King Duce built out and get it up and running. I was already starting to feel trapped inside a world I was trying to move away from. Sobriety was something I needed to master to survive. But the KD world was not conducive to sobriety. I knew this after realizing through rehab and drug and alcohol counseling that my mind was clinically fucked up and, left to its own devices, would inevitably self-medicate myself to death.

Duce's murder was still haunting me, and the count-less days spent in extremely violent black gang-run neigh-borhoods in California's toughest inner cities didn't ease the pain and trauma. Not being raised around violence, this took a heavy toll on my nerves. I was sincerely worried about being shot all the time. So many kids around me were either killing or being killed. PTSD is a term I don't use lightly or generically to dramatize my experiences or prognosis, but the reality at this point in my life was that my brain has suffered from PTSD, Paranoia, shakes, twitches, Tourette's symptoms, and other fucked-up neurological issues.

I said my goodbyes to the new acquaintances and walked out to find TK, Will, and Baber in the dark back corner behind the bus smoking a blunt. God, I wanted a beer! Trying to be sober in this amped-up social setting was brutal. This was new and scary territory; beyond the uncertainty I had launching a rap label and clothing brand sponsoring by X Games stars. I had a clear vision, but I was not financially or emotionally equipped to shoulder its weight without eventually crashing. But that's how life goes. We're never ready to manage a more sophisticated challenge until we've survived the struggles right in front of us. Learning is hard work!

I flew out to Vermont on my birthday, October 17, 2007, to meet Travis at his aunt and uncle's classic white Victorian home on five beautiful acres. I remember trees everywhere. Sugar, red maple, beech, and yellow birch and white pine. I had a terrible cold and had to stop off at a chain store with a name I didn't recognize to buy some cold medicine. I also picked up all the essentials I forgot to pack: toothpaste, toothbrush, deodorant, and a few white t-shirts. I was traveling all the time and always forgetting something, like the time I forgot to bring my wallet to Vegas for a meeting with a mafia family behind the El Portal Leather Luggage Company. Business as usual. I just wanted to do the deal and get home. I was in such a rush to finish that I couldn't even enjoy many moments and experiences in the fullest context because I had too much on my mind and shoulders. I wasn't managing anything well at that point. I was holding on for dear life with no easy way out. It wasn't in my DNA to not finish the job. I just couldn't. So, I pushed on into the unknown, often to places I no longer wanted to be, with money I no longer had.

For most people, the idea of visiting Vermont in the fall is one of those things on their bucket list. The beautiful fall colors draw thousands to visit every year because of marketing that guides them there. It really is a sight to see. But I could see through the evil veil of the liberal narcissism represented unapologetic promotion by companies like Ben & Jerry's and Subaru of "smart fun living" by exploiting nature and special-needs children to sell their brand. It disgusts me. Sadly, what they leave out of the picture they portray is poverty, drug addiction, and high levels of unemployment spattered throughout the canvas thanks to bad policy.

I stayed with Travis at his aunt and uncle's place. He spent the end of his high school years there to be close to the snowboard training school his uncle suggested he check out. He offered to raise TK for a couple of years to help him become a competitive snowboarder. Travis grew up in Alaska with pragmatic hippie parents, kinda like mine, and an older sister. He struggled in school but thrived socially and in boarding. His parents were in Vermont at the time, and I flew out there to personally meet them and the rest of his family, old school, face-to-face on their turf to understand what was important for their son and to come to a general set of deal points and a term sheet.

I remember talking to them about my value of protecting Travis from allowing people to take advantage of him. I didn't want to rush his parents or push Travis to sign something to "lock him in." I wanted to form a relationship that would transcend the shallow dollar showers of quick deals and cash that flowed in the professional sports world, especially in the red hot emerging extreme sports. The X Games and snowboarding were big, and Travis Kennedy was big. He and his family could see pretty quickly that the chemistry between TK and I, combined with my decade-plus in age and experience as a college football athlete and successful start-up business veteran, was real and exciting. I was asking for an exclusive apparel brand sponsorship deal, and TK agreed and eventually signed a three-year agreement.

When he was back home out west, my whole family went up to Reno to see Travis; Beck and I, and even my mom and dad. TK pulled up in his new truck, took pictures with all of us like family, then we set out to the Men's Club downtown with my brother Dan. We hung out and had some drinks. It was early, and we were the only patrons there, so the girls focused their attention on us. We signed the contract and celebrated by heading to the hills. We smoked weed and hung out at his new pad, high on what the future held.

I would be broke in less than a month, and TK would be injured during a filming session that put him out of commission and hooked on pharmaceutical opiates. The real estate crash forced my business partner and me to close Waterhouse, and my cash source was gone. The real estate crash not only killed the King Duce rocket ship, but it decimated the lifestyle apparel industry, and every other industry related to disposable income spending. So many athletes lost everything, living so leveraged financially, physically, and mentally. The fallout during this era was brutal. Lost jobs, lost homes, and lost cars.... destroyed relationships and marriages, shattered dreams, and suicide.

Travis clearly struggled with attention and hyperactivity at a minimum and ended up struggling with drugs and alcohol that landed him in prison; he lost everything. Like I said, we are alike in many ways. His mom and I kept in occasional contact, and she kept me up to date on how he was doing. She was a very mellow Liberal from Vermont. Nonetheless, Travis got sober in prison and was working as a cook in a fishing cannery and reconnecting with his family in his small Alaskan hometown of Ninilchik. I think of him often as I always had a soft spot in my heart for him because I knew he struggled like me. A fragile soul without the armor to protect him from the assault of evil ghosts of expectations that haunt all great athletes and artists. Like most young talent, no matter how well-intended parents and support systems may be, the machine will do its best to chew us up and spit us out. I just hope for the best for him and that he is living his truth.

The Perazas – A BMX Dynasty

Ty Callais – Team Above Self Achieves Gold Medal @ X-Games

I was having coffee and got a call from Ty Callais, one of the kids that I'd met down at the BMX and skate park with the early days of King Duce. I enjoyed driving down to the Bedrock Skate and Bike Park in the summer evenings to watch and meet the local kids riding and skating and hanging out. It had an element of the rougher street kids who grew up downtown where some kids drank, did drugs, and rode BMX or skated all day. Some rode to escape it. I found myself looking back and walking into that kind of intimidating social scene back in junior high with Matt Brandt and the crew. I would hand out King Duce stickers, hats, and other merch to the kids that were the leaders of the scene.

There were a few teenage boys that could ride. There was one kid named Ty Callais who rode with intense passion. He is the first kid I ever saw do a backflip. He was good looking and wore a mohawk with a bandana. He reminded me of a young Motley Crue drummer Tommy Lee. They both possessed a love of their craft, the thrill over the commercial fame and money, although both were born to achieve both because it was already baked into their wild DNA. Ty and I were kindred spirits and became close over the summer. Back to the phone call, fall was creeping in, and Ty was calling me to tell me about these brothers from Mexico.

"Hey Chris! It's Ty. Ya know, from the BMX park. Hey, these guys are really good. I mean, like the best by far I have ever seen. The older brother is about my age, and he's cool. His younger brother Kevin is the best. They dress in wild colors, and they're super nice. Everyone loves them. They would be great for King Duce. You should sign them!"

I was so proud of that moment because our best BMX athlete and the most dynamic personality was calling me to sell me on recruiting better riders than him! Let me take a moment to share what that means to my leadership and our team. It was because of how I established the King Duce culture from the beginning with the music and the artists that represented an authentic story, iconic logo, and premium hats, and other branded merch that expresses the identity and high expectations of the King Duce culture. I explained this to all the young athletes and artists I would meet.

But kids I wanted to rep seriously were given a deeper explanation about tradition and building a team that is better by realizing that we are stronger by attracting and recruiting better athletes from within our leadership, our top riders should be badass and team above self enough to want someone better than them; it makes everyone better. I talked about this all the time. I was not the typical lifestyle brand founder out to buy a good team. I expected the best, and I was being massively rewarded by my best rider calling me from Camp Woodward to recruit riders that were the best and would replace him as the face of KD BMX. My heart and soul were touched by this human proof of concept. No greater success, trophy, or win (validation)…

I continued with next steps

"Can you get the older brother on the phone with me?"

"Uh, man…like, when? I'll have to talk with him…um…"

"Ty!"

"Yeah Chris! Sorry man, I get distracted. Trying to pull a new trick in the foam pits. This place is amazing! The best riders in the world!"

"Ty!" I heard young girls giggling in the background, and they had Ty's already distracted attention.

"Oh man…sorry, Chris! These girls were… man, that foam pit is so cool…"

"Ty! Get David Peraza on the phone now."

"Okay, Chris"

Ty literally rode his bike over to David and Kevin Peraza and told the older brother, David, that I wanted to talk to him about joining our crew. We hit it off immediately. Both oldest of brothers in sports. There were more similarities than differences. I shared my sports experience of college football and modern media, and I was out to build the number-one brand through very high expectations and taking care of our family. I shared that I was only interested in building for the long term, starting with the best people—family.

"Yeah Chris, that's cool. We like the logo and Ty and the guys. The music... We would be stoked to be a part of the King Duce family."

We immediately mailed out KD hats, shirts, bandanas, and stickers. In less than two weeks, Fuel TV did an entire special on the Peraza family down in their hometown of Tucson, Arizona, by way of Hermosillo, Mexico. The entire time Kevin Peraza was wearing a black KD Cali t-shirt and even repped a Rasta bandana in shots. At the time, Fuel TV was the number-one action sports channel, owned by FOX, and reached millions of viewers in the U.S. and globally. Within weeks of talking to David Peraza on the phone, a verbal commitment was reached and bond to unite as a team to succeed as one family. And that's exactly what we did. As time flew by, the BMX world adopted King Duce and its riders as a force to respect.

To me, and this has never changed, this proof of our team family culture operating on a higher measurement of success was far more important than the inevitable byproduct of big sales and profitability.

Ty went on to explain that the Peraza brothers loved our logo and gear. They liked Ty and the other guys from my hometown who were not in league with Ty and the Perazas, but they all enjoyed hanging out as friends who loved to ride.

The final test would be recruiting the Perazas with basically no money, just some gear with a vision of building the best team to dominate BMX at the X Games.

I responded back like a proud big brother, "Thanks for thinking about the family, Ty!"

If you think calling this family a Dynasty is dramatic, then you haven't met the Perazas. I met them just before they started sending shock waves throughout the BMX world, and the oldest Peraza boy wasn't even seventeen.

When I met the Peraza family in Fresno after my brief introductory call with David Peraza in 2009, I could immediately see the similarities to my dad and my brothers. Victor Peraza was a good-looking former BMX pro and mentor and guide to his four sons. Originating from Hermosillo, Mexico, and residing in Tucson, Arizona, he's also a certified metalhead, made apparent by the Iron Maiden tattoos circling his upper right arm. I could easily imagine hanging out with Victor at a rock concert or riding quads in the sand dunes on vacation. He's fun to be around, and his positive attitude and smile are infectious. But, beyond the fun times, Victor is a solid father figure that leads by example. His boys have clearly adopted their dad's strong work ethic and adventurous personality. Maria Peraza is the quiet, solid foundation that allowed Victor and their boys to train and excel at the sport of BMX. She is a perfect match of cool and old-school mom, keeping her boys grounded while promoting their individuality.

David is the big brother; I relate to him because of this, but there is something beyond that fact that bonds us. He is a smart and thoughtful kid with personality and a sense of humor that is contagious. He paved the way by becoming a great rider in his own right. But he's constantly talking up his little brothers and pushing them to the forefront. He will be a big part of many different business ventures with us over the years.

Kevin Peraza is the BMX rock star. He has a look and riding style that is effortlessly cool. Kevin could easily be an actor or the lead singer of a rock band. But he'd rather be flying through the air, defying gravity like a fighter jet.

I notice when Kevin shows up to an event, he's clearly the crowd favorite. It's easy to see why. Despite his overflowing gifts, he's genuinely grounded by his family values and, at that time, realized that he had a long way to go to become one of the legends of his sport. That's why I think he's special. Now that he has proven to be one of the very best, he still works just as hard and has never let it go to his head.

Then there's little Victor Peraza. Since he was young, he would roll into the bike park like the big dog, calling out teenage riders using Spanglish slang for comical effect. His innocent swagger makes all the older riders embrace him like he's part of the crew. He's been a legit BMX rider since he was about seven years old, pulling backflips and other moves that seem unthinkable when you see his smiling face. Mark my words, Little Victor will be one of the biggest BMX riders in the world, *if* he feels like it. Or he might end up on a Telemundo Soap Opera as the leading man.

Eduardo is the youngest Peraza. He's more interested in the business side of sports and filming his superstar bros and their buddies, but he's a pretty good rider too. He's quiet and cool, confident without arrogance. He's a Peraza.

Coming from college football and sports media, I was used to the mega egos of the pampered superstars. I was pleasantly shocked and impressed with how the kids and their parents greeted me with sincere kindness, friendship, and appreciation. I met them at the Holiday Inn, where we were all staying. Becky and Maria instantly hit it off, and Victor, me, and the boys were instantly bonding. We jumped in our cars to head over to Logan's Steak House for dinner.

I was excited about the way we all connected so effortlessly. It felt right. It was the early days, long before the Perazas were a global name in BMX. I wasn't concerned with signing contracts to legally bind them. I wanted them to feel compelled to be a part of the King Duce/Chris Rockwell family. That evening and the following day at the bike park, we bonded over family and our collective adventure from humble beginnings. The fact that Becky was Mexican and connected culturally with Maria, Victor, and the boys made the friendship solid beyond BMX, King Duce, or money. We all felt it, embraced it, and celebrated it.

In June of 2011, as Kevin and David began climbing the ranks, they made a trip to Oroville just to visit us. I had just lost all our money with the real estate crash and was trying to find a way to continue sponsoring the Perazas when we all knew it just wasn't possible, especially now that Nike and Vans were paying big money to sponsor them. They drove to Oroville to see us and to show us they cared about us, even if we couldn't afford to sponsor them. It makes my heart swell, thinking back about how bad I felt and how much love and support—unconditional support—they showed me, Becky, and the King Duce family. Victor even got a KD logo tattoo during my darkest days. What superstars and their parents do that? I can't say enough good things about the Peraza family and the impact they've made. The world would be a better place if more people were like them.

Kevin would go on to win back-to-back Gold Medals at the X Games in 2016 and 2017.

REGGAE ROYALTY –
JUNIOR TOOTS

I met reggae artist Junior Toots while I was diving for abalone near Mendocino with my brother-in-law. After an
ideal day of diving, Butch and I decided to roll up the
back roads along Highway 1 to explore some unchartered territory as the sun was setting into the ocean. We had the windows down, listening to the *Slider* album from Mark Bolen of
T Rex. The smells of the cool, salty air and eucalyptus trees
were taking me back to my endless summer memories of
camping and diving on the coast. It was one of those perfect
days. So, I wasn't surprised when we stumbled upon this little
saloon overlooking the Pacific Ocean called the Caspar Inn, a
historic roadhouse that has been serving drinks and great live
music since 1906, back when Caspar was a booming logging
town. Legendary rock critic Joel Selvin coined the phrase
"Caspar Inn, where rock and roll meets the sea."

The place looked deserted, but we decided to stop in for
a drink and chill on the porch to watch the sunset. Before
we knew it, people were starting to roll in. Soon we were
surrounded by a crew that had just climbed out of their VW
van. It brought back memories of Reggae on the River in
Humboldt. It also brought back memories of my parents'
VW van, complete with four kids and my mom's surfboard. I

finally asked one of the dreadlocked locals lighting up next to me what was going on.

As he passed the joint to me as a friendly gesture, he said, "Bro... Junior Toots is bringing the Rasta vibes to the Caspar tonight!"

I said naively, "Junior Toots?"

And before I could make the connection, he and his buddies smiled at me and explained, "Junior Toots, son of Toots and the Maytals! You know, Marley, Tosh, Cliff...Toots!" I didn't own a Toots and the Maytals album, but I was familiar with Toots. I discovered later that they actually coined the word "reggae," and their countless hit songs are mainstays on all reggae stations. I was always into Sublime's cover of Toots and the Maytals, "54-46." Even so, I felt like I had just failed reggae 101 and disappointed the white dreadlocked Rasta master.

Butch and I looked at each other with big smiles and knew that we were in the right spot for a classic night of great music and positive people. Junior stepped to the stage a few minutes later and put on a show that filled the intimate setting with inspiring music and energy. While the band took a break, I went up to talk with one of the band members, a young Jamaican kid who was providing backup vocals and nonstop dancing with an infectious smile and vibe. After the show, he found me outside and invited me upstairs to meet with Junior Toots and the band. He led me up a steep and narrow staircase, disappearing into the dark. As we pierced the light of the doorway, I felt like the comedian/actor Chris Farley in the movie *Black Sheep* when he accidentally walks into the dressing room of a reggae band smoking a fat joint.

But before I knew it, the smoke-filled room was full of warm Caribbean smiles and laughter. The band made me feel like long-lost family, while Junior Toots and I talked about his music and what it was like growing up in Jamaica as a child. He told me a very memorable story of when he was about eight years old playing in the studio with the Marley boys while his dad, Toots, was recording with Bob Marley, Peter Tosh, Bunny Marley, and Jimmy Cliff. Led by Marley, they formed a tight circle with their arms around each other; with heads down, they prayed, smoking a traditional Rastafarian wooden pipe together while Junior and the other kids ran around as little kids do. It truly was a historic night in my musical journey. As we said our goodbyes, we agreed that we would unite our musical visions someday into a King Duce project.

I met up with Junior in his place in Berkeley to reconnect and talk about the video we wanted to create back at the Caspar Inn. In a sign of trust, he asked me if I was comfortable hanging out at his place with his two-year-old son while he ran down to the store for smoking papers. Before I had much time to process it, he was gone, and I was sitting in his living room with his baby boy standing in front of me in his diapers and a relaxed and curious look on his face. The room was silent, and we just looked at each other, both of us trying to figure out what was supposed to happen next. Then I said hi and he smiled back at my warm smile, and we just hung out like we had known each other for years. Well, at least two. A couple of times, he looked around for his dad, but he seemed okay and not nervous. I was enjoying his presence and started thinking about singing to him when the front door opened. Junior smiled big, and I smiled, realizing the trust he had shown me. We hung out smoking spliffs and talking about our first King Duce music video for reggae featuring him.

A couple months later, we filmed Junior performing live back at the very place we met on the Mendocino Coast at the Caspar Inn. It was a memorable project because my family came over for the event. My parents and Becky were there to support me as usual, and even my assistant Julie came over to help with all of the details and enjoy some reggae. Our film crew was led by Hagar Eliziz, who became as much a part of the King Duce family as any musician or athlete. She and her crew would become our go-to crew because she was a badass and was totally aligned with how I expected things to be done. The evening was not as laid back and easygoing as it was the first night I met Junior there because of having my family and crew there for work. It wasn't a vacation. Nonetheless, it turned out to be a well-done black and white video that captured Junior's positive energy on stage and our connection—*his* connection—to King Duce Records.

A decade later, when I was preparing for my visual art show at the legendary skate shop and museum aptly named the Santa Cruz Boardroom, Junior Toots and his band drove to the show for a meet and greet and a performance. I can't believe it had been ten years since we first met at the Caspar Inn in Mendocino, California. To reconnect for both of us is exciting. We both know that our combined energy is pretty powerful. We shared many creative ideas and projects we wanted to pursue before the recession. But now that we made it out of that we can explore lots of cool ideas, including a trip back to his home of Jamaica to film a documentary and create some music together. Either way, we just genuinely like each other and collaborating.

NEW YORK: SESAME STREET, VIOLATOR RECORDS, AND MADISON SQUARE GARDEN

I love New York. Maybe it's because my dad is originally from Kingston in Upstate New York, and my grandmother Dorothy was born in Brooklyn. I love its attitude, its cold truth, its brutal reality of winning and losing. No days off, and the lights never go out. I admire the tough, charismatic leaders on the biggest stage in the world. That's how I think, and that's what I respect. So, I was destined to set out on a late-night West Coast red-eye flight, landing in LaGuardia as the pinks and oranges of the early morning glow before sunrise fell upon the magnificent settlement of lights that never sleeps.

Each day provides a closing and opening to a new bold and bright prospect of fame and fortune. Here they are waking up and competing against the very best in the world, EVERY DAY. That suits me well. Every time I've landed in New York, I've discovered amazing people, opportunities, and success. Winning on the ultimate stage as a small-town country boy gave me tremendous confidence to envision bigger things than most others thought possible. New York makes crazy dreams seem possible, like LA and Silicon Valley.

The legendary film director, Martin Scorsese's, *Gangs of New York* paints a brutal but honest picture of what it was like during the time of the Civil War. It was a bloody fight to be accepted into the new world and an even bloodier fight to the top. This is New York in her bold, true colors. Over the years, I've spent time deep in the jungle of business and money, where feelings and empathy are a liability, and primal kill instincts rule supreme. There is an overt honesty to the truth of New York and her people. She's an intimidating woman who will slip you the tongue of demise as fast as she will hold you to the stars, until tomorrow when the next king of the mountain topples you with a bullet or a new hit single.

New York. It is a place that eats weak people, sacrificed at the altar of money and power, to feed the insatiable appetite of dark human desires. But the city calls you in, back to her opium den womb, with a soothing pulsating beat of immortality. Reality melts away and is replaced with an energy that takes over the soul and commands complete submission to her desires.

In contrast to my experience growing up in the California culture, New York is extremely different. The West Coast is deceptively "relaxed and chill," represented satirically by the typical slimy mindless and soulless Hollywood actor, agent, producer, and director and the worst of all, the Silicon Valley CEO—still wearing his Stanford hoodie and using politically correct catchphrases and style signed and approved by the far-left late-night talk show hosts spewing the mantra of the new power of Geeklandia, like Joseph Goebbels did for the Nazi movement.

New York is founded by bluebloods, thugs, and a deluge of poor immigrants that forced intense immersion competition and the resulting raised bar of performance and production. New York represents the human condition, human nature when things get fucking real, life and death every day real. That's what my grandmother Dorothy came from being born in Brooklyn illegitimately to an angry housemaid spinster who detested her and a father she never knew. I'm one degree from that existence, folks. I'm grateful for such proximity to the very bottom with people I respect and love. It has had a profound effect on my view at any level.

It was 2009, and everyone was starting to feel the reality of the real estate market and global financial collapse. It's strange to be insulated by the ravages of its societal effect on the people attached to its life source. I had spent a year and a half desperately trying to salvage the demise of my money, investments, and King Duce. That's when I got the call from Slim Dickman to join him and his team from Fox to help him with his revenue strategy for an on-demand Internet-based manufacturing company. I would join a team built out by Stanford multi-generational grads and lead financing by the venture capitalist godfather John Doer. I knew it was gonna be an exciting ride with cash and the ability for me to meet new people and build King Duce Records along the way. I would be paid by zazzle.com to be in New York to meet up with some young execs who were going to help me build out the company's music licensing division, but in my heart, I knew this was also an amazing opportunity for my record label. I was always up front about leveraging a trip to accomplish combined interests, and it always served my "employers" well.

New York and LA are the kings of media and content in America, especially when you are in the music business. So, here I was on a flight to the Big Apple to find my way through the jungle to introduce King Duce and the latest tech darling from Silicon Valley to the East Coast. I didn't have big expectations because we were just on the West Coast underground scene, although we did have the East Coast connection thanks to the Keak da Sneak video "That Go" repping King Duce hats and New York's own Prodigy. I knew cracking New York was the final test to see if our brand, logo, music, and backstory could be accepted by the East Coast and the world. My main objective was to hit a few music spots and introduce King Duce to some artists and fans. But that's not what happened.

It was October and raining when I got into my taxi to take me towards the flame of the city. Looming before me was a manmade silhouette surrounded by a low-lit canopy of rain clouds and a moat of fog. It felt very dark, ominous, and intimidating. To me, New York and LA are both extremely dynamic, creative, and violent places. But New York has a culture that is built out of the heart and soul of the mass immigration to America and the hub of the world. I love New York because she moves fast, and she's brutally honest. Culturally, New Yorkers are brash and go after what they want, and I have always respected that. I was nervous about how King Duce would be received and felt some fatigue over worrying about it for the last few nights. I knew I would walk away knowing the truth; that was my main objective.

I showed up to an apartment in downtown Manhattan where I would be staying for the next few days. I knocked on the door and heard nothing. Being in a big city at 6 am from a red-eye flight from the West Coast is always a strange out-of-sorts kind of feeling, but it's even worse when your bladder is about to explode from too many Jack and Cokes on the flight over. All I wanted to do was get in the place, but no one was answering the door, and I was seriously contemplating pissing on the side of the building like Ozzy at the Alamo. The building was eerily similar to the brownstone neighborhood on *Sesame Street*. I started humming the childhood anthem. Then I began thinking of the far-left government (PBS) funding and propaganda machine Kermit the Frog and Big Bird were selling to countless generations. The idea that we are all the same and should be fair and loving is a cool concept, but it was showing white kids as the second-class citizen in a smart and subtle way, and making blacks and minorities feel entitled.

I laughed out loud to myself and slurred, "Fucked up, but so true!"

I heard the faint creaking of old wood floors behind the door. I think a little pee came out as I anticipated the bathroom. The door opened but was abruptly stalled at about six inches due to the security chain. More leakage. The invisible shadow fumble fucked around with the chain until it finally released the door to reveal a guy in his tighty-whitey underwear and the look and build of a high school senior with no visible body hair except on his head. His skin reflected all forms of available light due to his baby white hue. The only color on his body was a little pink in his cheeks and on his forehead, where he passed out the night before. His eyes were still trying to open and focus while his black mop-top of curls was still formed to his pillow. Despite his groggy state, he displayed a warm, welcoming smile as if we had known each other for a long time. I introduced myself, although he was expecting me. I felt like I had just met a young version of my dad.

"Hi! I'm Mike Karns! Good to meet you, Chris!"

He smiled brightly and sincerely and welcomed me in.

"Sorry for welcoming you to New York in my underwear! Come on in and let me show you to your room. Jesus is still sleeping down the hall. He sleeps all the time, so don't worry about being quiet."

I found my room, and more importantly, the bathroom. Things were off to a great start.

I liked Mike instantly. He was a very smart, funny young guy with a law degree from USC and Stanford. Jesus was a young Mexican guy from a poor town outside Tucson, Arizona, that was able to rise up and graduate from Stanford as well. He was a trip. I liked his quiet, quirky ways and gave him the nickname Paco. The three of us hit it off and became close from then on. They were intrigued by my Internet start-up success and music business project and were like kid brothers in a world away from the warmth of our California sun and Palo Alto office. We spent the next couple days at a New York digital music symposium at a cool old university building in a classic New York borough, complete with the corner deli famous for pastrami on marbled rye.

We spent the days at a trade show booth with our Icelandic VP Mia (we called her the Ice Queen) networking with other companies connected to the digital music revolution. I was in the center of it all, just as I had done nearly a decade earlier with Rivals and Scout. Since I was the veteran in the room and our VP Ice Queen was caught up in her rise in the Silicon Valley game, I crept out and took a walk in New York to take in the vibe and find a bar to get well. I found an Irish Pub and ordered pints of Guinness until I passed out and was awoken by a young waitress asking me if I needed some water.

I had been around the digital music scene since Napster because famed venture capitalist Ann Winblad was an investor in Napster as well as my old company Rivals.com back in the late 1990s. This was the second wave, the "legal" approach to consuming digital content, whether it be music, movies, or books, after the rogue but natural evolution of file-sharing services built by geeks out to make a name for themselves in the new world unfolding while major record labels and movie companies tried everything in their power to stop the inevitable wave of change that was fundamentally transforming their industry.

I built King Duce Records based on this new and revolutionary business model of "give the music away" and monetize it with shows and merchandise. I was involved in the Internet Revolution from early on, and it seemed logical to me that the industry cartels were fighting a dying business model, refusing to adapt while fighting the change-makers. I was in New York for zazzle.com to negotiate licensing deals to produce and sell artist brand merchandise like shirts, hoodies, posters, etc. We were in talks with every major music label and ended up doing a deal with Warner Music, producing for brands like KISS, Skynyrd, Ozzy, Britany Spears, and more.

I spent that first night out with our chief revenue officer and my mentor, Slim Dickman, who just flew in from Seattle. He wanted to be in the mix of the New York media scene. He and I had just come off building and selling Scout.com, and he was rich and running with the elite of the modern media titans, including MTV founder/creator Bob Pittman. It was October 17th, another birthday 3,000 miles from home. Slim was spending his newfound stockpile of funds from the Zazzle.com coffers to finance his crazy plan of building the largest network of artist merchandise deals under one roof and monetize it in a bunch of creative ways.

Dickman had just left his chief strategy officer position at FOX, where he reported directly to Rupert Murdoch, the Czar of modern media, and worked side by side with the likes of Peter Chernin, then president of Fox (News Corp). We started out at an upscale restaurant with a group of ten, including Slim's new Southern California wannabe Hollywood blonde girlfriend, Lottie. She was hot enough to land a multi-millionaire CEO but dumb enough to not realize that it would end with one baby and a paycheck for his disappearance from her life a couple of years later so he could marry a twenty-five-year-old New York debutant connected to Bob Pittman of MTV fame. Slim was in rare form and letting loose with his Corporate AMEX, ordering drinks, constantly scanning the room to see who's who and who's looking at him, while enjoying his status as King at the table. Slim was trying to wear his New York media mogul look with a "me too" fashion sensibility.

I sat at the head of the table opposite him. Symbolically, I should have realized that it would represent the old saying that there is only room for one king at any table. I knew the Las Vegas swingers' sex club denial from my wife was still weighing on his view of me. I was out on my own building King Duce Records and taking chances that he and no one else at that table could fathom, so I just stayed quiet. Our group consisted of our executive team and a few big-name record executives. I couldn't remember their names after drinking shots at two separate clubs that were showcasing bands connected to the event we were involved with, and I really didn't care. I was focused on the weed in my pocket that I had managed to smuggle on the flight over, and when I'd get the chance to smoke it.

It was another memorable birthday, ending up with me puking between club stops. The bands were all alt-rock beta boy wimps singing about hating cool people and jocks, but Slim Dickman and our Silicon Valley geeks were in heaven. That was totally what they were. I was more interested in talking with the cool older record exec veteran Linda to get her take on the past, present, and future of the music business. She told me some classic sex, drug, and rock and roll stories. I was a sponge soaking up every drop of knowledge and alcohol I could absorb.

It was a great first night back in the Big Apple. But I had my focus on hitting the streets, clubs, and studios of the rap and hip-hop game. I was producing music and music videos with legit west coast artists and wanted to explore and discover everything I could about the New York scene. I wasn't sure where to start, but I was confident that I was going to get where I needed to go. I've always trusted that in myself. I'm not sure how I got back to our place, but I woke up to sirens and a dump truck that sounded like it was picking up the garbage out of our kitchen. After a couple of beers, a joint, and a piece of toast to mellow out my shaky hands and mind, I headed out to repeat the day before.

After surviving a hangover workday, me, Mike, and Paco hit the bars so I could get well, and they could try and pick up on some young Ivy League grads. The bars were full of young Wall Street bankers strutting classy suits, Rolexes, and cash. It was a boring scene, and I was itching to move on. We bar hopped the same type of places the rest of the night because the guys I was with would be scared shitless if we went into the hood or a real Irish pub.

So, after a final stop at a bar with half the women and men smoking cigars and drinking brandy, that was it. I said, "I'm outta here guys…I'll catch a taxi."

Mike pleaded, "No! Please don't leave us yet, Rock! I'm working on that girl over there by the Alec Baldwin wannabe."

Reluctantly, I caved. "Okay, I'll have one more drink, and you and Paco better close the deal. Hey, where's Paco?"

Mike smiled. "That Mexican hooked up with some analyst from JP Morgan, and they split while you were at the bar."

Mike knew he was up against the clock and had to close a deal with this chick before she got scooped up by Blaine from Goldman Sachs sporting the purple tie and Armani suit. I gotta say, I dig that New Yorkers dress to kill and live 24/7. They don't get the night started until midnight, and they keep the party going till the sun comes up. It's electric. It does make you feel like anything is possible.

In droopy-eyed contrast, Paco showed up looking for a drink and a hug from his rejection. We asked in defeated curiosity, "What happened?"

Murmuring, like Eeyore from *Winnie the Pooh*, he said, "Man…she said she had to get up early for a meeting." He looked down in defeat after such a promising start.

Mike walked over to the girl who had been talking to the Alec Baldwin guy and grabbed the window of opportunity while he was at the bar. I saw them both smiling, laughing, and exchanging numbers. He stopped at the bar to grab a celebratory round of shots before we headed out. We decided to walk back to our place since it was only a couple blocks away, or so we thought.

After three blocks that took us deeper and deeper into darker neighborhoods, we had a sidewalk showdown with a group of five or six black guys walking straight towards us. They were dressed in street fashion and walked with confidence. I was drunk and not quite sure what to think. I figured that we were either going to get jacked or walk past each other like nothing. It was 3:30 in the morning on a dark block in New York City; anything could happen. As we got closer, I could sense that these were young guys with their shit together. Their style made me think they may know where I should start to hit some clubs. Mike and Paco were silent and totally out of their comfort zone. I stopped these guys walking within feet from us and pulled out my King Duce business cards and sparked up a conversation. They pulled out their cards from Violator Records, home to platinum legend 50 Cent and a list of platinum players all the way back to LL Cool J. I couldn't make this shit up, folks; that's exactly what happened.

The next day, I was heading back to California, but I was able to convince the higher-ups at Zazzle.com that I needed to go back to New York to pursue this new lead. I knew I had to do it for King Duce Records and would make it a win for the company that was paying me to get there too. It was another month and a half before I could get back, but I eagerly jumped on another redeye flight to the city.

It was almost déjà vu as I hailed a taxi in the rain and headed for the city, but this time I was headed straight for Violator Records. I didn't bring an umbrella, so I was soaked before I got to the building. From the outside, it looked like a typical ten-story office building. As I entered the lobby, it looked more like a run-down government project building in the Bronx. I looked for the directory in the poorly lit lobby and found a discreet sign on the wall to the right of the elevator. I stepped in and hit the button for the sixth floor. When the bell rang and the doors began to open, I exited cautiously. In front of me was a giant steel door with an intercom. I scanned to the right and left as I thought of all the legendary artists that had passed through these doors and the crazy, violent history of the New York rap game. Behind that steel door is where so many platinum artists called home. I pushed the button on the intercom and took a breath.

The speaker exploded with a big black woman who sounded like she could kick my ass. "WHO IS IT?!"

I loudly but politely responded with, "My name's Chris Rockwell of King Duce Records. Damon and I are scheduled for a meeting."

The thunder of the tough black New York music industry receptionist let me know that this was the New York rap game I was walking into headfirst.

"HOLD ON..."

The door buzzed, and I pushed open the massive bulletproof behemoth. I stood there in a trance for a moment, in awe of the hit factory I was standing in. Right as I entered, the office was filled with a track leaking out of the studio down the hall. The bass was hitting so hard that it shook the framed platinum records hanging on the walls. The guys took me for a tour of the place and introduced me to the staff. I handed out King Duce hats as we sat at the conference table surrounded by posters and platinum records. The windows looked out on the hustle of downtown. It was inspiring to be around the heart of New York's' rap scene. Everyone was very cool and friendly, and we agreed to begin collaborating. And there forged our transcontinental bridge with King Duce Records.

I walked out, still stunned by what I had experienced, and had to find a bar to celebrate. Within two blocks, I found an Irish Pub with a big college basketball tourney on the TVs. The place was pretty busy and had a great vibe, so I ordered up a Guinness and found a stand-up spot at the end of the bar where I could watch the game and hit the bathroom all within a ten-foot radius. Things were starting off great. I stood there in deep thought about what I just experienced and where I wanted to go. The college hoops game was getting the crowd going since Notre Dame was playing North Carolina in the finals at the Maui Invitational, but I was in my own world after what I had just experienced at Violator Records.

During a controversial call, a guy at a stand-up table across from me, watching the same TV yelled, "Hey man, why don't you join us!"

I looked over, half-cocked from a few pints and the adrenaline of a New York Irish pub during a Notre Dame basketball game. Irish Catholics are a loyal and drunk crazy lot of hooligans. I could tell they seemed like good ol' Irish guys like me, so I grabbed my beer and took three steps to their table, and they reached out warmly and loudly to welcome me into their tight group of smiling red faces. One of the guys was about my age and wearing a traditional Irish tweed flat cap and had the graying red hair and freckles to confirm his authenticity.

After meeting the crew of four and having a few pints and laughs, the guys told me they had an extra ticket and invited me to join them at Madison Square Garden to watch the *National Invitational Tournament* LIVE! Next thing I know, we're heading out the door, the rain had stopped, and we walked down the street to Madison Square Garden.

We watched Oklahoma beat UAB 77-67 to move into the final, drank a few $10 beers, and then Danny Boy looks at me and says, "Hey Rock! Can you score some blow?"

"Me? I can try!"

We stepped out to hail a corner drug dealer. A giant black dude approached us, asked if we wanted anything. We said yes and he stopped, looked me up and down, and said, "You look like a cop!"

I said, "My grandpa was an L.A. cop. I like drugs."

My new friend gave him $100, and the black guy said he'd be right back. Bad bet. After 15 minutes, we knew that his $100 was gone and we weren't gonna get shit in return. We all left and headed back to the guys' hotel to have some more drinks and smoke some weed. I remember getting a little paranoid a couple of times hanging out in their suite, simply because everything was going so good and felt so natural that I was becoming convinced they were up to something and had some fucked-up Irish mob initiation planned. After going down that mental rabbit hole, I emerged with a grin on my face and rejoined the party front stage by taking another big shot of whiskey.

I woke up the next morning to discover that I lost my phone in the taxi! The trip was everything I had hoped it would be. I had successfully introduced King Duce Records to the legendary artists and team at Violator Records; our East Coast connection had been made and we were on our way.

Unfortunately, those amazing connections would have to wait for another time because I needed to handle the mounting personal and financial devastation that was about to unfold. I look back and think about how I used to believe that every cool connection I experienced would be the best and last, and that I would need to capitalize on it immediately or watch it disappear into the dreams of past days and lives. Instead, I now recognize that those experiences and connections gave me a perspective and confidence to envision and build on a scale that I would have never known possible if it weren't for the magical spell of New York.

E-40, TOO SHORT...AND THE
GHOST WOMAN OF TUPAC

"Hey Rock! What's a VC?" E-40 asked me as I was describing the Silicon Valley business.

"The drug cartels of Silicon Valley." I answered from experience and a matter-of-fact cynicism from years of the grind of pitching dreams to snakes with money.

I'm sitting in the front passenger seat of E-40's white Escalade complete with black tinted windows and crushing sound system. We were flying down Highway 101 southbound through the epicenter of Silicon Valley symbolized by the starship buildings lining the banks of the South Bay; Google, Facebook, Oracle. I look over at the driver and wonder how he got the nickname Shark. He was a bald muscle-bound white guy with a big silver chain and a black hood dialect

"They are the money that launches all the companies in technology. It's like the drug game. They risk big money on very unpredictable businesses. They win big or lose big. And they usually control the majority stake in the company, like the cartels do in the drug business. The employees and founders are the cheap labor, like the drug runners and dealers who work the hardest with the smallest payoff. Cash is king! Venture capitalists are the big ballers, making billions on one successful bet. Companies like Google and the rest of the big names on the 101 strip created more wealth and innovative value than any time in history."

"VC...huh? I like that. I'm going to use that in a song," E-40 said as he pondered a world and planets away from his upbringing across the bay in Vallejo. We met when I was building Artsprojekt.com, an artist's network that gave them the ability to create and sell their custom brand merchandise. E-40 was already showing love to our young King Duce crew, even letting them open up for him. I was working to recruit the biggest names in music and visual art to join the network. Our office was in another spaceship looking building just one exit up from Google and Facebook. I met up with lots of big names back then.

E-40, aka Earl Stevens, is from a good family in Vallejo, CA, an East Bay city known for being predominantly black and violent. E-40's father was a preacher, and his mother was loving, and both were encouraging. He shared a brief glimpse into himself one night. He called me up about a project we were exploring together, and the conversation flowed candidly and openly about where we come from. When I told him I was from a little town called Oroville, he gently laughed with sincerity, reminiscing, "I've got family from Oroville! I remember playing house parties back in the day there cuz my cousins lived there." He continued reminiscing and traveled back through his decades of hustling in the rap game. Working his way up the ladder the old fashioned way, from house parties to neighborhood bars and clubs to city clubs, fairs, car shows, selling CDs out of their trunk and hustling them on the corner outside stores and concerts, doing whatever it takes to learn and master the craft.

The more we talked, the more I liked and respected him. He was thoughtful, intelligent, honest, kind. His lyrics and style were uniquely E-40, and his loyal fans continue to follow and celebrate him into his third decade. That kind of staying power in the rap game, music industry-wide actually, is a huge accomplishment. E-40 has remained relevant in and out of trends because he's talented, works hard, stays out of trouble, doesn't blame others for his circumstances, and has positive confidence that inspires great things.

I learned more from E-40 than from anyone else in the rap game. He was an early supporter of my record label and helped me understand some valuable keys to success. In return, I shared my Internet start-up experience and the world of Silicon Valley, having him visit our offices, and discussing how companies are built and where the money comes from, and how much the businesses like Google and Facebook were worth, and how much the VCs made on their bets.

We shared similar life experiences and successes in our worlds of rap and technology. Driving down the 101, exchanging and sharing our knowledge with each other about our hits and misses, the highs and lows of our professions, and that we both loved to create, build and do it big. There were more similarities than differences, and we ended up with a friendship that I appreciate. The rap game, like Silicon Valley, is full of bottom feeders trying to suck the lifeblood out of good people and good ideas.

After building businesses from scratch in both arenas, I see the only true difference was that the shitty people on the Internet legally took your money with contracts and lies, while the rap game borrows the rules of the drug business resulting in guns and murders. I still don't know which world is more vicious. Serious. You have to be tough and firm with your principles and vision, otherwise the machine operated by ugly character defects will kill you. But that's in anything in life. If we don't have a strong sense of ourselves and self-worth, then we will invariably follow, submit, change to fit the person or environment we cling to.

His was another example to me of someone who created his own success by leveraging his creative use of the English language in a context that related him to his neighborhood and elevated the listener. Regardless of who the listener was, the message was of success through hard work and doing it in style, without avoiding talking about the challenges in his culture and society. E-40 is up on what's up and asked me questions when very few would even stop to recognize the opportunity to learn some shit that could help them grow. E-40 recognized the power of Silicon Valley. He even did a promo deal with Yahoo and Pepsi during that time.

The advice that I'll never forget that E-40 gave me about the music business was like wisdom from a big black Yoda: "Rockwell, slow down, don't rush, and it will happen." I loved it. I was used to moving at light speed in highly dynamic start-up environments. The rap music biz was similar in that it moved fast and was dynamic, but it was also relationships. It was so surprising and refreshing to hear him say it. We shared the view that when you're building for the long haul, it's all about long-term relationships and respect.

This sage wisdom was followed up by a ring on his phone. E-40 picked up and started talking and laughing with New York's rap star Busta Rhymes. I wish all the young rappers I was working with could've experienced the conversation because it showed me how the legends of the game handled their business. They were classy, polite, and connected with history, coming up together on opposite sides of the country but circulating over the years in the small community of rap artists.

I consider E-40 my mentor in the rap game and an example of a good man doing good work and inspiring others along the way. I admire that and strive to live that by surrounding myself with the best. It's so true what "they" say... "Winners surround themselves with winners." It's also absolutely true what they say on the negative trip: "Misery loves company." We choose. I got caught up in the game ill-prepared, especially when Duce was killed, and ended up with big money losses and hard-knock lessons that opened my eyes wide to the fact that I was in a jungle of hustlers, gangsters, and preachers all trying to be rap stars. I had to adapt to the rap "business." It was one degree more structured and predictable than the drug dealing business. I walked in, assuming I would be signing formal contracts with bank-wired funding and tracking, everything I was used to in Silicon Valley start-ups. It was like I had to unlearn and relearn how to do business. It taught me to trust my gut more.

Riding in the back seat with E-40 was his son Droop-E, a light-skinned mild-mannered eighteen-year-old kid with a slight build and a soft demeanor from an upbringing of protection and luxury. Despite their obvious physical and personality differences, they were very close and operated in the gray area of Dad or Big Bro, depending on the topic. In between calls from Busta Rhymes and our discussion about the Silicon Valley game, E-40 was talking quietly to Droop-E about calling his mom, about grandmother stuff, and apologizing for this morning. It was a trip. I felt like I was in a Twilight Zone of Silicon Valley and the hood merging in a private meeting by the ambassadors rolling down the 101 in a white Escalade, bumping underground Bay music on KMEL. We flew down the road, and I gazed out the window pondering the massive futuristic buildings lining the 101, housing the hottest new companies. I spent decades watching these buildings change hands, new logos trying to outdo the last like music promo billboards.

E-40 came across as a caring father and humanitarian in ways. He was aware of the world around him and where he came from. He also was unfamiliar with my world in a way that surprised me, probably as much as my rookie questions and ignorance about his world and business. I know why he was successful and recognized in him a similar passion and outlook towards life. We were both curious and interested in the other person's world. A true exchange that helped me realize that we are all people, regardless of the circumstance we are born into. We choose an optimistic or fatalistic view of ourselves and the world, and we fold that into every step we take, forward or backward.

E-40 raps to his people, his community, about what it takes to succeed like he did. He supports, encourages, and produces the young aspiring talent in need of guidance. And every once in awhile, as in any group, a kid will hear the message and follow his lead out of the hood and a negative way of life. Most won't. No matter what. E-40 is significant to my development as a musician and producer, and he is considered one of the godfathers of the Bay Area rap scene.

Too Short

I followed up my E-40 experience by spending a late night/ early morning in Too Short's recording studio. I met Ashara at my offices at Artsprojekt.com up the road when she and her ex-husband, E-40's manager, were negotiating a deal to produce and manage E-40's merchandise utilizing our on-demand print platform. We all hit it off, and Ashara was instrumental in connecting me with E-40 personally. She followed that up by introducing me to Too Short one late night at his studio in downtown Oakland.

I think she was Syrian. She was kinda rough around the edges in look, dress, and style, but she was symbolic of the rap industry. That's how it was. It always reminded me of a cheaply constructed palace shimmering of gold and diamonds, and just beneath the surface and seeping out of the cracks in the foundation was an unorganized desperation that was still poor and craving for attention and validation.

She picked me up from my hotel in Palo Alto and took me to the East Bay to watch a reggae show and meet some of her friends. Some of them were other Bay Area music legends. The club was cool; big, open Rasta-filled rooms with a good earthy vibe, a sharp contrast to the street outside and the downtown Oakland violence. The music was still going when Ashara tapped me to leave. I pounded my Red Stripe beer, and we headed out. We walked down the opposite way from her car, making me extra paranoid about what she was up to. She picked up the pace, her purse clutched tight at her elbow, and her high heels click-clacking at the same pace as my now nervous heartbeat.

I wondered out loud, "Where the fuck are we going?"

"Relax, Rockwell. You're in good hands. This is my turf."

She gave me a warm but confident smile and squeezed my hand to assure me that everything was on the up and up, and she was one of the people in my corner. Suddenly she darted out across the street towards a five-story building dragging me along with her. As we reached the sidewalk on the other side and approached a dark building, a black man came down the stairs out of the front of the building, and he was looking straight at us. My heart skipped and sank for a moment, cussing myself for getting mixed up with a rap stars manager's ex-wife! Before I could calm my head, we were face-to-face with Too Short! Ashara greeted Short as a sister greets her big brother out on the town.

"Hey Short, this is Chris Rockwell. He has a record label."

"Wuts good, Rockwell?"

I didn't know what the fuck to call him. I've always struggled to call an artist by their moniker since no one they know does, yet I don't feel right using a friendly nickname either, so I usually end up sounding like a total lame white guy. With Too Short, I decided to not sound like a dork and just kept it to, "Hey, good to meet you, man."

We shook hands before he hugged Ashara and headed out into the night. In the brief interaction with Ashara, I could tell they were close. He quickly returned, and before welcoming me into his studio, he gave me the skeptical once-over. I had met a lot of stars in my days, but Too Short is the original rap artist for my life experience. It was a special moment for me, and he didn't disappoint. He was the real deal, a true Oakland player. He didn't smile when we met, and he was serious and focused on his next step, not sure if it would be his last. He walked with urgency. That's what successful people look like in business. We walked up the steps to the second floor of the older downtown building. I walked in confidently since we had just met Short, as Ashara referred to him.

The best part of the night, besides meeting Too Short at the steps of his studio, was that I ended up hanging out with a talented eighteen-year-old artist who was finishing up a beat and wanted to play it for me. I have to say, this is why I dare to seek out places and sounds and people that are also out there exploring because every once in a while, the magical moment happens. This kid hit the play button, and his beat started rumbling through the professionally designed recording studio. The sound made me bob and smile at him. He was so proud! I was blown away by the beat and the moment.

I'm honestly not sure what happened after that. I know we went to go eat breakfast with one of the singers from the 90s group Toni, Toni, Toni. Ashara went out of her way to help introduce me to the godfathers of Bay Area rap and encouraged me because she felt I had something that was unique and rare.

"You have heart, Rockwell. Don't let these boys intimidate you. I used to be with Tupac back in the early days when we were coming up in the scene. He had that something special. An aura or charisma, call it whatever you want...he had *it*. Mr. Rockwell, you, my friend, have that special something...you have the *it* factor."

Ashara may have had her best days behind her. In many ways, she was a total disaster. But she had lived the Bay rap scene from its inception and specialized in that specific niche. She didn't have the tools to truly capitalize on it. But she saw something in me that gave me confidence in a world that I was still trying to understand and navigate.

HIP-HOP LEGEND – PHIFE DAWG OF A TRIBE CALLED QUEST

Phife Dawg is Celebrated at Memorial at the Apollo – Jon Caramanica April 6, 2016

...a rather astounding collection of hip-hop titans from almost every generation came to celebrate Phife.

In the audience and on stage were guests from across the temporal spectrum. Chuck D., Lauren Hill, the comedian Dave Chappelle, and the actor Michael Rappaport, who directed the 2011 documentary *Beats, Rhymes & Life: The Travels of a Tribe Called Quest*.

> *Without question the most intelligent, artistic rap group during the 1990s, A Tribe Called Quest jump-started and perfected the hip-hop alternative to hardcore and gangsta rap.* John Bush

> *Malik Taylor, the rapper known as Phife Dawg whose nimble, clever rhymes helped launch A Tribe Called Quest to both commercial and critical success...*

"Myself, Kanye (West), we wouldn't be here if it wasn't for Tribe's album," music impresario Pharrell Williams

Malik Taylor, the rapper known as Phife Dawg, has platinum records and industry respect that speak for themselves, but after getting to know the human, I can confidently say that he was one of the most loving and creative souls I've ever been around. Our connection was instant and real. The mutual admiration and our obvious differences created a powerful, trusting creative collaboration and friendship that still amazes me. We'd spend hours brainstorming ideas on music, fashion, and sports. Phife's outlook was about celebrating the best in people and offering up valuable ideas and wisdom without expecting anything in return. Plus, he had a sense of humor that could challenge the best comedians of today. He did a rendition of his mother scolding him as a child that is worthy of a stand-up skit. He could transform his voice into her Caribbean dialect originating from the island of Trinidad and then went into the back-and-forth dialogue between his Queens, New York accent, and his mother's Caribbean accent. It was classic.

I was first introduced to Phife while I was working in the Bay Area building King Duce Records and zazzle.com, and Artsprojekt.com. His agent got word on the street of some white producer making big moves with the big names in the underground music scene.

Fast forward one year later, my wife Beck and I are at Phife's place for a family barbeque with his wife Deisha and the kids. We hung out watching the Jets vs. Raiders and talked about King Duce and making music. Coincidentally, it was the one-year anniversary of his kidney transplant. His wife was the organ match and gave one of her kidneys up to save him. We celebrated the occasion with a sugar-free cake that looked like a kidney. It's an amazing comeback story that received national media attention. Deisha and Phife loved each other so much it was obvious and touching. Beck and I could totally relate. With renewed energy and inspiration, we found ourselves in a creative renaissance of sorts.

Phife was a sports fan with knowledge. He had a stint on ESPN and was passionate about the Jets, the Knicks, and Tarheels hoops. He knew how to coach it and analyze it like a pro. We stepped into the separate but connected dining room to talk and explore our creative, collaborative future. We were so connected and in the zone that we nearly forgot about our wives cooking and watching the football game in the other room. Deisha and Becky hit it off, sharing stories of their husbands' inability to remember anything domestically important because of our childlike hearts and attention spans. They were able to rein us in for the remainder of the night for an amazing barbeque family-style dinner. We genuinely enjoyed hanging out and knew there was more to come.

Phife and I decided to meet up at the Grill, a recording studio in the East Bay, a few nights later. We met up to film Phife for the King Duce documentary piece and to listen to some of his latest work. He had a young artist in tow that he was working with named Snack Box, and they were recording a new track that was making everyone move! Phife's manager friend Lamar invited me to a show the next night in Berkeley at the Shattuck Downlow to watch Phife perform with this raw group of musicians called the Kev Choice Ensemble. He hit the stage and showed the fans why he and his music are legendary and still relevant today. It was awesome to watch a sea of college-aged fans know all the lyrics to every track he dropped on them. And the ridiculously talented live band made the songs pop with rich colors and energy. It was one of the most memorable shows I've seen.

The bass player was amazingly talented and one of the nicest kids I've met. His future was as far as he wanted to go. He was gunned down a few days later heading to band practice by some thugs, content with the idea of snuffing out someone else's dreams instead of utilizing all that energy to do something positive for their community. The young bass player was doing something positive for this world. Just blocks away, a star senior high school football player was gunned down at his high school by some piece of shit haters who took glory in destroying a star that was giving hope and optimism to so many in his black community. But once again, the black community disposes of their very best. It's an inside job, not a white man conspiracy at this point in history. Wake up, black leaders.

Hip hop, in my opinion, was a response to the crazy times in 1970s New York. Murder rates, drug overdoses, serial killers, the beginning of AIDS, you name it. New York represented the depravity and horrors of a corrupt city gone liberal crazy. By the '80s, kids were sick of the fucked-up negativity and started singing/rapping about it and offering a positive message of hope and redemption. Think Kurtis Blow. Like any music, it was a direct reflection of the times. Then it evolved into a distorted, angry barrage of hate, violence, and sex being spewed to the public at large. That began the infiltration of the mob rule riot attitude towards the establishment that today's kids are trying to interpret with a manufactured idea of pain, struggle, and discrimination. You can see it metastasizing on college campuses like an aggressive liberal cancer.

As I was reemerging from my "Dark Ages Era" of my life, writing this book, and launching Manic Fusion Labs, I was excited to reconnect with Malik and Deisha to pick up our collaboration in music, branding, clothing lines, movies, and more...I mean, we had big plans. He was already trying to connect me and his close friend Michael Rappaport on a film project because Phife said I reminded him of his crazy white boy. Rappaport knew Q-tip and had mad respect for Phife and the whole New York hip hop scene, so it was natural for him to direct the Tribe Called Quest documentary, *Beats, Rhymes and Life*. Phife passed away unexpectedly on

March 22, 2016, due to complications from diabetes. He was 45.

Isn't that how life goes? One day you're hanging out and making big plans, and the next day—gone forever. It shocks me that we were so close to launching so much great work, but when I sit quietly and think about what we discovered, I realize that it was pretty amazing. We validated each other at crucial times in our life. I was still a young rap music producer trying to find my way with not a lot of guidance or frame of reference. Phife gave me confidence in my intuit steps on my creative journey. His success and gentle humanness embraced and encouraged me in a way no one could have. Phife proved that I could maintain a childlike love of music and creativity and be commercially successful.

Poignantly, Phife was living on borrowed time and knew it. He was alive in a pure way. Death summoning you can have that effect. There was so much he still wanted to do...so much love he still wanted to give.

MY VISUAL ART JOURNEY

When I set out on my creative journey creating and building King Duce Records, I had no idea that my visual artwork would explode out of me like it did. It really wasn't on my radar because I was focused on my true love with music and exploring that world with everything in me. Building King Duce as a multifaceted vertically integrated lifestyle brand and logo, I understood the vital role visual artists played in the world of creative brands, music promo, and identity. I grew up drawing a little, but not much. Music, social life, and sports were more interesting to me. I took a couple of elective art classes in school. The first class was in the seventh grade with Del Demeir. She was pretty cool and took her art seriously, even though our class was a bunch of stoners and jocks, more interested in drawing band logos and pot leaves.

I was aware of my mom and her big brother Jeff's artistic abilities in visual art. Mom's artistic eye was on full display when it came to her photography. Natural light was her thing, in life as in art. I'm the same. The "feel" or "mood" of a room, outdoors in a still or moving image, was critical to her. Mom's discerning eye and pallet demanded a richness of color, light, and contrast that mixed into a moment of lived experience perfection. Growing up in the golden era of Santa Monica and the surf, film, and music scene of the 1960s, she was exposed to elevated art and nature with the safety, support, love, and encouragement needed to allow her creativity to grow and flourish. Looking back, photography was a big part of my mom's creative outlet.

Mom gave me my creative foundation through her photography and explanation of what made it a great or poor shot taking pictures with her Pentax camera. I recall watching my mom spend hours working with other quality-obsessed artists at La Forces Photography to turn her shots into commercially celebrated artwork in fine coastal galleries. She also gave me the creative approach of getting it out on paper, as she helped me creatively write. She was a true creative in that she understood the flow of creative thought—from rough intuitive expression, then edited and massaged into quality work.

I laughed off art class to my buddies as an elective class I could skate in without getting into trouble. Being a sensitive artist as a jock in a blue-collar town doesn't come off real smooth. Nowadays, it's a little easier with more options and acceptable possibilities thanks to kids being connected ubiquitously and realizing that it's okay to be different and try "strange" or "weird" stuff like drawing or playing guitar. But it wasn't like that back then.

I didn't have the courage and self-confidence to show or really explore my creative passion thoroughly until I started King Duce Records. Coming from blue-collar men and working-class small-town USA, the pressure to conform to that cultural walk and talk made me feel like I needed to accomplish the expectation and success markers set by my dad and the men around me. So, I felt like I needed to be successful in sports and business before I could feel enough freedom to explore my artistic passions.

Graffiti with Greenleaf

I woke up in the middle of the night sleeping on an old musty couch that was a relic leftover from the 1968 "Summer of

Love" that Janis Joplin probably passed out on. I was covered only by a thin blanket sufficient for a warm night in Hawaii. The problem was I was in San Francisco in December. It was a cold that I hadn't felt since I was caught in a snowstorm on top of Squaw Valley skiing as a kid. I tried to focus my eyes in the dark and unfamiliar room only to find heaps of laundry and old beer bottles surrounding me. A warm yellow illumination was coming off a rusty iron street light that was casting an eerie haze of silhouettes that sent my brain to the 1800s in London during the reign of Jack the Ripper. I desperately searched my reachable radius for a blanket, finally settling on an old Levi's jacket and some dirty laundry to cover myself, and just dreamed about the morning light.

This was my first of many nights hanging with urban and graffiti art photographer Rob Greenleaf. With an introduction like that, most people would've run the other direction. But Rob and I were immediately connected and running like we'd been causing trouble since high school. We met working together at Zazzle.com.

It was 2009, and I was learning a lot about everything. Part of this education was Rob's insight into the urban and graffiti art world, and the artists leading the creative charge. We would cruise around the back streets of the Bay Area, searching out the latest graffiti that he could capture with his camera before it would invariably get covered up by another image within days or weeks. One of his classic moves was pointing his camera out his window at 60 miles per hour and machine-gunning rounds of frames at "graf art" that was only visible from the 101. It was a rush, like searching for gold nuggets in a rushing river. Soon, I started seeing spray-paint art everywhere, but in a totally different way. The artwork was amazing, and I was hooked.

This was at the same time that Zazzle was looking to attract artists to our on-demand product creation platform. Greenleaf suggested recruiting artist, former pro skater and founder of Element Skate clothing brand, Andy Howell, to lead a branded division called Artsprojekt. Just as this was happening, Zazzle fired Slim Dickman and almost our entire team because of huge cost overruns and internal cultural clashes with the Beaver family, who started and ran the company. Amongst the firing and restructuring mess, they asked me to stay, and I was introduced to Andy Howell. Andy respected what I was doing with King Duce. We connected as artists and entrepreneurs and he asked me to join him in building out Artsprojekt by helping him recruit the best artists to create the largest collective on the Internet.

Spray Paint Artist Chor Boogie

Little did I know that the guy I was hanging with had recently painted for the Olympics, Playboy, Jay-Z, the Prince of Dubai, and orphanages in Mexico, just to name a few impressive accomplishments that he never happened to mention the entire time we hung out the first time. In fact, the only piece of work he insisted I see was the mural he had painted for the Children's Museum of Art in San Diego. That's Chor Boogie.

I got to know Chor during an art expose with my Artsprojekt.com crew at the Agenda/ASR show in San Diego. Greenleaf introduced us before the show, and we ended up hitting it off and hanging out a couple of nights straight. There was no bullshit about this guy. Pure and honest energy flowed through his eyes, smile, and art. He had been to the edge, recovering from heroin addiction, and came back with a positive message about the therapeutic benefits of "color therapy."

Our adventure started when Chor and I cruised over to a hookah lounge at Med Café and met up with his long-time friend and painter, Evolve, for dinner. We ended up walking the Gas Lamp district of San Diego and then veered off onto side streets past midnight looking at work they had done, listening to nostalgic stories of walls and buildings they had painted over the years, stopping along the way to grab some grub at a Mexican joint and say what's up to some fellow artists they knew from the scene.

The final night we jumped in Evolves truck and rolled out to the only known legal graffiti park in America called Writerz Blok, where Chor had been a curator and mentor for many aspiring young artists. We spent the next five hours until almost 2 am as Chor, Andy Howell, Jim Mahfood, Evolve, Andy Brown, and LA's legendary graffiti artist Slick started doing their thing with over one hundred cans of paint. Evolves' truck bumped a mixtape from one of the OGs from Writerz Block. As the guys painted, Greenleaf captured the magic moment that was unveiling itself.

By the end of the night, there was a 15-foot canvas that was a magic mix of artistic styles and attitude. Chor's contribution was a sight to see. We all stood there at times dazed, partially from the fumes, trying to figure out how Chor could create images that seemed to defy what spray paint was limited to. It almost seemed impossible. But Chor looked like a cross between a magician and a composer orchestrating the paint as if it were literally flowing out of his fingers. You'd have to see it to believe it. I was lucky to witness him in the zone more than once.

Chor Boogie was exposed to the spray paint medium along with many other trials and tribulations that formed his life. As a self-made artist, his drive and his passion fueled his study from renaissance artists such as Michelangelo, Da Vinci, and Rembrandt to more modern artists like Klimt, Van Gogh, and Dali, combining a street culture of modern-day spray.

I reconnected with Chor for a King Duce documentary video shoot at White Walls Gallery in San Francisco a few years after we met in San Diego. We secured the location and the necessary film crew, headed again by Hagar Elaziz, who filmed the Junior Toots video not long before. We arrived in the city around noon to meet the team and set up for the shoot inside the open space of the gallery. After meeting Hagar and her team, the mounting pressure of this latest project had me shook. My pregame and alcoholic jitters were in serious need of relief; I headed out to the nearest bar.

Little did I know that I walked straight into a gay bar in the Tenderloin District. Two "friendly" guys bought me a couple of drinks for a chat, and I was having a nice time, totally oblivious until my assistant, Julie, walked in with a surprised, but not surprised, look on her face. I was stoked to see her and tell her about how nice these guys had been. By this point, I was feeling pretty good and not listening to anyone except my own thoughts of happiness with the temporary relief of my worries. Julie put her arm on my shoulder and whispered in my ear as she pointed up to the giant rainbow flag above the bar. I was in a gay bar called the Titanic, and those nice guys wanted to fuck me! She rounded me up since everyone was waiting for me to start filming.

Less than a year later, we were back at White Walls Gallery for an art show to support Chor's work and just hang out. I thought he had some really amazing work and wanted to see what else would inspire me. The art show was a collection of about eight Bay Area artists showing a wide range of styles from sculpture to spray paint to photography and some traditional oil painted pieces, almost seeming out of place next to the modern art display of a gorilla sitting on a pile of bananas and holding one like a gun. San Francisco is a place to see absurd as sophisticated. Chor was in prime-time form, and we hung out for a while in front of his pieces, laughing and drinking to ease the gathering group of people surrounding us. They could feel that this was big. Before we knew it, the momentum of curiosity drew cameras and more curious people to a perceived flame of artistic stardom. It's a gravitational force, just like being a big college football star. We are all drawn to people doing extraordinary things, especially in the arts, sports, and business. I'm more of a fan than most. Serious. I know what it's like to dream about my rock and roll idols then hang out with them, and them appreciating me.

Photographer Estevan Oriol

"Cartoon and Estevan are the DaVincis of our community; they have been the street chroniclers of our uniquely Chicano story ... our American story..." - George Lopez

After leaving Artsprojekt and Silicon Valley, I continued my creative journey and flew down to LA to hang out with Jim Mahfood, a comic book artist who drew a couple of custom pieces for King Duce. He was part of the Artsprojekt network of artists Andy Howell and I had recruited to leverage the on-demand platform Zazzle built. Jim and I hit Hollywood and a bar where we met up with a few of his friends for drinks. For some reason, I was not drinking at that rare moment, probably because I was coming off a bad run, and I was starting to get sick. I felt like shit. The bar was divided by a wall that separated the club part of the younger party crowd from the café where a stand-up comedian was performing. It was the famous Irish comedian Bill Burr, and he was crushing E Street goofball Springsteen.

I was on my way to my next meeting before the night was over.

Rolling into East LA solo at midnight was not something I was up for after a long two days of a really bad cold and traveling for multiple meetings, but I had a meeting with the famous photographer known for his gritty black and white images of street life in his hometown and of famous LA celebrities like Snoop, Ice Cube, and countless others. I became introduced to Estevan's work at the Agenda Show in San Diego when I met Mister Cartoon and his crew. They were cool and invited me down to their turf to meet Estevan. They gave me a premium black t-shirt with a black and white image of a Mexican chick throwing the infamous LA gang sign. The image was one famous shot by Estevan Oriol.

As I crossed into East LA, I was guided to the industrial garment section of the city by one of the guys who kindly stayed on the phone with me to direct me to the big imposing gate that looked like they got at a California prison auction. I walked in with a box of a dozen King Duce hats and met some guy downstairs who was big, tatted up, and not accustomed to smiling. He told me to wait in the lobby and he would go upstairs and get Estevan. I remember sitting there, sick and jittery from cold medicine, so I was also kinda out of it. But I was there!

One of Estevan's guys, who ran the business side of things, came into the lobby, first to feel me out and get my reason for being there. As we talked, we realized we knew some of the same people, and he began to warm up. Once he realized that I was there to meet Estevan out of respect, the gatekeeper allowed me to meet him. The meeting was brief but sincere on both sides. Estevan was a pro, a gentleman, but definitely someone you would not want to cross. They all dug the hats and my sincere appreciation for the meeting, and a friendship was forged for a future collaboration.

Bua

> *"As an artist 'for the people, by the people, of the people,' BUA's fan base is diverse and ranges from former presidents, actors, musicians, professional athletes, dancers, to street kids and art connoisseurs."* – Navarro, Mireya

I met Justin in Berkeley during my King Duce and Artsprojekt collaboration. I was a fan of his work as I got to know him, and he respected what I was building with King Duce Records. Bua grew up in the Upper West Side of New York City and listened to hip hop and performed with breakdancing crews worldwide, including having a part in the cult classic movie *Breakin.* His visual artwork was inspired by the sounds and motion of the music and dance world he was part of during the '80s in New York. Bua is down to earth and unpretentious, unlike so many artists I have met. He puts in the work and keeps pushing his game to the next level by staying true to his artistic truth. Our foundation in music connects us as artists and as friends.

My visual art journey required courage to get started with King Duce and then take the next step to be validated as an artist among artists I respected. And more importantly, I discovered my own voice and things about myself I would not have otherwise known. This brief summary of my experience hanging out with some of the best visual artists in the world is just a brushstroke that I will expand into an interesting journey of visual art and collaborations and showcases with artists I like and respect.

I now realize the artist needs the fan as much as the fan needs the artist.

It's not foolish that there are fans of stars; it's foolish to place our sense of self and identity onto our stars or fans. Optimally, it's an amazing collaborative energy exchange that produces sparks and fire of new ideas and creations. That's why I was at that art show in SF. I wanted to experience the heartbeat of the art scene with an artist I liked and admired. We were all inspired, fans and artists alike.

THE GREAT ECONOMIC
TIDAL WAVE

F lash back to 2006. We had just sold scout.com to Fox, and I had returned home to build a real estate investment construction business. Times were good, and we were building a solid business and creating jobs in my hometown. I started spending every penny in profits that we were making into launching King Duce. Fast forward another year to October 2007. We were just about to turn the corner when the Real Estate Bubble burst and the Great Economic Recession punched us in the mouth. We lost everything almost overnight.

In 2008, I ended up at the Zazzle start-up gig in Silicon Valley that lasted for less than two years. I learned a lot about human nature, spending over a decade in the crazy Internet start-up universe of Seattle and Silicon Valley. I've never met such delusional and self-obsessed people who claim to be ultra-giving and eco-friendly. They justify their self-obsessed lives by preaching to everyone about how much they "care" about the environment, how gluten-free and dog-friendly they are. Yet, these people taught me the truth about human nature as much as the streets of Oakland at 3 am. You can't hide behind status monikers that tell the world a half-truth of who you really are. It will eventually eat you up from the inside out, at least those of us who have a soul. The truth has a funny way of ultimately revealing itself. I know firsthand. King Duce was my attempt to shed that half-truth I was living. It was my attempt to challenge myself to dare to live fearless like I said I would as a child. I observe too many adults living scared and unwilling to abandon the false notion of job security and safety for the unknown and chase their dreams. Fear kills freedom.

The next few years drained my bank account; I got ripped off and lied to. It was a trying time because I went through a lot of costly trial and error, both with KD and in my personal life. It was a really tough time for Becky. It was the hardest on her, and I regret doing it because of the toll it ultimately put on our marriage. The recession was not nice to us in our real estate business, and we invested our free cash into building King Duce, right as the recession arrived at our shores. The apparel brands and retail stores were all dying a fast death. I was caught in an economic death spiral.

Nonetheless, I kept pushing forward out of a stubborn sense of obligation to my investors and to the memory of my best friend, and my steadfast belief in my pragmatic vision. The experience made me stronger and more certain of my creative path and life moving forward. I look back with a sense of pride with the quality projects we created, the amazing people I met along the way, and the lessons and wisdom I gained. There was a lot that was positive despite the loss of so much. Today, I am smarter about what projects I choose to take on and who I collaborate with. My circle is small and totally trustworthy now. I was so naive entering into those different extreme worlds and allowing leeches to suck me dry of heart and money. In December of 2011, I sent a letter to a small group of my investors thanking them for their belief in KD and telling them that it was over. Would I do it again? I would. But very differently. Hindsight is always 20/20. Now I know, and I don't forget those painful lessons.

People don't realize the ultimate toll King Duce took on my personal life and my marriage. We lost everything, and our relationship was in shambles from the years of being broke, sacrificing everything, and people demanding free gear and criticizing our good intentions and effort. Constantly. To say it was a rough time is a major understatement. I ended up literally living in my truck at times...crashing where I could; I was waking up drunk and cracking a warm beer to stop the shakes. I lost my hope. I lost my soul. I had seen too much greed, hate, struggle, death, and loss. My mind stopped working...and I drank myself into oblivion.

Through the years, the stories of how King Duce started, who started it, and why have been a source of comedy and frustration. When I decided to honor my fallen friend and name my record label and clothing brand King Duce, I had no idea the repercussions it would have on my life. For the most part, the support and love were overwhelming. But it became a huge responsibility with expectations I did my best to uphold while staying true to why I started KD in the first place. While the majority of folks took pride in something that bound us together, it was a way for many of Duce's closest friends and family to deal with his tragic death. Others turned their backs to my intent because of prejudice. Something that started as an innocent artistic journey turned into a tidal wave of dark reality and outside expectations from family and community that I was not prepared for. Some claimed they started KD. Some still do. That bothered me. Many assumed they had some family right to ownership and free KD gear that cost me thousands and thousands of dollars. I was heartbroken and totally blasted by a cold truth.

Pragmatically, I tried to monetize KD as a record label and clothing brand so I could create great artistic projects. That was the whole point. But the business side and investors, and people always demanding free gear wore me down and tainted the original reason I started my creative journey. At the end of the day, it taught me more about human nature than anything else had. I can tell you that the experiences made me a better person and much more grounded

For me personally, King Duce is a canvas that allowed me to create music, fashion, film, and collaborate with other artists who inspire me to explore and celebrate their work. I've never been interested in mastering one art form or defining art into suffocating categories. I just like the process of expressing what I feel, see, and hear, in whatever creative form it takes. Often, it's a mixture of art forms wrapped into a single piece. And that's why King Duce is a constantly changing collage made up of all the art forms that I explored growing up: music, visual art, writing, athletics, film, and photography.

I like coaching and inspiring young people to follow their dreams and teach them how to get there. I enjoy being around the kids' energy and their innocent love of the game. I wanted King Duce to be that creative incubator that gave kids a place to gain confidence and learn to follow their passion in a real-world kind of way. That's why, after working for a decade in Seattle and Silicon Valley, I decided to leave it all behind and combine my passions of music, teaching, and business. I wasn't sure what to expect, but I knew I couldn't go wrong if I was all in and just went for it, win or lose. I knew I would learn from the best artists and enjoy the ride. I chose to follow my heart and not the money. I chose right, even if it tested me more than I could've imagined. I would have lived in deep regret if I hadn't done it: risked it all and discovered my truth.

WHAT I DISCOVERED
BUILDING KING
DUCE RECORDS

My indoctrination into the rap game was no joke. I dove into the deep end of the pool, thinking I was an expert swimmer. The minute I hit the "dark side" in Sac with G Will and other young wild gangsters with nothing to lose and everything to gain, I realized this was a different world. Our first photoshoot was literally at the spot where a 15-year-old boy had been gunned down in a drive-by a few days earlier. It hit me hard then as much as it does now. I soon realized that violent death was not an occasional tragedy, it was all the time, and I was a target with money. Being white and doing big things, I was gaining enemies as fast as I was building a movement. I was producing a crew of rap artists who were not pretending. Their words were the reality they were living.

I felt like I had been dropped into an active war zone of killers, and my soldier in arms had already been gunned down execution-style. I was in a nightmare without a lantern. But I knew I was all in no matter what and had to lead a movement. I was very aware that I could be shot at any moment I stepped into the hood. It was a strange reality. As dangerous and unpredictable and tragic as this world was, it was alive and electric in a way that can only come from the mindset that your last day could be today. Say what you gotta say, and do what you gotta do, and don't cry to momma. It was an all or nothing game with winners getting respect and getting paid. If you lose, you're dead. It's that simple. And there are very few tears, regret, or remorse. It's a reality that white liberal people think they know experiencing the periphery of black culture, the mainstream immersed black culture brought to you by Bill Cosby, Oprah, and Obama. That's why you see white suburban church missionaries going to Peru but not Oakland or the LA inner city.

I walked through the hood late at night, spent time in bars, clubs, drug houses, strip clubs, and some real sketchy situations. I was on paranoid scanner always but also feeding off the insanity, excitement, and unpredictability of the moment, a stark contrast to the mainstream lifestyle of squeaky-clean preventative living. I loved it because these guys weren't fucking around; they talked about shit that was real, not the Williams Sonoma Napa wine and cheese culture I knew all too well. People talking about their carbon footprint, charity, running events, organic and gluten-free lifestyles all in a conscious attempt to passive-aggressively compete against their neighbors. They live to preach about how worldly, open-minded, and not prejudiced they believe they are.

I never saw any of these white liberal sympathizers visit the hood. The real hood. Never. I see their Facebook posts endorsing antifa and Black Lives Matter, but they won't cross Highway 101 from their ivory towers in Palo Alto to the real hood in East Palo Alto (EPA), a distance of about 400 feet! This is the epitome of talking big about diversity but full of shit. They're SCARED. So, if you don't experience the day-to-day reality of a culture or business or role in that business, how in the fuck can you preach about it? The next time I hear a spoiled kid from Stanford working on his first start-up as a 24-year-old CEO talking about diversity/politically correct bullshit, I am driving his lily-white ass into the underground rap game and inner-city neighborhoods and see how they talk about it afterward. The Far-Left don't have a clue about the brutal mindset and viciousness they are dealing with. Grimy is the word I often heard in the hood, and it perfectly describes the attitude there.

There are good folks doing good things, like E-40, but many are straight gangster gutter hood out for themselves. It's all good to me. At least I knew what I was dealing with; at least the game was more honest than the white-collar business game and the white middle-class world I grew up in, always worried about keeping their reputation clean, even if it was whitewashed. This is why Kevin "Duce" Kimble and I connected. We recognized and appreciated things in the other person and their world that we wanted. Kevin was attracted to the love, security, happiness, and good food at my home. We weren't rolling in money, but we always had plenty. I wanted the honesty and real truth like he had in the streets.

My dad grew up poor, so he felt connected to Kevin because he knew what it was like to be hungry. Plus, Kevin was always extraordinarily sensitive and loving to my special needs baby sister Nicole. It was very touching. I never knew the reality that Kevin was living, never knew until he died. He was beaten by his big brother like a soldier in training for the streets. He saw the real shit but kept it from me. My sister and Kevin would hang out playing blocks or Legos, smiling and laughing like they were kindred spirits. They were touching each other's lives since she was a baby up until Kevin died. I think Nicole and Kevin were both trapped in worlds they didn't choose, but they transcended that struggle and saw the love and gave it to people.

Duce and I established a trust and respect that allowed us to experience the other side in an honest and real way; good, bad & ugly. So, when I set out to launch a record label from scratch and jump straight into the underground rap game, Kevin trusted that I wasn't fucking around. He knew that I could handle it from growing up in his scene and my days running with the crew from South-Central LA when I was playing ball at Fresno State. I was coming off a big business win building and selling Scout.com to Fox. The trust and money were there, and together, we knew we had the partnerships to win. When Kevin was killed right as we were stepping into the rap game, I had to manage chaos in a tornado, while my income was wiped out with the oncoming Great Recession. I had no choice but to fight my way through it, adapt, and succeed against all the odds. I owed it to myself and to Kevin. That same decision almost single-handedly ended my marriage to my high school sweetheart.

King Duce became an all-consuming crazy train ride that I was holding onto for dear life, trying to steer as my personal life was collapsing. I had taken on extremely ambitious plans and couldn't see the perfect storm on the horizon. There were a lot of days and nights that I was asking myself why I got myself into this crazy life. I would picture myself living the safer, less adventurous alternative and concede that I was where I needed to be. It was a very challenging time, but made me grow in ways as a leader and person that I could never have received from another PowerPoint deck presentation at another Internet start-up ran by white boys who never left the security of what they knew—likeminded socioeconomic neighbors and friends who went to private school, walked over to Stanford with the same kids, and then commuted literally down the road to an Internet start-up with an office full of the same kids from the same background. These people don't know diversity. To be clear, Silicon Valley is racially diverse, but the culture is homogenously politically correct vanilla. They have no clue what our cultural and racial divide is really about in America. Being more compassionate for the sake of saying you "care" is a cop-out. Go actually experience it with your time and money, and then talk to me.

What I see in the culture I came up in is that people worked hard to come across as reasonable and thoughtful, but often, they are anything but. A pressure cooker of lies and self-deception only creates more delusional thinking and further divide. I remember the local Nazarene church pastors and other zealots criticizing me for going into the black hood to produce rap music. Talk about self-righteous. They couldn't understand that one of my reasons for doing it was to connect to the influential young black artists through their music so we could build trust and learn from each other and develop a new perspective, hopefully in a way that gave the kids the encouragement to chase a dream without a gun and the understanding of what it takes to get there. These kids were teaching me how their day to day was and how to hustle and survive in their world. We were teaching each other rules to the same game. Just different approaches and attitudes, but willing to die for a similar outcome—love and respect.

We *all* need that to feel good about ourselves. I was very conscious of the hard work I had put in to get where I was. But I was equally, painfully aware of the charmed life I lived. With every accolade and compliment, I winced at the inequality of life, not in terms of race, although I was fully aware of the inequality related to race, I saw it as more of a human struggle. I was aware of the socioeconomic differences early on and never wanted to be seen as above or spoiled. I dressed and acted according to the environment I wanted to be part of and get respect from. I think my dad's stories and attitude from being a poor kid from the outside had a major impact on the way I saw society's hierarchy, bosses and workers, and leadership. At a very young age, I was thrust into the center stage of leadership. I became aware of it the day I arrived at preschool. I was the oldest of three boys and a handicapped sister. I was very paternal and hyperconscious of the struggle exemplified every day in life by my courageous and inspiring little sister who battled life trapped in a physical and mental prison. She always smiled at the positive vibes around her and gave it back exponentially angelic.

A lot of people I was close with, including some of my family, didn't really understand my reasons for doing what I was doing. From conversations, I realize many thought I was chasing money and fame. We never could openly communicate about our very different view of the business world, socioeconomic issues, race issues, and the life I was interested in exploring. The funny thing is that I was basically following in my dad's footsteps, in the sense that I was attracted to black culture and wanted to teach and coach the high-risk kids. King Duce was my school operating in an unconventional way that scared and turned off traditional teachers, coaches, community church, and business "leaders." Ironic. I was putting my life and money where my mouth was when it came to my philosophy.

The virtue-signaling teachers that kicked me out of their "club" and out of teaching at the high-risk continuation high school in my hometown all went to Chico State, grew up in soft yuppie suburbia, and claimed to be saving street kids. The kids respected and loved me because I didn't talk down to them like they were dumb or below me. These kids had lived more life than the *Romper Room* gang of "teachers" combined, and the kids knew it. I walked onto campus with my King Duce Records street cred and had a loyal army by lunchtime. King Duce was the conduit that made these kids stop and listen, and once they got to know me, they realized I was for real and someone they could trust. One kid walked into class one day to show me a quarter pound of weed under his jacket as a sign of trust. I coached him but respected his sign of trust and commitment to me. I showed him respect. Today he works for me.

King Duce taught me the hard-knock lessons that strengthened my determination, focus, will, belief in self and others. It taught me to listen with my heart and to lead with courage even when everyone around me didn't understand me, and I could no longer trust their intentions. By challenging myself, I recognized weaknesses in myself and others.

Most deny their true passions out of fear. They never face it and go for it. I realized the world was made up of two kinds of people—those who live on their own terms, and those who conform to a way of life scared and frozen by fear but justifying the denial of their truth because of excuses like bills, kids, or their job and never really go for their dreams. It's not about going big or being rich or famous. It's about being alive to help others, pursue things we are passionate about, and continue to learn and grow until the last breath. Living our truth.

When Kevin was killed, I lost my trusted ambassador to the underground rap game and the black community. I was on my own and had to navigate a world I was not prepared for. And naming the record label in honor of my fallen friend only created an expectation that I would carry the flag regardless of what would happen to me. In the beginning, I felt a purpose that transcended death, but soon I felt locked and trapped inside of a tumultuous world of rappers, gangsters, and street elements that surrounded it. Spending over a decade on the Internet and major media start-up world, I was well equipped to negotiate multimillion-dollar contracts with some of the biggest names in the business game. In the Internet start-up world, I was used to taking big risks with talented people to achieve a successful end goal. I was even accustomed to some dishonest and selfish motives by investors and executives pushing their way to the pot of gold at the expense of others around them. But what I was now experiencing was a metamorphosis through my tragic experiences of human loss and violence without reason.

My lived experience gave me the confidence to create a record label that would compete in the rap music category or any other genre. But nothing could've prepared me for what I would experience. The minute Kevin was dead, I was aggressively approached by a deluge of rappers to make good on my plan. They wanted money and free gear; they expected me to produced videos and albums almost immediately. They saw a weakened player vulnerable to exploit, and I caved at times and lost discipline in my life. It seemed like I was being swallowed up by a force and group of people that would drain my blood if it gave them more money. Why? Because they all thought I was rich because I was a white guy with a plan and a BMW. Period. It never changed; even when my wife and I lost everything to the recession, I was still getting harassed for not doing enough. I felt trapped and frustrated and disillusioned. I look back and I don't lament the money spent; it gave me the ultimate education. But I do look back discouraged at the attitude and mentality I experienced. I was naïve and they knew it. I am no longer blind like the rest of mainstream America.

I lived and experienced the world I'm talking about, most people have not. And this bleeds into political ideology and polarized camps. If you haven't hung out in the hood over the years with street gangster black guys with guns, then how can you say anything with any lived experience or credibility? You can't! Theory doesn't cut it with this problem. From my lived experience in Oakland, Sac, South-Central LA, Chicago, New York…the inner-city black neighborhoods are totally fucked up, in big part because of liberal policy. It's the biggest lie in US history. Why are we trying to save third-world countries when we have a third-world epidemic right under our own roof? White Far-Left Liberals and Black race-baiters have convinced black people that liberalism is their way out. I hate to be the bearer of bad news, but it has only enslaved an entire people. It's a travesty. They gladly hand out money through a dirty payoff program called welfare, or any name they want to give it to sound better, so they can keep the black vote. It's bribery.

Rap music and hip hop both spend most of the time bitching about struggles and retaliatory violence. The more I was immersed in Oakland, NY, LA, and Sacramento rap scenes, I started to realize it simply was a larger cultural ideology of "the struggle" and being held down by "the man." Yet, what I observed were people taunting criminal behaviors and actions at the mainstream and law enforcement—boasting of killing cops, kids, anything, and then claiming the poor victim card. I walked away many days and late nights from the studios and clubs or streets with candlelight vigils shaking my head and wondering what the end game was. Everyone was just out for themselves and fucking over anyone in their way. It was all so illogical.

Violence and lack of cohesion within the greater black experience was my takeaway. To be very clear, I met some amazingly inspiring people along the way, as I do wherever I go. But I can say without a doubt that rap music, for all of the artistic brilliance, has a general testosterone-fueled message echoing a sentiment by black people that continues to divide and fragment a black society already in free fall failure. It goes back to my original point; the music isn't the problem, the attitudes expressed in the music are the problem. It is a direct reflection of the tired ideology of victimization, oppression, and "coming up" by any means necessary.

At the end of the day, I ran out of money and patience. The great recession and KD had taken its toll. I was tired of investing my hard-earned money into people who continually demanded more, sometimes with death threats, and never any sense of appreciation or pragmatic plan to make me a return for investing in them. They felt I owed it to them. They rarely showed a willingness to actually pay for my quality products, effort, and risk. It was a disappointing and eye-opening experience that taught me that we, as a nation, are more divided than I was raised to believe. The rap game is dirty but no worse than the shady and ruthless politicians and businesspeople I worked with and know personally. Both sides are out for themselves regardless of what they claim. That's the problem.

I felt crucified by many in my hometown including church zealots and folks who had a self-righteous disdain for the music and culture with no true experience in it. I actually lived it and put my money where my mouth was. The experience taught me to follow my heart and continue to stand up for the right people and causes. I spent way too many days and nights away from my wife with people who took property and life without regard for anyone or anything. It got old, and I changed what I invested my time and money into. I figured it out too late and ended up losing my wife, my house, my cars, and every penny I had. I was sickened by the state of the black community's lack of unity and out-of-control culture of ignorance, greed, and violence, totally fragmented by the Far-Lefts corrupt political agenda to divide.

For many, rap music is a means to an end; no more, no less. But for others, it's about music and creating. Many of the rap artists I knew wanted to be respected and paid. In theory, rap music gave them both. It took me a while to understand that rap music operated like the drug business. But then I realized it was all the same. In the rap business, you can get ripped off and fucked over if you don't stay diligent and disciplined and watch your back. It's a ruthless game, like the drug scene. I also saw more similarities to the Internet media business world than differences. The most notable difference is that in the drugs and rap music business, disputes are settled with guns and blood. In the New York and LA media business, they settle disputes with dirty lawyers and contracts that would make you pray for a bullet.

7

RUSTED, BUSTED, &
RECONSTRUCTED

Rusted, Busted, & Reconstructed

BECKY LEAVES CHRIS

It was March of 2011, or maybe it was April.... I was sitting
in my office, drinking Jack Daniels on the rocks, working
on a song. Posters of Bradley Knowles of Sublime playing on stage, passionately singing into the mic, and a poster
of Janis Joplin's famous naked shot wearing beads hung on
the wall for inspiration. I had a Howard Hughes room of
ripped out *Rolling Stone* pictures of different artists taped to
the walls, fat red marker arrows connecting the artists to their
relevant ancestor with words trying to describe their significance. Books on Howard Hughes, Carl Sagan, and the "Holy
Blood, Holy Grail" sat on the same table with my recording
system and whiskey. Sitting at the board trying to mix a song
and lay down a guitar track, I looked like I'd been up recording for weeks straight. Becky opened the door.

"I'm done. I don't know who you are anymore, and you're
going to kill yourself the way you are living. Why, Chris??
Why??"

Becky was crying but set on her decision. I looked up in
disbelief, partially irritated that she just interrupted a mixing
session and a good buzz.

"Babe, I love you."

"Chris, you don't love me as much as your music and
alcohol. Where are you, Chris! Where did you go? We had
a dream, and you decided to trade it in for something that

killed us. Go, Chris. Go follow your dream. I don't want to hold you back. I will always love you, Chris Rockwell. But I think you need something different. You broke my heart. I loved you with everything I have. And now it's over. I hope you get what you want."

The door shut. Still totally in denial, but kind of shocked, I took another drink straight from the bottle. I was lost and about ready to hit my first bottom. Little did I know that things were about to get really fucking bleak.

CRAZY CLOWN

After getting wiped out, I desperately continued working to make King Duce survive the inevitable tsunami of the Great Recession and my financial and emotional demise. Despite being a drunk, depressed disaster, admitting defeat with my marriage and my business in front of my hometown crowd was humiliating and devastating. I was drinking day and night, painting when I was awake, and trying to see a way out of the insanity and loss I felt. Drinking continued to erode my mind and moral compass. I couldn't be alone because I felt so absolutely alone.

I was an alcoholic, and I was going to die if I didn't stop. I was on the fence on how I wanted to finish the ride. I was a decaying corpse, pickled and wreaking of old alcohol, a drudgery of existence and miserable failure. I didn't know who I was or where I was going anymore, and when someone made mention of my dire condition, I would give a dead, emotionless stare of agreement. But it tore me up. Man, I was sick. The black sunrise from hell would greet me each morning with the four horsemen galloping through my mind, while my stomach, heart, and body were nearly seizing from my sky-high blood pressure and the need for more alcohol to quiet the insanity and physical shakes.

I remember waking up in my dank little studio at the Craggs in 2011 after Becky told me she was done. It was an

417

old Spanish mansion converted into individual apartments located on the Feather River, known to have historically housed a US president back during the heyday of the gold rush when Oroville was booming. The picturesque and historical highlights couldn't change the smell of a dying dog named Harley and her owner, who died there just before I moved in. My studio was covered in pounds of dog hair and was filthy. Despite having a north window and screened door that opened up to the river, I couldn't appreciate the beauty of it through the dander and my damaged mind and heart. None of it mattered. I was trying to see a way out of a darkness and sadness that blocked the sunlight to my visual perception. My heart was black. Most days, I would start my morning out drinking a beer from the mini-fridge, smoking a bowl to settle my turning stomach, and I would cry over the loss of my wife and pray for my reality to change or go away. The nights found me wandering and turning to more booze to keep me company.

When Becky left, all the world went dark, cold, and very lonely. I had just lost the woman that was the only true steady girl I'd ever been with and my true love. We started dating when I was sixteen and she was fifteen. I allowed alcohol, drugs, and my container shipment of ambitions and selfish insecurities destroy my marriage to this beautiful woman. In the middle of the night I would be begging with everything in me for the morning light; and the very next minute, I was up and screaming, twitching, crying, moaning at the depths of my soul for help and relief, which usually came in the form of more alcohol and bad decisions. To say it was bad is to say hell is kind of rough.

It was a nonstop manic roller coaster of loss, resentment, and depression. I was a mess. At that time, everywhere I traveled and stayed was a possible disaster waiting to happen, usually ending with a knock-down-drag-out argument and the eventual arrival of the cops. Things were spiraling down, and my blackouts, rage, and despair were starting to make me think and do things that were completely self-destructive and suicidal in nature.

I was walking but barely breathing and unable to see any flicker or ripple of hope most of the time I was awake, so I would sleep most days away. Wherever I woke up after passing out the night before or in my dusty riverside room, I would start the whole sad process over again. I would usually drink around the clock and pass out for a while, wake up and feel insane, and get more beer to calm my shakes and even shakier thoughts. It could be one in the morning or one in the afternoon; it didn't make a difference, and I usually didn't know. I dipped and dived my manic roller coaster drunken run until the lights would go out.

I felt like I had completely failed at everything in my life. It was as if I had hypothermia, numbed from the pain and loss, and I just wanted to go to sleep. I was making some vain attempts at finding work back in Silicon Valley, but things were quiet. Ironically, I was in talks with Yahoo and even met with them at their headquarters. It went nowhere, just like the company and the economy.

I was making decisions that were unnecessarily risky, although that's how I did things my whole life, but now I was crazy and financially backed into a corner. I had a run-in with the cops up at Oroville Dam for spray painting on state property. I was painting on a barrier wall in broad daylight, spray can in one hand, Bud Light in the other, when a young peach fuzzed DWR Security Guard rolled up and asked me what I was doing.

"Painting," I told him. He really didn't know what to do with that answer. I even offered him a beer. I left before the cops showed up.

Eventually, they caught up to me, and I was charged with vandalizing state property and fined by the DA.

It was a few months later I painted *Electric Sunshine* under the green suspension bridge on the far side of the lake. It's still there despite the local cops slashing it with paint.

They didn't remove it, just destroyed it, amping up my defiance once again.

As time crept on, I was literally losing my mind in the sense of being able to pick up and move forward. I was stuck on stupid. The only thing I could see was another beer and passing out and doing it all over again, with each day turning into a couple of weeks of a blur that seems like an endless dirt road with no point.

I was driving drunk day after day in the mountains, on highways, back roads, main roads, it didn't matter. Deep down, I wanted to just fade away. After a while, I didn't even care if that meant jail or prison. I wasn't opposed. I had lost the ability to put coherent thoughts together and make sense of simple topics and questions. I was also likely struggling with a form of PTSD from the years of death, trauma, and head injuries. But all I knew was that I was in a very dark place that only I could get myself out of.

Not only was I broke and defeated, but I was flopping around on couches and even spent a short stint with my parents until I pissed on their upstairs carpet while I was blacked out sleeping in my childhood bunk bed. Talk about feeling like a total loser! I wanted to scream, cry, fight, kick, and drink even more. I was so disgusted with myself and feeling sorry for my losses that I was beside myself.

I felt very alone and misunderstood by my town, investors, and family. It was a brutal time at the bottom. During that time, a lot of hard truths had to come out. And at times, it felt like each day was only arriving to slam a hammer down onto my heart with another round of sadness and despair over losing Becky and trying to keep above water wading through the 25 years of lived emotion and life that was suddenly gone. I know the fact that I was staying at other women's places was killing Beck, on top of losing me over alcohol. The world and universe felt incongruent and totally fucking insane and pointless.

After a particularly bad New Year's Day, drinking a half a bottle of Tequila before noon, getting kicked out of a bar for talking shit about the bartender's husband's union retirement from Anheuser Busch, I drove back to Julie's place in half blackout and proceeded to spray paint a crazy clown art piece on the back-room wall. It was basically a self-portrait of how I was feeling. Then I went apeshit crazy and punched and kicked a bunch of holes in the wall and then passed out.

Julie came home with her kids, then eight and ten, to find me unconscious and the house smelling like a toxic lab, not to mention the scary as shit clown I painted on her destroyed wall. When I finally woke up, I felt like I was on hell's back door, smelling like an old drunk and feeling like the devil was playing a sick game with me. I knew my reckless and futile ways were numbered. I didn't care, and it showed. I was done...but I wasn't. Julie endured some really bad times during this period. I was always drunk and going off negatively about what life had dealt me, or I was super high and in a good but short-lived and unpredictable mood before I would black out and escalate my depression, anger, and fear. It was literally the worst time in my life, and probably hers too. There is no other way to describe it.

Although I was still a long way from my final road to recovery, I had a moment of clarity that day that forced me to make a move that would shock my system and get me to a healthier place. I needed to leave town and get clean. And it was settled—I was off to the Eastern Sierra Nevada Mountains.

But, wherever you go, there you are.

DONNER SUMMIT IN
A SNOWSTORM

Julie and I had road-tripped over to Mammoth and the surrounding area, including the June Lake Loop, Bridgeport, and my hallowed hunting camping grounds of Monitor Pass just north of Bridgeport a couple of times for business. The Eastside was a special place to us both, so it seemed like it made sense. We spent the next couple weeks packing up my truck and preparing my Lance camper with a supply of food and gear fit for an Alaskan Expedition. Julie was able to get me a job working for an old ski patrol friend they called Wing Nut. I soon learned that it was because he was off his fucking rocker! He owned a fishing marina and campground on the world-famous trout fishing reservoir in Bridgeport. It was a high desert landscape of sage brush, obsidian, and granite rocks scattered everywhere. It's kind of like a moonscape except the horizon to the west and east towered giant snow-capped mountains and pine trees that put the meadow and reservoir into a picturesque context of the Wild West in its pristine form.

I remember the day we drove over, Julie followed behind my truck and camper in her beat-up gold Ford Expedition. We hit a heavy snowstorm on Highway 80; we were stopped with hundreds of other travelers on the road for over an hour, and then finally allowed to exit the highway and pull into Colfax for dinner and to camp out in the Lance for the night. We pulled off just in time and found two seats at the counter of a tiny diner with a white and red 50s feel to it called Colfax Max Burgers. The snow was coming down like heavy balls of cotton.

The little room full of weary travelers trying to get over the pass that night to reach Tahoe and Reno were all unanimously shocked that the pass had been closed. Not sure why anyone was surprised, really. I mean, we were trying to cross over the Sierra Nevada Mountains at night in the middle of a snowstorm. Gee, I guess that's why Donner Pass got its name! Pioneers thinking they could beat Mother Nature. Never. I looked back out to see the snow falling and contemplate the interesting news from the unofficial source that just entered our tightly packed café. The windows were fogged up from all the hot breath and laughter emanating off of everyone, which gave me a claustrophobic feeling, especially since we were sitting at the far end of the narrow train car-designed building, and I was wanting a beer real bad but knew I couldn't.

My mind started racing, yelling at me to get the fuck out of there. I was starting to feel a panic attack coming on. Julie gave me a warm, reassuring look that helped me come down and settle in and enjoy our situation, despite the noticeable tension and fear she could sense in my nervous ticks and sounds. The moment was smashed and lifted up into happiness when our hamburgers and fries showed up, to the envy of the starving travel-weary comrades who still hadn't found a seat or menu with the flood of people taking cover from the road and storm.

It was like a big loud family reunion. The couple next to us were passing through visiting their daughter attending college at Nevada (UNR), where my baby brother Dan played football and earned a degree in how to get really high and play Frisbee during class. As I zoned out on my food, I started to drift into a quiet place, pondering my life's next steps and saying goodbye to the past. For that moment, I felt a sense of peace and hope, as slight and fleeting as it was. I appreciated it and took a deep breath and a drink of my Coke and knew that I was going to be okay.

For now, I was going to enjoy the impromptu pit-stop adventure and the anticipation of sleeping warm and cozy in my camper. We enjoyed our meal, paid our bill, and said our goodbyes to our new gypsy family in the café and walked outside into the muffled sounds of Sorels in the soft falling snow. The faint sounds of laughter and good conversation back in the train car drifted further away as we neared the trucks parked in the Safeway parking lot behind the diner. The fact that my heater in the camper was not working, coupled with the snow and falling temperatures, made me realize that we were all in on this journey. My cold breath was like billowing steam, and I mused at the adventure I was on. I felt another spark of happiness and warmth at that moment.

I climbed inside the camper, up into the queen size bed directly above the cab of my truck, where I had laid with my wife on many camping trips during our marriage. A dagger struck my heart. It was freezing outside, but I was warm under layers of blankets. The light through the windows my breath glow yellow and white with blends of luminescent colors that swirled like the thoughts racing through my mind. I figured I could lose my mind tomorrow. I drifted off under the layers of camping blankets and sleeping bags protecting me from the frigid reality of my future.

Sunlight and blue skies greeted me through the east window headboard. The warm illuminance filled the camper with hope. The fresh white snow was like starting over with a brand-new canvas. I smiled for a moment, before hurling my thoughts down a steep mountain, watching it roll out of control as I started feeling anxiety over not drinking and the terror of not having a fucking clue what my life was about. We hit the road after grabbing large coffees at the local drive-through and stopping to smoke a bowl and take a leak with a view. The crisp, clean air and the smell of the pine and cedar trees grounded me and let me know I was headed in the right direction.

After the Crazy Clown incident, I continued to drink uncontrollably for a while, but now I was about a week sober and fucking miserable. Being a heavy daily drinker, I was in a total physical and mental state of hell. It's a place that feels infinitely dark and hopeless. Why do you think alcoholics and drug addicts keep doing something that ultimately kills them? Do you think they do it because they are dumb or weak compared to the average human? I can promise you it has nothing to do with intelligence or normal strength and discipline. Imagine a physical allergy and mental obsession that is beyond medical explanation or solution. The "regular" person can't grasp the unimaginable mental grip that takes over. But stopping does require a true willingness to want to heal from the inside out and hit the restart button by taking some action and discipline to live a different way.

I have excelled at most things I've focused on in my life, but every ounce of my stubborn persistence was going to be needed to fight my battle with alcohol. It owned me, and I knew it. It was a love-hate obsession that ruled my days and nights with an iron fist and a seductive kiss. Nothing was going to change for the better if I couldn't kick this demon bitch alcohol in the fucking head. She ruled my every thought, step, and word. She loved me and coddled me, she adored me and hated me with hell's ugliness and rotting death. I hadn't hurt enough yet to completely surrender to it.

After we hung out for a few minutes drinking our coffee and talking a little about life and the adventure ahead, the mood got serious and focused as we confirmed our plan if we lost contact since our cell phones were useless through the thick forested Western Sierras. We jumped in our separate trucks and looked through the rolled down windows to wave goodbye. We hit Highway 80 towards our destination, and honestly, I wasn't sure where that was. My mind was focused on the monumental life changes facing me. I felt a frigid darkness creep down my spine and settle deep into my soul.

The morning light hit the fresh snow on the trees and high mountaintops in an indescribably beautiful way. In that moment, my icy outlook thawed into a smile and a glimmer of light that gave me a few miles of relief from my impending thoughts of doom and gloom. I just knew I was in the mountains of my childhood and was heading to a familiar place, not far from where we bow hunted every year since I was born.

"WING NUT"– MY
SUICIDE ANGEL

His mind was disturbingly fragmented, wired to self-destruct with the simple daily decisions, like how to handle an unscheduled phone call during his strict morning regimen of coffee and reading his morning prayers and meditation. He would lose his fucking mind and could never regain any semblance of his day. I suffer from that to a slightly lesser degree. When I met Wenger, he was twenty years sober. He survived fetal alcohol syndrome along with his twin sister. They were adopted by a loving family who brought them to grow up at Convict Lake in the cradle of the Sierra Nevadas. He lived in and loved the outdoors and the serenity, solitude, and isolation he could achieve there. He was a good, caring soul with a mind that rarely slept or cooperated with his true intentions.

Jeff's parents owned a fishing marina and resort at Crowley Lake, world famous for its trout fishing and located near June and Mammoth Mountain Ski Resorts. In fact, G'pa Lee used to spend a week every year fishing Convict, Crowley, and the neighboring lakes with his buddies during the 1950s when he was an LA cop. Growing up on Crowley allowed Wenger the necessary space in nature to help regulate his damaged brain. From my talks with him during our breaks from preparing his docks, store, and campground for the upcoming May 1 opening day of trout season, I could tell that Jeff was a good soul trying to right things that couldn't be changed. He was painfully aware that his mind was his enemy, but he lived with colorful passion and kindness when his mind granted it. Sadly, peace and focus evaded him most of the time.

Wenger's twin sister, Ruthie, was a crazy bitch who thrived on chaos, destruction, and taking. Apparently, she duped their parents to will everything over to her just before they died, cutting her brother completely out. Jeff didn't care about money, and it broke his heart in a way that I could still see on his face as he stood in the midday sun sharing his life with me. I related to Jeff in so many ways it scared me. Looking back as I write this, after his suicide and my recovery, I feel closer and more similar to him than I did that day he shared a part of his tortured life with me. He basically lived out on the reservoir alone much of the year in his fifth-wheel camper trailer. I don't know how he did it. I couldn't do it alone. It takes only one day of overwhelming brain activity or tragic news to take someone like us out, back into the hell of self-medicating a clinically malfunctioning brain. The average person has no fucking concept of what that reality feels like—to battle the constant swings and agitation. It's brutal.

Life is a trip. Julie had connected me to the place and the person I needed at that very moment. Wenger was exactly the extreme case that I needed to be around. His temper, lack of concentration, and inability to effectively communicate without losing his mind made the experience challenging at best. I think back to all the days I had exposed the people I loved to even worse drunken rageful behavior.

I was equally as disturbed as Wenger by the time I staggered into Bridgeport, but at the time, I didn't believe that. I figured I just needed to dry out and get my money situation figured out. Looking back now, I was completely fucking disassociated from reality in many ways. My alcoholic mind had me believing things that were simply not real. I was a broken soul landing at the shores of a familiar and scary new world. Julie stayed for about a week, helping me get the feel of my new home and getting everything set up for work and life.

My first day in Bridgeport after Julie left started out with beautiful high desert spring weather. The sun was shining, and the snow was melting and flowing into creeks, streams, and lakes all around me. I remember waking up before daylight and brewing a pot of coffee on my Lance camper stove. I turned on my Pandora station to listen to some music to fill the silence. John Denver's "Country Boy" was playing, and I found my foot tapping and a slight smile chiseled at my granite stone thoughts. I suddenly had a newfound connection to the song and its lyrics of a simple country boy being thankful for his good, simple life on the farm. Julie had left the evening prior to return to Oroville to get back to her kids, dealing with a divorce and home in foreclosure. I was so caught up in my losses and struggles that I didn't consider the weight of responsibilities and adversity she was dealing with. I jumped in my Chevy diesel truck and headed out of camp before the sun was up.

The moon was still visible to the west, and it cast a bone-white glow over the expanse of sagebrush, water, and mountains that surrounded the giant meadow. I decided I was going to drive south out of the little town to a small lake and stream that I had discovered a few days earlier. I turned up the heater and turned on my CD player. The growling scream of Phil Anselmo came blasting out of my speakers and about gave me a heart attack while I frantically punched the stereo to shut it off. I ended up ejecting the stereo face, and it fell to my boots and the floor covered in volcanic dust and sand. My temper soared to red as I tried to get out of camp without waking Wenger and the other camper, apparently some other guy there for the summer to help out. Cliff was an old friend of Wenger's' from the Crowley days. He accepted Wenger's

abuse and ridicule because they had known each other forever... and Cliff needed a friend just as bad as Wenger did.

After reattaching my stereo face, I replaced Down's
NOLA album with Willie Nelson. My heart rate settled as
I sipped my coffee and crept past Wenger's gigantic camp-
er-trailer parked right at the entrance to the marina. As I
turned off the gravel drive and onto the blacktop road, I hit
my headlights and accelerated up to a nice rhythm. I lit a bowl
and inhaled a mellow tingling sensation that helped take a
slight edge off my raw nerves. I started to lose myself in the
solitude and surroundings that were so familiar and nostalgic. Growing up deer hunting just north of Bridgeport made
the Eastern Sierras my home. The sagebrush, deer, and aspen
trees were the things from my childhood, and I was doing
exactly what I dreamt about doing as a kid, living there with
my hunting truck and no one to hassle me. I always dreamed
of being a cowboy out on the open prairie around the campfire, probably because I did get some of that camping and
hunting with cowboys like the Brandts and the Mastelottos.
I was reminiscing about playing with my brothers in the hills,
running through the sagebrush, charging down the hill up
from camp, crashing through the aspen quakies.

I started to cry. I didn't know it at the time, but I had
become far too dependent on Julie, taxing her every move
and thought with my fear and insanity. I looked to her to kill
my pain and loss, and then I would condemn her for it all.
Suddenly, the safety of her kindness and caretaking was gone,
and I was very alone. As I drove through the early morning
light, the rays of the sunrise touched the green pastures and
the cattle grazing like they have been for over 150 years, back
when Mark Twain passed through Bridgeport on his way to
Mono Lake and the many hot springs surrounding the volcanic lake.

I felt a spark of myself experiencing a moment in an environment that felt right. I felt connected. Listening to Willie
had me beginning to think about the lonely and courageous

path he traveled to discover and live his truth. He never gave up, no matter how bad it got, because he knew his calling and had to live it out. There was no other answer after he discovered his love for music—a life calling. I suddenly felt sick, realizing my music dream had died in the great recession. King Duce flooded my mind; the angry investors, rappers, gangsters, and the local community as a whole.

I started to have a panic attack and fell right back into the depths of pain and darkness. My heart and mind were broken over the demise of my marriage and the life I so carefully planned. I was totally devastated and couldn't logically rectify the damage and hurt I had caused. Picturing Becky living with her parents while some insecure bitches were pushing her out of her job made me long to hold her and tell her everything would be okay. But we both knew it wasn't. I knew she was broken, and there was nothing I could do to make it better. I had failed her. I let her down.

Tears were obscuring my vision like a windshield in a storm without wipers. I pulled over and stopped my truck to breathe and finish my cry. I started to dry my eyes and looked around to see again. The sunlight danced on barbed wire fencing and the morning dew glistened on the grass that stretched brushstrokes of greens for miles in all directions. Suddenly, I became still and felt a calm enter me and lure me out of the black hole that had engulfed me once again. I would feel the tug and pull of calm and darkness fight within me over and over again; this was just the beginning. But at that moment, I knew that I was going to be okay. I changed the CD to Skynyrd, got a second wind of self-confidence, and continued down the timeless country road to a destination that I would have to find on my own.

I never realized how much I had looked to others to fix my problems. It was like living with a fifteen-year-old—frustrated, pissed off, mad at the people he loves and needs the most. All I wanted was for the world to fall in line so I could make some money and get back to "livin' the dream." Classic alcoholic thinking. I was clueless about how fucked up, burnt out, traumatized, and in full-blown denial I was about how bad things were. It's funny looking back. It seems like so much wasted energy. But when you are going through loss (I'm talking about the kind of loss that makes you reconsider everything about life), you are living in a state of incomprehensible misery and pain. It's real, and it fucking hurts. The only solution is to get back up and move forward. I was fighting to live, and I knew that this morning would be an emotional adventure to face without alcohol or Julie's shoulders to hold me up. Man, I wanted a beer!

The grassy pastures turned into sagebrush, pine, and aspen trees as I came upon the edge of the great Sierra Nevada mountain range. I rolled down my window and my pulse mellowed as I exhaled and then breathed in the crisp high mountain morning air. It felt amazing to my traumatized senses. I just needed to go where my heart led. The energy of the hills called me home to a simpler time and rhythm of my spirit. The sunlight was pulsating through the tall pines casting beams of soft light and silhouetted trees on the dirt road. Suddenly, a blast of white light filled the cab of my truck and momentarily blinded me. The trees had opened up to reveal a high mountain lake nestled into granite spires a thousand feet high. I literally lost my breath and let out a "whoaaaa…"

The lake's edge met the road on the driver's side of the truck, giving me the opportunity to slow down and peer into the crystal-clear water. I struggled to see the bottom only because of the dancing diamonds of morning sunlight shimmering atop the nearly still lake. There were a few cabins placed just so, including a quaint old red and white fishing dock and bait store. The imposing granite peaks cradled the other side of the lake's edge with a few trees and morning shadows. The natural beauty and solitude were filling me with a joy that I knew and longed for. I was that young boy running around those same hills, dreaming of becoming a great hunter and warrior long before the many battles and casualties beat me into what I had become—broken and defeated.

I flipped my truck around and rolled back to nowhere in particular, gazing off onto the water and the little fishing dock near the small dam on the north shore. The road soon exited the tall pines, so I decided to take the next dirt road that would lead me back to water and trees. Reminiscent of driving dirt roads as a kid on deer hunting trips with my dad, the road entered aspen groves and then into sage. I came across the creek that was originating from the little lake. I hadn't showered in a couple of days and could smell toxins leeching out of my pores. My body was still not well, and I needed a refresher, so I stripped down and took a bath in the icy mountain morning stream. I will never forget how good I felt afterward, standing there with steam emanating off my body, tingling and revitalizing my soul. I felt a self-sufficiency and independence that had eluded me for so long. I was smiling as the cold water ran down my face and beard. I took a deep breath and exhaled the dripping water off my lips into a fine mist that turned rainbow colors when the morning sunlight hit it. Talking to myself since no one was around, "You made it over the mountains. You made it. You can do this." I spent the day driving back roads, soaking in the beauty of it to keep me going.

I remember that night, walking out of my camper and making my way to the lake's lapping edge under the glow of the full moon and nearly treeless landscape of sagebrush and pumice. It was a perfect evening, but as I looked up at the moon and the silhouetted mountains looming to the west of the reservoir, I felt totally alone. The moonlight was dancing on the water as the slight breeze rippled the surface just enough to give it character. The sound of the water gently caressing the shoreline attempted to keep my mind off the loneliness creeping in as I stood before the universe, a broken man with no place to call his home. I was too sad and lost to even cry at that point.

Over the next week, the early spring weather was turning to outright winter with snow and fifty mile-per-hour winds ripping across the lake and into my camper, filling it with icy air and sand, freezing everything it touched. Did I mention that my heater was not working? Unlike my mechanically-minded father, I was fucking worthless at wiring and engines. I never had the interest, even being around a dad and grandpa that fixed those types of problems on a daily basis. My ingenuity did help me figure out that I needed my thick beanie and every blanket and sleeping bag I had to survive the below-freezing temperature that the barren landscape was enveloping me in.

As scared, lonely, sad, and lost as I was, there was a glimmer of solace and a fragile freedom from demon alcohol and the train wreck of a life I had just left behind in my hometown. There was so much unfinished business that I needed to circle back to address if I survived the next twelve months. I honestly wasn't sure if that was going to happen. Maybe it was a sign of growth, not knowing and admitting it.

During calm moonlit evenings, I would stand by the water's edge and feel the quietness of the night air and the soothing sounds of the lapping water. It wasn't peace. I was a pulverized soul begging to find shelter from the hell in my mind and heart. I couldn't take a step without sobbing, asking and pleading to a still unknown power to show me a sign. To give me a second of peace. To not feel hopelessly dead from so much loss and destruction. But deep down, I knew I was exactly where I was supposed to be. Writing this is difficult because I'm still recovering from my alcoholism, and I realize that every day I could lose the battle and end up like my people do. In psychiatric facilities, prisons, or dead.

Wenger was a beautiful soul who gave anything he had to anyone who would take a moment to listen or care. I remember arriving with Julie and watching how happy he was to connect with someone from the past. She was kind to Wenger. He really liked her, and I know it's because she had always been kind to him despite his wacky and volatile behavior. That's why she thought Wenger might actually be a good starting place for my new journey to sobriety and a new life... and that's why Wenger took a chance on me. At that point in my life, I was unemployable. Really. I was clinically depressed and drinking thirty-plus beers a day, all day, and starting up again in the middle of the night to calm my racing mind and nerves begging for more poison to feed the six-headed dragon. It was the spring of 2012. I had no idea how much more fucked up my mind and life would get from that point. I truly believed that I had experienced the worst of it.

Having the gift of recovery and hindsight, I was so consumed with my selfish ego and pride I was literally spending years swimming in a self-created sea of misery so consuming that I couldn't genuinely care about anyone else around me, especially the two women in my life. I was trying to come to terms with losing my wife. It's all a blur of drunken insanity that destroyed everything I touched. Learning to become not ragefully angry and resentful at the world and myself was a very difficult force to overcome, especially as I consumed more and more of the anger and misery. It's a drug and habit as powerful and manipulative as anything we can ingest.

I hated everything at that point in my life. I had failed in every major pillar of my adult male life—marriage, career, babies. Absolute failure, and no way out to a better day. I knew all I could do was wake up and take a step forward. Still, I hated every breath, every step. Deep down, I knew my road back to a "normal" life was so far away that I wasn't sure if it was even a realistic goal anymore. Thinking about living in my camper on a fishing reservoir in the high desert of the Eastern Sierras offered my soul a quiet respite from the daily habitual triggers and stressors that I used as excuses to drink away the loss, pain, and utter confusion that had become my life.

Julie showed up a week later to visit me and help Wenger with some organizational tasks for his business. It was a painful blessing experiencing life without her. I was so used to her doing so much for me during my bad days that I unintentionally became dependent in unhealthy ways. I needed to fall alone, and this was the next phase of tough growth after drinking my way out of my marriage and home. I had become totally reliant on her in ways that were not good for anyone. We were both struggling through loss, but I was dealing with it like a crazy man. Somehow, Julie believed in me. I gave her every reason to walk away and never look back, but she could see beyond my warped words and anger.

I would only stay at the reservoir working for Wenger for a short time due to his inability to work with me or anyone without losing his mind over the simplest of work-related questions for clarification. He just couldn't manage basic stuff emotionally because his brain wiring wouldn't allow it. Wenger was on the phone with Cliff and me as he was driving back from Reno to pick up supplies; we were trying to figure out if we were supposed to paint the women's bathroom stalls or not, and Wenger couldn't communicate what he wanted done. He began to get riled up and was screaming at us over simple questions. After a long, hot day cleaning and painting the marina bathrooms and having him yell at me over basic questions, I decided it was time to go, or I was gonna lose my shit.

My temper exploded like a dirty bomb. I looked at Cliff. "I'm done!"

Cliff looked at me as if he were saying, "I don't know if you can do that..." Poor guy had been manhandled by both an overbearing wife and Wenger his entire miserable, passive life. He was the kind of guy I couldn't stand to be around even though he was nice enough. Cliff had no balls and no fucking backbone. *I would rather be dead,* I thought to myself. I gave Cliff a smile and a warm handshake, genuinely hoping the best for him. The afternoon winds had created a sandstorm that was pulverizing our cheeks and teeth as we said our goodbyes. He was in disbelief that I was actually leaving. I seriously don't think he believed it.

I looked at Julie and said, "Let's get the fuck out of here!"

I threw Julie the keys to my truck and told her to back it under the camper. She reminded me in the middle of my cussing tirade that we needed to raise the camper with the electric jacks (that worked sometimes). With Julie on one end and me on the other, we coordinated the control levers to make the bottom of the camper high enough off the ground to load it into the bed of the truck. The electric jacks were stalling our momentum, and I was losing my cool. Julie gave me a calming smile to let me know that everything was going to be okay. I believed her and smiled at our situation and regained my focus on the task of lifting and then loading up my camper. Sand and wind whipped and swirled around us so loud that we could barely hear each other from only ten feet away. *Click, click, click* went the the jacks as they reached their maximum height off the ground, suspended on four flimsy metal stilts, when a gust of wind charging off the eastern side of the Sierras smashed into the side of the giant camper and literally lifted it off of two stilts, pushing the two-ton behemoth with an invisible force that nearly tipped the camper to the ground.

Suddenly I heard my diesel truck start up and saw the reverse lights and Julie in the driver's seat. She turned and connected her eyes with mine, and we were totally focused on the project at hand, guiding my truck within inches of the camper on both sides of the wheel wells in the bed of the truck. With only a couple of slight hand gestures, Julie placed the truck bed perfectly to drop, lock, and hit the road. We couldn't believe she nailed it on her first try. It usually took me a few frustrating tries to succeed. We secured the lockdown bolts that held the camper to the truck, both happy about our pit stop speed and precision under pressure. We went through the storage space where I had stashed all my gear and systematically loaded everything into the truck and camper, closed the door, and jumped in.

"Where to?" Her wind-swept hair brushed across her sunglasses as she wondered aloud where our next journey would land us.

"South..."

Within minutes, the adrenaline and endorphins from the exit from my new job and home were gone and were quickly replaced with dire thoughts of the unknown. I felt pretty fucking bad that my job and new home only lasted two weeks!

Julie pulled the heavy swaying house on wheels out onto the main Highway 395 that cut through downtown Bridgeport, and we turned south. The Blue Rhino bar sign caught my peripheral vision. I rubbernecked with some impossible hope that we would just call it a day and go have a beer and a burger. God, I wanted to drink! Thankfully, Julie was there to hold me accountable to my goal of sobriety. I was becoming convinced that I simply couldn't drink. But early sobriety and trying to figure out where in the fuck you're gonna eat, sleep, and work is a pretty overwhelming ordeal, not to mention my mental state was pretty bad. I was stuttering and couldn't connect basic thoughts with conclusive outcomes half the time. I was extremely depressed and on the verge of being incapable of finding and climbing my way out.

Julie patiently guided me to safety. I didn't have the energy to think or speak, so I just stared ahead at nothing because my eyes were blurred from my tears, and my mind was shutting down sensory intake. She drove without a word, only to check to see how I was doing with worried glances in my direction. The truck began a downhill descent that jarred me from my self-consumed thoughts long enough to see the giant lake at the bottom of the grade. Mark Twain wrote about it in *Roughing It:*

> *"Mono, it is sometimes called, and sometimes the 'Dead Sea of California'. It is one of the strangest freaks of Nature to be found in any*

438

land. ... It is an unpretending expanse of grayish water, about a hundred miles in circumference, with two islands in its centre, mere upheavals of rent and scorched and blistered lava, snowed over with gray banks and drifts of pumice stone and ashes, the winding sheet of the dead volcano, whose vast crater the lake has seized upon and occupied."

Like Mark Twain described the unique landscape of Mono Lake, I too felt dead and ugly. Within a few days, I was just down the highway in a new location with a new gig.

WALKING WITH JOHN MUIR IN THE SIERRA NEVADA MOUNTAINS

I was living alone and getting clean in one of the most majestic backdrops in the world. Granite spires cradled pristine glacially formed lakes amid a horseshoe of mountains set within the great Sierra Nevadas. The peaks rise thousands of feet to the south, north, and west of the tiny mountain village and wrap the lakes, speckled with conifers and aspen trees. The mountain breeze provides a spectrum of greens, yellows, and whites as leaves flutter against the salt-and-pepper granite that make up much of the mountain range.

The four-lake loop includes the town's namesake and most spectacular June Lake, a miniature version of Lake Tahoe but stuck back in 1950s nostalgia. It has a white granite sand beach and crystal-clear emerald water that dives deep to ever darkening shades of blue. It truly is a sight to behold as you turn off Highway 395 and leave the desolate high desert landscape to begin the short but relaxing drive west. The high desert is brushed with a sparse lay of pinon pine and the gray-green of sagebrush holding down the long sweeping expanses of Eastern Sierra landscape. Then the road drops gently into view of the exquisite lakes and majestic peaks that embrace the village, making the perfect setting for tranquility. The old-time trout fishing/snow skiing town is welcoming to the heart and soul needing healing.

I would spend four months rediscovering myself through many lonely days in this beautiful area, but I learned that changing my geographic location, no matter how beautiful, would not fix the stuff inside of me. That kind of change requires more than an alteration in the environment. I was trying to get sober, but still fought the idea of going to twelve-step meetings or reaching out to other alcoholics. I read a little, but I eventually drank.

Within a few days, totally thanks to Julie's help, I was able to land a job at a local resort called the Double Eagle. I worked with a young group of snowboarding gypsy guys and girls who were all pretty cool. My job was at the spa/club, making sure all the visitors were kept happy at the pool or weight room; making smoothies or running their food and never-ending resort vacation beverage orders out to them, bringing them towels and pretending to listen to their inebriated stories and accepting their snobbery and flirtations. I booked their luxury treatments, then scrubbed toilets and washed and folded towels with the Mexican ladies. The people I attended to were often my age with families and money...a life. They were tourists visiting the Sierra Nevadas to "get away from it all." They were leaving the stress of the city to sit at an indoor pool and have manicures and massages while they sipped their $10 fruity alcoholic beverages and tipped me to dote on them.

I found the attention from the young girls and even the older women nice, and the tips were an almost embarrassing bonus. The men would claim to be fishermen but would have the resort staff bait their hook and clean their fish. They would extract the joy of catching a high mountain lake trout and then sit around the pool, drinking their pitchers of beer and flouting their money and false trophies to one another. June Lake was a critical crossroad moment in my life. Despite all the rhetoric I saw at work, I actually found myself for a second.

Julie found me a one-room studio at the Barracks, an old two story dormitory-type house that was formerly the party house for Danny Way, the pro snowboarder and founder of Grenade snowboarding gloves and boards. I loved my room. The little studio was painted a cheery yellow and white and consisted of a twin bed, a tall narrow freestanding wooden closet with a full-length mirror, a small dining table, a desk, and a big metal framed picture of the Eastside taken by local folk hero photographer Ansel Adams. A small counter with a tiny sink and a cupboard for dishes and food lined one wall and an attached bathroom with a strangely large tiled shower and two sinks. There was a mini-fridge and a mini-microwave to match the mini room. The two small windows looked out onto the mountains. It was a breathtaking view right out of the movies where some eccentric artist lives to work and heal and find his way forward. That was my story exactly. It was cleansing and renewing for me, and by the second or third month of my stay, my mind started to open up, and my visual artwork, writing, and guitar recordings were breaking new ground. It was a truly special time. The quiet alone time for days at a time allowed me to meditate and get into a groove that produced work that challenged every boundary I thought I had.

I was either at work or alone at my studio. The owners of the resort where I worked were a mother-son team, and they took to me pretty quickly. He was a rich, soft, pampered goof-ball who liked people to know that he ran marathons and was important. He tried to buddy up with me right away, inviting me to play golf and taking me behind the scenes on the set of the Tom Cruise futuristic armageddon movie *Oblivion* that was being filmed on resort property and nearby Silver Lake. He took me to all the exclusive locales just to show me that he could, even to the hut Tom Cruise was staying in. He was that guy back in high school that had to buy his friends... some things don't ever change. Mom was fairly smart, well, she was rich. Some of the decisions she made regarding parenting and running the business proved to me that she married money. She was an old Mormon ditz who limped around with her son in tow, wearing her jewels and expensive clothes, and they lived in a spectacular log home between the resort and Silver Lake.

The gypsies, snowboarders, and ski bums that lived and worked in the community all co-existed, most of them at poverty level, just eking out enough money through seasonal work throughout the year to live in a breathtaking outdoor utopia. As we all crossed paths either at the spa/gym, the General Store, or at Tiger Bar, I realized that there were a few lifers, but most were like me, searching for something… in my case, something or someplace that could fix me. Since the Eastern Sierras was such a big part of my life, deer hunting just a stone's throw north at Monitor Pass since I was a child, I figured that if I got so low I felt like dying, at least I could finish it up in a beautiful place that was sacred ground that comforted me.

I found peace in the anonymity I had there. No one knew me. Well, I found out that my old college football drinking buddy Marty Thompson grew up in June and went to Lee Vining High School just up the road. It was a big deal to the little town at the base of Tioga Pass because their Marty went on to play a couple of seasons for the Detroit Lions. They were so proud that they still had a banner posted in town. His mom still lived in town and I dropped into her real estate office just once to say hello, but then returned to being the man no one knew. It was a relief almost.

But for my brief stay and exploration, I discovered how lonely I could get. I had no idea how alone and lonely I would feel until after I fell off the wagon and started drinking again. I still had my truck, my driver's license, and no serious criminal charges to my name…yet. I had some sense of freedom.

I didn't realize at that time how much I still had to still lose and destroy before I would truly get sober.

June Lake was a gift in so many creative and healing ways at a time when I needed to find my own space, no matter how small or insignificant it may have looked to anyone else. Nonetheless, during that time, I continued to struggle with the loss of Beck. It sparked an explosion of creative exploration through drawings and writings. It was a brutal shock to my system being without her, but it was also very healthy for me to learn to walk on my own again.

I began to slowly develop a daily routine that incorporated my job at the Double Eagle Resort, taking hikes and walks and doing something creative to regain my battered health from drinking every day for years. I would write or just talk into the recorder for hour-long thought sessions while I looked out my window to see the moon's glow on the mountains with pure neon blues, pinks, and purples. I would draw incessantly and started to record new guitar riffs at all hours of the day or night. When the creative urges hit, I just stopped anything else I was doing to let it pour from my soul, to grow with each moment and opportunity to tap into the healing power it afforded. Each creative thought and my interpretation of it, whether written, visual, or musical, was an inspirational stimulant to express the broken but blossoming fearlessness I found in being alone and no longer accountable to anyone but myself. I was lost, but I began to cherish being alone, at least when being alone worked for me. The rest of the time, I was painfully lonely and shattered.

I was quickly discovering actual healing and joy coming out of my boldness, especially in drawing. My creative explorations sans boundaries soon dominated my time. I unveiled a new level of raw emotion and risk in my work. My proximity to the truth became intimate by comparison to where I had been just months earlier. Life does that. It shocks us into crossroads moments that we either continue with the least resistance or courageously choose to seek the path less traveled. Suddenly, I found myself living alone, totally free to do anything I wanted. I sat in my studio one early morning, sipping my coffee and journaling to get my brain started. I was trying to figure out what I MUST do. Nothing. It was the first time in my life I turned off the switch temporarily and plunged into letting my creative force manifest into whatever it was going to be. I felt a release of tension, expectations, distraction, competition, superior/inferior complex. I began to feel alive again. And the freedom and space to explore that alone, by myself, with no-day-to day person requiring or wanting something I couldn't give.

Being self-consumed is much easier, and at times, enjoyable when doing it alone. Causes less damage and more and better creative work production in some cases. But spending too much time alone in that wide-open freedom with self can also be a prescription to the asylum. I was leveraging my moments of appreciated freedom to dig deep into my creative guts, using the daily pain and rage to carve and bleed paint and ink onto paper and canvas with a passionate force. I decided to let go and create fearlessly and passionately—no boundaries. The themes often centered around the struggle, sex, fighting the good fight, aliens, and space, and for the first time ever, I started to create at a deeper and more honest level. I was challenging my truth. I had been putting in a little time with my visual art to that point, just enough fundamental knowledge and direction to know what turned me on visually, intellectually, and emotionally. I challenged myself to create something new or continue working on something new every day. It got to the point some weeks that I could hardly focus at work and couldn't wait to get through my shift and get back to my studio and create.

My well-known self-portrait of a decapitated depiction of me holding a gun to where my head once was and a knife to the once existent throat was created during this time. Colorful flames are shooting out of my neck with my bare-chested body, a backdrop of blood red with black thunderbolts, and the name Create or Die. It became my theme, my life…Create or Die!

Growing up, I used to watch movies and read books of rugged men facing the wild world, courageous and alone, guys like Jack London, Ernest Hemingway, and Mark Twain, and other explorer romantics. The idea of being totally independent and free from people, places, and things seemed like the ultimate goal. But the reality is that most people strive for security from perceived risk and never reach that painfully enlightened state of reality. I was forty, and it was as if I had landed alone on a remote island and had to figure it out by myself.

My internal alarm clock would go off, and I would have no choice but to occupy my brain and time somehow productively. I would occasionally read some recovery, but I was still so newly sober that I wasn't craving but leveraging my relatively clear mind and physical strength and stamina. I ate simple, but healthy. I was training to complete a mission few men have: sobriety. At the time, I did not make sobriety a priority. I had a long way to go. I continued to think that financial stability was *the* critical factor in my long-term sobriety. Wrong. I conveniently fooled myself with that bullshit lie for a decade as I said hello to more alcohol hell and goodbye to the things I cherished the most. But being alone to sort out a few things and take a breath away from the pressure cooker of my hometown helped me. I started to meet people without my status shields and insecurities. I was a broken, middle-aged guy working with mostly twenty-something free spirits. As free as I felt, I was trapped by my alcoholism and financial devastation that was never going to sort itself out if I kept destroying my progress with my destructive drinking. For the moment, I was clean but not going to meetings. I was working full time at a job that checked my eroding wall of pride.

As much freedom as I had living alone in a picturesque Sierra Nevada ski village, I was also haunted by many ghosts that I would have to rectify, one step at a time. I had left Beck with the fucked-up struggle to navigate herself after 25 years of being together. I had taken all my loss and pain out on Julie, letting her hold me up while disregarding her personal loss and struggle. I had issues with my parents that I needed to at least address. My mind was shattered and struggling to make sense of the amends ahead of me and the work and courage it would require. Getting out to walk, hike, or drive out into the mountains was a revitalizing part of my healing and exercise. I grew up hiking through country just like the hills around June Lake. As I would hike up a mountain, either on a well-marked path or not, I realized that it had been a long time since I had hiked in the mountains just to hike and experience nature without the principle objective of hunting, stalking, and killing a deer. I really didn't know what to make of it at first. I mean, if I wasn't laser-focused for the hunt, I was in football training mode, using the mountain as an obstacle course to prepare me for a future physical experience. But that all changed for me.

I took my time and soaked in the experience of the hike. I learned to stop for a swim in a glacial pool or check out an eagle's nest. For the first time, I was off on a hike into the eastern Sierra Nevada mountains just like John Muir. I remembered reading his writings describing his hikes and the majesty of the nearly undiscovered cathedral he spent decades living, praying, and exploring in. Exploring is cool. I like the description exploring better than hiking. Hiking reminds me of nerdy teachers and doctors I grew up around who measured everything in milestone accomplishments, like hiking the seven peaks of who gives a fuck.

One morning I got up early, before the sun as usual, and decided to hike up to Horseshoe Falls, a picturesque waterfall I could see from my studio window. Julie had a friend named Pete, who had been killed ice climbing the falls one winter, so I was called to it for many reasons. I drove down to the base of the granite spired mountains that cradle aspen-lined

Silver Lake. As the sun was waking, it lit up the peaks and cast shimmering colors and reflections onto the near-glass surface of the lake.

Providence guided me to the mountain that morning, with a simple plan to hike up to the falls, or at least start up in that direction and see how my body felt. I was still weak but starting to regain core energy and a little motivation between heavy swings into depression. I locked my truck and sneaked over the PG&E gate guarding the downstream powerplant fed by some mysterious backcountry lake high up in the mountains. I was wearing my Levi's, high tops, and a hoodie; not the modern-day picture of a Patagonia outdoor enthusiast requiring a $1,000 outfit to take on anything the mountain can test you with. I spent my entire life facing harsh terrain in this same outfit with a Copenhagen in my back pocket. The more things change, the more they stay the same.

I followed the creek up through the thick of conifers surrounding the base rim of the June Lake Loop. I walked at a quick pace to get past the *Do Not Enter* zone of the PG&E yard, downshifting only when the roar of the crashing water and turbines swirling at the base of the mountain started to drift away. Before I knew it, I had climbed a few hundred feet up and was set just high enough to look back down at Silver Lake and the surrounding village of lakes and cabins. My legs were on fire, and I had to stop and gasp for air. There was one small aluminum boat carrying two silhouettes, slowly trolling for trout. The sun had risen above the White Mountains east of the Sierras, and I could feel its warmth basking me with healing energy that commands gratitude deep in the soul. With my eyes closed and my chilled body recharging its heat core, I imagined what it was like during the night for all the animals around me hidden from sight. I thought to myself that deer must have a unique warming system or nerve senses that deal with cold in a more advanced manner than humans, even accounting for their fat and fur-covered body. Then, as I shivered briefly and glanced up the mountain to see the snow-capped peaks despite it being late spring, I thought about John Muir hiking all over these mountains wearing an astonishingly simple getup of old leather boots, Levi's jeans, a rope for a belt, and only a thin button-up shirt over a t-shirt. He would spend countless days and nights exploring the highest peaks with a hardtack biscuit in his pocket and some loose-leaf tea. He kept it pure and simple.

I closed my eyes again, the sun lifting me into a state of near meditation. I thought about John Muir's journal book and his contribution to sharing the majesty and wisdom of the Sierra Nevada mountains. With each deep burning inhale of chilled fresh alpine air, my body, mind, and soul were being regenerated. I was reconnecting to nature's grounded energy frequencies that I had cut myself off from. With a renewed tank of oxygenated blood and inspiration from the gratitude and joy I was experiencing, I wanted to keep climbing, but I would stop to watch the animals playing and drinking in the creek and waterfall pools of granite.

The revelation to me as I could feel my life force reigniting was that it did not matter if I had money or not. Easy to say, really different to feel it click in the brain and repair the soul with freedom from all the insecurities, fears, pressures...it vanished. King Duce didn't matter. My goals didn't matter. My status, reputation, and pride *did not matter*. I was not special and apart from, but an infinitely small and connected vital energy to the greater one. I watched a chipmunk scurry out to the edge of a flat granite rock anchor. It was set perfectly to allow the critter to drink then get back to the big boulder towering behind him that made up part of the five-foot waterfall, winding its way down the mountain like a water slinky cutting back and forth with ease and grace. The chugging and babbling of the concert of natural granite falls and pools filled the quiet with energy and action, urging me on up. The high altitude and my shaking legs were telling me to call it good and start back down the mountain, but I couldn't. I wanted more of what I was experiencing. Being all alone on that mountain that morning was a moment for me to commune with the great spirit in her cathedral. John Muir's descriptions of this are beyond eloquent.

I was allowing my spirit to walk with him and experience the mountains as he did, just appreciating it for the awe-inspiring creation they are. Being alone on that mountain that morning with each step and breath of fresh, clean alpine air, I was reconnecting to an energy around me that was undistracted and true. I felt normal, alive. But not preoccupied with getting to a preconceived destination or maximizing my time by hiking to get in shape and say I climbed it—an autopilot thought process so many are trained to do in society. People are completely consumed by framing their lived experience in filtered Instagram highlights driven by the need to feel accepted, liked, admired, and respected. All the ego, pride crap the Silicon Valley mind criminals like Twitter's Jack Dorsey and Facebook's Mark Zuckerberg helped metastasize into a cultural meltdown of family, community, and human empathy and connection to something bigger than self. Nature is a status showpiece the Liberals love to tout when in reality, I was the only one on the mountain in a village full of "caring, natural people," California shoptalk for selfish people who spend a lot of money on Patagonia and the new Tesla SUV, only to live stuck in their alternative reality brought to you by the newest trend in social status and traffic jams on the 101.

I was momentarily free of the bondage of alcohol, self, and the flood of people, media, goals, and deadlines. For the first time since I could remember, I was free to be... just be. I glanced up to the spires that make up Carson Peak. The late spring weather had melted much of the snow, revealing cleansed and blooming patches of green shrubs and trees and flowers of the Sierra Nevada kind. John Muir wrote that the Sierra Nevada Mountain range was "...the most attractive that has yet been discovered in the mountain ranges of the world."

Range of Light – "After ten years spent in the heart of it, rejoicing and wondering, bathing in its incline the trees and rocks and snow, the flush of the alpenglow, and a thousand dashing waterfalls with their marvelous abundance of irised spray, it still seems to me above all others, the Range of Light, the most divinely beautiful of all the mountain chains I have ever seen" (pg 4., *The Mountains of California*).

I could imagine Muir's voice describing the sunrise as I witnessed it at that moment.

"How glorious a greeting the sun gives the mountains! To behold this alone is worth the pains of any excursion a thousand times over. The highest peaks burned like islands in a sea of liquid shade. Then the lower peaks and spires caught the glow, and long lances of light, streaming through many a notch and pass, fell thick on the frozen meadows…"

I feel strongly connected to the mountains and the Sierra Nevadas, and rediscovering it through reading descriptions of the very place I was exploring like Muir had over one hundred years earlier was special.

I kept climbing up the granite slope with patches of exposed soil and trees until I reached a large sheet of snow that stretched a few hundred feet to my destination, the crest of the falls. It was steep and dangerously slick. At its edge was a cliff that dropped into the rocky pool of water flowing out of the falls. I felt very small and vulnerable to the mountains will. The landscape that surrounded me was built by a master architect with quantum dynamic force, and I was inspired by the amazing beauty and power that surrounded me. My legs were shaking, and my lungs were on fire, but I knew I would surge forward. I raced out across the snow and ice-covered incline. The power of the mountain and my precarious footing on a dangerous point of no return sprint pumped me full of adrenaline. I was at the point where the risk of moving forward equaled the risk of turning back, the point where facing the fear rather than letting fear own you become the overpowering motivator to keep you moving onward, risking everything to cross the final and most dangerous part of the journey. Such is life—an adventurous journey or a stagnant life where fear keeps you from truly living.

Fatigue is a deceptive killer to many men who have tested their will against Mother Nature. I knew I was stronger than the ache in my muscles or tightening in my chest. The fear of losing my footing and sliding off the slab, plummeting thirty feet to rocks below, gave me a shot of focus to dig in and make it to my destiny. Within a few make or break steps, I landed on an opening of exposed earth just above the falls. The trees and shrubs accenting the ridge were alive with songbirds welcoming a new day. Gratitude filled my heart as I fell to my hands and knees. My asthma was constricting my ability to breathe, which exasperated the alarming need for oxygen to my starving muscles. I was inhaling so hard that I was dripping drool and snot, and then the tears began to flow. I was purging pain and sorrow, but with each painful breath, I was overwhelmed with emotions of gratitude and joy for being alive. I began to sob. I soon found myself smiling through the streams of tears flowing down my face as I looked up at the life-giving mountain. I felt a sense of peacefulness come over me.

John Muir describes a similar moment of terror and then calm on the mountainside where his mind was suddenly full of fear, "My mind seemed to fill with a stifling smoke. But this terrible eclipse lasted only a moment when life blazed forth again with preternatural clearness." He describes a sense of clarity brought on by his "other self, bygone experiences, instinct, or Guardian Angel—call it what you will…" I, too felt that surge of clarity and the sheer will to move forward, to explore, to risk all to reach my destiny.

I took in all that the mountains were offering me at that moment. I paused to pay my respects to Julie's fallen friend Pete who had met his fate on the frozen falls. I closed my eyes, prayed, and I knew Pete's spirit was alive and well in the mountains he loved so dearly. The energy from everything elevated my spirit like the rainbow mist rising from the cascading wall of water behind me. A surge of happiness filled my heart as I looked out on the town far below and scanned east beyond the high mountain valley that is protected on the north, south, and western boundaries by the grand Sierras.

With renewed energy and inspiration, I decided to hike further to find the source of the falls. Scaling and climbing boulders like a seasoned mountaineering guide, I was reminded of my childhood exploring the eastern slopes of Monitor Pass, scouting deer for my dad and his buddies, or exploring with my friends after the hunt. I reached a little wooden bridge that crossed a granite crevasse and then traversed along the slope until the lake came into view. The high mountain lake was right out of a movie. The little concrete dam formed a spectacular reservoir. On the southern side was a beautiful grove of high mountain fir and pine trees that would be perfect for camping and fishing for months. It was breathtaking. I stopped long enough to stare at trout swimming lazily along the edge of the small dam. I smiled. The dam had an old wood pump station with a narrow metal walkway, and a small aluminum boat was tied to it.

Besides the absolute natural beauty of the mountain lake, the coolest thing I saw was a small mining car that was built in the 1930s to haul all the materials and men up to construct the dam. The railway was still there, and I began to follow it back down the mountainside until it turned too steep to navigate. Nearby I saw a well-worn switchback trail that headed back down the hill through waist-high brush with an occasional patch of aspen trees. The mountainside was now well exposed to the morning sun, and it made for a perfect walk after a tough climb. With each step, I found my mind dancing with endorphins and an energy that was not only within me, but all around me. I smiled as I walked and then skipped like some happy-go-lucky Johnny Appleseed joker. Just a few hours earlier, I was in mental anguish. I had climbed the proverbial and literal mountain, and I suddenly felt totally alive and allowed my downhill momentum to be filled with unbridled happiness, and I was skipping down a stretch that lasted a couple of turn backs. But then my oxygen depletion alarm finally overrode my spirits joy of floating my physical being down a mountain on a perfect morning.

As I stopped to catch my breath, I looked at the birds flitting around the pine trees and brush and pondered their life and admired the pure existence they lived every single day. I tripped on the mastery of nature's system and rules. Each day was a gift, and the animals had to earn it, often with everything in them, to eke out an existence in a brutal seasonal war of life and death. I contrasted how I had lived my life out of sync with nature's basic rules. I lost my discipline. Simple. I had been successful but cut my talents and opportunities short through ego, fear, and alcohol. I imagined the mountain lion, deer, bear, and fish surviving the harsh summers and brutal winter nights on that same mountain, the savage death, the survival of only the smartest and strongest. *Humans are pathetic,* I thought. I've been pathetic. But then I remembered that I was sober and on my way to living a truer life.

A surge of fire coursed through me, and I began charging down the mountain, running, jumping, sliding, and falling hard, getting back up and running and whooping and screaming "Hell Yeah!" I couldn't believe the gift I had been given, the energy, strength, vision, and awareness to listen to the mountain as I began my new life. I was coming to terms with the past I needed to face and the man I was going to discover through sobriety and an honest and relentless search to live my truth. Freedom sparked through my soul. Running, skipping, slalom skiing the dirt and rock trail like I used to do as a twelve-year-old kid on the hill outside of camp. Descending into the aspen quakies, I gazed upon Silver Lake and to the aluminum boats trolling back and forth for trout and realized that my exuberance had an audience. As crazy as they must have thought I was, for that moment, I didn't care what others thought of me, and that in and of itself was very freeing.

My stomach growled and directed my attention down the hill toward the Silver Lake Café nestled in a pine and aspen glen on the north edge of the lake. Having eaten a few meals there, my taste buds lit up, imagining the Spanish omelet with crispy fried potatoes and perfectly brewed coffee. The café was famous for unbelievable food and amazing customer service, and the wait time alone was proof of that. It was like going back to the 1920s with the historical photographs on the walls throughout the café and the connected general store. The combined store and café were built in an old cabin that takes up less than 1,000 square feet and is full of memorabilia as well as everything you need to compliment your high sierra camping and fishing experience. The family that owns it not only runs the store and café but an entire camping, cabin, and fishing resort, including trail rides and backcountry mule train experiences, and they manage it with a pride and care as stewards celebrating how life was lived back then when people worked hard and treated others with common courtesy and goodwill. It was and still is a place that honors hearty pioneering spirits, the strong work ethic, the struggles and joys of life.

The irony, as I waited for a seat at the counter, was that I was observing a room full of mostly city folk tourists talking loudly and glancing at their phones, kinda listening and kinda engaging, but distracted by the fact that there was no Wi-Fi. I realized the romance of that time was still attainable, and to me, desirable. But most people choose to play it safe and live in the box where they are trained to stay. I was struggling to find my way because I did not want to go back to that mad rush sprint through life, enjoying only snapshot moments like camping for a week at the Silver Lake Resort to living the experience. I wanted to live the experience, period. Every moment. To breathe. To think. To live. To beat fear and risk all to reach my destiny.

The problem with modern mainstream programmed living is that the speed and expectations of fulfillment in that societal context make taking time a liability and not an asset in experiencing deep, meaningful relationships and work. The modern-day machine of society is a script and mechanism designed to enslave people's minds and time to an impossible happy ending. I sat at the end of the fifteen-foot slab of hemlock counter in the small and crowded café pondering this for a few minutes. Then I glanced up to the photos of the resort's original founding family members. In one, there is a family happily displaying a stringer of trout. Another photo shows the proud smiles of successful hunters and their kill. The black and white photos were simple but striking images of a real family living in tents on the edge of the lake during the summer months. It revealed truth and honesty of daily life, of chores and of recreation, together. One photo shows a woman doing laundry by hand. Another is a shot of a boy and his dog by a campfire with the lake in the background. Another yet shows a man shaving using an old mirror hung on a tree. Nostalgia warmed the atmosphere. The staff was mostly made up of multiple generations of the founding family, and they maintained the proud tradition of hard work and modest living. The welcoming attitude and courteous manner of the establishment brought people back again and again. I enjoyed sitting quietly and observing the families enjoy the experience, and I hoped that their memories were framed with the view of Silver Lake in all its shimmering splendor.

I watched as the down-to-earth waitresses worked swiftly, yet courteously paused to make eye contact and give me a smile and shy hello between high-speed maneuvers in tight spaces to move people and food around like a choreographed performance. The smell of bacon, coffee, and pancakes created a warm, sentimental finale to my predawn hike and charge down the mountain. I ordered the Hungry Hunter Breakfast, complete with a slab of ham, sausage links, bacon, country potatoes, three eggs, and pancakes. I was still jacked up on endorphins and was savoring the entire experience with each sigh of contentment. I had discovered happiness on my own. For that moment in time, I had shed layers of my past and felt like I had achieved a solid step in discovering me and my way forward.

After boxing up the half of my behemoth breakfast I could not finish, I set out to walk back to my truck at the PG&E trailhead. The lake shimmered with purity, and my soul felt free. My legs wobbled a bit as I made my way along the edge of the lake, stopping off to say hello to fishermen posted up along the bank. As I walked down the middle of the quiet road cradled by Aspen trees, I found myself walking with my eyes closed and feeling my heart soar with the breeze that swept across the lake and up the mountainside that challenged and changed me.

The elation of that morning kept me in a positive and happily sober state for a while. I worked and spent my free time creating. Creativity was bursting from within me. Everything was so great that I decided one night that I deserved to celebrate the best way I knew how. I lit a joint and a few candles, gifts from one of my new friends, lowered the lights, got out my guitar and recording system, and started in on a hard-earned 12-pack of ice-cold Budweiser. I was back in Oroville within a month and crashing hard again.

BASS THRASHER

Once I got back home, I was in full swing again. All in, as usual. All in with my music, spending multiple days and nights at the Electric Canyon Studio completing the songs I started in my little eastside studio. All in with my visual art, exploring different styles and mediums and creating like a madman. All in with building new business concepts. As I was finding my way out of divorce, foreclosure, and the death of King Duce Records, Julie and I began to develop Manic Fusion—a creative lab that brings together likeminded individuals to build and create great brands, content, and technology. We had multiple brands that we were developing. It was a creative hurricane.

I was also all in with my drinking again. Between the strengthening bond I was forming with Julie and my still broken heart over the loss of Becky, I couldn't make sense of any of it. I was running from both the pain and the potential happiness. I felt guilty that I could have feelings for someone new while I had failed in my marriage and in love. Not to mention Julie had two young boys. What a mindfuck to a guy who had wanted kids and didn't have any. As much as I knew we were connected, I was mourning the loss of not having kids and I was sure to let her know on a daily basis how fucked up that felt. I didn't want to love her, but I did. It was heaven and hell all rolled up into one big fat ugly mess. Through it all, her patience and support of my crazy ideas made great things possible.

We spent days on end working side by side on all of our projects, either in the home office in our mobile home or on dirt roads all over the county and beyond, drinking and coming up with even more ideas. It was a crazy time, perfect for my crazy as fuck mind.

It was a Monday night. Good enough reason to drink. It was November 26th, 2012.

"I've Got It! Bass Thrasher!"

I was pacing the floor while Julie worked at her desk in the entry room of the double wide mobile home. Broke didn't even begin to explain the sad state of our financial situation. Times were tough, but she believed in me and us. She had worked by my side, managing and closing up King Duce and looking to the future with some final work and drawn-out pain as I tried to reach the other side to a new life.

The name hit me that night the way things do, like a bolt of lightning from somewhere far away. It seemed unexpected, as always, but my mind is obsessed with creative wordplay. My mind loves to creatively build multidimensional, vertically integrated concepts—whether building a treehouse as a kid, complete with a giant old-school TV and a twenty-five-foot antenna—or creating a song, a painting, this book, or a lifestyle clothing brand. At the time, I was in a creative storm, in the early development of an unnamed creative lab I eventually established as Manic Fusion, named after a crazy, beautiful self-portrait I created while I was drunk and naked in the crazy clown back-room after losing everything.

When Bass Thrasher clicked and locked into place in my mind, I felt an explosion of creative passion from memories of fishing with my grandpa, dad, brothers, and buddies. The experience of building the King Duce lifestyle clothing brand gave me the sixth sense, and I knew this was it. Bass Thrasher was the big bang that instantly validated my expertise in the outdoor world. The minute the words came out of my mouth, my mind could see everything clearly. I knew it was huge. I was especially excited because, despite being broke, I had emerged with a brand that would give me the opportunity to reinvent myself.

Bass fishing was my refuge and hobby when I first moved back to my hometown from Seattle and launched my real estate investment business. I was enjoying some moderate financial success at the time and bought an old Skeeter '21 Bass Boat. It was 2005, and I was sitting on my boat in the launch area waiting for a friend to return from parking my Chevy truck and trailer up on top at the main spillway launch ramp parking area. I had unknowingly launched my boat during an evening bass tournament. I sat there sipping on a beer and observing brand new bass boats being unloaded into the water by brand-new full size four-wheel drive Chevy, Ford, Dodge, GMC, and Toyota trucks. I suddenly felt embarrassed by the tattered condition of my old bass boat and used diesel ranch truck. At the time, I was making decent money and didn't appreciate that my stuff was paid for. I was witnessing staggering amounts of money, undoubtedly much of it on borrowed money, being spent on trucks, boats, tackle, gas, lodging… It hit me like a freight train; bass fishing was big business! I didn't grow up fishing with fancy bass boats. Like most people I grew up with, I usually fished from the bank and wasn't targeting a specific species of fish. I grew up with a grandpa that caught everything with a "rooster tail" lure. He even held a few records on Lake Oroville for a time.

Suddenly my mind started seeing that evening bass tournament as some beacon of light pointing me to an opportunity literally in my backyard. I remember being stuck on it that evening; I couldn't stop thinking about it. I intuitively felt like this was an opportunity worth exploring. The more I thought about it, the more I realized how limited my knowledge of bass fishing and the bass fishing industry was. I had a bass boat, I grew up bass fishing with my friends on the lake and the old gold dredging ponds out along the south end of town along the Feather River, but I hadn't seen the potential before this. My twin black friends Rodd and Todd were totally into bass fishing. They watched *Bill Dance* TV shows on weekends and had tons of tackle and the latest gadgets and topwater baits. It was pretty cool that when I eventually launched a bass fishing lifestyle brand that Rodd was the first friend I called to invest.

By the time I came up with the concept and name, it was five years later. I was flat broke and didn't even have enough money to register a ten-dollar domain name. Serious! As always, Julie scraped enough together to grab the domain name and gas to drive down to Los Banos to meet up with Rodd. I remember that night vividly. Rodd and I hadn't seen each other in a long time, and we were happy to reconnect. But I was tired, stressed beyond belief, drinking tons every day, and just wanted to snap my fingers and get to the finish line, whatever and wherever the hell that was. After a few beers, Rodd handed me a personal check for five thousand dollars. I cried inside and started to choke up. He could tell I was hurting, but he believed in me and my business judgment despite the commercial failure of King Duce and my personal life disaster. His belief in me and that check sent my spirits soaring.

As we drove away from Rodd's house that night, my brain was in overdrive thinking about possible investors and relationships that would take my idea to the next step of development. Feeling drunk and high coming off a big win for my vision, I was air drumming and guitaring to Ozzy's "Over the Mountain" on Fresno's ZRock station 103.7 while I sifted through the Rolodex in my mind of possible investors.

5150, MY HIGH-SPEED COP CHASE

E ven though things were looking up, the day-to-day was not pretty.

I had been drinking all day. I was staying at my ex-wife's house while she was on vacation with her family. I was treating myself to a little vacation of sorts as well, on my own, enjoying my sense of freedom. But all too soon, I just wanted to be back at Julie's place. As much as I wanted to be on my own, I wanted to have her by my side. She refused to come to me, so I decided to go to her. I jumped in my old BMW and hit the road. Soon after entering the highway, I was cruising at 120 mph with not one, but two cans of beer open and flowing. Freedom! Or so I thought. The cops lit me up before I knew what was going on. I was out of my mind at this point and didn't really care what happened to me. I slammed on the brakes three times, trying to get them to hit me. Finally, I pulled over and jumped out of the car, yelling at them to pull the trigger. It was July 2013.

"Suspect is 5150. We have suspect restrained and will be bringing him in. We're gonna need back up!"

That's all I remember hearing the cop saying into the radio attached to his flak jacket with his gun pulled, calling for back up as his partner was struggling to handcuff me and try-

462

ing to calm me down. I was shouting disconnected thoughts about the brilliant flashing colors of light; something about how Van Halen's *5150* album was the best Sammy album...I miss my wife...but Pantera still ruled heavy rock music.... Bottom drops out to the black, wondering how I got here, then snapping into a manic rage, yelling at the cops about how fucked up the state of the country was. Then I brought it home, telling them how cops are outmanned and under-funded on purpose by our government to keep our society in a state of fear and paralysis...on and on until I was stripped naked in my jail cell and searched, as they removed my over-dosing heroin junkie cellmate leaving a trail of blood from a gash on his head as the cops dragged him out.

The police report stated that I kept telling the cops, as if it was a premonition from God, "This isn't what I worked my ass off for! This isn't what they fought and died for! Our Founding Fathers would be disgusted!"

Through losing my wife, money, and home to the economic crash and excessive drinking, I had become that unemployed, broke, homeless, no car, no driver's license guy who loses everything and goes off the deep end into the black hole of drugs, alcohol, insanity, and jail. That's a very dangerous man. It wasn't always this way. From early on, I was outgoing and trusting, but I also possessed a very confident but manic disposition. The result was social and commercial success to mask my hidden shyness, pain, and insecurities. I felt different than most of my peers from day one, ahead and behind, every day.

It only got more intense when I started self-medicating with drugs and alcohol to calm the highs and lows at fifteen. It was about the time sports started getting really serious, and we were having growing pains at home from the strain of three boys involved in multiple sports plus taking care of my special-needs sister, who required 24/7 care. I chose a solution that only made my mind and problems more scattered and manic. I've been diagnosed most often as bipolar by psychiatrists specializing in the field of drugs and alcohol addiction. But when you crash hard, it doesn't matter why. The pain is bigger than a medical diagnosis or solution.

Strange thoughts floated in and out of my mind in my jail cell as I paced in figure eights naked and freezing and half wrapped in a green padded 5150 robe. I heard the fat-neck sheriffs discussing the upcoming presidential election; three years away but already an important and historical event... everyone knew it. I heard a voice reminding me of the stoner film actor and director Seth Rogen. I randomly thought to myself, *I wonder if this cop's Jewish...*

"I wouldn't be shocked to learn that Obama and Hillary had an affair and even considered running together as secret lovers. I'm sure he cowers from his big-toothed bully of a wife by hiding out with the butlers and kitchen staff to sneak a smoke break and a moment to feel normal. Then I thought, 'Maybe he would feel more appreciated by the white grand-motherly Hillary, who would have a little black Eurcle to play with.'"

"Billary and Vanilla Nig are lynching the American dream with a Coke and a smile."

"More serious crime, fewer cops, and they're trying to kill the second amendment to render us helpless to tyranny."

Then the cop with the fattest neck I ever saw jumped in with his take on the situation to articulate his unscripted thoughts. I heard someone call him Bubba, and I laughed like only a crazy drunk naked man in jail could.

"Well, they ain't takin' my guns. Period. I will fight again for what this country stands for. We're facin' a war on our own soil. And this time it's goin' to be an all-out war. Instead of a couple hundred thousand casualties, we're looking at millions of dead Americans. Obama doesn't know what it's like to struggle. I ain't gonna let some spoiled caramel white boy who grew up surfing in Hawaii smokin' fuckin' pot and snortin' cocaine, had all his school paid for, claiming to be black, like he grew up on the south end of Chicago take over my life. Hell, I'm blacker than that idiot, and I'm a redneck. This fuckstick just slapped my kids with a giant tax he calls Obamacare…no concept of money, what it takes to earn it and pay taxes on it. It's easy to talk about wealth redistribution and healthcare for every deadbeat American when it ain't your fuckin' money!"

The cop who recently transferred in from the Bay Area mildly offers his perspective. "Well…I don't know if I agree with your assessment. I'm a fourth-generation cop and union member. My uncle was the head of the union and believed that they protect the rights of the working man. I agree with that."

Even in my fucked-up state, I thought to myself, "Okay, Jimmy fucking Hoffa! This isn't 1930 for fuck's sake! Different times…back then, unions were organized to address the savage working conditions. We forget that there was a lack of good jobs and health care prior to the Industrial Revolution. But let's blame the evil entrepreneurs. We forget about Henry Ford's $5 workday, unheard of at that time. He didn't need a union to strong-arm him to do it. He was smart and realized that he needed motivated and committed employees who would produce and then be able to buy his cars. Liberals think that they have to save the world from evil business owners. So backwards. Liberals and their mafia counterpart we call unions don't produce, they take your hard-earned money and spend it and redistribute it for their delusional vision of a socialist America, until they destroy the goose that lays the golden egg."

Turns out that I was thinking out loud. The cops all listened and considered my slurred words but continued their conversation without me.

This dialogue continued until I saw sunlight through the bars of my cell and the dispatch window. I was actually impressed for the most part of what I could comprehend, through the noise of the other inmates, the sounds in my head, and the fat-neck drawl that the cops were speaking made me question what I had heard.

My heart was starting to flutter, my body was starting to shake from the DTs, and the meat locker temperature was shriveling my balls and pride into oblivion. Being locked up is bad enough. But being stripped naked, searched, and guarded by your old classmates is a nightmare.

Julie was able to bail me out, and they sent me to the emergency room to make sure I wasn't going to die from withdrawals. I was in pretty bad shape. Shackled and handcuffed, I scuttled into the hospital with no help from the sheriff's deputy, who told me to step carefully because if I started to fall, he would not stop me. I looked at him, deep in his glazed and alcohol-drenched eyes and bloated red face, and smiled, knowing that we were actually more alike than different. I was listening to a doctor telling me once again that if I didn't make some serious life changes, I was going to die. Just then, Julie appeared in the doorway and came to my side, held my hand, and promised both the sheriff and the doctor that she would take responsibility for me and for my care, and they reluctantly released me to her. She took me home, fed me a home-cooked meal, and let me sleep while she went to get my ex-wife's BMW out of impound.

Months later...

SCOUT 2.0 – DRINKING AND DYING IN SEATTLE

My nights living back in Seattle coked-out with Wall Street boy and drinking with the producer from the rock band Alice in Chains in a corner bar 'til 2 am.

I was freshly sober...again. I was so burned out from struggling through the manic ups and downs of my chaotic mind.

Things were looking up with Bass Thrasher, but I was out of cash and bummed out that I had to halt my momentum because I was underfunded and broke.

And then I got a call from El Diablo. "Hey Rock! It's Dickman. I've teamed up with MTV founder Bob Pittman to buy our old company Scout back from Fox and merge with North American Media Group. I need you to help me roll up the top outdoor publishers." I needed this for so many reasons. Despite being exhausted of the Silicon Valley rat race and wanting to get on with creating and building my own businesses, in my environment, and live a life that inspired me again, I was broke and broken. I accepted a consulting position to lead the build-out of an outdoor network for what Dickman called Scout 2.0. He even agreed to help us push Bass Thrasher. Dickman appointed me Director of Network

Development for Outdoors/Fishing, and I brought Julie in as my research assistant. We needed the money to get caught up from our struggle, and this would help us promote our new clothing brand, but there was a catch. There's always a catch with Dickman.

The first couple of months were like being back running and gunning with the original Scout team. It was electrifying to be out of my despair and rocketed into cash, challenge, and respect for my skills. All day and night on the phone recruiting new high-level deals with the biggest outdoor sites on the Internet, doing three-hour-long conference calls with the team connected by our offices in New York, Seattle, and Minnesota; including multiple remote home offices throughout the country like my home office in NorCal. I had a green light to fly around the country to close the deals we needed to build the network out, including trade shows, entertainment, travel, flying clients to our New York office at Rockefeller Center, right next door to the *Late Night Show* on NBC with Jimmy Fallon.

I was able to excel at my job simply because I had executed the same business model and role three times before with Dickman. And, at first, I was so excited to be pulled up out of the deep poverty depression that I wanted to believe it would be different this time. I blasted onto the scene less than four months sober and ready to dedicate my life to El Diablo and the collective project. I recruited the biggest names in the outdoor world simply by evangelizing my passionate belief in our CEO's vision and our past success and my legitimate connection to the outdoor world. It felt so exciting and rejuvenating. It felt like the band was back together.

In addition, the authenticity of our bass fishing brand, Bass Thrasher, gave us and Scout.com industry credibility and helped to recruit the top names in the industry. Since I had successfully built very similar companies with essentially the same executive team, I figured it would be all good, and we could build two great companies as one big happy family. I forgot that I had signed a deal with the devil.

Despite the excellent progress my team and I were having establishing our presence in the outdoor market, developing key relationships, and signing long-term partnerships that would establish the gravitational pull to attract the key players in the industry and markets like bass fishing, Slim began to drop me from key team meetings in our Minnesota and New York offices. I couldn't understand why. And I certainly didn't connect the Las Vegas swingers' rejection from a few years earlier.

But then it began to dawn on me. Dickman was treating me like something was up, and I started to put two and two together. Plus, I could tell that he had changed, and he was more power-hungry and belligerent than I had ever seen. He dressed much more New York metropolitan, but he had grown stranger and slimmer. For some reason, he began to press for me to meet with him and work out of the Seattle office. Slim told me that he wanted my energy in the engineering office because it would inspire the team. Then, on New Year's Day 2014, he gave me an ultimatum. I either moved to Seattle or I was out. It was too much to bear knowing that I would have to uproot again and take on the city life alone... just the thought of it all hit so hard I buckled and drank.

Reluctantly, I moved up to Seattle from NorCal. I was forced to uproot my fragile recovering life, just months sober and getting my DUI jail shit figured out, to move and dive headfirst into a high-speed and high-stress start-up turn-around. I didn't know exactly what to expect since things were happening so fast, as they predictably do with an Internet start-up, but I knew that this would be my final stop before going solo for good as an entrepreneur.

I had only signed the deal to get out of the financial and mental hell of being unemployed and broke for so long. The little Napoleon Hitler knew it and sadistically forced me from the stability of Julie and our home and office in NorCal to join the engineering team in Seattle. I'm not an engineer. I can't read code. I'm an entrepreneur and CEO. But he never thought about how it would take my inspiration and kill it with zombie engineer personalities and a cold rainy city that was six hundred miles from my girlfriend and business partner and only sense of security after losing so much and barely hanging on to sobriety. Looking back, it was a suicide mission that nearly killed me. For that, I still consider Slim Dickman a little reptilian with no soul.

Sometimes we need our lives totally disrupted to make things clear about the direction forward. I was being manhandled and controlled for his power-trip kicks. I took it bending over when I was a young twenty-something punk under his tyrannical rule because I wanted him to pay me for his knowledge. I extracted it by infiltrating his compound from inside his home. His ego and greed blinded him to my true value, and it hurt him in the long run because he never fully utilized my talents. Weak people stayed "loyal" to his mind control manipulation. I saw the end as I packed my bags for the city.

As I sat in the silent office of code theorists who grew up playing video games, I began asking myself why Dickman would make me move away from my home, my business partner, and productive environment, just to be in an office that he rarely visited, opting to work and party in the New York office instead, with his new 25-year-old debutante socialite wife? Julie and I were kicking ass for the team out of our humble little home office in NorCal, and she couldn't leave town to join me in Seattle because she was raising two young boys. The same CEO that forced me to move to Seattle ended up never being there. It was the beginning of the end. My patience AND sobriety ended. I was done playing games with this little boy. It was time to grab my life by the balls and make my move and leave his twisted world behind.

I sniffed out a shitty dive bar called the Anchor on a prime real estate street being renovated with yuppie condos and organic markets. They were about to tear it down when I arrived, and I remember feeling bummed because I felt comfortable there. Most of the other bars in Queen Anne were yuppie spots that held professional thirty/forty-somethings, working hard to impress one another. In a dark, shitty bar, other fucked up people couldn't see my loneliness, and I was too lost in my own dreary thoughts to recall anyone from that place—except the bartender. I didn't care. I just assumed everyone was perfectly content drinking alone and feeling miserable like me.

The bartender was this old Irish guy with a permanent scowl and the red face of an alcoholic with stamina. He sat there on his stool behind the bar drinking his Scotch whiskey right along with the other customers and me, gazing up at the fuzzy TV screen hung up on the wall to his liking. All of us ending the night in a shit-faced whiskey stupor. No one cared. Not even the owner. He had just made millions selling it to a developer out of China. The pain and loneliness of trying to exist and work in Seattle alone forced me to take control of my life and walk away from the insanity, no matter how badly I thought I needed the money. The toxic culture was becoming so revolting and off-putting that I became physically ill being associated with the kinds of people who treat others poorly because they pay them for a service. The arrogance and lack of humanity and leadership became so appalling that I had to jump ship and swim alone until I found my way.

I decided that I would never give bad people my heart and production again. I accepted that I made the choices to end up where I was and made a change, despite it being one of the hardest things I've ever had to do. It ended up showing me a world and a courage and sense of direction that I never would have found if I had remained enslaved to a subservient mindset connected to a paycheck umbilical cord of poisoned personalities, greed, and fear. Dickman was running the business into the ground by treating clients and employees like lower-class citizens, and it was affecting my ability to recruit the partners we needed. Word on the street was spreading fast that the CEO was "a fucking liar." I'm quoting a client that turned down a huge deal because he didn't trust my boss. It was that simple.

And things were getting crazier. Word was that Dickman had joined the New York and Hollywood media elites in style and carnal extravagance with drug and sex parties with the biggest dirtbags in the scene. I couldn't sell something, and especially people, that I no longer believed in. And that's coming from a full-blown alcoholic! But this guy was a time bomb. He had railed against drugs and excessive drinking his entire youth and adult life, harshly judging his older brother and mother for their addictions while idolizing his German nuclear physicist and Stanford socialist workaholic father. Now he was just like them, but worse. This dude was out there, and he hadn't even crossed the point of acceptance or awareness that he might have a problem. In all honesty, how could he possibly see the signs? He was a neurotic media start-up junkie addicted to constant forward motion to quiet the wreckage of his buzz-saw thoughts and actions. Money can soothe the pain and regret for a while, but there is always a day of reckoning.

I was done with this way of life for good either way. After having to listen to him disrespect us unmercifully, and without merit, except to quench his savage thirst for control and power, I was done. I quit in the Minnesota Airport, returning from a big outdoor show in Orlando after closing some major deals for the company. I got a call from my colleague in New York, who I originally brought into the original Scout Sports Network years prior. He was calling to advise me that he was now my boss.

After losing my cool, yelling on the phone at my "new boss," and getting frightened looks from the nice Minnesota folks eating dinner next to me, I was escorted to my plane seat by security with a stern warning that I would be arrested and kicked off the plane if I opened my mouth one more time. People in Minnesota are so nice. Seriously. They basically hugged me because they could see how visibly upset I was. I knew I had to dramatically change the people, places, and things I was surrounding myself with; otherwise I was going to wind up dead in my posh Seattle apartment, complete with hardwood floors and a southwest view of the Pacific Ocean's Puget Sound, the downtown skyline, and the famous Seattle landmark Space Needle.

None of it mattered anymore, and I was drinking myself into oblivion and beyond. Hell, I would take anything anyone offered me. I was at that dangerous place where I didn't care anymore, and I was sliding fast into a black hole. I had become a slave to my alcoholism and a perverse and extremely insecure CEO, whose mind and life were quickly coming off the tracks, too. I called Julie at 3 am, gacked out on blow after a night out with my new money manager hanger-on and the producer from Alice and Chains.

I was dying and called Julie. "Get me the fuck out of here!"

She stayed on the phone with me all night, listening to my paranoid panic and then my passed-out snoring until I woke up in the morning, and she knew I had made it through the night. I packed up my bags and walked out of my empty apartment. I wasn't there long enough to buy furniture or even set up cable. I guess, deep down, I knew I wasn't gonna be there long either way. I quickly settled on it just being a drunken rampage of destruction, paid for by Slim Dickman. I decided that this was the last time Dickman would fuck me over. Never again! Julie had me on a plane and home within hours.

I had been disrespected by these dorks with money for the final time. Never again would I give my heart and skills to shitty people. It was war. I told them to fuck off, moved back to NorCal without a second thought, accepted the inevitable firing, signed the "mutually agreeable" separation, and I launched Manic Fusion Labs, finished this book, and built a ground breaking green technology company. It was a prolific terror of creative force and competitive will.

I now know, more than ever, that my approach to leadership and company culture is all about team above self. I played college sports and have come to realize that few people in business have strong teamwork or leadership skills. Being exposed to greatness as well as dysfunctional leadership has reinforced my leadership style of identifying amazing talent with heart, and inspiring and cultivating their potential, simply by helping them see it and providing a framework to feel inspired to create amazing things. At the end of the day, I'm extremely grateful for my last experience working with a crazy CEO and his yes-men storm troopers. They unknowingly made me a much better leader and person.

BUTTE COUNTY JAIL

Not long after a stint in a Nevada jail, I was back in Butte County Jail. I was working on the book, sitting at the table in the living room, when I saw cop lights reflecting off the mirror on the wall to my right in the dining area. I walked out to find two cop yelling at me to show my hands. They told me to walk down the steps to the asphalt and to get on the ground. They cuffed me and then started asking questions.

For me, being held captive is a spirit-crushing force of concrete, steel, and submission that turned the screws to my already damaged CPU of a brain. It was taking everything I had to simply make it through an average day as a "free" man, living and attempting to stay sober while I finished the book, launched businesses, and tried not to lose my fucking mind. That day, the force and anger built up inside of me, and with nothing to escape to, I snapped. I called up my buddy, and he came by with a case of Budweiser and news that he was going to be a dad. We started hanging out; drinking, laughing, and celebrating his news. I remember feeling so happy for Tyler and at the same time, totally sick to my stomach about the whole baby thing. I drank until I couldn't see straight and had a very loud conversation with the asshole neighbor next door. This fat fuck uses a decades-long fraudulent workman's comp claim to sit in his house all day except to waddle out onto his broken-down porch to smoke cigarettes and shoot his pellet gun at birds and deer that dare trespass on his half-acre domain. I told him how I really felt about him, including that I would fucking kill him. Oops. The cops that arrested me that night were not fucking around, and they dealt daily with someone like me.

Cops have been put in a position where they need to be on full alert no matter what situation they are responding to. When they get a call that a very large drunk and angry man with a shaved head is threatening someone's life, I'm sure they are on full alert. It was not the first time in my life that I had lost all my power and freedom. This was also an exclamation point to my view that once you are in the legal court system, it is extremely difficult to get out, especially if you're poor. And at the time, I was penniless. I was served a warrant for my arrest because I had violated my DUI terms, and they slapped me with every possible criminal charge they could stack on me, including a felony terrorist threat and strike for the California prison system. I couldn't believe what was happening.

When they got me to the station, I stared at the one cop and said, "What's your name?"

His partner ordered me, "Shut your mouth!"

The Sheriff hard balled me for the rest of the night and left me in the holding cell to freeze. He was the guy that makes the good cops look bad; fifty pounds overweight, a ten-pound mustache, and an awkward walk and talk of someone in authority who has no clue about being a leader. He was about as smart as his fucking combat boots and his tired stories of being a vet and how he would kill anyone trying to step up on him. He drove the point home by bragging to us all night about how he deals with people who talk back to him in 'his' jail. I wanted to laugh at him, but I looked at him and nodded as if I was really impressed with his manliness and smarts. Fucking idiot. He lapped it up all night and just poured it on like he was the star of his own Barney Fife show.

Jail was a wild trip, to say the least, but it was also really interesting and a life experience that everyone should have to go through at least once in their smart-ass arrogant existence. Having your freedom stripped from you is no fucking joke. After spending twenty-four hours in the county sheriff's icebox holding cells (the same place where I was held on my 5150 DUI), I was given a bag with my new orange jumpsuit, blankets for my cot, kinda-white shower towels, and orange slippers and ankle socks. I was escorted by a Hispanic sheriff who I've partied and ridden quads at Sand Mountain with. Quiet, but generally a friendly guy. Anyway, he had to watch me strip naked facing him. Jail is always freezing, so dick shrinkage is guaranteed and adds to the humiliating and psychological degrading factor of the experience. It took everything for my brain to not explode into a million pieces as the old drunk from Willows sat in the corner singing a song and calling me and all the cops "Scudder." It was a term of endearment; most drunks forget or don't ever care to remember anyone's real name since it won't be relevant within minutes of any discussion. So, my name was Scudder, and I was trying not to lose my mind while listening to old boy sing a sad Neal Young song at the top of his lungs. His mess of a body, red and bloated, disguised the fact that he had a beautiful voice and great ear. He could sing a song with perfect pitch and started over anytime he missed the octave by any degree that would go unnoticed by most sober ears. I smiled at the mind trapped inside the alcoholic cage that shackled our dreams, intelligence, and heart to a concrete floor in a jail cell.

This is why only a true alcoholic or addict can help by sharing their struggle with someone like them. To "normal" people, this all seems like weakness and selfishness run wild. And they're right. But they also are oblivious to the glaring mental obsession and body allergy that is more powerful than a normal person's will to live. It's a mental illness. Think about that. An alcoholic like me is like a possessed soul with a metastasizing cancer of the brain that fails to stop us from doing things that will destroy us. This is one of the major reasons I wrote this book. I am one of those dirtbag low-life alcoholics society cast out as a lost cause, never to return back to normal society...thank fuck!

I want to help the country understand the drug addict, alcoholic, the mentally ill. Talk about prejudice! I've been showered with accolades, alcohol, chicks, and drugs most of my life. Being an alcoholic drug addict was a bad boy image both girls and guys loved, as they watched me win big college football victories and consume whiskey and blow like Ozzy. I was struggling with normal life, but my drug-fueled mind told me to get right by doing more, and more, and more, to oblivion. I know many intelligent alcoholic/addicts who went from millions to the gutter. People don't realize that people who are high performers, extremists, alcoholics, drug addicts... are addicted to adrenaline and the chase of highs and lows to get there one more time...that high...money, a win in sports or business, women, sex, cocaine, sugar, alcohol, diet, health, ideology of any kind...all an addiction to keep us preoccupied from our true self and the search, time, and care it requires to get to know and love ourselves. I mean, truly like who we are and not *what* we are to society.

I know that skin shedding metamorphosis painfully well. I went through the breaking down of all the social status that made up my identity. It was all a lie. I had to keep challenging myself—my true self—to become what I was made to be and do. I knew deep down, like most of us, but I was too scared to go all in, and I'm a guy who has lived all in my whole life. But I was conflicted between what I thought I was and who I am supposed to be. Now, I'm just me. And that mindset makes me happy. I don't have to feed myself whiskey, blow, women, and lies to get through the week anymore. I hit the wall going a hundred miles an hour, and it smashed my delusion, pride, and self-hate, all my fear-laden bullshit to protect me from the truth and what I needed to do to become the man I knew I was capable of becoming. This was when I learned to work really fucking hard. My struggle is not unique. How I chose to face it required courage and a commitment to a new way of life.

Funny thing is, if you look at the macro view of America's people, their mental health, their personal contribution of production and consumption, their personal GDP, in every category, you will see that, as a whole, most Americans are cross-addicted to various overindulgences to feed unhealthy thinking and behavior (selfish inferiority narcissism complex...whatever the right definition is). Think about how our financial system swings like a stripper on a pendulum in some high-dollar Washington DC strip club for the power brokers and dealers. Think about how the average home buyer dropped to their knees to suck out every penny of equity in an over-inflated real estate bubble, created by that very greedy behavior, that they and the media and Obama so conveniently blamed big banks and Wall Street and the Republicans for. I blame the dark side of human nature and the men and women who sell their souls to the devil to feed their carnal desires. They come in all forms and at every socioeconomic level.

Back to my old drunken cellmate. I couldn't help thinking about this old man's sad, predictable life of alcohol and high school football memories. As I looked at his swollen and discolored feet, I was shocked by this guy's memory. He was rattling off dates of significance, at least in the history of his little farming town of Willows. It made me smile with how sharp the old man's mind actually was. He remembered fifty years of high school football with about the same effort as their school's mascot, the Honkers, a Canadian goose, exerts to fly. I'm surprised Honkers is an acceptable term in our politically correct era. NorCal is a funny thing. We are a collision of the richest Far-Left Liberals on the planet with old-school blue-collar "deplorables."

I started humming Neal Young's song "Old Man" and imagining myself twenty years down the road, realizing that I would be him soon, one way or another, either rich or in a jail cell, maybe both, but hopefully happy and free. At the same time, I didn't see a sadness in the man that I had. He didn't seem upset or discouraged with his situation. In fact, it seemed like he saw it as par for the course and was content to have a dry place to sober up before he found a ride back up the hill to Paradise. The old man could tell I was in a bad place, smiling gently, remembering the fiery ambition of his younger days before the world and the booze stole it. He finally sat down to take a break from singing and standing on his swollen purple feet. He took a few deep breaths and looked up at me, standing and pacing to nowhere.

"What's wrong, Scudder?"

I didn't even know what to say. This old guy was being kind, but I just wasn't in the mood to share my feelings about the situation. I was just trying to talk myself down and think about being in a meadow in the mountains or standing at the edge of the ocean with no one around for miles. Freedom. It's like breathing oxygen. Doesn't mean shit until you have it taken away. And then shit gets real. I have struggled with claustrophobia from a couple of traumatic experiences as a young child. But even more than that, I was raised from birth to run and think free. Remember, I didn't wear clothes on a regular basis until I was four. I was allowed to think and speak about things that had no boundaries. I was free to explore the world and discuss my thoughts with my parents as a free, independent person since my baby eyes connected with theirs.

Jail didn't feel much different than 5th grade with my underachieving small man Mr. Vaughn reigning over young alpha boys like the punk bitch schoolmaster in Pink Floyd's song "Another Brick in the Wall." Authority was a dubious monster that I was taught to respect, fear, and conform to. But how could I when I felt that some of those in authority positions did nothing but apply for a job just to have said authority to kill my independence and command my respect? I couldn't. I was given too much freedom and confidence as a baby boy to ever be able to exist inside the confines of the normal school or social framework of the middle-class community designed by the reigning powers of our system. Spending my time in jail felt just about as relevant as sitting in school or a Silicon Valley office. Suffocating.

I kept challenging and asking why, until a risk-averse elementary teacher or well-intended mother would give me the "Now, Chris, you need to pay attention and apply yourself more." I can't tell you how many times I heard that, even into my high-tech career with a quarterly review of "Needs to apply himself to being more organized and write better plans," when I had just signed the largest revenue producers in the country. They didn't have a clue that my mind was possibly on the spectrum and not clicking at the same right lane speed or low altitude as theirs. I look back and feel a little resentment at these mindless scrubs telling me that I wasn't applying myself; to what? A system and plan that I disagreed with in its most fundamental form, even at my earliest age of exposure to it? Intuitively, I knew that the system I was raised in for the first four years of my life, and the world I was tossed into after that, were diametrically fucking opposite concepts. And my mom and teachers wondered what was wrong with me. I was a leader. They were followers. I see things from a higher altitude with a broader view. It's that simple.

Now I know the real question is, "What the fuck was wrong with you guys for not seeing that I didn't fit in that system?!" Jesus Christ! Seriously, I was a personality of explosive color and action before preschool. Then, all of a sudden, I have problems with my environment? You mean the sterile box of linoleum tiles, chalkboards and uptight teachers who are rewarded for not taking risks in their adult life? Give me a fucking break, folks. I've heard it all and having grown up around it, I know it when I hear and see it. Conforming to the mediocrity of the masses was what that was all about. Puke.

I have always had creative ways of thinking and a lot of sensitivity. I get lost in my world of a million thoughts coming in all at once and not knowing how to connect them to the reality processing that must happen at the same time. It transcends the spoken language because my thoughts move faster than I can convey a linear verbal thought without distraction. My mind, like my dad's, is like a vacuum sucking in stimulation and information (data) from the world around us, all the time at hyper speed. My dad shares the story of walking up to his mother at about twelve years old.

"Mom, I think too much. How can I turn it off sometimes?"

"You can't, Dear. You need to accept that's how it will be, and you need to work with your mind."

Sounds simple, but it's not.

Back to jail with the old man. He and I were the only guys in the holding cell. Those rooms would be awesome to record some rock or opera vocals in. The echo from the imposing concrete block walls, acoustic friendly ceiling tiles, and a slick concrete floor that created an echo box chamber that amplifies and layers a sung note that only a modern effects processor could artificially emulate. The old man was utilizing its recording potential with his string of KTEL's drunk bastard hits from the 1970s. I stood on the other side of the door looking at him with a cold dead stare, studying his red face and thick wavy grey hair like Grandpa Rockwell's. All three of us alcoholics suffering the life of insanity, highs, lows, destruction, and fear, but I doubt my Grandpa Rockwell ever went to jail or got into trouble. Back in those days, a working man never got into trouble for driving home from the bar after working in the hills for the lumber company all day. That was just part of the gig.

I'm surely not endorsing drunk driving. We've all learned the horrific results of those statistics. I am truly thankful I was caught, punished, and never hurt anyone. I know people who have killed people driving drunk. There was a 20-year-old kid in my jail pod that just killed his girlfriend and paralyzed his best friend. He's fucking done. He's going to prison and worse, he wakes up to it and lives with it every day as do the victims' families. I watched his young dying eyes, looking for answers that no hardened criminal could give him. I just hugged him and told him that my heart went out to him and everyone involved. His baby face looked up at me with welled eyes and said thanks without a word. He made me grateful. I experienced so much pain in that jail caused by addiction and alcohol, self-medicating chemically imbalanced people struggling with the day-to-day shit that mainstream brains can't understand, in many cases. Others just don't give a fuck about human life and piss it away, living a self-consumed existence of degradation. The contrast was startling, I wasn't sure where one ended, and one began.

The thing about jail and a wild animal like me is that it's like caging a lion who is used to owning and dominating his domain. To suddenly take that from me is like shooting me with a stun gun, or an injection of some fucked-up psych med and a crisp white clean straight jacket to muffle the force of nature surging through my veins. I would rather be dead. Not even a question to me. Give me freedom or give me death.

So, old man started tuckering out from his singing and last flash of drunken exuberance before the sad and ugly crash back to reality. He plopped down on the concrete floor and kicked out his mangled feet and let out a big gasp of air, realizing reluctantly that he was right back where he said he would never be…again. That was also the case for me; I swore I would never end back up in a jail cell after my first DUI and night in Santa Rita Jail, an East Bay stop off for serious criminals passing through to San Quentin or Folsom Prison. Talk about a fucking trip! I was the only white guy in a holding cell of fifteen black guys.

Here's the deal: trying to adapt to those kinds of crazy scenes was nothing new or shocking for me by the time I ended up in jail that first time. College football brought me face-to-face with the criminal element. Jail was just the same group of guys who got caught. That's it. Period. In Santa Rita, we hung out and talked King Duce Records; everyone in the cell was either a rapper or their cousin was. Most of them were from Oakland, Vallejo, Richmond, San Jose, and Sac. I was entertained all night with stories from the streets and freestyle battles until they moved us along to our next holding cell, one step closer to our fate.

"Hey Scudder... where'd you say you played football for?"

I looked at him in disgust, probably because I saw me in twenty-five years with the same fucked up life and swollen feet if I kept drinking. He asked me the question a few times, which felt like a million needles shoved into my eyes and eardrums. I snapped and screamed bloody murder at him. I'd gone into total red blackout rage from the fact that I was trapped with my claustrophobic thoughts and old boy who kept talking about football and calling me Scudder. I lost my shit, and next thing I know, there is a loud crack on the window next to my right ear, and a loud but muffled scream from Barney Fife....

"Hey! Knock that shit off! Or I'll knock it off for you!"

Did he really just say that while I'm caged up like a tiger with my mangy cellmate, who was driving me to insane thoughts? Now I wanted to fucking kill the sheriff and use old boy as a human shield as I broke out. All these thoughts raced through my mind as I took the stare of the cop while he let me know who was boss. He opened the door and took us into the main waiting room just down the hall, where they book us. There were freezing steel chairs, three rows, and a TV on the wall with a Butte County Sheriff's department public notice about the fucking diseases you can get in jail because it's so filthy. Half the people in there could give a fuck about germs because they're already decomposing from meth or heroin. Fortunately, another set was on NBC Sports, and the show was Bass Fishing with Scott Martin. It was a very familiar and almost comforting world with our recent launch of Bass Thrasher. I smiled to myself, recalling the endorsement of Scott Martin with Bass Thrasher sponsored angler and owner of *Bass Angler Magazine*, Mark Lassagne.

The release from the eight-by-twelve holding cell and transfer to the main lobby with a TV felt like a sense of freedom. Funny how we normalize and quickly become satisfied with what seems to be an improved environment or situation. I appreciated the extra space and a few other nightcrawlers and their stories…but, honestly, it was too cold in my paper-thin black t-shirt, Levi's jeans, and bare feet on ice-cold concrete to care. It's hard not to feel like cattle waiting for slaughter. I thought about what it must've been like for the Jews who ended up in the Nazi death camps like Auschwitz. Then with a lightning bolt of karma, I started to feel like a dick for feeling sorry for my situation.

Hell, I challenge any of you to try and sleep a wink in meat locker conditions you have no escape from. It was fucking hell. My bald head felt like a snowball leeching the warmth from my body. I tried enveloping my arms and head inside my t-shirt and breathed my hot breath in hopes it would warm me up, just a little. It worked! I smiled like I had just figured out a survival skill for jail…wait! I said I would never go back! Now I'm saying "next time?" I've got problems. Anyway, I tried lying down and stay tucked in my little world inside my t-shirt, breathing hot wet breath onto my stomach and arms. It actually works if you're in a bind, folks. Not saying it only works in jail. Believe me, I prefer this technique when I'm outside deer hunting early in the morning way better than utilizing it in jail!

"Rockwell!"

I popped my head and arms out of my shirt like a frozen white turtle…I was just getting warm…well, not warm, but fuck, I wasn't freezing my dick off for just a few seconds! I was drifting off to a warm beach somewhere with all the things that would make me smile and laugh. The sheriff's stupid tough guy baritone announcement snapped me back to the fact that he controlled my life at that moment, and it was taking everything in my body and mind to keep calm and make him feel important, by using my "Wow! You're smart and tough!" Do you know how hard that is to do for someone like me? This is why I laugh when people, who think they know me, will say that I'm rigid and won't listen. I do talk a lot and listening can be a challenge for me at times when my mind is flowing with ideas or really fucking pissed off. But I am generally pretty flexible and willing to reach a compromise. But in terms of my fundamentals, I never sway. It's the infrastructure of truth that allows me to test waters outside my comfort zone…like jail, high-speed cop chases, creating a new song, or writing this book.

Guys like this cop revel in this moment. We both knew what we stood for, and this night was his moment of glory and vindication against all those nights that he hung out with his shit-kickin' buddies working on their trucks instead of trying to risk rejection and hook up with some girls. None of us really change when we get older. Think about it. Even though you ran away from your hometown, changed your hair or clothes, and made more money with a cool title compared to your parents, did you really change? The more we try to escape what we come from, the more it stalks us like the dark shadow of Jack the Ripper.

This guy was young, but he had settled into his grand-pa's slow and steady world war two generation thing like my grandpa. Man…I just don't know how my grandpa did it. I'm serious. He loved to fly his plane, sail the ocean, build houses and churches. *How did he put up with these fucking meatheads?* I thought. I guess he put up with it kinda like I put up with the Silicon Valley start-up slapdicks for over a decade. Suddenly, I understood. It was a means to an end for him to retire in Northern California and chill out. And that's exactly what he did. So, I figured I'd ride this wave, let homeboy do his boss hog thing, and take it all in, including the other people arrested and sitting or lying by me.

There was one chick who looked familiar. She was an older brunette with a sucked-up face. She was all fucked up for being out there running and gunning for a while. She looked at me with shy embarrassment. I smiled warmly back. We recognized each other and found comfort in knowing that we were the same in there and just helping each other out with a smile of encouragement. Being poor and down and out helped me realize how fucking close we all are to the bottom. It's like swimming somewhere and not knowing how deep it is because you can't touch or see the bottom as you tread water. I kept my head just above water for years with no rudder. I'm thankful I was able to sink to the bottom. I knew my purpose would eventually surface if I didn't keep lying to myself and others just to keep achieving the goals of a society that I didn't respect.

My mentor, who survived a machine gun for breakfast in Vietnam, helped me strip the need to please the outside world of ridiculous expectations by telling me to simply be true to myself. For me, it struck a nerve that nothing else could touch. I had been hyper-focused on achieving to please my dad and trying to live in accordance with what my parents thought was acceptable until it started to backfire. I finally figured it out. But I was tired of people climbing onto my wave and kicking out my board as I lined up a perfect ride. That's what coming back home was like for me after riding so high for so many years. Coming home showed me the dark side of men and how they see other men in a competitive state.

Being under the control of a cop can be a harrowing experience. But here's my tip to all the people blaming cops for violence against criminals. Don't put yourself in the situation. Believe me, the Far-Left are making them an enemy of the state, which has escalated cop killings and fatal confrontations. So, while I was not happy that I at the mercy of the cops called on me by a dickhead neighbor, I also understood their position. Traditionally, I've had good luck with cops. There are only two situations that rookie cops heavy-handed me, but I'm big and sometimes pretty crazy.

At least I was in a controlled environment now and I minded my Ps and fucking Qs and stood where they wanted me to and looked into the camera and turned when they told me to. Since this wasn't my first rodeo, I took it in stride the best I could and tried to make it an adventure and not fight every second of it. I kept telling myself that I would be a free man soon, I didn't know when, but I knew it would be relatively soon, compared to other guys rotting away for years. I was dreaming about being in the recording studio and dreaming of standing on the coast, breathing in the salty air and feeling elevated and free. The thought crossed my mind about the fucking neighbor responsible for getting me locked up, claiming that I threatened to kill him. But I was past that; I was focused on freedom.

Living on the edge doesn't mean living reckless and stupid for the sake of it. It means not living like a scared bitch. I know too many people who live scared and 'safe'. They make or inherited plenty of money to be comfortable, yet they don't really live. They are so consumed with not dying, preparing for possible risk scenarios by working super-duper hard to pay for all the insurance, long term investments for retirement, scrimping and saving like they are guaranteed at least fifteen years after the official retirement set by the IRS. These folks save for a rainy day, not just with money, but with their spirit and soul. Saving it out of vanity and fear.

These same "educated and successful" idiots would constantly preach to me to be more sensible and smart with my money. If that means inching my way to a nice comfy retirement at seventy, no thank you, and by the way, go fuck yourself and the life you preach to me. Go worry about your kitchen remodel and insurance premium rates and off the solar grid fad sweeping the nation. Go ahead and chase that carrot. I will be over on this side, diving headfirst into the unknown with a pragmatic view and a burning desire to discover something out there and in myself that lights me up. Sitting around hedging my bet to not die and not get hurt or not lose money is worse than death to me. So, go ahead and preach to me about how I need to get with *your* program. My response to you: grow some balls, ladies and gentlemen, and start living and stop playing to not lose. What the hell are you waiting for?

Funny thing, in jail, I observed that the cops and most of the jailbirds all lived half-ass. The difference between the two is that the many fat lazy cops are legally bullshitting themselves as a legitimate contributor to society and use it as a crutch and insulation to protect them from the truth that they traded their dreams for a predictable paycheck and retirement when they threw on their gun belt and gained fifty pounds. Same thing for the fucked-up addicts I was camped out in jail with.

There was this young mixed brother from a few backgrounds, from the good looks, tan skin, nappy soft fro curl, light Irish freckles hidden under his Black-Mexican skin tone. He was a heroin junkie that had been living off the system and landing where they gave the freest benefits. He was a smart young guy, passing the time away with dirty needles, welfare, and the Bernie Sanders socialism view of the world. Of course, he was the beneficiary of the socialist economic plan, he gets to live for free and the people who work for a living feed and wipe his ass, while he talks shit on the hand that feeds his sloth and sin of wasted life.

As I wasn't listening to him he proceeded to tell me for the third time about his fucked up right forefinger that looked like a meat grinder had taken off the tip and the nail grew back abnormally curved over the tip. Heroine junkies have some of the most gruesome physical deformities and illnesses from dirty needles and sticking them into bone and veins and nerves that cause permanent damage, and often a slow and very painful death.

I finally got my orange jumpsuit on and threw my nap sack of cot blankets and stained towels and boxer shorts over my shoulder. The thing I experienced in jail was not only the mental damage from my freedom being taken from me, but I also walked out with quickly diminishing etiquette and table manners and slang that was noticeable to my friends. I was walking, talking, and eating differently. Believe me, it only takes days to adapt to new social norms if you have to. I realized I was reverting to a primal survivalist behavior that matched my surroundings. My outward actions reflected the declining thoughts I was exposed to. I was also quickly learning a world of commerce inside that was a continuation of things I observed out in the streets, particularly with the black inner-city rap music gangster scenes I spent time in. Criminal thinking is not dumb thinking. Don't even get it twisted. The prisons, jails, mental institutes, and homeless communities are overloaded with smart people. Many are simply, or not so simply, enslaved by their mind and, in many cases, end up declining into the abyss through a well-intended, self-medicated routine that ends in predictable horror.

The sheriff marched me down the hall towards my final landing place. I had no idea what to expect but imagined classic prison cells and bunkmates. I was already deciding how I was going to handle the first guy that tried testing his yard status with me. None of this was new to me, being a former college football player and rap music producer. I've had my showdowns and occasional fights to establish respect and leadership, but I'm a good person who sees good in others, and that speaks louder than a puffed-up chest looking to fight. I prefer collaborating or just having a good time with interesting people.

The giant steel door with *L Pod* painted on it opened up to reveal a big steel and concrete room the size of a two-story weightlifting gym. I took a deep breath and said to myself, "Game on, let's do this." As I looked forward, I saw a mob of forty fucking inmates, all talking loudly. It fell silent as the door banged open. The lights were bright white, and every single one of them was instantly focused on me, the new guy. I thought to myself, *Man, I'm fucking tired of being a rookie!* I remember composing myself as I stood tall and walked in as if I belonged. But for now, I was going to learn the rules of the game and do what I needed to do to establish myself in those walls as someone to follow and not fuck with. I've always had that attitude, and that's probably why I haven't had to hurt too many people along the way—well, except on the football field. I don't play dirty, not in business or, more importantly, in life. I believe in honorable competition. To me, that's all there is, especially in this fucked-up world. And the thing I like about the illegal and rough side of the street is that, as Willie Nelson said, you have to be more honest on the wrong side of the tracks.

Before I could focus on the faces making up the crowd of men, I heard, "Chris!"

Although my name is very common, I knew the tone. It was someone who recognized me. As I homed in on the direction of the voice, I saw a big intimidating white dude with neck tats stepping out of the group and up on me like a grizzly bear. My fear and insecurity of the new playground quickly dissolved into confidence when I realized that it was my buddy Rodger from recovery. As I scanned the guys, I could get a sense that Rodger was one of the baddest mother fuckers in the entire jail. He was not only battling fierce meth addiction, like so many good guys in my hometown, but he was dealing with some serious head trauma from using his forehead as a giant baseball for a Louisville Slugger in a fight. Worse yet, he was still reeling from the horrible tragedy of his sister shooting and killing their own mother in a fit of meth rage. His entire family had been destroyed by meth. Rodger was big like me, about 6' 4", 250 pounds, depending on if he was clean or running and gunning. If he was all tweaked out, he could weigh a buck eighty. I was relieved and energized by Rodger's welcome, and within seconds, I was being welcomed to the pod by the rest of the guys. It was a moment that I won't forget.

I was at another low point and was picked up and hugged by the very people society says are the bad guys. Now, before I start sounding like a bleeding-heart Liberal, these men, including me, can all do some serious destruction and damage when we're whacked out of our minds on drugs and alcohol. Bad shit. And that stuff can't be excused or undone. Believe me, you have to deal with it, ask for forgiveness, and pay for the damage caused. It's the only way to get right. But these guys, free of drugs and alcohol, can be completely different people than the day they were arrested. Jekyll and Hyde. One day I'm a respected CEO of a legitimate business, employing lots of amazing people, and the next day I'm sitting in a jail acting like Charles Manson because I drank and lost my fucking mind for just a few hours. But that's all it takes. I used to scoff at a saying in recovery: *The first drink will get you drunk.* But now I get it. I have friends who have served twenty-five years for a moment of rage and the death of an innocent person. These stories are sobering to me. But they only affect me because I've faced a small sample of what my future looks like if I choose to go back to drinking.

After Rodger welcomed me, like only a lead warrior of the streets could, he proudly presented me to the men as his friend, Chris Rockwell. What Middle America and the wealthy spineless business dorks who hide behind money and slimy misleading contracts miss is that the streets are based on one simple principle, respect. I mean real respect. Not, "I have more money than you and a bigger title, therefore I can treat you like a fucking peasant." I've lived that in school and then again in business as I worked my way through the start-up high-tech media scene. I wanted to punch them in the mouth for abusing their moment of false power and disregarding all the truths that the playground taught them.

I've done business in a gangster's house in Oakland and at Internet billionaire's oceanfront water offices in San Francisco. The difference? Nothing. Everything. It depends on the person you're doing business with, not so much the industry you're dealing with. Liberals forget this basic principle. Shoving an inept employee down my company's throat just because she's a black woman to meet a racial quota is about the most racist and anti-competitive policy they could think of. The thing I respect about jail, the hood, and the poor, is that the people living in it are real about living and dying and how to survive in between.

I met one guy in jail who looked like Layne Staley, the lead singer of Alice in Chains (I'll refer to him as Layne here). He had bleached-blond hair that he cut short on the sides and left a little longer on top and an almost white goatee. His eyes were sunken into his ghostly white face, and the dark rims gave him the appearance of Rasputin's albino kid brother. Layne was funny, smart, and lived his entire life earning his way into the brutal Peckerwood gang indicated by a six-by-four-inch image of the gang's trademark woodpecker logo tattooed on his stomach. We would spend hours walking the pod, and I would listen as he would share sad, rough, funny, and crazy stories of his dope runs, battles, run-ins, and getaways from the cops.

The more I listened sincerely to him, he could see in my eyes that I wasn't bullshitting him like so many people had done to him all his life. He knew I didn't want something from him. He could tell I actually gave a fuck enough to sincerely listen to him about his life. He rewarded me with his truth, the stabbings, gunfights, murders, beatings he took as a baby, overdoses on heroin; you name it. Everything. He knew I wasn't a snitch. He knew I actually cared. That was it.

He finally, quietly, confessed with a serious but vulnerable look and said, "I know how to survive, but I never learnt how to succeed. You can show me how, Rock!"

My world fucking exploded and reassembled into a new perspective. I looked at him and said, "We're teaching each other, dude, but from the flip side. That's how it works in any game."

Layne smiled enthusiastically and then gathered his next step with new self-confidence.

"Being around successful people, right? Can I get your number so we can hang out when we get out? I can figure out anything. I'm good with figuring shit out, ya know? Anything bro! Like cars, that's kinda my thing. Did I tell you about the time I hooked it from the cops out off South Villa in Palermo..."

The dude could tell a getaway story like Michael Rappaport, the hyper Irish actor known for his dramatic and comedic characters.

Layne told me a couple of stories, back to back, that kept my attention away from the fact that I was in jail. He had this shit-eatin' grin that reminded me of a kid I went to elementary school with but can't remember his name to save my life. It'll come to me. Anyway, the funniest story Layne dropped on me was the time he was driving out on Lower Wyandotte road, pulling a boat he just bought and fixed up to go fishing with his buddy. Well, they were pulling it with a stolen Toyota Camry with a trailer hitch and no tags. No big deal.

Anyway, Layne and his passenger, a kid he grew up with and did crime shit with, were flying down the road, caught a bump where a big oak tree root grows under the road. We smiled at each other, both knowing that oak tree and bump in the road from our childhood. He said the trailer popped off his car hitch, and the boat started drifting into the oncoming lane right as a 1970s Chevy truck was coming the other direction. The truck collided head-on into the boat, the outboard engine launched over the cab and exploded into a million pieces. He said he stopped briefly to see if the truck and passengers were ok, even backing up a few yards as his emotions started to get the best of him. If he was to get caught chasing down his runaway boat now scattered all over the road, he would be looking at serious time. Layne dropped the car into drive and punched it, seeing that everyone was fine, and his boat was destroyed.

He said he took off like a bandit to his place around the corner, parked the car in the back, locked the door, and continued doing whatever shit they did when they weren't running from someone or the cops. Usually smoking meth, drinking, and planning the next robbery or drug deal. He mentioned as a side note that he had a quarter pound of dope (meth) and a couple of guns with them in the stolen Camry to top off all the possible charges and prison time facing his already two strikes.

If I hadn't grown up around this crazy redneck tweaker culture, I wouldn't believe the shit I was hearing. But since I knew he was the real deal, I was glued to his next performance as if he was doing a stand-up in front of his gang around a bonfire after a fucked-up initiation involving shit you don't talk about. I think I never got caught up in meth because I left to play college football right as it decimated my town and a lot of my friends, many of them smart, motivated kids.

The first time I smoked that shit off a foil with a hollowed-out Bic pen; the rush hit my head and body like electricity, rushing water and sunshine. It was like the natural adrenaline rush created by working out or playing sports or music. So, for me, I never had a big draw to meth. Plus, coming from health-conscious parents, I just instinctively knew, even though I was young and invincible, that crank was poison. I also knew I liked stuff that made me feel good more than the average kid. So, with that, I made a conscious effort to stay away from that stuff, and I continued to abuse whiskey as my primary drug of choice with blow and other shit tossed in. For guys like me, more is never enough.

Layne could tell I was up with his lingo, and I think it made him feel safe to let loose and tell someone from the "Ville" how fucking crazy and skilled he was at driving a getaway. Despite the comedy factor of his animated story, his dark eyes showed a beaten but loveable dog who was still playful. But I guarantee you that Peckerwood would not hesitate to shove a big fucking knife through my chest for snitching or stepping up on him with disrespect. Not a lot of people can be real with someone like that because you fear your truth and fear exploring people, places, and things that are outside your immediate safety bubble of family and work. I know so many people, white upper-middle-class homogenous intellectual theorist types, who talk all day about diversity and cultural immersion, but they can't even spend a night in a dive bar full of hardworking blue-collar folks because it's scary and below them.

Layne knew I was different. He could see it and feel it. He knew I was a leader, I was white, and that I could be trusted. For you uptight super politically correct idiots, there are strict rules in the jail/prison system with regard to race. It's real simple. White people stick with white people, just as blacks stick with blacks. You can speak to another race group, but you can't share or trade food or open items. You can only share or trade items that are sealed. There are certain tables, beds, etc., that are designated for certain ethnicity or gang affiliation.

My lesson to the liberal idealists: You have to earn respect. You can't pander, coddle, feed, and expect a strong independent human to develop. The street knows this, only out of life and death struggle. I had no idea what that world really looked like until I lived it and then experienced poverty and real struggle, after much success, money, and notoriety. I felt the pain and hopelessness and my resolute persistence to not let anything define my life but me and the bigger energy that I try to align with.

"All right, all right, listen up. We want to welcome the new guy Chris and lay out the rules of the pod."

It would be a few days and a few court appearances in my highwater orange jumpsuit, flip flops, and shackles before I was afforded the opportunity to be released on bail. Again, Julie was there to post bail, pace for hours in the jail parking lot waiting for my release, and then get me to the next steps towards freedom. I was crashing at Becky's place because there was a restraining order from the neighbor keeping me from returning to my place. She didn't feel comfortable letting Julie stay with me, so it was just the two of us. We were able to reconnect and work through some heavy shit.

The next morning, I woke up to shocking and disturbing messages from friends hitting me up about my friend and artistic collaborator, Phife Dawg, from the legendary hip hop group A Tribe Called Quest. Phife was dead.

THE EGYPTIAN EYE &
MY MEXICAN ANGEL

My Last Day Drinking - January 16, 2017

I had been drinking all day, as well as the day before that... and the day before that...and... I had worn out my welcome. Julie had driven off three days earlier after a tearful screaming match of insanity that I was probably mostly responsible for, but oblivious as to why. My alcohol-drenched mind demanded that I fight anything that stood in the way of my life or my next drink. I was sitting alone in our mobile home, miserable, but posting on social media how amazing life was and getting the positive feedback I needed from every possible source I could. Julie was sleeping on the couch at her friend's house, three days in the same clothes, tired, and devastated at the loss of sanity we were both experiencing. Like me, she was hoping and praying that things could get better. I sat at the kitchen counter, talking to myself and listening to music, singing along at full pitch as I drank my days and nights away, only the dogs to hear me and sigh, wondering if I was going to remember to feed them. I finally heard from Julie, and her message was clear: she was coming back, and I was not to be there when she got home. I was lost in what to do and where to go. Then it happened.

A symbol appeared in my vision like the all-seeing Egyptian Eye. I drew what I was seeing. I remember being taken aback with amazement, literally gasping, "Whoa!" It was like a white hologram right in front of me. I blinked to erase the image and resume my vision, but when I opened my eyes, the symbol remained. Now it was there whether my eyes were open or slammed shut. I panicked for a moment, trying to come to terms with the permanent scar that would haunt me for the rest of my insane life. I was scared. I was coming to terms with the end of my sanity, if there was any of it left at all. The eye symbol was seared into every frame of vision imprinting in my brain. I was crazy.

My life, the life I had worked so hard for, sacrificed myself for...that life was over. I had lost everything. I tapped out. I knew that I could continue drinking and die, or stop. Those were the only options left to me. I needed serious help. My parents would not take me in. I was angry and devastated. How could they abandon me at my greatest time of need? My mom said my dad's heart couldn't take it. I used my tablet to Google Call the one person who might possibly take my call. Maybe.

I was desperate. My hands and voice were shaking. I had been drinking my days away, not only forgetting to feed the dogs but failing to nourish myself. I was hopeful that she would answer the call.

"Connie?"

She answered. I don't even know what I said to her or if it was halfway intelligible. I told her that I was seeing shit, that Julie had kicked me out for good this time, that I didn't know what to do. I told her I was done drinking. Done for good.

Connie and Del, my in-laws, had taken me in a few months earlier when Julie couldn't take it anymore. I remember watching the 2016 Election on November 23rd in their living room. I spent a few sleepless weeks there until I promised Julie that I would be better, that I wanted to be home, and promised to stop drinking, raging, and blaming her for my misery. She believed my promises one more time and let me come home. But back then, my promises were made to be broken.

Connie told me I needed to get a job—any job—if I were to be staying with them. They didn't expect me to pay rent or for food, the just knew I needed something, anything, to get back on my feet again. My first step back to work was spending weekends in a nursing home that filled my soul with the repulsive smell of death and decaying old minds and bodies. I spent days playing bingo with old ladies and one old guy named Henry, known for walking down the hall in his old sweatpants sagging past his ass and shit running down his leg. I wanted to scream and run away to drink as fast as I could. It was the most depressing and humbling thing I had done in my long stretch of jobs. I ended up drinking and walking away from that place.

I honestly don't understand how or why my former mother-in-law was the one who was there for me when I was desperate. She showed an unconditional love and support that bordered on godly. I'm not kidding. I personally witnessed and experienced the actions of truly unselfish and good people. I was helpless, and they fed me, loved me, encouraged me, drove me to my job interviews, drug tests, physicals, and finally my job. They believed in me and kept encouraging me to fight on when I wanted to throw in the towel. There were a few evenings Connie held me as I cried and moaned from the despair and the pain I was in from feeling so alone and reeling from alcohol withdrawals. My father-in-law would get up every single morning before sunrise to get me to work by 6 am, including his day off on Sunday. Who does that? Their lived example and no-nonsense attitude guided me back to daily action that forced me to focus on getting my basics handled, like get a job, pay off my DUI fine, and get a car and place to stay. They literally had to hold my hand and help me start completely over as if I had suffered a debilitating stroke.

They were kind and loving to me, and deep down, knew that I was a good and decent man. They loved me. But Connie had the expectation for me to better myself. She agreed to help one more time.

"Chris, if you drink again, I'm done!"

This time was different. My body and mind were starting to shut down, and I was running out of time. I was desperate to do whatever she told me. Connie is old-school Mexican and she meant what she said, and I was ready to listen and to do whatever she told me. I trusted her and promised I would not drink.

As soon as I knew she was on her way to get me, to take me in and help me start on my path to recovery, I slammed as many beers as I could before she got there. I knew this was it, and the comedown and comeback seemed an insurmountable wall. It was 4:00 pm as I saw the headlights of Connie's car pull into the driveway; mid-winter dusk was already upon us even though the weather claimed it was springtime. I grabbed my backpack and Kiva duffle bag and stumbled and staggered out the sliding glass door onto the covered front porch. I gashed the top of my head as I failed to duck out of the low hanging door frame, but I was just happy to see Connie. I was drunk and scared, but happy she had answered my call. Before I could even close the door behind me, she laid down the deal; if I drank, I could not stay at their place, and she wouldn't be able to help me. I agreed wholeheartedly because I truly meant it. I would not drink. I was done. I would not drink again...after I finished the beers that I had stuffed into my backpack. I told her I needed them, all twelve of them, to keep me from having the DTs. She quietly poured them out the next morning, but she still laughs about it today.

My vision was still messed up, but I had a glimmer of hope that I could be saved, and maybe brought back to some reasonable level of sanity. I felt safe, loved, and hopeful. I was still drunk, so the tough road ahead was a blur. I was in the moment, as if it was one last drunk road trip. I was reminiscing on the good old days on the way "home," going back and forth from road trip bliss to the black abyss of destruction, loss, regret, and unimaginable sadness. Connie would shift the conversation to a funny memory that could connect us, bringing my mind away from the spotlight focus of the devastating loss of my wife—her daughter—and back to the family that loved me unconditionally. Without knowing it, Connie's love and understanding were therapy for a very sick man. She was gracefully and brilliantly keeping me off the rocks while helping me to come to terms with the way things were. Helping me to be okay because no matter what, they loved me. No matter what. The fact that she had just scooped me up, once again, and was bringing me home was proof of that.

Looking back on that afternoon, Connie was showing me what love looks like, the kind of love that surrounded me, but I couldn't see it. I would hang on to Connie for the next few weeks; she was a godsend. I had absolutely nothing to offer her except a daily in-home reminder of the pain and struggle her daughter had lived through.

We arrived at her home, the same humble house on a nice country road, only a few miles from my childhood home where I would visit my high school sweetheart.

Del, my former father-in-law, was not home yet. He was old school and couldn't understand what the hell was wrong with me. I was relieved that I did not have to face him just yet. Connie opened the door and welcomed me in. It smelled exactly like it did thirty years earlier. I remember being there a lot when I was a 16-year-old punk, wanting to spend time with Becky. Because she is a year younger and was not allowed to go on a date until she was 16, I was constantly at their house. Smart, loving, vigilant parents sure can make a teenaged boy's life challenging! But now those same people were taking me into their home to nurse me back to health and sanity.

Only a few things were different. The modest home was typical of the working-class family homes in our town. Rather than moving into a bigger home, add-ons were common. The fairly new kitchen remodel and expansion was one. It was nice, and as usual, home to a pantry and refrigerator filled to the brim with the essentials and then some. The garage had been converted into a spacious family room where everyone would hang out. The wraparound couch brought back memories of holidays and many family get-togethers; everyone lounging and laughing, and love radiating from every cushion and throw pillow. Ol' Del would sit in his corner Lazy Boy with his slippers dangling upside down on his toes while he read a book on World War II or a new magazine featuring fast cars or guns. He would glance up to catch the sound bites of Fox News or a Nascar race. He rarely spoke, but when he did, it was either to fire back at the TV about an opposing liberal view that was fundamentally hurting his lumber construction company or to sternly ask his wife and daughters to keep it down so he could hear the news anchor issuing a warning about this or that. They would fire back at him for being rude or because he had lost his patience with the lively conversation seven feet away from him at the loveseat social hour.

When the whole Mexican family would get together for the holidays or other celebrations, the entire house would be overflowing with love and laughter, boisterous conversations and kids giddily running around everywhere; There would be Del, sitting in his Lazy Boy with a couple of kids dangling off him as they laugh and play.

There was a big open fireplace with a stone hearth in the new family room, but it was for ambiance alone. The classic closed-door fireplace in the smaller entry room and former family room was the one they used for heat.

Connie led me past the fireplace in the entryway to the north corner bedroom that used to be Becky's. The room I was to live in was her childhood room. Not much had changed at all. Memories would flood into my soul over the months that I lay in her bed and regained my strength and mind.

The bathroom was right outside the door and the kitchen was across the hallway. I dropped my bag and backpack on the bed and went to the bathroom to pee and wash up...I think I took a shower. I felt safe. I remember telling myself, "All you have to do is not drink for the next couple of hours." I was still drunk and talked to Connie in the kitchen while she fixed me supper. I don't remember much, but she said I played Pandora on my tablet, loud, and I sang enthusiastically in between talking about everything and nothing. It was just gibberish drunkenness—a drunk trying to celebrate and sing his final glorious day of drinking to a close.

As the evening wore on and my buzz wore off, I began sobbing and shaking, my broken heart awakening to reality. Connie held my head in her lap as I held on to her and sobbed over my losses. I was coming to the realization that I had burned up something very special, a second chance, because of my drinking and rage. I just wanted to die from the weight of the destruction that I had caused. The whole time Connie rocked and consoled me, a grown man blubbering in her lap. Del was sitting in his Lazy Boy, slippers dangling off his toes and reading a new Bill O'Reilly book, *Killing the Rising Sun*, while Fox News blared above my crying and moans. At one point he got up, walked over, grabbed my shoulder, and said, "You're a good guy. You're gonna be alright!" Despite his frustrations with me as a father-in-law, he loved me and knew Connie and Becky wouldn't let me fall into the black hole without one final attempt to help me. I fell asleep in Connie's arms.

Connie let me sleep most of the next day away. She cooked me dinner, and then I attempted to sleep again. I was having terrible sleepless moments. I was alone, without alcohol. My mind was hell personified. By the second day, I was able to wake up in the morning and take a shower. I even managed to take a few sips of coffee. My hands shook and my dexterity, vision, and thoughts were retarded by the alcohol-saturated brain and body. I was involuntarily making spastic jerking moves and sounds. I felt and looked crazy. Connie treated me with kindness and love. She fed me and put me to work. She had me clean my bathroom as the first chore under her roof, knowing that I wanted to earn my stay. She not only expected me to clean, she walked me through each step, including using an old toothbrush to get to all the cracks at the base of the toilet and the tiles around the shower and sink. When I was done, she would inspect every inch of my work to make sure it had been done properly. By the time I finished, I was ready to puke and pass out, still hungover from a few days earlier. I was sweating so bad it looked like I had just walked out of a shower, but my body was leeching out toxins that smelled worse than the household cleaning chemical cocktail I was mixing as I cleaned the shower, sink, floor, and toilet.

Connie is maternally militant when it comes to cleaning the house. About keeping anything orderly and together, actually. Growing up with a single mom and six siblings, she was the second oldest and took on the role of second in command to help her mother, Juanita, take care of the rest of the kids. She would take jobs cleaning for others; cleaning bedpans, bathrooms, kitchens, bedrooms, and doing load after load of laundry. She took pride in the cleanliness and order of her home. A dirty bathroom or kitchen is a sign of laziness and sloth, and a lack of pride to her. Being married to her daughter for over a decade and being around their family for more than three, I knew and appreciated the high expectations for excellence.

Connie had me focusing on baby steps. Completing a project that mattered in real life. Over the next few weeks, I was regularly attending 12-Step meetings, and Connie and Del brought me along to my nephew Ace's high school basketball games. In my current state, I was socially reclusive and terrified of seeing anyone I knew, much less an entire basketball gym full of people my age there to watch their sons play basketball. I fought and tried to stay in the house, but Connie made me go because she believed I needed to re-socialize and see that I would be okay.

The final step was getting a job. I still had the shakes and a fragmented mind. My stomach was constantly upset, and I was in and out of the bathroom all the time because of it. Good thing I knew how to clean that bathroom. My nerves were totally wrecked, and I couldn't take anything to ease the pain. I was so accustomed to alcohol taking the edge away, and now that lubricant was gone. Sugary snacks helped. The stocked kitchen pantry and backup pantry in the garage kept me alive and sane. Ice cream gave me the sugar I craved and the calories I needed to bring back some of the weight I had lost during my last binge drinking run. Drinking a 30 pack of beer daily leaves little room or time for eating. I had a plethora of fun foods for me to dig into. Cookies became an after-dinner favorite. I would crush a container of cookies, sharing with Connie, of course, during an evening in front of the TV. I was learning to sit and relax and enjoy quiet family time. But the fear of finding a menial job in my hometown was nearly unbearable to face. Connie kept me calm, and over the next few weeks, she helped me find a job at a local plastics factory called Roplast.

ROPLAST

R oplast felt like I was working in a prison factory stamp-
ing out license plates, awaiting my release to return to
my freedom and my life's work. I was physically ill
from stress the first week on the job, resulting in a cold and
a bout of third-world diarrhea. I was not very grateful about
landing a shit job in my hometown, and I felt like a dead
man walking and working. The job required twelve-hour
shifts with a constantly changing schedule of days, nights,
and weekends. I couldn't believe that this was the job option I
was afforded after all the sacrifices I made to do challenging
work and the dedication I gave to my craft.

In the first two weeks, I struggled to control my anxiety and verbal and physical response to my fragmented and
stressed out mind that resembled a form of Tourette's syndrome. These increasingly uncontrollable ticks looked like I
was having a strange outburst that seemed like I was panicking from falling off a cliff in real life. My mind cracked in
2011 from losing so much so fast and drinking like a freight
train. I called it a nervous breakdown. I could feel my mind's
fragility. Now, I was being expected to go from being unemployable to working hard labor for twelve hours a day with
fast-moving and dangerous machinery. Being a rookie at the
bottom of the pay scale in my hometown was almost more

than I could bear. Deep down, I knew it was the next best step on my long journey back.

I worked with a bunch of good dudes, the classic mix of characters that are made for a sitcom. You've got the burn out stoners, the ex-cons, the goofy happy strait-laced family guy. Lots of rough and tough guys from around the area that were not sure what to make of me when I showed up. I stayed quiet and tried to learn my job through countless missteps, working hard, and being positive, even though I wanted to run out of the fucking building and go straight to a liquor store and drink the day away down by the river.

The lesson for me was that life could give a fuck how hard or easy reaching our goal is. It's up to us to choose the outcome. It's a lesson that sometimes we must go through hell before we can get to our concept of a happy and successful life. I took my early success for granted in ways and was not emotionally equipped or prepared for major setbacks in life. I just assumed that life would be one grinding success after another until I reached my youthful ambitions of the million dollars by thirty, the family, the big house, pool, property, and to take care of everyone—the symbols of a successful man.

"You throw like a girl!"

Her deep sultry voice parted the factory noise to insult my failed attempt at sliding the bander under the pallet, supporting the pair of six-hundred-pound plastic roles of soon to be Nike retail bags. Feeling frustrated, and now confused by the voice, I looked up to see an old childhood friend, Heidi Allen, walking by to give me a shit-eatin' grin of cold humor and a wink. I instantly smiled and lightened up, seeing her tough love grin and comforting eyes. Heidi was a big Nordic tomboy chick from the logging hills that could destroy boys on and off the soccer field. Nick played on her team back when they were about ten years old, and they dominated the league. Heidi was also a talented softball player that could've played big-time college ball if she would've had any inner motivation to see and go beyond what she knew.

Despite throwing her talents away for a life of factory work and raising kids without a husband, including a son who suffered a tragic car accident at sixteen that left him a quadriplegic with mental disabilities, Heidi seemed to shoulder it with strength and working-class grace. The years had been hard on her. She was carrying an extra hundred pounds of well-distributed weight, and each step taken, and word spoken was strained with jaded exhaustion. Heidi was nearly six feet tall and weighed an estimated two hundred and seventy five pounds. But she carried it like a retired offensive lineman would: in the legs, hips, and arms. For some odd reason, her face did not look fat. I've always thought that was interesting how certain women don't carry weight in their face when others can get a puffy face just by eating a little too much salty Chinese food.

One of the funniest things I observed on a daily basis at the factory was Heidi and her little chubby Mexican sidekick, Martha. Her double-stuffed face and four-foot-ten, hundred and seventy-five pounds justified a comparison to a Mexican Cabbage Patch doll. Watching them walking through the factory next to each other was hilarious. Martha never spoke, except to acknowledge with a very slight head nod as she ate her one-pound Reeses peanut butter cup. I am not exaggerating. This overweight midget chick was sitting at break outside next to her giant Arian sister, quietly chomping down on a one-pound Reeses peanut butter cup! I didn't even know they made them that big! I watched her sneakily break off pieces and nibble them up like a rat with a piece of cheese. It was repulsive and comical.

I wondered how the liberal mentality would blame the big greedy corporation for selling a one-pound peanut butter cup to a defenseless Mexican woman. As a capitalist accountable for my own actions, I applaud Reeses for their success and crafty marketing to sell a one-pound Reeses Peanut Butter Cup. Obviously, they didn't picture Martha the Mexican cherub eating one by herself in one fucking day! But, hey, that's her decision, that's her freedom of choice. I also noted that she chose to leave her home in Mexico for our freedoms and opportunities.

As I watched people limp their beaten bodies out of the factory and into the sunshine and fresh cigarette smoke that filled the break area outside, I couldn't help observing that many of my co-workers chose to feed their bodies and minds processed crap. I would watch them consume Red Bulls and candy at each break and lunch; this was their meal. And they would polish it off with a pack of cigarettes and negativity-filled discussion with their likeminded commiserates. But you know what? I respect their right to treat their bodies and time however they want. Let's not act like they don't have the necessary intelligence and information to make healthier choices.

The reality is social group dynamics are extremely powerful, and habits are extremely difficult to change. They can purchase and consume whatever the fuck they want because they are paid slaves to a big noisy machine twelve hours a day that beats the hell out of their bodies and spirits. Their reward most often, unfortunately, is to treat themselves to short-term feel-good ailments that predictably make them feel like shit within hours and even worse the next day. It's a cycle of extremes that deform the quality and performance of life and cuts it predictably short. But to be clear, these folks chose this life. And I can respect that. They literally work their bodies to the bone and should enjoy whatever the hell makes them happy. Remember, these folks work hard for their money! Hell, I justified my poor habits of drinking, drugs, and women just the same. I simply convinced myself that I earned it!

Over time I noticed that there is this strange blue-collar culture defiance, almost a juvenile rebellion toward adapting advances in knowledge on health, finance, or any subject relating to improving wellness and quality of life. Of course, there are deeper issues and more dimensions like group influence, fear, and addiction, but the result is people cope with temporary problems or urges with the wrong shit that puts them one step further behind every day. I knew I was the same. In fact, I'm one of the worst offenders. I hated when some squeaky-clean health nut on TV would preach about how fucking happy and great his life was because he eats healthy and works out every day. No one likes to be told what to do from people they can't relate to, especially if that person is stoked, and we're not feeling great about ourselves. I worked hard to change those poor habits in me that I could so easily see in others. As depressing as it was, being around so many unhealthy struggling people provided me with a burning motivation within myself to fight the good fight to simply live and feel better.

The joke at Roplast was that you needed to be a felon to get a job. There were over one hundred people working inside a building of giant plastic extruders and presses that created much of the reusable plastic shopping bags used in grocery and retail stores, including big sports lifestyle brands like Nike, Puma, and Converse. The factory was loud, and the air was clouded with poisonous chemicals used in the manufacturing process. Keep in mind, though, that most people working there were used to ingesting far worse chemicals outside of work.

The mentality I witnessed at the factory reminded me of being in jail or at a high school party. Most of the people working there were cross-addicted and working their way to nowhere. Most would end up back on the run, chasing hard drugs and running from chaotic lives and the cops. The conversations at lunch were typical, talking about who was more violent, crazier, tougher, who had spent more time in jail or prison...same people, same shit. I wanted to cry and escape to the ocean every day. I desperately wanted to be free of the negative survival attitudes and lifestyles that surrounded me. I also realized that I was just like them, a cross-addicted criminal working a shitty factory job at 45 years old because I fucked my life up. I even needed a ride to and from work from my in-laws because I still didn't have a driver's license, car, or money. I felt pretty fucking low. But with each passing day, I felt glimpses of pride and accomplishment, albeit small victories; I was where I needed to be. Sure, I needed money, but I really needed the regiment and humility to stoke the burning desire to kickstart the next phase of my life.

I'm naturally attracted to people who live on the edge. It's a different culture and mindset, and I respect it. It is often earned from people who have been flopping on the ground, writhing with death in their hearts and souls from overdosing on too much poison-chasing and escaping themselves and the world around them. I know these people. I have the scars and street credibility and have lived comfortably inside that world. There's a sinister dark comedy in the lifestyle of the street tough. At the factory, there were some bad dudes and chicks from gangs and prison, tattoos of kills and hate. I was at a new phase in my life, and all of it repulsed me. Those same behaviors I adopted to earn my street cred had taken me down. Being around it made me angry and motivated to climb my way out and away from it as fast as humanly fucking possible.

Working at Roplast was like being sentenced to hard labor in a Stalin era Russian prison labor factory. I had never felt so claustrophobic and frustrated, except when I was in jail. I could see the beautiful pinks, purples, and blues of the early morning sky peering through the loading dock roll up bay doors on the west side of the building. It was tantalizing and cruel. I tried not to get lost in its alluring beauty and freedom. I thought of the life I had created through drinking and irrational thinking and the repercussions I was living. I had destroyed everything around me and was now working a "real" job. I had spent the last few years dedicated to drinking like a mad man, writing my book, developing my rock album, visual art, and Manic Fusion Labs. All of that, besides the alcoholic madman, was the reality I needed to return to, but I had a mental crash that required a total restart from scratch.

Getting sober and learning to walk again was all I could do at that point. I had to in order to move forward. After my weekend job working at the nursing home and my hit-and-miss flooring gig with my tweaker buddy, I finally had a consistent job that provided me with structure and a way out of being stuck. My first paycheck was $1,060 for two weeks' work. It was hard not to get bummed out when I saw the amount. But deep down, I felt better knowing that I earned it and was making positive and measurable steps forward, back to an independent life. I paid $700 on my DUI fine with the county courts and paid Beck back for money I borrowed months earlier. I had enough left to buy my sponsor a coffee and take Julie out to dinner as we slowly tried to figure out what it all meant.

There were moments that I felt good about myself, deep down. I wasn't running from my shadow of lies and self-deception anymore. It was brutally confusing being in my hometown, watching people's lives appearing to make sense through a lens of traditional life success, complete with a nice house, truck, kids, and baseball games. I was starting from the very beginning, literally, as if I were 18 years old, leaving Oroville to go play college football. I had lived nearly full circle and returned to my spawning ground to die and then rise from the ashes. Complete with working at a job that paid about equal to what I was making at 18 years old working at NorCal Lumber. Having my pride and ego tamed in my hometown created an irreversible sense of urgency to stay sober, finish this book, and begin monetizing my Manic Fusion Labs business portfolio.

I had to remind myself that when I was standing on hard concrete for twelve-hour days in a factory, it was temporary pain, temporary setbacks, eternal rewards. Although I felt behind, I was exactly where I was supposed to be. I fucking hate that saying, usually because it's coming from some out of touch, Bible-thumping clown that says it without any sense of empathy or awareness. I've had it preached to me a million times when I DIDN'T want to hear it. But the hard truth is that I have had to experience some fucked up shit to desperately want a dramatically new way of thinking and living. One thing's for sure; it's easy to allow the outside forces of work, friends, family, social media, and marketing to make us lose ourselves and self-destruct.

As I prepared to fly over (cut the plastic coming off the press with a K-knife while it rolled towards me at a fast clip), I kept imagining the roll was printed with one of my company logos. As I waited for the press operators subtle head nod to notify me to press button #1 then button #2 and prepare for the roll to be cut and transferred to start a new six-hundred-pound roll for Nike or some grocery store from Texas that I've never heard of, I could see my future in my Manic Fusion Labs office, listening to music and feeling inspired as we brainstorm new ideas and the next steps for one of our successful businesses. It's my destiny. So, all the crazy, seemingly irrelevant time-wasting detours were part of my training to see what I needed to see and feel to know myself and my path forward. Seemingly insignificant in ways, my job at the factory represented a very significant, vitally constructive launch pad for my next stage of life.

I was forty-five years old and working twelve-hour days doing physical labor; it was a grind, to say the least. Standing on a hard concrete floor and lifting fifty-pound steel pins and loading six hundred pound rolls of plastic all day long for $12.50 an hour was a true test of what I'm made of. I may have been broke, but I never felt stronger and more grounded with my eye on success in every aspect of my life. I focused on my emotional and physical health, finding that it positively impacts all my relationships, my art, business...everything I touch. I was hustling and disciplined like I was back in college football.

"Hey! My name is Mike! I just wanted to let you know that if you have any questions, don't hesitate to ask me! We were all new here once, but some guys don't want to take the time to teach the new guys. I think some see it as a threat to their job or something. I'm a positive guy who is pretty much cool with everyone as long as they don't steal from me or fuck my girl."

I smiled and nodded with an acknowledgment of appreciation. The one thing I knew for sure, no matter what industry or level I've worked at, there seems to always be the same ratio of good guys, bullies, and haters in every group. The group of workers reminded me of the same people from my time in jail, lumber yards, or running King Duce Records. There are a lot of hard and rough walking and talking characters at the street level. But after one or two discussions, I find that most of them are pretty chill but equipped with a tough exterior of armor and guns to survive in their environment. I was the same person they were, standing but beaten and bruised through the rattling experience of life's ferocity.

I finished my first night-shift off by getting high in my co-worker's car, then we both stood at his print press talking about movies and music. Mike's a drummer. He looks, acts, and has the upbeat "live for the moment" personality. He has no kids and lives with his mother-figure chick, who is twenty years older than him. He spends most of his time hanging out in his man cave, smoking the gravity bong he made in woodshop and watching movies or playing his drums. He's permanently stuck back in junior high. He even referred back to those days when he was "killin' the pussy."

Mike was short and younger but looked older due to his lifestyle and scars from acne. His dark hair and big ears framed his friendly smile. He approached me on my second or third day to introduce himself. I noticed him throughout my first days because his printing press was directly opposite of the one I was working on, separated by a busy thoroughfare of speeding and honking forklifts. The presses were so loud we had to wear earplugs and yell at each other from only a couple feet away.

I walked over to him and belted out, "What's your favorite movie of all time?"

With a visible shock from the overwhelming number of amazing movies, he firmly said *Dazed and Confused.*

I wanted to go, "Are you fucking with me?" But he was dead serious. I really liked Linklater's biopic story about growing up in rural Texas in 1976. A classic stoner high school movie that is definitely an all-timer in that category. But best movie of all time? I smiled at his youthful enthusiasm and genuine excitement, despite his fast-approaching thirty-fifth birthday and an ailing heart from excessive drinking, cigarettes, and a past life of meth. Mike was a good dude who just wanted to be liked and be kind to others. His body would fail him faster than he would realize.

When I mentioned I didn't drink anymore, he looked up at me with serious sincerity and said, "I drink too much...my heart is already doing fucked up shit."

He wasn't saying he wanted to stop his deeply ingrained daily habits, but it made him consider, for a split second, what it was doing to him. I have many friends like him who are just grateful they could kick their meth habit. Weed and beer are like cookies and milk after living through the black hell of meth. He even referred to his past and being done with it. Kicking meth is something to be very proud of. It is overwhelmingly powerful and destructive shit. It certainly ravaged our community and multiple generations of families. It's like the grim reaper brought hell to our doorstep and started consuming souls and leaving a zombie culture of crime, violence, and death. Sick fucking shit.

The more I listened to Mike talk details about his man cave and his gravity bong and his simple apartment over by the jail and the aqueduct that facilitates the outflow of Oroville Dam's water and distributes it to farmers' crops, desalinating the bay area delta, and providing Southern California with water, the more I realized that he was just a kind and simple dude. Mike didn't think about where the water was coming from or where it was going. He just knew it was there and that it was a lot of water, but no further thought about why or what it was for, despite his apartment sitting right next to the state's most expensive concrete infrastructure project in California and US history.

Mike was thinking about getting off his job and heading home to spend his free time "chillin'" with his "ole lady," getting "ripped," and watching movies. I can't say I blame him. Why should we need more than that to be happy? I envied his vision of fulfillment and happiness for a brief and confusing moment, realizing it was a warped junior high dream of being independent, young, and free. Unfortunately, that life vision ends as a burned-out middle-aged slacker like Jeff Bridges playing "the dude" in the classic Cohen Brother film, *The Big Lebowski*. I found myself being happy for him but took pleasure with the changes I had made to my life. I was growing up and finding my path forward, and it felt good. Working at Rolplast reminded me that we're all working hard and just trying to feel a little fun and fulfillment along the way. But that wouldn't dissuade me from my destiny.

As I took a break from loading a six-hundred-pound roll of plastic to be printed and then cut into bags, the whir of the machines humming me into a trance state of action, I found myself thinking about the similarities of working in a factory back in the industrial revolution. With respect to the role of the factory worker, not much has changed. And that fact depressed me immensely. I looked up to see the new robot being tested to replace a portion of the workers: no one fought it because they couldn't. I was now among the new class of working poor...powerless cogs...fucking peasants.

I went through waves of sullen reality that I was grinding out life and feeling its daily strain and demands without relief in sight. It was the working poor's endless cycle of overworking and then offsetting it with days of overindulging and lethargy. The results showed on their faces, greasy and red from toxic chemicals they inhaled and absorbed all day long, whether on or off the job. Ragged and consumed were descriptive words that fit most of the people there. But the press operator that worked across from us seemed to be different.

Jamie seemed to be a happy, clean, relatively healthy, and together guy. He was a former newspaper press operator, and when the Paradise Post shut down, he found what he knew: printing presses. Jaime had a wife who was the store manager for the Kmart in Paradise. They had four kids, three boys and a daughter, ages ranging from fifteen to twenty-one. All three boys wrestled competitively at Paradise High. The oldest was an assistant wrestling coach for his alma mater, and they had just won sections for the first time in over twenty or thirty years…I wasn't sure with the blaring press we were standing next to, and I didn't feel the urgency to ask him to repeat it for clarification. One of the boys was in the Marines, and the twenty-one-year-old still lived at home.

I could tell Jaime cherished his kids and enjoyed helping and watching them grow up and go through the daily challenge of life. His crooked and unclean toothy smile showed me that he was happy with his life. It was a trip. This guy looked kinda odd, with an incongruously shaped head, shaved to override his bald pattern. He wore his tattered and too tight clothes out of practicality, completely unconcerned and unaware of how it looked and what it said about him. It had no value to him. His identity and value were defined through being a good providing father and husband. Like the blue-collar roots he represented, Jaime was well versed in NFL team analysis and seemed to have a good head on his shoulders.

Jamie was a transplant from the blue-collar Salinas Valley, where everyone I've ever met claims to be from Santa Cruz until you press them. Jamie spoke with an exaggerated effort of speaking that sounded like he had a dad from Michigan who could've been an assembly-line guy in a Ford auto manufacturing plant in Detroit. Good, solid, and reliable company guy. I bet Jamie is a lot like his old man. I worked under him one day when my printing press was down. He was very friendly and willing to teach me what I needed to know. He wasn't the guy that you'd want to party with or get crazy with, but he was the guy that would show up early on a Sunday morning to help you move because he said he would. He was sincere about helping other people. He didn't have a cunning ulterior motive to benefit himself. He simply liked the feeling and habit of being helpful to others.

With each passing moment, listening to guys talk about shit that was cool back in the day was starting to drive me insane. The passive, fearful, and lethargic mentality of the working poor was grinding me as much as it was inspiring and humbling me. I recognized our similarities as well as our glaring differences through a blend of choice and fate. Beyond judgment, I simply knew that I was destined to be leaving the factory soon and moving onward and upward to a world that allowed me to sail the creative space and time continuum. I had traveled miles to be so close to my new life chapter, to do what I was born to do, create, lead, and inspire.

I had come full circle in my life, working a job that I could've been doing right out of high school. I realized that I had to continue to work hard and overcome any challenge standing in the way of my dreams. It really takes me back to the hunger and ambition that I had as a kid, full of fire, ready to head out into the world to test myself against the best. That has never changed. I have just gone through periods of my life where fear and addiction held back my true self-actualization from fully developing. I'm just grateful that my personal crash forced me to restart my life by getting back to the fundamentals of sobriety, commitment, and hard work.

I had been forced to buckle down and prove once and for all that I was retired from thirty years of alcohol-fueled chaos and destruction, finally surrendering to live life on life's terms. I no longer felt a sense of control over anything except my choices. I could get started with my life moving forward in a much simpler, healthier, and happier way. I violently fought the painful loss of alcohol and the change that I needed to go through to gain the enlightenment that I've experienced. I now see myself and the world around me differently. Less combative. I see more open space and opportunity that connects me to people and true intentions and reality. I see the world through new eyes and a dedication to thinking and doing the next right thing for myself and others. It's starting to make sustainable sense to me.

Working in a loud factory for twelve-hour shifts, rotating days and nights, with no weekends or normal schedule to function with the flow of normal working family society, the workers are an outcast group of misfits like they've always been. As I took breaks in between loading and unloading my printing press, I would observe people grinding out a life to nowhere. As I began talking to my co-workers, I started to realize that this was the new working poor in America. I was experiencing the cold and harsh reality; that this was the best job they could get after years of bad decisions that got them drug addictions, jail, unwanted babies, child support, and raising kids as single moms. Tough stuff that makes the day-to-day a struggle reminding us to appreciate the simple things.

I found myself between feelings of worthlessness and gratitude. I was grateful that I wasn't in jail and finally had a job and a paycheck, as small and soul-crushing as it was. I knew that I was just like the rest of the people working there; I was there because I had no other reasonable option. I was trying hard to tell myself that the two thousand dollars I was making a month was honorable. But deep down, I kept comparing my compensation to the money I was used to making in the business start-up world, where six-figure money was my baseline. Talk about humility. Not only was my sense of career and identity stripped away, but the money symbolized how far I had fallen as well. At moments, it was almost unbearable. I found myself debating with myself about staying or leaving, always finishing my inner conversation with the reality that I needed to stick it out until I got on my feet with something better. It felt like a place that I never wanted to be in again, and I knew I had miles to go and many days and hours to grind out before I would taste my new life of happiness and freedom.

Like most men, my job is a significant factor in defining myself to the world around me and how I perceive myself to the outside world. As much as people try and act like they are different and above this, the reality is that as competitive males in America, we define success and failure very clearly: job, money, and kids. Everything else that a man does throughout his existence on this earth amounts to nothing measurable in a mainstream human social context. As I looked out across the toxic cloud-filled factory, I saw people of all kinds with all kinds of reasons to be there, working for a paycheck to cover their existence, and many times paying off their past.

THE MORNING LIGHT OF WORKING THE NIGHT SHIFT

There is something truly special about working a night shift and coming home to unwind and watch the sunrise and listen to the world wake up. I've always loved the mornings. I spent my youth up before daylight heading out on adventures with my dad. But as I got older, the beautiful mornings became a period of time that couldn't be truly appreciated because of the day of responsibilities that lay ahead. It was only on my weekends off or vacation where I could enjoy an early morning without distraction.

I dreaded working a night shift since I had never done it before, thinking there was no upside to it. But it turned out to be a pleasant surprise. I have always struggled with insomnia, or wakeful sleep around the 3 am time zone; sometimes earlier, sometimes later. But generally, that's my witching hour to creatively write, ponder and contemplate the shit that haunts me or inspires me. So, working through the middle of the night for me in a well-lit factory full of people was a nice use of that often lonely and introspective time. Instead, I was interacting with other people and feeling productive. I would get picked up by Del, and he dropped me off back at the house where Connie would still be sleeping. I would quietly go in and start some coffee, jump in the shower, and then sit on my bed for a few minutes to gather my bearings in the luxurious silence and warmth of my in-law's home.

After throwing on my mainstay outfit of original black with white striped Adidas sweatpants, Supra black high tops, Bass Thrasher beanie, and hoodie, I would head outside with a cup of coffee and listen to the birds and animals greet the day as I watched the sun begin to fill the sky and land with light and beautiful spring colors. I sat out back and felt so much simple contentment to be able to enjoy the amazing warm spring weather and smell the sweet star jasmine. I truly appreciate, now, how precious these moments are, to experience the power of the natural world around me without distraction. It is brilliance in motion.

I knew at that moment that I had found true peace and happiness, whether rich or poor. I, like so many in our society, have expected those euphoric moments of money and "stuff" to be a perpetual reality. I don't condemn that thinking because I have chased the wicked illusion as much as anyone. We have been thoroughly conditioned by a lifetime bombardment of propaganda to believe that to be important until it is disproven by a life crash. I have been given the gift to return to my earliest experiences of the joy of being outside and simply taking it all in and exploring it without any outside distraction or expectation.

The factory was a necessary stop off along my twisted travels. I found a comradery and confidence that revitalized aspects of my bruised manhood. I could feel the work, the sweat, and satisfaction that comes from enduring the grind. Working hard, no matter what it is, offers a reward deep in our bones that pay massive dividends throughout every aspect of our lives. It provides a self-sufficient strength that is extremely powerful to our conscious reality. I know the difference in my own thinking and behavior. Night and day difference.

So, with each passing day, or night, toiling in the factory, I was feeling an escalating desire to fly away and march onto the global field of competition and brave the uncharted waters once again. I owed it to myself and the guys I worked side by side with. They knew it and encouraged me to lead on. They were my brothers, mentors, and my fans. We all knew our place, supported each other, and played our roles accordingly. It was honest, real, and affirming to my life vision. I needed to remember the working-class roots I proudly came from and never forget the people who proudly make this world grind forward.

Sitting outside, listening to nature's intelligence and beauty inspires me to listen and observe its message intently. The more I quietly observe the more peace, joy, inspiration, and direction I gain. I find my "stinkin' thinkin'" trying to creep in with negative thoughts, but I consciously wash them away and realize that life is happening now, and there isn't time for anything but positive, forward thinking. The world doesn't care about my selfish woes and isn't waiting on me to get started. My journey and observation of nature are that we all must wake up every single day and earn our way for that day, with no guarantee of tomorrow. The script is written deep inside of us, but most of us think that it comes from the outside of some guy in a New York advertising agency or a Hollywood movie studio.

I was watching TV one night after a long 12-hour shift, about to fall asleep, when this disheveled war correspondent dude from Australia was interviewing the Dalai Lama. It appeared an odd match. The two men looked so far apart in every way. But it ended up being a very real and refreshing hang out session with the living Yoda. His Holiness emphasized that living is suffering, and we must let go of what we want to hold on to in order to find true freedom and happiness, enlightenment. He said he almost never feels anger. I could see it in his eyes. He was serious and telling the truth. I have an old friend who helped me get sober, who says, "My life is perfect, as long as I don't think about it.'" That works for me.

I spent most of my life worried about failing or feeling scared about disappointing people around me. It was an exhausting way to live. The moment I began to truly stop thinking about myself in that way and started thinking more of others, I began to feel better, like almost instantly. It allowed me to release so many unfair and unrealistic expectations in my mind that were making me very unhappy, scared, and constantly at odds with the world around me. The minute I let go and started flowing with the positive energy around me instead of fighting myself and standing in my own way, things began to take off.

And here I am, after years of being penniless, drunk, and brutally depressed, I am finally and truly sober and feeling okay about myself and financially successful again. I've done the work, and consequently, many good things started happening.

As I write this at 4 am, picture me sitting in my ex-wife's childhood bedroom where I stayed for three months getting sobered up and cared for by her parents. They are saints, all of them. I'm not kidding. They took me in despite failing their daughter in marriage and gave me everything necessary for a restart. Experiencing this kind of unconditional love, support, and encouragement has changed everything. I have faith in love and forgiveness because of them. To make critical amends and receive true forgiveness and unconditional love and support from my ex-wife and her parents has been the gift that has allowed me to begin my life over. Instead of saying goodbye and moving on separate with our lives, we rediscovered a loving friendship that has allowed us to support each other as we navigate new people and challenges in our lives.

I've learned to wake up wherever I am, with whatever I may or may not have, and live my day with courage and action forward so I can respect myself at the end of the day. The trophy is the peace of mind knowing that I participated fully in my existence and interacted positively with the world around me. It's such a better feeling than the self-consuming hell of alcohol and selfish, ugly thinking. To have experienced both sides intimately provides a euphoric element to the new dimension I've entered. It's a wave I don't want to fall off ever again. Next time I'll certainly drown, and I've realized how much amazing life is in front of me. I am truly grateful I have this perspective and opportunity to give life on Earth my best effort.

After a couple of months, I had all my bags packed and headed home. Within a week, I re-tore my bicep muscle on the job -- I left the job without filing worker's comp. They were shocked. I was on a principle-fueled mission to win the right way for me to feel good and sleep peacefully.

MY PURPLE HEART SAVIOR

F inding sobriety has been the most challenging and free-ing experiences of my life. There is a reason Ozzy calls it "demon alcohol"; it's cunning, baffling, and powerful, as they say, and it is out to take some of us down. Alcohol was my best friend for over thirty years, helping me to cope with everything from social anxiety, work stress, family and rela-tionships, to devastating loss, and it did not want to let me go. My recovery has required a team of sober veterans of recovery, and one very special Purple Heart Vietnam vet.

Richard "Dick" Coughlin was born in 1942 in Boston into an Irish-Catholic home, the son of a business agent for the AFL, and a mother he can best describe as a saint. His dad was 54 when Dick was born and drank heavily until Dick was five years old. The youngest of three children, having one brother and one sister, Dick excelled at sports—playing foot-ball, baseball, and boxing—until ultimately, his father made him focus on baseball exclusively. His dad started drinking again when Dick was sixteen and died within a year due to lung cancer. Dick's talent as a pitcher earned him a minor league contract with the Pittsburgh Pirates farm league.

His Irish-Catholic upbringing and thick Boston accent add flair to his colorful storytelling. He reminds me so much of Coach Sweeney in demeanor, the way they say things, both boxers, fighters…winners! The spirit of my Irish boxing middleweight champion great-grandfather Bryan "Groco" Downey must connect me to similar Irish fighting spiritual men.

After a year in the Appalachian League playing and traveling through parts of the segregated South, Dick's contract was not renewed. Nonetheless, he learned a lot during that first year away from home. He was exposed to things he had never experienced before; things like racism, segregation, and moonshine.

Upon returning to Boston, he was ready for his next endeavor and went to see the Marine recruiter at the post office. The sign on the door read *Out to Lunch, Back in 20 Minutes*. When he turned around, he saw a poster of a young man parachuting out of a plane. He heard a voice say "You like that?" "Sure, I like that", he replied, and within 48 hours, he was shipped off to Army boot camp at Fort Dix in New Jersey. It was October of 1961. He made it through Advanced Infantry Training at Fort Dix, then on to Jump School at Fort Benning, Georgia, and landed in Kentucky at Fort Campbell. Dick went home for a week and a few weeks later got a call from his high school sweetheart; they were going to have a baby. They got married, and his son, Michael, was born, but the marriage wasn't meant to be, and the two separated soon after.

His platoon was on alert 24/7 and could be called out at any moment. They had drills at all hours of the night, never knowing if it was just a drill or a legitimate mission. So, when they were sent on their first assignment, they had no idea where they were going. As it turns out, they were sent to Mississippi, on the order of the Kennedy Administration, to guard the University of Mississippi and James Meredith as riots broke out. It was October 1, 1962. Meredith was the first African American student admitted to the segregated university after much persistence and deliberation on his part. Meredith had armed guards with him during his entire period of study at the university. Dick was assigned to check all vehicles entering the campus as riots and violent clashes broke out in protest. A young man, he was more intrigued by the girls in miniskirts he met as they searched under seats and in the trunks of their cars. The girls would return with cookies to visit the troops during the six weeks they were stationed there. He had no idea at the time that he was in the presence of a historical moment. It wouldn't be his last.

Dick was a sergeant in the elite 101st Airborne, 2nd 327 Airborne Infantry. From April through October of 1965, Sergeant Coughlin was stationed at the World's Fair in New York City. There were twenty guys and three girls representing the Army in their Class As. The three gals were manning an exhibit called *A Walk Around the Moon*, promoting their collaboration with NASA, and they were chosen both by skill as well as because they were all gorgeous. Dick was there to meet the public and inform them of what the Army was doing abroad, showing weapons seized from the North Vietnamese and answering questions about the war. Being there and meeting parents whose sons were already on the ground in Vietnam was a huge mental strain.

Dick also met Joanne while working there. She was one of the women working the exhibit with him. They hit it off, and a romance was started. She was recruited from the Fair by Robert McNamara, the United States Secretary of Defense, to come and work for him as his secretary assistant at the Pentagon. Dick would visit her there, and he met both McNamara and United States Deputy Secretary of Defense Cyrus Vance. Dick said Vance was a good man, and McNamara was the numbers man, and a total asshole. When he met Vance, he looked at Dick over the rim of his glasses, stuffed Indochinese Tiger looming behind him, a gift from the South Vietnamese, and told him straight up, "It's not a picnic over there." He was a straight shooter and a good guy. Nonetheless, when his stint working the fair was over, Dick worked hard to go to Vietnam. He felt that it was his duty; he wanted to go.

JFK was working towards decreasing the numbers of military in South Vietnam, there only to train the South and offer intelligence support, but not combat. On August 2, 1964, the Gulf of Tonkin incident supposedly occurred. There, three North Vietnamese torpedo boats approached the USS Maddox and supposedly fired on the U.S. ship. Authorities announced that a similar incident occurred on August 4th as well, but it didn't either. As it turns out, on August 2nd, either we fired first, or we fired at nothing, depending on the account told, but nonetheless, the public was sold the lie, and the number of US soldiers in Vietnam escalated dramatically. McNamara and other US policymakers feared that the fall of South Vietnam to a Communist regime would lead to the fall of other governments in the region, so the story was manufactured so we could go to war. War is a huge moneymaker and a devastating and evil business of the elite. LBJ's wife just happened to be the owner of a construction company that made a shit ton of money on the war, as did many others in high places after the big Texas oil thugs, CIA, and Mafia had JFK killed and blamed it on Lee Harvey Oswald. Over 58,000 US military were killed in the Vietnam War, a war we entered as a sham. It's the same story every time. Even McNamara finally admitted near the end of his life that it was "wrong, terribly wrong."

In the U.S. Army, NCOs are enlisted soldiers with specific skills and duties such as training, recruiting, tech, or military policing. The Army refers to them as its "backbone." NCOs often supervise lower ranks to ensure the assignments are done properly. When Dick was sent to war, he and five other NCOs were flying out together from Travis Air Force Base in Fairfield, California. Just before the flight, they got a taxi, went to the closest liquor store, and bought all the small bottles of alcohol they could stuff in their pockets. Arriving back just in time to catch their flight, they sat three and three in seats on the plane and started in on the alcohol right away. Military flights barred the drinking of alcoholic beverages, but they were on their way to the combat zone and needed the lubrication of the devil's nectar to keep their spirits up. Bobbi, the stewardess, questioned them and told them they were not supposed to be drinking. They pretended to oblige but drank all the way there. Upon their arrival, it was 6:30 am, and it was hot and humid. Suffocating, sticky HOT!! They were transported in trucks with chicken wire on the top, and when they asked why, they were told because of the hand grenades that would be thrown at them... welcome to Vietnam, boys!

The 101st was hit hard, and Dick was a part of the troops that were sent over as reinforcements and replacements for lost men. It was Nov 1965. They were in Saigon for four days before being sent into the jungle. He had a buddy, Jerry DeMello, who was an MP at the Capital Hotel in Saigon. Soon after they arrived in the city, they found Jerry. He was on duty, so after quickly catching up, the guys went in for a few drinks at a bar in the Chinese District. Dressed in army fatigues, they came upon six to eight truck drivers, or "Legs," as they called them. Callahan, knowing as Airborne they were considered elite, said, "Up! We're taking this table," but the Legs wouldn't get up. Callahan broke the table, and a brawl ensued. MP DeMello came in and took Dick and his buddies out of the bar, appearing to bust them, but actually keeping them from getting into unnecessary trouble. Fifteen years later, at a reunion, Jerry told Dick that he *was* engaged to the bar owner's daughter...but not after that!

It was a few weeks later that Dick got notice that Joanne was pregnant. They tried to get married through proxy, but it didn't go through.

Fast forward to February of 1966. Dick was 22 years old. That made him one of the older guys in his platoon. Because of his age and rank, he felt a sense of responsibility for and to the soldiers he oversaw; each was someone else's child. He also had a clearer view of what was really going on, which added to his need to watch over and take care of these young men. Before going over, they were told not to get close to anyone, but that was virtually impossible! They were in an atrocious war and were a band of brothers.

Doc, as Dick called Marty Eastham, was one of his closest friends. They were the same age, giving them a common and very strong bond. They shared many stories together. Dick told a story about Marty being sarcastically defiant of orders from a superior. Doc held the rank of private. One night, Marty was wearing a beret and was told to take it off or dig a hole. He refused to remove the beret. Dick, siding with his buddy, said, "If Doc goes, I go..." Not long after, they found themselves digging a hole. At one point, Dick was down in the hole, digging, and he looks up to see Doc with his beret on, laughing. Here was a Private, looking down on his Sergeant digging a hole because of the trouble he caused. That's just how it was. Dick described many funny and tragically horrifying stories of drunken escapes back into the bars and getting caught and reprimanded for being disorderly in war... ironic.

The North Vietnamese were relentless. Unlike in WWII, when a battle would be fought about every six days, in Vietnam, battles were a daily occurrence. Green troops were sent over every 12 months to replace the war-torn troops. Those who had spent 12 months in combat, and survived, were returned home. It was wet, hot, and either open or steep terrain. The men had horrible foot fungus due to the constant moisture but marched on and continued their offensive. It was early morning, and they were on an offensive move towards a village through a rice paddy, the enemy firing from the front and then from the right flank. They could hear shots but just didn't know if they were going to be hit or when while they made their way to their objective. Three rounds went straight through Dick's helmet, knocked his sunglasses clear off, and knocked him to his knees. The shots came from his right flank. Having been a boxer, he knew how to take a hit and what it felt like, and this was one impressive blow. It was crazy! He'd been shot. He asked a black kid named Runderson, "Where am I shot?" It was hard to tell because they were *always* wet and with the adrenaline constantly running through them, masking pain and keeping them going. "You're not hit, Sarg!" The three bullet holes through his helmet proved otherwise, but his flesh had been spared... this time.

Although his own life was spared, Sergeant Coughlin would experience death almost daily during his time in Vietnam. The first man to die in his arms was a young black man, 19-year-old private first class Harold T. Edmondson of Charleston, South Carolina. He was just a boy. His death, and the many many others, on both sides of the battle, would haunt those in combat for the entirety of their lives.

In June 1966, just short of a month after his 23rd birthday, the Second Battalion 327th Regiment 101st Airborne fought in Operation Nathan Hale. A remarkable example of the day by day combat United States forces experienced in Vietnam.

A guerilla attack from three hills northeast of the Special Forces camp at Trung Luong Valley began Operation Nathan Hale, a series of battles fought for nameless ridges and nearly deserted villages. The Viet Cong excelled at fighting in the extreme heat and through the rank elephant grass. The air cavalrymen and paratroopers—PFCs, NCOs and officers— became veteran fighters overnight in a war in which the enemy is virtually invisible, even when dead, graves having been carefully dug beforehand so no one would know the numbers of casualties they suffered.

From *In the Fields of Bamboo* by S.L.A. Marshall, pg. 42–43

"Either the Charlies had been set to box them in when the platoons came out of the river trench or the gun had been swiftly moved to the rear position unobserved. Anyway, it was damnation.

"Sergeant Richard Coughlin was hit by (three) machine gun bullets through his mid-section. He called out: 'Medic! Medic!'

"The aid man, Spec 4 (Martin) Eastham answered: 'I'm coming,' though he had taken rifle bullets in both legs.

"Eastham crawled to Coughlin.

"As he made it, and got out some bandages, a bullet swarm caught Eastham in the head and neck and he died instantly.

"The undeviating faithfulness of the United States aid man to his duty is a phenomenon beyond explanation."

On June 20, 1966, Dick had a machine gun for breakfast. Their platoon was surrounded by enemy forces in numbers that were incomprehensible. The jungle looked alive as it appeared to breathe and move as the camouflaged troops stalked them. He was shot five times, thrice in the mid-section, and then twice more in his side as he ran to the chopper. He was shot at such close range that the bullets went straight through his abdomen area, missing his spinal cord and vital arteries and organs by millimeters. The three shots to his abdomen were instantly cauterized, but his backside was literally blown out. "Marty was all in and ran straight into bullets. He was shot three times in the head, trying to save me."

Dick called out to Flemming, an Irish buddy of his from Boston. Both Flemming and Dick had been shot once before. Dick took a fragment to his leg, and Flemming was shot in the ass while digging a latrine. They each received a Purple Heart. After that, they made a $10 bet. Whoever received the next Purple Heart owed the other the $10. There was a lot of black humor just to make it through the day. Flemming ran out to save him and to retrieve Doc's body, even though Dick was yelling for him to turn back. Flemming was able to grab both men and got Dick to the safety of the creek bed. Dick still owes him that $10.

Off in a creek bed awaiting medevac, another medic gave Dick a dose of plasma…then Dick was gone. So pumped with adrenaline, he was running to the chopper on his own. The medic recalls seeing just Dicks' rear end and legs hanging out of the chopper door as he leaped onto the hovering beast.

Sergeant Richard "Dick" Coughlin was medevacked to 8th Field Hospital in Vietnam, then on to Boston Naval Hospital. Joanne was in Michigan, but because his paperwork noted that he was from Boston, they sent him to the hospital closest to what they knew was his home. He had the Red Cross send a letter to his sister to advise her that he was there, but also to have her let Joanne know that he was on a mission and she would not hear from him for a while. He didn't want to jeopardize her pregnancy. Maureen was born on July 16, 1966, while Dick lay unconscious for months after enduring multiple surgeries to remove shrapnel and scar tissue from the machine gun bullet wreckage. Even though coming home medivac spared him of the hate spewed on those who returned and arrived en masse, the war left permanent scars, both physical and emotional.

He didn't get to see Joanne for about four months, and then met his first daughter, Maureen, when she was about six months old. During that life and death experience, he developed a serious opioid addiction healing up in the military hospital. After recovering, Dick and Joanne married and went on to have another daughter, Dawn. He stumbled drunk and loaded through a second marriage and two daughters and began working for the U.S. Postal Service. Sgt. Coughlin, a drunk Irish bloke, became President of the Postal Union in Detroit, MI. His old man was a hard-hitting union president in Boston, a legendary tough guy in one of the toughest towns, and Dick wasn't going to let that legacy end with his pops.

Doc's sister was sixteen when he died. Two military officers came to the house, and she was excited because she thought they must be Marty's friends. When she yelled to her mom about the uniformed men approaching the house, her mom knew instantly what it meant. When Onie, Marty's sister, realized he was gone, she ran out the back of the house and into the woods, devastated by her loss.

The battle when Dick was shot was a total disaster caused by political battles between the Marines and his 101st Airborne Army men, 2nd 327th Airborne Regiment. The big wig of the Marines that were desperately needed to help Dick's platoon fight off the overwhelming number of enemy troops that had them literally surrounded for five days refused to come to their aid. Dick describes the blatant internal strategic warfare driven by bureaucracy, pride, and fear and the death and destruction of lives and families back home from the unaccountable savagery of self-serving people in power, especially in war. That's an extra level of sin. He tells me that some of the hardest parts to deal with are the lies that were, and still are told here. The lies the media have propagated, and some people who were never there claiming to have been, telling stories they never experienced. He lives daily with what he did and saw in combat. As Dick gets older, he tells me that the struggle and pain over killing men who would be grandfathers and fathers and husbands today gets harder every year that passes. The evil that handed this type of struggle to great men like Dick is beyond me.

The entirety of the Vietnam War was a disaster, unnecessary from the start and propagandized throughout the media. "Journalists" like Walter Cronkite "reported" what the government wanted U.S. citizens to believe. Many of the soldiers and officers knew how fucked up it was by the wasted battles and lives for nothing. Team morale was never great… there was never any momentum to build off, just a lot of really bad leadership decisions. Dick said there were never drugs being used while he was there, but maybe more later on with continued corruption and the fact that they knew it was a war that couldn't be won. He thought that maybe they needed the assistance of mind-altering substances to cope with the knowledge that they were simply there as pawns, waiting to die for no cause at all.

The U.S. set up the Vietnam War with the Gulf of Tonkin incident. The original American report blamed North

Vietnam for hostile action towards the USS Maddox while performing a signals intelligence patrol as part of DESOTO operations. LBJ was behind it, right after the JFK assassination. In 2005, an internal NSA historical study was declassified. It concluded that Maddox had engaged the North Vietnamese. Despite the inconvenient truth, LBJ and his deep state dirtbags passed the Gulf of Tonkin Resolution, which granted President Lyndon B. Johnson the authority to assist any Southeast Asian country whose government was considered jeopardized by communist aggression. The resolution served as Johnson's legal justification for deploying U.S. conventional forces and the commencement of open warfare against North Vietnam.

And through this unnecessary war, Dick lost many men, including his best friend. Doc was killed saving him. It was the ultimate sacrifice. They had made a promise to each other that if one of them were killed, the other would find their family. Due to misinformation, Doc's family thought Dick was dead, so they never looked for him.

Not knowing how to cope with the aftermath of war and his injuries left this courageous and decorated soldier a broken man. Unfortunately, Dick's alcoholism and other drug addictions finally landed him living under a bridge in the Bay Area with other Vietnam Vets, drinking from leftover beer bottles behind local bars, covering the top with a cheesecloth to keep from ingesting the old cigarette butts and debris leftover with the few drops of alcohol. Dick was dying from damaged internal organs and the alcohol killing him faster for it. He looked for Doc's family for 15 years, but was incessantly drunk and never made the connection. His sweet older sister knew the true man he was and bought him a ticket back to Boston in hopes that he would get his life together. She believed in him. She gave him a card and told him not to open it until he was on the plane and in the air. When he did open it, he read, "No one knows you like I do. No one loves you like I do. Make it work this time." And a $100 bill fell out. Touched by the words, upon landing, he found a bar and promptly bought everyone a round.

Back home, he stayed with his brother for two weeks, went on a final run of debauchery, and then decided he was done. It was May 1st, 1980. He walked down the front steps of his brother's house, looked his brother in the eye, and said, "I'm done! Take me to the VA." Before the hospital, they made one stop. Dick surrendered at the graves of his parents, sobbing that they had not raised him to be this man. He quit the bottle and returned to California to be with his wife and kids. At the start of his sobriety, he was 38 years old, riding a bicycle through Silicon Valley looking for menial work to get started again after having been a union president, then going deep down the rabbit hole and living beneath an overpass. He found work at the *Mercury* newspaper, managing all the paperboys. The first three years of sobriety were hell, but he knew that it was all or nothing, sobriety or death. Although working to find healthy sobriety and save his family, the relationship was not able to endure the damage that had been done; Dick and Joanne divorced after 22 years, eight of them sober. It's real, and it's brutal, and only someone who has experienced it can truly understand. Dick is a fighter and a winner.

He stayed true to his buddy Doc, and miraculously went on to find Doc's family from Minnesota in 1995. He had written an article in the hometown newspaper where Marty grew up, asking for help in locating the family. Chief of Police Ron Nagel, a high school buddy of Marty's, saw the article and was instrumental in uniting them. There was an instant connection of love and honor between Dick and Marty's mother and sister. They are family.

At a reunion, Dick told a story about how Doc owed him 13 cans of fruit from sea rations for different bets they had made. Later, Doc's mom sent him a case of fruit cups. She understood the friendship that her son had shared with Dick and the humor that went along with it.

Through all that Dick has lived, he was somehow there to help me find my way out from the exact same affliction and very similar backgrounds. Like I said, it took a three-time Purple Heart Vietnam vet and a team of other recovering badasses to get me sober.

Dick stood by me patiently while I clinically denied my alcoholism and roared off in my new BMW 530, cash in the bank, and a beautiful and loving wife at home. Twelve years later, after countless attempts, I finally lost enough, felt enough pain and despair to become coachable and sober once and for all. This man stood by me through many days of hell while I screamed, cried, got kicked out of my place, and locked up in jail. Finally, the day came that my thinking and vision collapsed, and I was done with alcohol forever. January 16, 2017, was my very last drunk. Desperately, I took control of my sobriety like a possessed man. I had become resolved to win the day in sobriety, relationships, and serving by working a 12-step program that gave me the rock-solid proven steps to a happy, joyous, and free life from alcohol and drugs and fucked-up thinking. I've been fortunate to finally use the tools so freely given to me.

This man never broke me down or belittled me, even after a hundred attempts at failing to recognize my alcoholism. He patiently let me lose everything as I tried desperately to hold on to the old ideas and ways that ended me up in jail and facing serious time. This man showed me a way out of the bottle. For "normies," or people who are not alcoholics, the idea of someone destroying their lives from booze seems totally weak, selfish, and stupid. Dick was different. He had survived war and the hell of a true alcoholic; he understood my pain. By sticking close to him and really listening to his suggestions, and slowly adapting his critical examples to my life, I am finally experiencing freedom and happiness.

8

Manic Fusion

MANIC FUSION

M anic Fusion was spun out of the inability of my mind to accept what reality was showing me. The incongruities of life that are real, but in my heart and soul knew are so wrong. It is wrong for evil to take over and masquerade through the streets as if they are good. It is wrong for people to work so hard for others and then end up with nothing while others pretend they have done something real and significant and for the greater good when they haven't. It is the mission of Manic Fusion to celebrate those of us who are truly living who we are, despite society's desire to label us as strange, different, eccentric, or crazy. We are creators and innovators. The masses flock to what we bring to them without recognizing that we are the ones they mock, bully, and try to destroy. Manic Fusion is the deliberate act of bringing together the best creators and innovators, artists, and thinkers, those who have fought to be true to their heart and dreams, and to applaud, praise, and celebrate them. To bring together a tattered group of social dropouts to create a place, a company, a community, a family—where great ideas, companies, brands, entertainment, and innovation occurs.

Manic Fusion is a self-descriptive name I first came up with to title artwork of mine that visually described the manic world of my mind and being, my crazy or different energy frequencies and thoughts fusing into an innovative concept or idea. The Fusion of Manic ideas into simple brilliance.

I remember creating Manic Fusion, the art piece. It came through me with no preconceived idea of what it would be. A door that had been used as a desktop lay on its side on the floor of the back room of Julie's house. I spent many hours in that back room after being kicked out of my house, my marriage, my life as I knew it. I was devastated beyond comprehension and was drinking every waking moment. Then I saw this door. A blank canvas. I had oil pastels from different art pieces I had done. I picked up the pastels, and the piece just started to happen. Hours, days, nights, sweating half-naked in the non-airconditioned back room, Manic Fusion came to life. A creature filled with electric and colorful energy screaming out to the universe. If was full of a force, a power that was driven to be seen, heard, and understood. It was like the phoenix, rising from the ashes of my loss, struggling, and determined to just be. I started to see. To see me. To see truth.

Manic Fusion is a return to my roots of what it means to work as a family, a team, to produce championships...to win consistently with no excuses. It is a return to family and team above self. Walking through tough times and growing from it.

Manic Fusion is a philosophy, a culture, a way of life. Its daily and eternal foundation is built on honesty and trust. The people and the process and the expectation. Starting with the founders, the people that are attracted to Manic Fusion, people that build a diverse mix of innovative businesses to disrupt markets and win, are grounded, positive, smart, passionate, confident, competitive, hardworking, and *honest* with self and others. Integrity truly is Manic Fusion's competitive edge and core value proposition in everything we do. It makes things simpler, efficient, effective with clear fact-driven results, and learning opportunities to improve—relentlessly.

Living what I believe is paramount to the success of our team. Words are cheap on the football field and in business, as in our personal lives. *How* we win, to me, is as important as the win.

I write this as our country and the world have been hit with a socioeconomic meltdown due to the pinprick of the Coronavirus, a financial reckoning due to the massive over-leveraged U.S. dollar. The stock market crashed worse than in 1929. The fear, panic, and irrationality are predictable and sad. Watching regular folks and the business world hit with a tsunami and how they are reacting, in a general sense, points to irrational fear driving short-term decisions that negatively affect their long-term goals and momentum. This is why it is critical to live and work daily with a solid foundation, fundamentals, and expectations. A team cannot do great consistent work if they are emotionally and/or financially compromised or leveraged. Desperate decision-making becomes irrational and self-serving; dangerous to the individual, family, and team. I know from experiencing devastating personal pain and cost. Manic Fusion is the result of the thrill of victory and the agony of defeat. We can weather cyclical and unprecedented economic and geopolitical storms if we drive our own market disruption and innovation. We are proving that in the worst of times.

The long view of Manic Fusion is about creating a winning track record that attracts the best and brightest and fosters an environment that celebrates winning thinking— risk-taking using sound fundamentals and making something measurable happen in the best interest of the team.

Pride, ego, and selfish gain must be honestly acknowledged by the leadership and team and checked at all times to ensure the integrity of Manic Fusion's foundation and work product.

We incentivize Manic Fusion talent to stay by rewarding them for new ideas, regardless of whether it's for the project they are paid for or an entirely new business idea. I want to reward people who create positive value and energy to our company. The reverse is also true; I will eliminate anyone who commits treason to our team, our family. One bad person can sink a ship. That's why our team protects and rewards the good people, and it's also why a bad draft pick is eliminated quickly. Great teams self-regulate based on the attitude and expectations established by the day-to-day example of leadership.

Built to Last, by Collins & Porras (1995), was a book I read not long out of college. I also read In *Search of Excellence* by Tom Peters and Robert Waterman. They left profound impacts on me; I agreed with the principles they were espousing because it's what I knew, it's what I came from, and it's how I had done it consistently in athletic competition. The book *Built to Last* focuses on the deep reasons behind American long-term corporate success stories. Drawing upon a six-year research project at Stanford, Collins, and Porras studied each exceptional and long-lasting company in direct comparison with one of its competitors. Throughout, the author asked, "What makes the truly exceptional companies different from other companies?"

Visionary companies display a remarkable resilience, and ability to bounce back from adversity. As a result, visionary companies attain extraordinary long-term performance.

– *Visionary companies have done more than just generate long-term financial returns; they have woven themselves into the very fabric of society (pg. 34).*

Manic Fusion is a visionary company.

I played college football for a great head coach who was successful, consistently, because he knew his job was to lead by example and demand obedience to the principles of team above self, the six Ps, and no excuses. We won three championships while I was there. We beat USC in the 1992 Freedom Bowl as major underdogs. I earned a starting role at D-line and gave all to the team. I suffered a major neck injury, multiple torn ligaments, and major concussions. I fought through very real injuries and fear of paralysis to make it back onto the field to help my team. I earned an honorable mention nod for All-Conference due to the productive season I had when I played even after being injured and missing four games. More important to me is that I earned a coveted award as one of the team's captains for our defense. That's leadership acknowledged by great leadership. My head coach offered me a coaching job and said I had what it takes to be a winning head coach. Even after two decades of building industry-leading companies in technology, media, domestic manufacturing, entertainment, and more; I never met a more honest, direct, passionate, tough leader who won championships in a more challenging industry, college football. Leadership and team built on honor! I approach Manic Fusion with this experience and philosophy.

Ten years to create our first certified "hit." Think about that. Julie and I relentlessly worked on developing business and brand concepts as if we were in a laboratory using the scientific method to discover new fundamentally sound ideas until something monetized on scale. It worked, validated by the market and the target consumers. We are both former college athletes and share a similar obsessive approach to practice, preparing to compete and win. We've always approached life this way. Together we are a machine that churns through ideas, problems, and solutions in real time, all the time. Now that we've been able to settle into focusing on building out and launching "Urban Lumber Network," we are hitting a new level of collaboration, delegation, and leadership for both of us in our respective roles. Manic Fusion is maturing into a culture and process-driven business.

Creative content, telling stories, is the future of Manic Fusion Entertainment. It's our long-term secret weapon of value. Making music and movies has always been my natural calling. King Duce Records gave me the platform to deeply explore and learn about making music and music videos. I also learned about attracting and recruiting the best creatives/

artists. Over time I envisioned a creative compound that would inspire me as an artist, and an architecturally inspiring business and multi-media center, like the best in the world, to produce music film (traditional film, digital, and animation), video games, and the marketing of all forms of creative content. We will push R&D with a state-of-the-art center for new technology and inventions.

Financially frugal leadership is paramount to Manic Fusion's success. Co-founder, President, Chief Operating Officer, and Chief Financial Officer maintain a lean, mean operation that expects the team, especially the artists, to create cost-effectively. Disney would have never seen success without Walt's brother Roy. Julie IS the Roy Disney of the company.

Feathervale Drive is the original address of Manic Fusion headquarters. Unlike the cliché Silicon Valley tale of starting the next tech company out of a Palo Alto garage, Julie and I started our company out of a double-wide mobile home while raising her two boys and homeschooling one of them, a creative prodigy who is developing an original animated show. I always tell Colton that Manic Fusion Entertainment will be the house MineBros built. We didn't have a garage, only an old metal storage shed big enough to hold a couple of bikes, kid toys, and a weed trimmer and blower. We didn't own a lawnmower. The only income we had was thanks to Julie working for the local SPCA. She kept a household as a devoted mother and partner, but she worked tirelessly to drive and do much of the heavy lifting to make our business and this book come to life. The daily process of Julie and me, working independently and collaboratively is showing a positive, dynamic, attractive environment that is producing amazing results.

The Feathervale humble beginnings is the formula for a globally scaled company that can grow and thrive through economic volatility and will create original, authentic content that attract and retain loyal customers through trends and fads. No matter how extreme and no matter how out of touch our company may seem at moments to mainstream fans, our loyal customer base will remain happily paying fans for the experience we consistently bring to them. At Manic Fusion Entertainment, the artist, the talent of any kind is not the star; the work product is the star, and we serve her so we can keep the destructive forces of ego, pride, selfish, self-serving, and team killing energy where it should stay—in the shower! We are all the same when we show up every day. We are fortunate to work with the best to build the best creative product for our fans and family.

HOW ULN BEGAN

URBAN LUMBER NETWORK

I never set out to change the world with our first profitable business. We made many attempts using the Manic Fusion formula of building only market-disrupting businesses that can see a clear path to number one. In 2013, we knew we had proven the formula with Bass Thrasher. The industry pro anglers and everyday bass fishing folks across the U.S. and countries all over the world validated Bass Thrasher as an authentic and attractive bass fishing lifestyle clothing brand. We developed a complete brand, multi-season designs, and tons of demand by stores and the 40,000-plus social media community Julie had built organically. Even after talking with many industry insiders and outside investors, we couldn't get the necessary funding to capitalize on the demand we experienced while at the Bassmaster Classic in Birmingham, Alabama, in 2014. We had to shelve Bass Thrasher. No matter how good something is, you need cash to fuel the idea into reality.

We reset our sights and focused on the cut and sew and screen-printing factory angle, a natural part of a vertically integrated lifestyle brand company. My domestic manufacturing experience between Kiva Designs and Zazzle gave me a clear vision of what Manic Fusion would ultimately need in order to have control over product creation and customer service and satisfaction. I learned with King Duce, and the street brands I respected, that high-quality, limited edition/small batch is where it's at. Julie and I dedicated some serious time to putting a plan together.

I was having a conversation at a local coffee shop with Kevin Penton, a Bay Area consultant with expertise in designing and building screen print and cut and sew businesses with the biggest names, when the woman at the table next to us interrupted us. She was very intrigued by our conversation and said that what we were talking about was exactly what she was looking to be a part of. She promised us the world; she had the industry connections, tons of knowledge, energy, and cash. She was excited about the plan and assured us that funds were on the way. We began to recruit industry experts to build our factory. We had the facility picked out and were taking steps to move forward. Unfortunately, Valerie Navarro is a true business viper.

In desperate times we open ourselves up to people who will try, and often succeed, at exploiting that vulnerability. I now more accurately see it as my selfish pride clouding my judgment. This woman is truly despicable. A classic woman empowerment "I can do anything a man can do...and do it better" kind of lady who still wants desperately to be one of the guys while needing love in a way she could never reciprocate. She was crazy. A compulsive liar who really took us for an emotional ride when we least needed it. Now I know that's precisely *why* we needed it. Nothing she said or promised was real. Without notice, she literally disappeared. She left us wondering what in the fuck had just happened and owing more than a little money to those we had recruited. Julie and

I were exhausted, and this blow really hit us hard, to the point where we weren't sure where to go from there. Really. We just kinda walked around with the wind knocked out of us for a while, trying to make sense of the hard work and passion resulting in losses. At least temporarily.

At the time, my drinking dominated my ability to see that I was the obstacle, not money or Valerie Navarro. Finally, in January of 2017, when I was getting sober at my in-laws, I got the idea of trying to help my father-in-law with driving some business for his lumber and truss manufacturing company in town with the ultimate goal of bringing Becky in to lead the company as her father and his partners moved closer to retirement. Del liked the idea.

During the few months that we dedicated ourselves to working with his company, we ended up at the Auburn Home Show. It was June of 2017. I was right around six months sober and had more energy than I knew what to do with. Positivity and excitement to be back building businesses got my blood pumping. We were out to meet people and build opportunities to grow and expand their production. We met a family in the lumber business, a father-daughter team similar to what we were proposing for Becky and her dad. It gave us the inspiration to push forward. Jennifer Alger and her daughter Alyssa were inviting attendees into a cute tiny log cabin, and it drew Julie's eye almost immediately. We went over to hear what they were offering. We also met Jim Evans, Jennifer's dad. He was outside the cabin running a huge Wood-Mizer portable sawmill, explaining that there is no bad wood. Jim and I hit it off immediately with his manic energy and passion for wood and guitars. He talked excitedly about the things he's made and how unexpectedly beautiful the different woods could be. We learned that day that it's not just any wood they work with, but urban and salvaged woods.

Jennifer passionately explained how wood that would normally end up in the waste stream could be saved and turned into beautiful products; slabs, tables, bowls, even pens, or $30,000 visual trusses. She also explained that when this wood is saved and milled into usable lumber, it sequesters, or holds onto, a ton of carbon. Tons, literally tons of carbon are now stored in the wood products and are not released into the atmosphere as it would have been if left to rot at the dump. We knew instantly that this could be a connection. Over the next few months, we worked to figure out exactly what it was that we would end up doing together. Jennifer and her dad visited and toured the facility with Del, Becky, and me. Everyone got along great. Del agreed to buy saw blades from Jennifer, and her brother Jason bought trusses from Del to rebuild after he lost his home to a wildfire.

We proposed using the Oroville facility for the production of tiny houses using urban lumber, making pallets using beetle-kill trees, utilizing the warehouse to store lumber, and even utilizing urban lumber to build and sell man caves and she sheds. All our ideas fell flat. Regardless, we felt that we met Jennifer for a reason. We were meant to do something together, to build something great.

Julie and I got to work putting together a presentation to pitch Jennifer on repurposing "blue pine" beetle kill wood into other products. We met up at a restaurant in Wheatland that was a family favorite of theirs. It was July 26, 2018, just over a year from meeting them at the home show. She brought her dad, Jim. He is truly a character out of a wild west pioneering movie; a life-long logging man who had been nearly killed multiple times working in the hills and even had to have a hand reattached after a gnarly accident. Jim is a good Christian man who lived wild but grounded to the trees and his family. Just like the day we first met, we hit it off immediately.

Julie and Jennifer sat across from each other, and Jim and I sat facing each other at the edge seats of our booth. As chips and salsa hit the table, the conversation was light with meaningful discussions about family, current events, and even God came up. I remember admitting I had a cussing issue and that I was trying to cut back on bad vibes in general to walk in a better light. I was open about my battle with alcohol and my sobriety... cleaning up my life and starting a new chapter, my second half. They smiled warmly and kindly offered their less than perfect truths. There was a genuine caring and connection between us. The conversation moved into work mode effortlessly because no one was trying to posture, exaggerate, or intimidate. It was loving, trusting, and open for collaborative energy, thoughts, teamwork, family, and success.

The topic moved to the repurposing of the beetle kill wood they were being paid by the U.S. Forest Service and Cal Fire to remove from the Sierra Nevada Mountains. We were discussing the area it was coming from, how much there was, and where it would be stored. One thing led to another, and Jennifer began to tell us about a non-profit she had just started called USRW, Urban Salvaged and Reclaimed Woods, casually referred to as the Urban Lumber Network. It stopped me in my tracks.

She had started the first of its kind network in the western United States, but her expertise and influence were recognized throughout the country and beyond. If it had to do with urban lumber, Jennifer was the sought-after authority. She knew she could help people market, grow, and monetize their small businesses because she understood that the "urban, salvaged, and reclaimed" category is huge, global, and profitable. Jennifer was describing an emerging market at its tipping point, and she had developed critical relationships with other influencers that were part of this emerging "green" industry. Jennifer needed an inventory management solution and a way to gather all the small businesses together to better market each business and the industry as a whole. She had talked to developers to create an inventory management system for this unique industry but was faced with a lack of understanding and development and cost overruns.

The stars aligned as Jennifer described her challenge of trying, for over twenty years, to educate people and bring the industry together to help it grow.

"We can do that!" I interrupted. With a big smile of confidence from past experiences of aggregating and monetizing high school recruiting and college football insider information from independent journalists. What Jennifer was describing seemed more similar than different. I saw it all clearly in my mind that day, and the fundamentals have never changed. The way my mind saw the value proposition was simple brilliance thanks to Jim Evans.

I continued with amped enthusiasm. "Jim Evans told me the first day I met him that there is no bad wood. I'm picturing a pile of urban wood the size of a mountain, every type of wood, all in one inventory, all in one place, every piece maximized for its value and utilized... logs, rough cut, finished products, and more."

From that moment, we never looked back. We agreed to join forces officially and disrupt a global market, to offer a superior product and service, and to give the world a real and honest green solution to improve small business owners' lives and the environment all at the same time. Our combined experience and aligned hearts and life principles forged a spiritual bond that would see us through to victory. Looking at Jim's eyes and then Jennifer's, I knew our team would win. We all smiled at each other and shook hands in a moment of true understanding, connection, and deep purpose; a commitment that was bigger than us.

That day we set out to change the world. We didn't have any money, but we had something much more powerful. Faith in team and purpose.

We left the restaurant with victorious joy, and I was met with a desperate phone call from a guy dying from alcoholism.

Journal Entry October 11, 2018, 2:00 am

… I met that victory with a phone call from a guy dying of alcohol. I must remember that my primary purpose is to be of maximum service to my fellows and the next suffering alcoholic. I walked with him through his struggles and he made it to the next day.

Success is measured in many ways, and on that day, I felt holistically triumphant.

In the next few months, we put together a team—a project manager of sorts that I know in town, and his talented engineer brother in Idaho. We worked together to get our system figured out, prepare presentations for Jennifer to take to conferences and trade shows, and to get started on the build-out of the inventory management and network platform systems. We all seemed to be working together well when the wheels came off. We had one engineer, Brian, confirmed and all in, but then the second balked. Matt started to act as if he were more important than he was and that he was indispensable to our project. He refused to work on our terms. Immediately Brian went silent, and progress slowed to a halt.

In the meantime, Julie's mom was taking a turn for the worse. Her organs were shutting down, and her mind was following with memory loss and dementia after a life of alcohol, cigarettes, and condemned dreams. Julie was homeschooling her youngest son, a freshman in high school, and they had to make a few trips to San Diego to see her mother. The second trip, they missed seeing her due to fog cancelling their flight. They took a later flight into LAX, landing at midnight on November 5th. While completing the rental car process, she received the call that her mom had just passed. She spent a few days helping her sister make final arrangements before returning home to the terrifying Camp Fire burning just north of town. Despite Julie's sadness and loss, she trudged on and did everything she could to keep the trains moving on time.

Journal Entry December 31, 2018, 3:15 am

... The day to day at our Feathervale mobile home in Oroville has been insanity and game changing in all aspects of life. It has tested every ounce of my being and smashed my paradigm of what I thought possible.

...After a few false starts, either because we didn't have the cash or the wrong people coming at us, claiming to be something they were not... the greatest frustrations bring silver linings in new and unexpected opportunities.

Journal Entry January 13, 2019, 6:00 am

We were fed up with the lack of communication and the arrogant and shitty attitude of the back-end developer Matt S., and Brian S. the UI developer has basically gone silent on us after we told Matt we were not going to work with him. They have acted like small town hacks in the heat of the start-up of this business. All this, while the rest of the Urban Lumber Network team is forming and synergizing almost effortlessly. It feels right. We made a decision to eradicate the cancer and bring in my trusted friend Andrew B., a former product manager at Boeing Satellite Division.

These are tough decisions that drain energy and cause bad energy. Not surprisingly, I felt my body starting to feel stressed to the point of illness. It hit me and I literally felt tingly and exhausted. I was getting sick after feeling healthy for a long period of sustained health from good diet, exercise, and better thinking and positive action forward and no more lies. All of a sudden, my body and not to mention my mind, began to short circuit from the illogical conflict and uncertainly from the fall out with the engineer team, one of the critical columns in the company's successful buildout.

Journal Entry January 16, 2019

…Yesterday after a week of cutting and recruiting a new engineering team led by Andrew B., a musician buddy from our Fresno State days, we had a team conference call to introduce Andrew and Jennifer and talk through the next steps with me and Julie. Everyone hung up feeling stoked and confident that the project was back on track and shifted into a new gear. I was proud of how Julie and I handled that situation.

My leadership lesson is to keep cool and steady during times of adversity and focus on the solution to the problem and not the other way around. The outcome will be what is manifested in the mind of the leader. The experience of people who were bad fits to the team drove the point home that our company culture and higher aligned vision remain our most valuable assets.

We were off and running once again as a family with team-above-self vision and purpose. Then tragedy struck once again.

In January, as we mourned the loss of Julie's mother and I celebrated two years of sobriety, we got the news that Jennifer's older brother had been killed in a horrific welding accident. A devastating blow to her extremely close family and community. We stuck together and shared our love and prayers once again for an unexpected loss and grieved for all who were impacted.

Journal Entry January 20, 2019, 5:15 am

Overcoming adversity is what life is about, learning to be of service during tough times is the test. Do we fall or rise to the occasion? This week we overcame a challenging situation with a rogue engineering team, firing them, and replacing them in one weeks' time. I was certain that was going to be the biggest obstacle we would face in the early stages of building our new technology company. I was sadly wrong. Friday was a day I won't forget. (January 18, 2019) Dick picked me up at 8:15am and we (Dick, Skip, Kirk and me) drove up to Paradise to help Bill, a recovery buddy, move to Oregon. His duplex survived the fire by inches, not feet. The development of approximately 50 units, half of them, randomly chosen by the fire that engulfed that town in November were gone.

Driving up to Paradise and around neighborhoods was like being in a war-torn country. It was an emotional start to helping people move who were clueless about where to go next. Bill's wife was worthless at this point... she hadn't packed anything and expected us to load a truck that hadn't even arrived. It wasn't just the fire that had her unprepared... a year ear-

lier we helped them move and she was equally demanding and unappreciative. She made my skin crawl. I was angry I just wanted to run away and curse my circumstances. I was a bitter motherfucker... oh, and it started raining. My phone rang between carrying crap furniture and unboxed items into the late arriving U-Haul driven by Bills overachieving son, Billy, a retiring contractor from Fremont. He reminded me of the guy that takes pride in working all the time and staying busy... boring personality but nice enough guy. After a bad start to the morning with Julie, I was surprised she was calling me.

"Chris... Jennifer Alger's brother died yesterday... not sure how yet...". Jennifer, our business partner, and friend that we were launching ULN with. I couldn't believe it... "What?!" I shot back. My heart broke and I was transported to another person's loss from an unexpected accident. I stood frozen, looking out the back sliding glass window that framed the trees and manzanita brush that was like charred black corpses from the deadly flames that licked the six foot concrete patio walkway space that separated total destruction and a standing home... I was surrounded by death. As Julie was trying to talk with me about it, I snapped and went off about how fucked up the world is, being stuck in Paradise, broke, wet, frustrated... I was in a blackout rage of sadness and confusion.

I rocketed back to the loss of my big brother Rusty in a tragic bowhunting accident... Just when I thought I couldn't take any more, I was standing alone in the universe with the great spirit, quieted with the truth of how I was to lead in this time of struggle and adversity... sadness and loss. I thought of the night under the stars and moon when Rusty died and I swore to myself that I was going to live fuller and bolder and tell people I love them in the now, everything in the now... I was trans-formed that night. After making things worse with Julie from this morning, I refocused and got back to work. A few hours later I headed home with the guys feeling a little better from the camaraderie of sober, unselfish guys show-ing me how to love and give in adversity. As I listened to the near death experiences of Dick and Skip on their death beds, not from alco-hol but crazy medical shit, I looked out at the black and newly green contrasted hillsides as we drove down the ridge and I smiled, laughed a couple times from Skip and the guys telling funny drunk stories, and I found a moment of gratitude.

We forged our way through loss and tragedy as a family to come out victorious. Our team is truly special.

Black Hole Sun – Coronavirus Global Crisis

Despite the real impact the crisis caused millions of hard-work-ing people, it turned out to be more manufactured fear-mon-gering and evil profiteering, like every time before. Watching so many innocent people negatively impacted, especially the vulnerable and the best, the small business owners have been hit with a tsunami wave that will ultimately eliminate many of them unnecessarily. It's sad. But it is also a brutal lesson.

9

GOOD VIBRATIONS

Good Vibrations

OUR HEALTH—THE TEMPLE OF HEAVEN OR HELL

W anna save money and feel better? Nutrition, rest, positive thoughts, and actions equal success and happiness. Stop eating crap and paying bad companies a stupid premium to kill yourself. That shit will slow and deform the body and mind's natural ecosystem and ultimately cause a system failure. I don't want to gross you out, but we are not one individual human being, each of us, we are made up of trillions of creatures that all symbiotically co-exist. Through a very complex balance of proper whole foods, minerals, and water, we can keep our body and mind operating at a level most of us have never known. If we do not properly take care of our bodies, they will fail us. It's ironic that we say it that way when in reality, we are failing our body, mind, and soul when we don't care for ourselves the right way. I was raised by parents who were health minded and athletic and who shared their love of the outdoors, interacting with nature constantly. I know the proper rhythm and feel when all cylinders are firing inside me, when I'm alive and exploring and challenging the world and myself.

I constantly hear people tell me, "Yeah, Chris, that all sounds good, but I got bills, bro! The IRS and my boss are not just gonna let me slide because I'm eating better, resting, and thinking more positive!" You are totally right! We didn't put ourselves in a challenging financial situation overnight. Well, let's be honest, most of us did! Our cars, our home, kids, insurance, sports, hobbies, and all the crap we spent and committed money to that we will have to work forty fucking years to pay off. "It's too late, Chris, I'm too far deep into raising a family and my career that I can't change my circumstances like that!" Total fucking bullshit excuses! I know because I said all the same shit, in one way or another. I was scared to go for it and start creating the real Chris Rockwell. But I did, one step and day at a time. It required pain, struggle, perseverance, hope, belief in myself, and a stubborn persistence to see it through when I literally had no money and had to figure out how to start my life over from scratch. It's been a lesson that has taught me extreme gratitude for the simple things in life.

One big but very easy change was how I nourish my body and mind. My eating and health are now a top priority in my life. I eat much healthier than ever, and I am spending a fraction of what I did when I ate out all the time. I used to snack on ice cream and processed munchies of all kinds until I would pass out from a food coma. Now I eat to feed my body, mind, and soul so I can perform at my optimal. Almost everything I eat now is organic and humanely raised with no antibiotics. We shop local. We are really lucky to have so much available to us close by. But I am no elitist. I still crush dark chocolate and food that is offered to me by friends and family. I just realize I will either benefit or lose a step depending on the food intake I choose. It's about caring for the machine that gets the work and fun done.

Again, we do as much organic as possible, and local, free-range, pasture-raised, nutrient-dense meats, raw dairy, and eggs. We do our best to balance Omega-6 and Omega-3 fatty acids so they can work together rather than against each other, and we grow our own vegetables and fruits and shop local farmers markets and stands for items we don't grow.

We eat whole foods more than processed foods. I find that in properly providing my body with the nutrients it needs, I actually spend less money. The nutrient-poor foods I used to eat not only wreaked havoc on my health, both physically and mentally, but they emptied my wallet faster as well because I needed more just to feel somewhat satiated. Now, I eat nutrient-dense foods and don't overeat or overspend.

Total cost for the day is around ten dollars for amazing nutrients and mind and body healing. I used to spend over twice that much just on alcohol every day, three times as much if I made my way to the dive bar down the street, then add a shit ton of food and junk to feed my mind what it told me I needed. Some days I spent over $100 just to get a ride to the shitholes I would rot away in. We're talking hundreds of dollars every week to feel like shit—mind, body, and soul! Now we shop frugally, making sure to get the most for our money. Even our dogs are eating better!

Pharmaceuticals and bad food destroy our good probiotics and make us ill and malnourished and unable to think and behave as the mind and body should if fed properly. As my dad always said, sugar is a killer! Alzheimer's, dementia, depression, diabetes, obesity, heart disease, and so much more. In the 1960s, the sugar industry-funded research that downplayed the risks of sugar and highlighted the hazards of fat regarding their impact on heart disease. They actually paid scientists to refute studies and experiments that stated sugar's major role in heart disease and instead highlighted the hazards of fat, concluding that cutting fat, not sugar, out of American diets was the best way to address coronary heart disease. They knew that if fat was out, something had to replace it, and sugar stepped in. They also knew that America's per capita sugar consumption could go up by at least a third. Remember all the packages that have that bright label shouting NON FAT at you? Well, hello sugar! Hello, heart disease. Pretty disgusting and disturbing to realize how many lies we are being told. Pay attention and be vigilant about your health.

It's a fallacy that you need to be wealthy to eat healthy. We all have access to inexpensive, healthy foods. Most people simply choose to reward themselves with a big bowl of ice cream or chug down chemicals we wouldn't put in our truck's gas tank.

Because I have alcoholic and concussion-related brain trauma, I have a vitamin and supplement regimen that I take daily. It is based on a study on pro football players who also struggle with the disease of alcoholism. (**Reversing Brain Damage in Former NFL Players: Implications for Traumatic Brain Injury and Substance Abuse Rehabilitation** Daniel G Amen 1, Joseph C Wu, Derek Taylor, Kristen Willeumier)

My daily routine:

- Vitamin B complex supplement
- Ginkgo Biloba
- Acetyl-L Carnitine and Huperzine A
- Alpha Lipoic Acid (ALA)
- N-Acetyl Cysteine (NAC)
- High-quality fish oil
- Vitamin C

I am on a schedule where I take the supplements four different times during the day to ensure that I am getting the most from each while not suppressing the benefits of the others. I am able to get minerals, probiotics, and other essential nutrients to heal and ensure my brain is functioning at top capacity through my diet of natural, fresh, unprocessed foods. Lemon juice and raw organic apple cider vinegar every day keeps the doctor away! And a green leafy veggie diet while eliminating processed foods and refined products. We make our own kefir, an amazing probiotic that goes back to the days of Plato. The gut-mind connection is real. If you take care of your gut, eat what it and your body needs, your brain will function at a higher capacity, and don't we all want that! I know I do.

Physical exercise outdoors is fundamental to feeling good. Save money and drop the gym membership to destroy your joints, lifting heavy weights and overexerting on the treadmill inside of a claustrophobic germ-ridden gym where most people are there to socialize and obsess over how they look. Taking a walk, hike, swim in nature, or just outdoors in the metropolitan areas gives us sunlight, fresh air (even in cities, it's better than staying indoors). I live in the country, back to my roots after city life and wasting time in gyms after being stuck in an office all day. Crazy and not my idea of health.

Even when I'm working indoors and traveling, I choose to take a break to take a walk around the hotel or office building. It gives me a mental break to breathe in some air, let the natural light provide me with Vitamin D, and mentally relax while my body is in motion. No matter what I'm doing, I turn it into a mini-exploration or adventure away from my task at hand, which is usually work that requires a lot of mental and physical energy and stamina. Moving the body is more important than pushing our body into the red to show the world our muscles or data tracking score on social media. I no longer see it as a competition or ego-driven body sculpting task. Now that I am eating good food and not drinking alcohol or using tobacco, I don't need to go to extremes with working out. I now take my dog Bradley out early in the mornings and sometimes evenings too, to go swimming and hiking in the mountains. It's a complete body and mind cleanser and healer, and it saves money. Getting outside of my little world wakes me up to the reality, beauty, and gifts all around me.

I now basically follow the example my dad has always lived—eat right, think right, and keep the body in motion. Physical labor and exercise through runs or walks and outdoor adventures hiking, fishing, hunting, swimming, skiing, diving, and sports. Justifying spending hundreds and thousands of dollars on stationary in-home work-out equipment is isolating and constricting us to the same indoor environment that we are stuck in (home office) most of the day. That's good marketing and a great business for the companies selling that concept. Even in a metropolitan city, there are parks to take a walk in and get a shot of nature, sunlight, and looking around at the world around and outside of ourselves, even if it's just for 15 to 30 minutes. It's part of a healthy, productive day that I need to feel good.

For folks that do physical labor for a living, you are ahead of the game, as long as you don't fuel it with energy drinks, sugary snacks, Bud Light, and ESPN after work. pH Balance devastates disease in our body. The crap we drink and eat usually throws our pH balance into an acid bath. We don't need to be health experts to realize that the basic concept makes sense. The science is simple but hard to do if we are stuck in our mainstream eating and drinking habits. As I got older, I heard more about this and watched my parents eat a diet with the goal of balancing their alkalinity. I didn't need proof. My dad is 80 as I finish this, and he's kicking ass!

It's not easy to do, but I see the results, and I'm striving to continue, like my parents say about health and about life, to make it a fun challenge!

MONEY—GRAB THE BULL BY THE HORNS

Money is not good or bad. It's not real, except in the eye of the beholder. Value is perceived very differently by different people, even within the same family. Growing up, I assumed everyone thought about money in similar ways. I couldn't have been more naïve and wrong. I now realize money can be used as a tool or a trap. There is no excuse for allowing personal desires, even with the child excuse, to steal or shackle our self-worth and personal freedom. Debt is the trap.

We allow ourselves to become slaves to our lower desires, in a lot of cases. I realize debt can come in all sorts of forms, often from unfortunate events. But the majority of debt, and I include myself in this, comes from poor thinking and usually selfish thinking. Money and marketing can make us feel like total losers or false gods if we buy into it. I did, for years, even though I denied it and acted like I was different. I lived most of my adult life in debt due to my ignorance and erratic selfish thinking.

As I finish up this book and our technology company ULN is growing into a market leader, my financial life has returned to a place where I won't struggle again if I choose to. The big question I have been quietly pondering is how to deal with money now that I have it again, and at a level that is growing far beyond anything I knew before. As I'm experiencing my metamorphosis from absolute poverty to "riches," I get overwhelmed with the way it makes me think. For a guy like me, like most people, really, it would never be enough. The time creating, protecting, and growing my wealth is something that consumed me from a competitive sport measuring success kind of way. It's a trap for a guy like me. My mind won't turn off or turn down the intensity of the chase to do bigger and better. If ten million dollars is good, then one hundred million dollars is better. Really? Why? If my ego and self-will make that my goal, then I'm dead before I start.

Living and working in Silicon Valley, LA, and the New York media and entertainment world, I am so jaded from reptilian money fiends using charity and philanthropy as a public relations and lobbying strategy and often using it for a tax shield to pay self and cronies the lion's share of the money supposedly used for charity. It makes me sick. Free money is bad money. And It's rampant. It's the way people see themselves and live, claiming virtuous intentions when the truth is covered with malicious, greedy actions. The lines on their faces and plastic smiles tell much of the story. Their lifestyles, what they have and consume for self is the rest of the story... their truth.

If someone wants to work hard, earn a lot of money, and spend it on themselves and or their family, that's cool. I don't care. What bothers me is when people are not honest about it. It's not up to me to judge the true intentions and actions behind others. But I choose to associate myself and business to people that see a bigger picture. There are two types of people; those who value human bonds and relationships and those who value money above people. It's easy to be misled *if* we are living in that philosophical seesaw of people vs. money.

I must treat my closest loved ones like gold, instead of sacrificing them at the altar of money and status. For me, I realize that the less I personally need, the more I can give, the better I feel. That, in its foundation, is self-serving. And that's how I must align my personal and altruistic desires and purpose. I have no desire to continue the futile race of amassing wealth and feeding my ego with a big charitable donation "celebrating" *me* at the end of a life consumed with making money and never getting out of the race. I have the desire to use my skills to help the most people possible. I have learned the art of uniting and leading great people to build innovative and valuable companies and future leaders.

That's why Manic Fusion exists. At its core, it is tasked with creating value to feed our people and our purpose to help our own and others succeed. Living happy, healthy, productive lives to be an example to the people around us. That's winning. Wealth. It's a mindset, a paradigm shift in how I wake up and see my place and purpose in the world today. Instead of my old game plan of waking up and feeling behind, I am starting to wake up with a reserve of hope and energy to share with others, all day, every day.

The minute I wake up and start thinking about a bigger, cooler house, truck, trips, chicks, bank account, and lifestyle, it inevitably takes me down a dark path of my desires but also my worst insecurities. The competitive poison of ego kicks into an insatiable vampire hell-bent on sucking out my life force for a few bucks and glory moments.

Rebelling from the consumer machine is where the gold and riches are at. It's about owning less to own more of our most valuable resource, time. The funny or paradoxical thing is that this gives us peace of mind, happiness, and freedom to use our minds much more creatively and productively, especially when the true intent is producing maximum value to help others. Sometimes I leverage a public platform to achieve a worthy goal. But anonymous help and giving are where most of my effort and money and time is spent because it produces the deepest change and enlightenment for all involved. I believe pushing myself to teach, mentor, and help future leaders, entrepreneurs, and today's struggling kids and alcoholics daily is where I discover my gold and sunlight. There is a correlation, folks.

Own your decisions and choices about money! Stop chasing the billion-dollar business and perfect family success story being sold as the concept of happiness. It's a marketing scam, ladies and gentlemen. The point is to lock you into a low wage (based on your potential) job and debt, secured with a wife and kids like everyone else on TV and your social media feed. Everywhere you look, you are told that you need to work harder to make more money to become a success, and show your family that you can be the provider and protector. And it's all measured by the crap you buy to satisfy your need to feel ahead of the game... all the while feeling totally behind. The sad part is that the poor and working-class usually give more for less because they do what they are told to through mainstream media and deep seeded habits.

Take back control of your financial life! We spend nearly all of our waking time enslaved to a job we hate to pay for the shit we don't even want anymore, and never really needed, just to fit in with the idea of who we are supposed to be. Stop and take a breath! It doesn't have to be like that.

Imagine simplifying your life by 50%. Think about it. Imagine having free time to do what you always dreamed about doing. What would you do with the time you used to spend working your ass off to make another payment on a status trophy item at a compounding interest rate that steals your most precious gold—YOUR TIME. YOUR LIFE!

We must stop wishing we made more money to buy more ego-driven shit and start taking internal stock of the things we need versus want. Marketers love parents because they know that they will spend anything and everything on their kids to give them that extra edge to win or just to fit in. They spend thousands of dollars in sports gear, a car when they turn sixteen, and a college fund as everyone—the parents, grandparents, and society—give them more unearned money and praise. The kid thinks they have it all together when they never worked for or learned the appreciation for all the shit handed to them simply for being a good student in a corrupt, dumbed-down education system that fails to teach kids and the teachers the truth about money, capitalism, and life. These attitudes are the training ground for internal and external factors that create working slave consumers, disconnected to the cause and effect of their concept of time and money. There ends up being a total lack of understanding of the true-life cost of becoming a toiler for their sick and unscrupulous greed.

Wanna beat the system? Stop allowing evil outside forces to trick you into giving your money to them when they will use you and your money for evil and give you nothing but fake security and respect. We care about our hard-earned money a hell of a lot more than some big bank crony connected to the evilest people on the planet that finance death and misery for a living.

Parents, wanna help your kids be truly successful? Teach them how to value and manage their money and their purchasing and thinking related to it. Teach them the difference between wanting and needing. A hard lesson to learn if you always get what you want. We must share value in hard work and frugality. It's not about living miserable. It's not about scrimping and saving and starving our whole lives to reach this nonexistent pot of gold at the end of our miserable grind. That's no payoff. But that's how we do it. It's how work and retirement have been sold to us. It's the formula of working super hard all the time to buy the things we need while having no time to truly enjoy the most important people and moments in our lives. We are too busy working and end up paying with the shackles of long-term choices we made for short-term gratification.

We as a nation, and individuals, have a divided culture and attitude toward money because some people work hard for their money, and some expect it given to them by some invisible god of entitlement through the ugly sales pitch of being a victim to the system. Most people today, especially the kids, are growing up pampered, protected, and celebrated for false victories and effort. I grew up like a lot of kids I knew in my hometown. We did a lot of manual labor, whether it was helping our dad or parents around the house and property or jobs in the summer before football and school started. I also grew up with kids that had parents that convinced themselves and their kids that they were above physical or manual labor because they were college-educated and self-identified as the upper class, even though they were teachers, doctors, and sales guys.

My dad grew up poor and worked his ass off in fields picking fruit, working in canneries 12 hours a day, six days a week, or setting tile in the blazing summer heat. He eventually earned a master's degree and became an amazing teacher and dad. His example was not lost on me. I also had a grandpa who grew up in the Great Depression, leaving home at 11 to work on a ranch to help earn money for the family. Both men were in the military and then worked a career helping others as teachers and police officers. They were well-rounded men that instilled the honor and value of doing tough work and doing it right. They didn't preach it like many disconnected self-impressive guys who walk and talk a fragmented delusion of what hard work and teamwork mean. The value of hard manual labor, at any age, but especially for developing kids, is that it teaches a person to get humble, take direction, and think about working together with other people to get a job done when it's not easy or convenient. Like life.

Unfortunately, especially in today's ideologically divided nation and technologically isolating jobs at the white and blue-collar sector, people are disconnected from what made families, communities, and this nation strong, working together towards common goals that ultimately benefit us individually. The powers behind our economic system, who also control the media propaganda we consume, want us to be passive and entitled. We are a nation of softies that expect a free ride. The majority of kids and adults in 2020 are zoned out on their idiot phones and rewarding their toil of going through the motions, lying to themselves on social media, while they are too busy buying a Starbucks frappuccino and posting selfies about their unique individualism, forgetting to get off their ass and actually work to build a financially independent life. They are subsidized by clueless and self-serving parents doing basically the same shit. A recipe for disaster. That's the plan. Sheep arrogantly thinking that they are smarter than the wolves.

As I finished this book in the summer of 2020, I went to work for a logging crew in the same mountains where my dad's family lived and worked in a logging camp back in 1947. I worked for an old crusty big bear of a man named Big Jon. He reminded me of the old logger Oliver Elam "Bear" who lived next door to my parents in the original Tucker house across the irrigation canal from our property. These men were hard drinking and hard working in a business that killed and maimed many good men because of the inherent dangers of logging. These men were battle-scarred and leathery, aged beyond their years by the back-breaking work, sun, and alcohol they endured daily. They didn't talk like most men; they growled with a booming profanity and words of direction at the crew throughout the day to keep the operation pressed at full speed to maximize the ever-shrinking profits and suffocating regulations that were impeding their craft and way of life, cutting and hauling the logs that eventually make their way down the mountains to the mills that cut the logs into lumber that would ultimately become the homes in the San Francisco and Los Angeles to the very elitists who were sitting in their posh life of luxury hating on the very people and industry that provided their beautiful homes.

California *is* the land of contradictions, dreams, and hypocrisy. My stint working for Big Jon was short-lived but memorable. I worked with two guys from Mexico. Ivan was my 26-year-old supervisor who had turned his life around after getting caught up in the brutal drug cartel world that ran his hometown Sinaloa led by the infamous drug lord El Chapo. The other man I worked side by side with was Ivan's soon to be father-in-law he referred to as Don Lupe. The prefix was a sign of respect for the older and wiser man. Don Lupe looked like he was in his sixties. His old, wiry body was broken like his English. He was missing many teeth hidden behind a long and unkempt goatee. But his tan skin and green eyes showed a kindness and resilience few possess.

Ivan coached me like a calm and seasoned leader, far beyond his years, because he understood through his life in the drug world, that calm thinking and motion produce better results with fewer mistakes. Big Jon valued Ivan, but he showed it with insults and hung-over rage without logical guidance. Ivan didn't seem bothered by it. He understood who Jon was, a gentle heart protected by a big bad and loud coat of armor that was transparent at moments when Jon would realize what he was doing and who Ivan was, joking off his disrespectful tirade because he felt bad and slightly worried about pushing Ivan back into his dark past solution of sticking and dumping his fat ass in an old mining ditch that traversed these mountains from the gold rush days.

My job part of the day was setting chokers on logs after they've been felled and bucked. That job consists of, in this example, hauling a big steel cable up a mountain to the downed logs and wrapping the separate choker cable around the butt end of the log and hooking the winch cable connected to the skidder tractor winch to drag the 10,000-pound log down the mountain. This is where shit can go bad. If the choker isn't locked in right or the cables are compromised, they can break and turn into deadly flying steel that can decapitate or maim you if you are in the way. That means, after I hiked the mountain and locked the cables and hooks into place, I would give Big Jon the thumbs-up to pull the log down the mountain. I'd be so gassed and exhausted after dragging thousands of pounds of steel cable up a mountain and setting the choker that I would barely have the strength to run up and over to the side to get out of the way in case the cable snapped.

Just before I started setting chokers on those logs, they were felled by an animal of a man named Forrest. We met and shook hands before he headed up the mountain to fell the trees I'm describing. Forrest could easily be an MMA fighter but preferred wrestling giant trees to the ground. On this particular day, Forrest came down the hill after doing his job, and I noticed that his right hand was red with fresh blood running down his forearm and onto the ground. I walked over and put my hand on his shoulder to check on him, and he didn't even seem shook by it.

But as I looked closer at his injury, I realized that his fingers were nearly cut off, and his hand was shaking. I asked him if he needed help, and he smiled and told me, "I'm good...this is logging" and then he described how he finished the cut and his foot slipped out and tried to catch his fall instinctively, and his hand landed on the saw blade still spinning at high speed. He nearly cut his fingers off and calmly, with a little "no big deal" shrug of his shoulder, told us he was gonna go get stitched up and be back to work in no time. He had no choice. It was his craft and livelihood. His son and helper, Austin, watched quietly, trying not to act too concerned, knowing the ways of the logging man. Forrest was a seasoned professional. The trees and terrain are very unpredictable and unforgiving.

BE HONEST... WHO ARE YOU?

Wanna be happy? Stop consuming and criticizing and start creating and building! Get started on your dream instead of running from it, being distracted by everything society told you was truth and using the weak excuse that you're "too busy"! It takes work to stop the idiot inertia we are programmed with.

Changing our time killing distractions and justifications is extremely difficult. Take me, for example. I finally chose a path of sacrificing my short-term, feel-good fixes that would coast me through another wasted day of denying my truth, dreams, and potential, my purpose. What I can do to feel good about myself now is to give back and challenge myself to live up to what I am capable of doing to lead and serve others—my family and mankind. I can't do that if I live the way I used to. Now I use the formula that has been proven through the history of mankind. Live true and free from the rules of success taught by mainstream society. Financial wealth at the cost of relationships and time is not success or freedom. It's a scam and suicide of the soul.

We are being led, mindfucked, and enslaved to feel the desires of evil intentions that have distorted our natural energy connected to our mind, body, and soul. Feeding our selfish wants to fix our insecurities and moral conflicts. I know from trying to live both ways, and now I can say with confidence that there is only one formula for true happiness. GIVE IT AWAY and start loving ourselves and the people that actually give a fuck about us. The cost of our choices must be analyzed in a more holistic way. Why spend money on Red Bull and fast food to 'hurry' to a job that we sacrifice our life getting through for scraps? It's not about working harder with more hours if you are never truly present with the ones we love. It's crazy.

I rebuilt my life by getting back to the basics of hard work, clean living, and giving back what was given to me in every facet of my life. Funny how little we can live on when we are forced to and not relying on government handouts to keep us stuck in a victimized state of mind. Fuck that! I had to get up and get started on rebuilding by living with basically nothing for years and realizing how to walk and talk and think as a sober human and relearn how to see money not as the answer but as the problem. It was not going to fix me, even at the bottom! I experienced it! How humble are you willing to get? How little are you willing to have around your peers and friends?

Today, people can tell me anything they want about who they are and what they've accomplished. I don't hold much weight in rhetoric and sound bite clichés. I was given the gift of objectivity, which gave me a unique perspective starting way back at preschool. Everything I need to know I learned at preschool, right? I observed adults and kids my age saying the same self-deceptive half-truths about who they are, what they stand for, and what they are going to be. I observed, and still do observe, especially with the proliferation of social media, people measuring their self-worth with stupid certainties based on delusional criteria that come from a mixed bag of compromise and denial.

Most people walk through this life in absolute fear and never really live one day out loud and naked to the wind, but nonetheless yell really loud and tell us how adventurous they are with their latest Vegas sky diving crazy pic. Masks and cover-ups. Literally. Come on, people, be real. It is hard at the beginning. We need to figure out who we really are underneath the lies of who we have become to feel safe in society. Working through the fear of letting the real you be seen and heard by the rest of the world is the next step. It is scary, but we start to feel momentum and confidence that propels us to confront the truth of our soul and purpose in this world.

Our purpose, our calling, is already in our hearts. We just spend most of our life running from that truth because we are afraid that we won't be accepted or liked. We are afraid to be a disappointment. Too many times, people judge someone by their appearance, their job, or the things they like to do. Too many times, people hide their true selves to avoid being judged for who they really are. It's shameful the way we pretend to be something we're not out of fear. I can appreciate that. I ran from my truth for years, trying to please people and expectations that were half-truths. I was scared and paralyzed. Then one day, as with each stage of my life since I was conscious, I dove headfirst into the unknown because I had to. I couldn't live with myself if I didn't take the chance to explore something amazing and life changing. I realize everyone has a different pain and risk threshold. That's cool. But if we want freedom, we must confront what scares us and face it and take it on, one step and day at a time.

I'm stoked and scared all the time. But it scares me even more to not live my truth. That can wake me up at night. At least these days, it's not because I'm fucked up and praying not to die from taking too many drugs. My experiences have brought me to my knees and face to face with the end. I'm not leaving this amazing crazy fucked up world without dropping some thoughts into the universal pot of time and space. My hope is that my experiences can inspire others to find their truth and live it.

I have learned that many people are simple and predictable, no matter what their intelligence. Intelligence is an interpretive thing, believe me. I've met and worked with a shit ton of well-educated idiots with zero life experience outside their Stanford dorm walls and all-night coding marathons, as well as a number of very smart junior high school drop-out street gangsters that could run 'intelligent' laps around those Stanford grads. Perspective defines intelligence.

It all boils down to one simple fact that we can't run away from in the midst of all this confusion about self; no matter how much we want to elevate ourselves above the granite foundation of human nature, we can't. Many men have lost their sense of manhood. They have been stripped of what sets a man apart, and they are trying to figure out who they are. Most men today have never experienced the battle of a warrior. They are simply getting everything done to please the wife and conforming to a female-driven marketing mindset and lifestyle. This means reducing risk and spending most of their time working their ass off trying to be a reliable provider and completing all their honey-dos.

People blame marketing. I do too. But the reality is that the "Mad Men" ad agencies simply tapped into the social psyche destruction plan that was set in place to destroy our sense of self and makes us question our instincts rather than acting on them. Modern consumerism and Madison Avenue's advertising agencies create a delusional fantasy of dreams, entertainment, and unattainable expectations for people. No one escaped that indoctrination into modern consumerism, including me, and social media has put this sick trend into hyper speed.

People chase status marks to elevate self within that particular social group. We all do. It just looks different based on the team we are trying to be on. Some show their stripes with a Chevy truck, and some do it with a Subaru and others with a Rolls Royce. For example, I buy Chevy trucks because my dad has always driven Chevys. Can I justify that they are the best full-size truck? I guess, but that depends on who you're asking, and honestly, that's not why I bought it. I bought it because it looked cool, and like I said, my dad drives a Chevy. Now, when I was making the purchase decision, was I consciously telling myself, "Gee Chris, Keep the family tradition going and buy a Chevy." No. My inner dialogue was more like, *Man, I'll look cool in that truck, working men I respect will dig it and see me as one of the "guys."* And whether we want to admit it or not, this is a natural human process.

Most people I talk to claim that they don't buy things because of the brand name despite the fact that every scientific, consumer, psychographic analytic result on the planet points to the opposite. WE ALL BUY BRANDS THAT WE IDENTIFY WITH. And yes, that goes for everyone. No matter what people say, even if they drive a Subaru and volunteer at the food bank. In fact, many times, those are the worst offenders. People rarely buy things without considering price and, more importantly, the brand name. Everyone claims to be above that stuff. Virtue and dominance signaling is a human nature thing.

Of course, for some, price is the top priority. Brand and price will adjust their weighted ratio by the level of necessity versus desire. The poorest communities prove that poor people spend their money on name brands as much as wealthy people. They choose brand in every area, even when many of the commodity food staples are identical and often significantly cheaper with off brand bulk packaged goods. But no, poor people, especially on welfare, choose brand names which tend to be more expensive when purchasing food, clothes, electronics, and soda, etc. I've seen it with middle-class half-asses, living in perpetual debt and working just to keep up with the Joneses. If everyone would quit trying to act like they are so righteous and telling the world how together they are, we'd all get along better. The truth is we all feel fucked up inside and pretend to be okay on the outside. It's just not real. The façade needs to come down!

Experiencing and analyzing the world outside ourselves can help improve self. But far too often, pointing out other people's shit instead of focusing on self can become the obsession. When people don't pursue their life on a daily basis, they want others to share in that guilt and self-loathing. Misery loves company. I'm guilty of this ugly attitude at times, just like anyone. But my saving grace is that I'm painfully aware of it and choose not to live like that, most of the time. The difference is that most people either don't admit it or more often, they are not aware of it.

It's time to wake up and start living who we are. We can change our consciousness by being true to ourselves, and positivity will follow and attract other positive people and opportunities. When we all live true, the world will change for the better.

INVISIBLE WAVES
OF LOVE & WAR

As a musician, first and foremost, I have always been sensitive to sounds and people's energy.

I always wondered what music was: what was sound, where did it originate from, what did it mean, why did some sounds carry me through a gateway to enlightened consciousness, while other sounds and songs opened the dungeon gates to a dark demonic energy?

The visual translation of the rock music I grew up on, starting with album covers and magazines, posters, and eventually MTV Head Bangers Ball and live concerts, introduced me to a seductive fantasy world of the sex, drugs, and rock & roll lifestyle. I was hooked by the powerful force of sound, and visual waves manifested in the form of the 1970s rock band KISS as a child and Pantera in the 1990s. I used to think about it in-between plays when I was playing college football. I saw the game from an aerial view and perspective that it was a performance... entertainment for the masses. Just like in Rome's Coliseum, the gladiators battle the opposing team and fans scream, booing and cheering to each win or loss, except we played under lights with rock songs blaring between the college band fight songs. The music was there to pump up the teams and the crowd, readying us for battle. ESPN would

flood this experience into millions of homes with an artificially enhanced blast of play by play and film angles that tells
a story, highlights key figures, personalities, fans, and cheer-
leaders. Add co-sponsored beer commercials combining more
music with the latest super model and multi-million dollar
ad budget to entice the viewers of the football experience to
equate Bud-Light to the already amplified state of sex and
violence, boldly staged as "normal" family entertainment on
Thanksgiving Day. Sounds, music, can either soothe us, or
ready us for the fight.

In my research I found that music tuned to 432Hz creates "feelings of ecstasy, compassion and altruism". Listening
to music tuned to 432 Hz has been scientifically proven to
decrease feelings of anxiety, paranoia, and depression and to
actually heal DNA. It has been noted that over 4,000 years ago
Sparta had all the instruments tuned at a higher frequency so
people would NOT be anti-war. Nazi's Goebble knew from
military acoustic research that A440Hz tuning was the most
dissonant, psycho-social, demonic and stressful mass hyste-
ria-inducing frequency, and chose said frequency for standard
tuning "to craft specific mental and psychological conditions
that predispose us to be self-centered, narcissistic, materialistic and aggressive." This is what music is tuned at today.
Service to self is what holds this together at every level, which
is what this plan is all about. Getting people to disconnect
from nature and create self-serving individuals is just part
of the plan. We can all agree that music can evoke emotion
without understanding any scientific reason. But the truth is
that there is science behind it. Music is vibration, and the
vibrations are measured in the frequency of the sound waves
created by different instruments. The way the instruments are
tuned determines the frequency of the music created. When
the A note is tuned to 432Hz, the tune is in balance with
the vibrations of the natural world, it is "in harmony with
the vibration Universe"... "and combines the properties of

light, time, space, matter, and gravity into biology, DNA and consciousness".

Freedom Slaves

"A really efficient totalitarian state would be one in which the all-powerful executive of political bosses and their army of managers control a population of slaves who do not have to be coerced because they love their servitude." Aldous Huxley, *Brave New World*.

You don't have to take my word for it. Call me a conspiracy theorist, and I'll laugh at the ignorance.

It may sound crazy, but there is a plan that was put together by the elitist of the elites a long time ago, and most of the world has fallen prey to it. If you really think it is about red and blue, then you are blind. Rothschilds, Rockefellers, Bushes, Gates, and the like are evil greedy, weak, effeminate little boys who win by stealing and destroying. It doesn't take a brilliant mind and deep insight to look at 2020 and miss the signs of our world being intentionally more fucked up than it should be. Unassuming people, too busy to take even a second to think about it, have let the world change over the past sixty or so years into a state of oblivion that they are completely unaware of, but fundamentally responsible for due to their lack of paying attention. We have all fallen for the evil script at some level, but now we must wake up to the reality and take it back, starting with ourselves.

The elite social engineering is designed to make us feel scared and need to run around in this sick rat race, always trying to keep up, always feeling behind. They want us to feel so shitty that we turn to excessive drug and alcohol use in the attempt to deal with the mind fuck they are feeding us. They want us to kill ourselves and each other to help them with their eugenics goals to decrease the population and keep the globe theirs. It's truly disgusting, and it's real. But whether you do or do not believe, it doesn't matter. The facts are that what we live today is right on course to what seemed even more insane back then. While most people don't plan much beyond what time they are eating dinner, the elite plan long term. I'm talking plans that span over multiple decades and generations.

On March 20, 1969, Dr. Richard Day, an insider of the New World Order, gave a talk to about eighty students and healthcare professionals at the Pittsburgh Pediatric Society who were destined to be leaders in medicine and health care. He requested that no notes or recordings be taken during his address, indicating that it may be detrimental to him if what he was going to tell them went public. Nonetheless, one Dr. Lawrence Dunegan made notes on napkins and later recorded them.

Dr. Day stated that he was able to share what he was sharing because "everything is in place, and nobody can stop us now." He made it clear that there were always two reasons for anything the Illuminati do: the pretext, which makes it palatable to the gullible public and the real reason, the reason that gets them what they want. The truth is that a handful of powerful people make decisions that will become our reality, and shit rolls downhill.

The beginning of the change was to impose a morality revolution on the world where all morals would be shattered and reconfigured into what we see today. It was already in motion, and the '60s were in full swing breaking down the established principles of our country and world; free love, including sex with anyone, anywhere, any way. Day said that sex would be separated from marriage and reproduction, "abortion, divorce, promiscuity, and homosexuality will be made socially acceptable" with the intention of making it more difficult and less desirable to permanently bond with one another. Sex education was introduced in the schools as a way of getting young people to think about and want sex at younger ages and to make contraceptives available to them, so the point is sex and not procreation.

More and more people will seek personal and individual satisfaction via career rather than family. Dr. Day made it clear that females will be encouraged to take part in sports to make them feel more masculine, and they will be taught that they are the same as boys—women's and gay rights movements will become prevalent. The family bonds will be broken down, and extended families will stay divided in order for individuals to "survive" in this new world they have planned for us. Work will require relocation and travel, making it even more difficult to stay connected. More women will work outside the home, and many will choose career over family. All of this is happening, and we are scrambling around and trying to keep up, thinking we are doing what is best for ourselves and family. But if we stop to think about it, we have been scammed, people. We need to wake up! I know I have been feeling behind, working my ass off to catch up and losing the most important relationships along the way, but at the same time saying "What the fuck?" for a lot of years, and finally, it is all coming clear.

Keeping people from forming bonds with others in how they would be able to easily make people work against one another rather than together (i.e., 2020 "Social Distancing"). Introducing violence, pornography, and obscenity to the masses by slowly increasing its presence on TV, movies, advertising, and all forms of media has desensitized folks to all of it—it seems normal, and we laugh at what is truly vulgar and unacceptable. We introduce it to our children at younger and younger ages, precisely following the plan (think Disney). It is sad and maddening when we realize what we have allowed to happen to us.

It was stated that education would change. Unsupervised education is known to stimulate greater learning, but schools will decrease unsupervised learning and increase supervised, in the box, analytical learning (think distance learning from home with Zoom). Students will be in school longer; specifically, summer vacation time will be reduced with a lengthening of the academic year, but students will intentionally learn nothing. Better schools will be in better areas with better people—their kids will learn more. The plan is to create a superior race and eliminate those they consider to be inferior. Classic literature, including the Bible, will be subtly changed to promote globalist ideals, some books will disappear altogether. People of all ages will feel the need to continually educate themselves, and once they can no longer do so, they will be considered useless and will willingly hand over their "space" to younger people by agreeing to be "humanely euthanized." Sounds crazy, right? Laugh all you want, or pause to ponder what we call "normal." Too many obvious facts. Here's another one based on history's sick truth.

It was stated that music would get worse and be used for indoctrination and that we will become disconnected to nature. The fact that in 1939, the Nazi minister of propaganda, Goebble, had the standard tuning changed from 432Hz to 440Hz fits right into this plan.

People will be implanted with ID cards (microchips), watched via surveillance and by their TVs and phones (i.e., 5G rollout during COVID-19 shutdown in 2020). Drug and alcohol use will increase. There will be more violence, and more jails will be needed. People will be incarcerated in hospitals, medical care will be difficult to obtain and tied directly to employment, diseases will be *created* and increasingly difficult to cure (AIDS), Ebola, Swine Flu, COVID-19, thus aiding in the depopulation of the world. There *is* a cure for cancer, but only available to the elite, again, enhancing the depopulation efforts. Weather can be controlled to wage war or create drought (and hence massive fires) and famine, ensuring the food supply is controlled as well. LBJ bragged, "He who controls the weather will control the world."

> "Control of space means control of the world, ...
> From space, the masters of infinity would have
> the power to control the earth's weather, to cause
> drought and flood, to change the tides and raise

the levels of the sea, to divert the gulf stream
and change temperate climates to frigid... It lays
the precedence and foundation for the develop-
ment of a weather satellite that will permit
man to determine the world's cloud layer and
ultimately to control the weather; and he who
controls the weather will control the world".

It goes on and on. They spray shit in the air on a daily basis. Geoengineering, aerosol injection, etc. This is all happening whether we want to acknowledge it or not. The environmental elites of the Sierra Club choose to pretend it doesn't exist while the forests of the Sierra Nevada are dying a quick death and then burning into uncontrollable infernos. Get it?

Dr. Day stated that each part of the world would have specialties and thus become interdependent. The U.S. will remain a center for agriculture, high tech, communications, and education, but heavy industry would be "transported out." He spoke of mass unemployment and social change starting in port cities and moving towards the heartland; hence the East and West Coasts being more socially liberal and considered progressive. Again, this is happening.

We are living this nightmare reality because we bought into the powerful illusion. There are some who are trying to make a difference. Most people sell out. We choose to opt-in or opt-out of the plan; to submit or to live our truth.

GOOD VIBES

Kids on surfboards floating on the Pacific Ocean like my mom and her friends growing up in the LA surf culture of the 1960s noticed the waves of the ocean. Scanning the horizon revealed the undulating heartbeat of the ocean in wave form. It looks like vibrations before the final exit of energy near the shore as the big crashing waves surfers live for. Someday the ocean had good vibrations that made for a magical day of riding the waves of energy. Other days the heavy energy made for less predictable and dangerous riding. My mom and her LA classmates, many famous musicians and actors, strumming their acoustic guitars around a campfire on the beach, translated this visual energy to people's energy. I also believe mind-expanding drugs like marijuana, LSD, and mushrooms helped them see energy fields that were undetected before. They coined the term "Good Vibes."

I followed this path naturally, spending much of my life in the ocean and growing up in Northern California with my counter culture of weed and other psychedelics like mushrooms and acid and mother nature revealing her truth in visual energy, people, places, and things. Now it's becoming widely accepted "Science" thanks to the brilliance of Nikola Tesla. His famous quote, "If you wish to understand the universe, think of energy, frequency and vibrations... It's our doubt and changing frequencies and our inability to hold thoughts and visions for extended times that takes us off our path."

Experiencing the viciousness of high school and college football and Silicon Valley startup tech media culture, I began to meet and feel energy that was different, and NOT in a good way. I discovered innate bad vibes and bad people. Selfish people pretending to give off cool or chill energy when it was only a false vibe to cover a darker demonic self-serving energy. I talk about this earlier in my book because this IS why we are so fragmented as a society... people trying to virtue signal a good vibe for self-serving purposes. It's a very California thing that started in Hollywood and metastasized throughout the music scene in LA and Silicon Valley tech scene years later, eventually infecting the entire media, tech, and mainstream family community and individuals. Syrupy sweet, artificially-flavored bullshit.

The reason I got crushed, woke, and eventually beat them at their sick game was by calling it out and being kicked out of the "club" so to speak. I realized, like it's been proven in scientific tests, my vibes and frequencies began to change and adapt to their sick energy. I came to realize that I was destroying my naturally good intentions and energy by conforming and tuning into bad people with bad energy and selfish intentions. I had to confront my own distortion and retune to people that were living, generally speaking, with a vibe and energy more aligned with my truth and natural vibrations. As a leader, for example, I had to really take a look at my intentions.

Thoughts are vibrations. Our thoughts start a wave of energy that physically manifests precisely in the direction we choose. It must be a conscious decision.

I have discovered that good vibes happen when I want to give more than I take. I have good vibes when I am consciously aware and focusing my thoughts on guidance and direction to help others more than my personal desires. The more I practice this, the more good vibes I give and receive. And what I selfishly desired ultimately faded, and a new and improved payoff revealed itself from places never imagined. I can't have and project good vibes if my intentions are not pure. If I allow *any* unacknowledged selfish desire to invade a good thought or action, it will invariably come back to haunt me. I know from experience.

I grew up with a stoner friend who always seemed to have good vibes. I didn't realize it was because his intentions and actions, despite not doing a lot, were solid for the most part. He didn't have to set the world on fire to be okay with himself. I always admired that. It's taken decades and serious work on my thinking and patterns to change fearful, selfish, and negative thinking of self to produce consistently better energy and performance in all aspects of my life. Cleaning house and helping others produces the foundation for good vibes for me. Simple but hard to keep self-desire out of plans.

In finding myself, and having faith in what that means, beyond my nagging interfering negative thoughts about what other people are thinking about me and what I haven't achieved or created, I began to heal. All that shit about what other people think or expect is just a distraction from being honest with self and having the courage to march forward into the unknown and achieve some measure of worth and purpose at the end of the day. And if I'm not a drunk fucked up mess, I will keep climbing and growing into a man I like and respect and create a life that I could've only dreamt about not long ago. I surrendered my old game plan and started listening and relearning how to think and walk again. It was nothing short of a miraculous recovery from a truly hopeless state of mind. I had help, but I ultimately had to do the heavy lifting. As slow and painful as it could feel sometimes, many good things were happening, never fast enough, but they were proving to me that living this way is a much healthier and happier way to approach life.

The next chapter of my life is drastically different than before. I have been given the ultimate gift of losing all to learn gratitude and a happy, healthy way of living. Now I'm focused on the right goals, most of the time, getting my work done and not trying to escape from the self-imposed expectations and ego-driven chaos associated with textbook alcoholic and mainstream societal thinking. Today, I'm not as distracted by selfish, self-destructive thoughts and behaviors. Being able to re-channel that energy to tranquil thoughts and effective action is encouraging a new surge of creative work that is exciting and very fulfilling. My focus, energy, and outlook are positively primed and pumping. In many ways, I've arrived at a place where I've retired from crazy. Now it's about assimilating my lived experience and giving my best today, every day, one day at a time.

"Live your fantasy." I can hear my dad telling this to my brothers and me as kids. He wasn't some effeminate man selling us a fairy tale from Disney. As an athlete, outdoorsman, and psychology teacher, he talked about visualization as an important part of performance at a high level. Most important to me is the example of him growing up poor and making very challenging changes to live a happier life doing good work helping kids.

Self-esteem is the key ingredient to all successful people. Some were born into a loving environment to have organic self-worth and confidence. Some were born into totally fucked-up environments and built self-esteem through positive thinking, action, and successes. However we get it, we must start and end and live our day-to-day with a concentrated vision of what we want to achieve. Otherwise, we are a disposable cog for someone else's vision, regardless if we are the employee or the boss. Positive affirmations, and just as important, eliminating negative self-talk, is the foundation to manifesting success. I'm not describing anything new. My dad believed firmly in self-visualization related to sports but also changing deeply ingrained negative behaviors of poverty, poor habits, and thinking.

My morning routine consists of coffee and sitting quietly in my studio before the sun comes up. My mind is often awakening to misfires or unfounded fears or confusion in what to do next—all or nothing, extreme manic swings. I get quiet and sip my coffee and think about the amazing life I have and the opportunity to help some people today if I just do what's in front of me and not allow negative thoughts to creep in and take over my outlook. I think about the special people in my life and send them good thoughts of happiness. And I do the same for anyone I know who is struggling. May sound cheesy to some people, but it totally does have a measurable positive effect on my day, my productivity, relationships…success!

I like what Einstein said: "Imagination is more important than knowledge." Dreams are important because they can be premonitions of truth if we have faith. Dreaming and taking relentless forward action to build it into reality is the one-two punch required to win. In my case, to offer you an example, I wake up and confront whatever is keeping me awake. This truth knocking on my door, helping me rise and face the obstacles stopping me from my destiny. In my role and out-look, it is an all-or-nothing game.

Transitioning from a dream state into a competitive state is not always easy for me. I would prefer to stay on the creative aspects of the business as in life, but I must suit up and take action on the things that are not always comfortable like picking up the phone and calling or meeting with people about investing in my business ideas to make them come to life. This has been a true character builder that makes me confront the weakest aspects of my being—fucking pride. Having people judge my ideas, as potential investors, is humbling and maddening. But I have also learned the rules of the game and choose to accept the terms of the deal, being an artist in a fear and money-obsessed world.

Courage is the essence of fuel in the form of facing fear and overcoming it by walking through it. In the spring of 2020, the stock market was crashing, people were panicking, and the food bank lines were unreal. Friends were getting laid off along with millions of others. We entered June 2020 with race riots over the cop-killing of George Floyd: very questionable optics and media fanned flames. It's a dirty scam to fragment a country that actually gets along pretty well, considering we are human. I'm not feeling the impact because I'm just starting to rebuild my life from scratch. Our business, ULN, walked through hell to arrive united and stronger on the other side. I spent my time focused on being productive while I took stock of what was going on; spending time researching and studying the major markets and gauging the fallout and what it means to my team and me. It's a time to be alert and aware of the micro/macro threats to our financial and health ecosystems. It's also critical to stay calm and steady. So much destruction has happened so fast. The positive people in tough times do exponentially better than those focused on what is wrong. The changes and shifts in our world are opening vast opportunities. If you can look and see them. We can. I learned from the great real estate economic crash in 2008 that I must live below my means and have cash reserves because a cyclical crash *will* happen.

A positive outlook and daily measurable action that I can build momentum from is the game-changer. It's not easy to do consistently, but the results are proven. It took me years to start over. I chose to stay stuck in my negative outlook. After I stopped drinking alcohol, a lot of the negative shit that comes with that world went away, for the most part. I got to work on doing the next right thing. I started developing habits in my thinking as I wake when my greatest fears are upon me, and my conditioned thinking starts to panic and self-hate. I now realize that with a little discipline and action-driven daily routine, I can completely change my outlook and production literally overnight. Linking days to weeks to months and years results in a golden life. Moral integrity and action equal billions. Keeping cool in crazy times has given me optimism and a clear vision to walk calmly to my destiny with my team. I get a great feeling to meet this economic crash with a humbled and forged way of life and experience that enables me to provide hope and calm guidance by the truth that I am living. I lost everything, and now I am rebuilding from scratch.

Patience takes courage. I struggle with patience every day. I want it all right now. That's how my brain works, and that's what I got for the first forty-five years of my life. Unfortunately, mountains cannot be built overnight, and neither can successful businesses. Giving all I have to people and my craft also requires letting go of the outcome. I play to win, nonetheless. I now realize and have faith in waking up with a deep purpose to help people. When I start to see the world and try to bend it to my will, I am setting myself up for massive disappointment. It is in direct conflict with the will to help others. Of course, I have big dreams and go after them, but they are aligned with building value for the greater good.

Think good thoughts about yourself and others, especially the ones we do not particularly like for whatever reason.

Try it. I swear it works. It takes power away from negative people and thoughts. Learn to think about how you can help the people closest to you in whatever you do. My experience is proving that monetary success is ironically a guarantee if we are living right...in tune to the bigger energy...voice... infinite power we can all access and leverage to a higher consciousness.

The key to success and happiness is inner peace. Not the "I love you, baby...honest! ...Now will you have sex with me?" or "I love you, son. We'll play catch later". I'm talking about the kind of love and honesty that can leave a person who is utterly broken and hopeless with unexpected gifts through faith and optimism, commitment, patience, and forgiveness. It's like a magic carpet ride of joy, security in the eternal sense, peace, harmony with self and our closest loved ones and more importantly in our mind. We experience a higher level of consciousness!

You wanna know the fucking "secret"? Quit wishing for selfish crap and feeling behind and resentful all day long because you don't feel you are where you should be. I totally get it! I have spent most of my waking and sleeping hours consumed with this mindset. My own transformation with how I've become aware of the way I thought and acted and the changes I must continue to make on a daily basis – changing any negative thought into positive, seeing through a new lens-free from negative blockage (people, places, things) that can consume the real estate in my brain if I allow it - has been life-saving. I let that shit consume me and it really damaged me. I changed... because I had to. My thinking was gonna kill me. It's propelled me into a higher dimension of thinking and action that is producing unlimited possibilities.

WHERE EAGLES FLY

It was June 2020, Julie's oldest son Ritter is graduating high school and moving out to live at his dad's full time while he goes to the local JC, Butte College, to play baseball and figure out his next steps. We've been through some tough times, to say the least, but through the years of getting sober and changing slowly, something crazy happened; He started to change his view of me. The best example I can give is one evening after dinner. He was on the couch with his girlfriend looking at publicly traded companies on his laptop, and he asked me a question about the stock market. We started to look at graph charts together. Oil prices were another timely topic because of the economic crash at the writing of this book. We started to talk about some companies that would be good for him to study (long-term charts and deeper dives reading annual reports, etc.): Tesla, Berkshire Hathaway, Bitcoin, and a couple of other companies and their long-term stock charts and talked about the fundamentals of Wall Street, of investing in the stock market, versus building your own business.

This parlayed into talking about his future. It was the perfect moment and opportunity and window in his life as he was getting ready to transition into adulthood and discover the world of capitalism, politics, and self-will. And it opened the door to this world that I have been a student of ever since

I was his age reading the *Wall Street Journal* and *Fortune* magazine in high school. Sharing with them how I used to watch CNBC in the very beginning when a young Maria Bartiromo would stand on the Stock Exchange Trading Floor and report the winners and losers of the day while getting knocked around by the old school male traders.

And at that point, I was able to look up at Ritter and tell him he has the ability to lead in business, and it's very rare. It's about bringing people together and being able to create value. There's a lot of money involved in that, but there's also a lot of responsibility. It gave him and me an opportunity to connect in that moment, to have him recognize what his mother and I are doing in business, respecting it, and asking me for advice.

That's full circle to where he and I were when I was drinking a few years ago. There's no better example of the gifts getting sober and really working on getting outside of myself to try to help these kids when I myself was struggling. The payoff of that moment with him was a tremendous gift.

As he packed up his truck with his clothes and baseball gear bag, we had a one-on-one moment that I seized as an opportunity to tell him what I felt. I started by explaining to him how much he meant to his mom and how hard this day was for her. I explained that I hope that he didn't forget her and made time to see her because their connection is special. I told him that he meant the world to her, and I paused for a moment. I looked up at him and told him that he meant a lot to me, too. And then I slowly walked away back towards my studio, in the back-room addition to the little mobile home that we were living in at the time.

A few minutes later, after Colton found his bag of action figures, we all reconvened outside at the truck as the boys packed up for the final time. Julie was in tears as we were both saying our goodbyes. As we all stood there in that moment of silence, I stepped forward to give him a hug. He hugged me back with sincerity and warmth.

As the boys jumped in the cab and started up the engine and slowly backed out, I asserted to the boys, "I love you guys!"

And what came back was one of the great surprises and rewards I have I've had so far in sobriety. I heard, "I love you!" I just remember thinking, *Did he just say he loves me?* It was a very special moment, and it's something that I will never forget.

Julie and I watched them back out and drive away, waving and wondering what the world was going to be like for him; I was also wondering what it was going to be like for me. Despite our age difference of thirty years, Ritter and I were in a very similar parallel of life, getting on our own feet of independence and flying away to discover our own world through the help of a very special woman.

My heart warmed, and I felt good. We had been through a lot of rough days. And the tension and mutual disdain brewed as time went on. But I got sober. I started acting differently, slowly, and things started to change. I started to treat his mom better. The house felt a little happier and less chaotic. I couldn't see my changes affecting Ritter for a very long time because he had seen a lot of years of bad times, and it required a few years of a new walk to have any faith that I was a different man. A man that they came to like and respect. We started having dinner at the dinner table and having conversations, even sharing jokes and laughter.

From where this all started to how it ended is all due to sobriety and realizing that my purpose is to help the ones in front of me. The boys and I share so many similarities and conflicting overlap of lived experience that it required a brutal confrontation of my pride and ego, to see past my lost dream of being a parent and focus on giving them my lived experience and guidance that they need to be solid leaders and build a happy life.

Around that same time, Becky called me to tell me that our childhood friend just lost her firstborn to a tragic car accident on his way to pick up his new girlfriend. He was so excited about life and had just told his mom about his girl-friend and that she might be the one. Becky and I cried on the phone.

Life's highs and crashing lows...

Being sober and present through these experiences of life are intense, but being present and able to share in the flow of life with my loved ones is priceless.

Talking with Beck about our friend's devastating loss somehow brought us to the shared sadness of our loss. The loss of our marriage and the babies we were not fortunate enough to have. Sensing my loss for coherent words, Beck, as she always does, eased me off the jagged rocks of the regret and pain I still live with over destroying my marriage, my life. Becky calmly said through tears, "You were sick for a while. That's how I see it, Bubba. I know you have always loved me. Football, alcohol, and the outside world of business was just too much. It's pretty amazing that we are able to be trusted friends we can lean on. Don't be sad and live in regret. We're solid." I write this through a veil of tears. I miss her and what we had more than I will ever be able to express. I'm experiencing life on life's terms sober and feeling all the intense, insane confusion. But I'm FEELING, and I'm participating in the good, bad, and fucking ugly moments of life with the people that loved me when I was broken. As crazy as it can feel, I am experiencing the joy of living in the now. The tears, the laughs...life's little moments that become a beautiful song or painting of meaning... love.

My dreams and plans are important to give structure to this ethereal journey of infinite chaos and order. But I now realize that they are delicately woven into a web of loving people that help me walk through this world and the effort I give back to them and anyone struggling that I can help.

Wanna know the magic source of living life to its fullest? Cherish the ones we love by making them more important than selfish dreams we chase every day with more effort and sacrifice—usually sacrificing the people we love the most. I got caught up with competing, and I lost the most cherished person in my life. There is no success if you can't share it, especially in tough times with trusted people that love you. Thinking we can walk through this world on our own self-will, led by society's insane machine, is a one-way ticket to a lonely and lost life. Trust me.

Family matters. My dad and I are in a solid place. We've been able to talk about my alcoholism, and I have been able to apologize to him for how I had him constantly worried and how it affected our relationship. He acknowledged that we had some rough times because of the responsibility and challenges of Nicole and how that affected our family. We've had some special talks, and my dad has told me multiple times how proud he is of me getting sober and living how I now live. That's all a boy is ever looking for.

I called up my dad the day before the 4th of July just to say hi and check in. The COVID-19 pandemic has surged, and the elderly are classified as a vulnerable group… "old people," as my dad would say comically since he is in the high-risk zone at 80 years old, despite being physically fit. He was actually digging footings with his backhoe and jumping off the full-sized tractor to dig out the remaining dirt with a pick and shovel. He was excited to talk and reminisce about our traditional 4th of July weeklong trips to the coast, usually camping at MacKerricher State Park, a beautiful stretch of coast and wooded beachfront that provided protected campgrounds from wind and other campers.

There was a small lake full of planted trout and bass and perch that I would fish for all the time. There was a trail that circled the lake. Much of the trail was a dirt path cut through a thick and lush ancient forest complete with giant ferns and flowers. There were many sections along the trail that were like a marsh, and the park rangers built nice redwood bridges and walkways that made a perfect ride all the way around the lake on our BMX bikes. My brothers and I loved riding through the trail near sundown because it was a scary and exciting adventure. As the ancient forest would grow dark, we could hear new animals and the crashing ocean waves just five hundred yards away, literally on the other side of the old train bridge that used to run lumber south to the mills in Fort Bragg. When I was a kid, the old train bridge had been converted into a logging road until it was turned into a part of the Pacific Coast Walk.

During the mornings, we would wake up to the smell of campfires, cooking bacon and coffee, laughter echoing through the coastal pine trees. Many mornings, Dad and I got up early, before most campers and the sun was up, and we would head out to fish the rocks at some of the same places we would dive.

My dad started telling me about the time I caught a big Cabazon rockfish at the mouth of the cave at Buckhorn when I was about ten years old. My dad continued telling the story from his crystal-clear mind as if it were yesterday. "You pulled in this huge fish and we were so excited. You got quiet, looked at the fish, and then looked up at me and asked me if we could let it go. I remember thinking, 'This kid's got heart!'"

Another classic and funny early morning fishing expedition dad brought up was the time I slipped off a kelp covered rock trying to jump across a trough of ocean water rising with the tide. I was wearing a thick jacket, jeans, and high-top shoes and was packing my ocean fishing pole and a bag of bait, hooks, and sand-filled Bull Durham sacks for weights. I vividly remember how excited I was to be at the hot fishing spot as the sun was not yet up, but the pink and purple sky and the birds and fishing boats let me know the timing was perfect. As any young fisherman on a mission, I scanned the rocky shore for the best place to drop my bait.

I saw a point and started skipping over rocks until I landed on a slippery as ice kelp covered rock that sent me flying horizontally back flat first into the trough. The water was receding as I fell into its black unknown only to feel the thud of my mid-back landing on a rock hiding just below the water. Just as I landed, the ocean decided to fill the trough with one big surge, knocking me off the rock only to be nearly drowned. My dad was there to save me if the adrenaline didn't launch me out of that trough after a few gulps of saltwater to start my morning off. My dad and I laughed then, and we laughed at the memory that is special to us.

My dad and I share the great moments of achievement, but oftentimes, we share the vulnerabilities and comedy of growing up and being a man in this world. My dad always had this perspective because he was aware of the illusory hierarchy of life, and he knew where he fit and was vigilant to live it daily. I feel connected to my dad in a very special way. I had no idea or perspective about truly how special it was until I could finally get wiped out financially, sobered up, and worked through my past resentments and expectations, whether they were actually real or perceived through a waterfall of alcohol, social pressures and trophies.

As Dad and I are talking on the phone, I hear my mom in the background sharing in the good vibes, and Nicole is sitting at the table next to them, making my dad laugh like a kid. My dad paused to interact with her. "I get a kick out of her... She's funny!" Dad started joking about Nicole wanting him to sing "Itsy Bitsy Spider... a new song I'm learning..." since it was just about the only song she likes to sing and hand gesture the spider crawling up and down the waterspout. Every day, approximately ten to thirty times...conservatively speaking.

"I don't know how you did it, Dad!" I started to get choked up and cry in appreciation of his journey growing up poor and giving his children a positive, loving, and stable home life and guidance to navigate the world and live this life adventurously. I was one of the lucky ones...and I know it.

July 9ᵗʰ, 2020 Manual Labor in the Summer Heat & Colton's First Day of Work

During the launching of ULN and finishing this book, I started doing different types of physical labor jobs, from a logging job to cutting weeds and general labor for lots of lifting and digging. Being back outdoors working with my hands and working in the 100-degree summer heat like I did back when I was a teenager. It shocked my body and mind into elevated states. My pride fought it all the way until I put in a few days and felt my being changed. By looking for basic labor work in my hometown forced me to crush my pride so I could finally see the opportunity versus the humiliation I imagined in my mind that my ego was manufacturing. Working outdoors with people and making a few hard-earned dollars was a breakthrough…a strength and freedom…an independence I have not felt in a very long time.

I was working for an older couple putting in a water feature and walkway in their yard. The job required lots of shoveling gravel into a wheelbarrow and hauling it around to the back of the house. I asked the owners if Julie's now 16-year-old son Colton could work with me, and they agreed to it. We spent a couple of days a week for his first real paid job. He showed up dressed and ready to work. I wasn't sure what to expect. He worked hard and did a solid job loading, hauling, following directions, and not wasting time. Learning to work is a lost art to so many video game couch kids. Colton was changing with every load of broken concrete he was hauling from the bottom of a hill up to the job site. I watched a sixteen-year-old boy transform into a hardworking, conscientious young man. Firm, loving, and trusting coaching and his willingness and desire to do a good job. I watched him struggle from the grueling nonstop physical work; he was drenched in sweat, even his jeans were wet from sweat. The midday July heat blasted us. Colton would start to slow down or lose focus, and all it would take was a little, "Come on, man! Let's go!" and he would pick up the pace.

Our connection and years of spending time together and working together on other projects, created the bond that he could trust as he tried something new and very uncomfortable. And Colton has observed my work ethic over the years and listening to me talk about it related to the work I do on a daily basis as he was homeschooled with us in the same work/home environment. He had a frame of reference, and he understood my way—my true intentions. Colton is very perceptive, and he would shut down if I just barked orders and disapproval at him. Most people do. He watched me work, and I coached him to learn to be aware of what he can do to help us get the job done. Colton was learning to work on a job with me and an energetic 25-year-old named Nick. It was hot without a trace of a breeze. I had Colton shoveling gravel and hauling broken concrete slab. We traded off so he could see me do it. The hard work and pay and sense of accomplishment were written all over Colton's face at the end of the workday.

With his first hard-earned cash, I seized the opportunity to help him understand taxes and his hourly value based on supply and demand an basic principles of capitalism. With taxes, I gave him the comedian Bill Murray's concept that any kid can understand instantly. A kid has an ice cream cone of three scoops, and the government takes one of the scoops of the kid's ice cream, leaving him in tears. It's a funny and brutal reality for kids and adults. I grabbed one of Colton's twenty-dollar bills as if I were the IRS taking the 1/3 of his earned money.

He looked at me like it was excessive. "What do they use it for?"

I replied with, "Some good stuff like law enforcement, but so much is spent on bad stuff that only pays and helps the people in power at that time."

We continued this conversation with his mom when we got home, arriving sweaty, dirty, and exhausted but feeling good, accomplished. We talked about the money we use to build our businesses and how he will use some of his money to build his business, an animated show he's been working on for a few years. Colton was learning how it all fits together in a very simplified and pragmatic way. He was learning that he could do it, and he would be okay no matter what.

Colton watched me write this book over the years. He was watching me work hard labor to pay for the book to be published. I was living what I was coaching, and we both benefitted exponentially by sharing the experience.

FIRE, FAMILY AND FREEDOM

September 11, 2020

O n this 19th anniversary of 9/11, New York and the fraudulent "government", or actual oligarchs in power, remind American citizens how their sacrifice of money (taxes) and 3,000 plus lives paved the way for "patriots" like Larry Silverstein and his arch-angels to be paid to demolish and rebuild World Trade Center One. All to provide the perfect story of an attack on the US, thus giving the Bush, Inc. the justification for a multi-trillion-dollar war. And if you believe this, you're not a "patriot" – get it?

All over the country cops are being assassinated, riots rule the streets, and we have been impacted by the COVID/ societal 5G shutdown. Out west we are experiencing rolling "blackouts" and devastating fires. Just a typical day in the "Golden State" of California. Mafia Governor Gavin Newsom, nephew of the "godmother" Nancy Pelosi, took the media opportunity of the "natural disaster" called the Bear Fire, or North Complex West Fire, to come to my hometown after our foothill neighbors had just been wiped out, to condemn the townspeople, the state, and the nation. He came to NorCal sporting a designer version of a military type coat that might be worn by us folks here in the hills as if an attempt to connect with the "common man". He spewed about his intolerance of those who dare to see any point of view other than "global warming" as the cause of the fires. WTF? Extreme disconnect. Using the classic arrogant and condescending tone that he consistently uses towards his "ignorant constituents", he went on a rant:

> *"This is a climate damn emergency," Newsom said in remarks during his tour. "This is real and it's happening. This is the perfect storm. It is happening unprecedented ways year in and year out.*

> *"We're experiencing what so many people predicted decades and decades ago... all of that now is reality, it's observed...you can exhaust yourself with your ideological BS by saying, well, one hundred years ago we should've done this or that... all that may be true and I'm not gonna suggest for a minute that the forest management practices in the state of California over a century plus have been ideal – but that's one point... but it's not THE POINT..."*

We choose to live where we live because of the beauty of the area, the space, and shared beliefs of much of the community. We realize the threat of forest fires, earthquakes and dams breaking. But we also drive while realizing the risk of being in an automobile accident, which happens to be a higher risk than fire, flood or earthquake. Nonetheless, we have been evacuated multiple times in the past few years, and we were evacuated once again and at the mercy of the North Complex West Fire.

It was September 9th. We calmly loaded up the truck, Julie, Colton and I, with our pre-packed bins, each one marked with the words "In Case of Evacuation - Take This" on a bright orange note... it has become such a familiar routine. Our most cherished items, photos, artwork, this and that, were first staged in the front room. As the wind grew stronger and the emergency warnings continued to blare from every cell phone in the house, we decided to at least load the truck. Just in case. And then the red growl of a beast of a fire snarled from the top of the hill above us. As I looked at the glowing night sky to the east of us, ravaging the foothills of the Sierra, I knew it was time to go. I thought about the generator I just borrowed from my dad so we could run a few fans and the refrigerator once the blackouts hit us. It was of no use now and there was no room in the truck. I thought about the house on the ridge to the east, and directly in the fires path, where my grandpa once had a home. I have many fond memories of playing and working there. I thought about G-Pa and how everything goes away in the end, except those memories and the legacy of a life well lived.

Becky had called to check on us, knowing our proximity to the fire. She opened her arms and her home to us – which included me, Julie, Colton and our two not so small dogs. We had a few other friends offer for us to crash at their places, but Beck's was the one place where I felt the most comfortable, so off we went. We locked the house up, chained the gate and made the slow drive to safety. We joined the hundreds of others fleeing the foothills. I checked in on my parents and Nicole earlier and as we drove by their house, we confirmed that they had left town, so I knew they were safe. All too familiar with devastating wildfires, not many waited for the officials to begin cruising the street to demand that we leave, most had already received the text alerts from PG&E telling us to expect power outages and then the Butte County Sheriff texts to notify us of the fire evacuation warning which was quickly upgraded to an order. The evacuation was methodical and precise; our town has become accustomed to evacuations and everyone seems to know to be cautious, courteous, and controlled. Ashes rained down so heavy it looked like snowflakes and the tires of the escaping cars and trucks threw up ash as if it were snow on the asphalt. It was truly surreal. My thoughts went back and forth between "the house will be okay" and "this is the one that will take us out." The fire was moving over two thousand acres an hour and was less than two miles away from our home, the winds were raging, and the foothills were aglow. It was fifty-fifty at that point.

As we pulled into Beck's driveway, I felt safe, but I also felt anxiety. I wasn't only worried about the human dynamics of it all, but more about how the dogs would get along. I quickly realized the insignificance of my worries and knew that we would figure it out. We had a safe place to stay whereas we had passed by numerous people parked on the side of the road and in open parking lots with nothing but the clothes on their back and the few items they could escape with. I replaced my lower vibration worries and fears with thoughts of gratitude. Feeling vulnerable in a life and death kind of way and walking through the moment with calm and purpose is very connecting to self, to family and to the humanity around us. Of course, plenty of people struggle through experiences like this to justify fucking terrible behaviors. It's like the old saying goes, "when the going gets tough, the tough get going." I also like, "tough times never last, but tough people do." I found myself in a tough time with tough people. It gave me strength and calm focus.

We spent 5 days in our communal living situation. Becky and Julie are cool with one another and easily got along and figured out how best to manage the dogs ... including me. They handled the temporary circumstances as if it were just another day and for the most part had positive attitudes and make the best of it spirit. Julie and I only fought a few times, and Beck and I only once... or twice. I spent a lot of time in the garage with Bradley, not because I was in trouble, but because I just need my own space to get out of my head sometimes. When it comes down to it, we are family and have a healthy amount of respect for each other, and when it *really* comes down to it, we've got each other's back!

Once more, we were spared from the wrath of another forest fire. We were among the lucky ones. The truck remained packed for a few days, but when we unloaded, we only unpacked the absolutely necessary items, knowing fire season had barely started. Everything else stayed packed, labeled, and ready to go.

This and many other events of our times caused me to think about how our day to day lives as Californians, as Americans, have been pounded by assaults and how it has taken its toll on the masses, forging the country into two camps. It's not by accident. It is basic human psychology played out with the same predictable results in every human era. It's a tired drama of destruction and retribution ad Infinium. It's about two teams: short-term self-servers and long-term team players. Other interpretations might suggest a Star Wars or Bible analogy of good vs evil.

WAY OF THE FUTURE

I'm excited to hit the road and share my story and creative work with you in person. At my core, I love meeting new people, exploring ideas, and connecting the best energy together to create magic.

I spent years in the studio creating work that will allow me to spend a lot of time on the road, old school, touring the United States, city by city, town by town, sharing, learning, and hopefully helping.

Maximizing my time and effort is critical to achieving great things. The general plan is for me and my Manic Fusion Team, which is made up of many amazing independent companies, including all of my personal brand and creative work products—*Civil Bullets* (book), artwork (Chris Rockwell Originals), music (Guns of the Revolution) to hit the road. A typical week for me on the road will include visiting multiple towns and cities as an ambassador for our companies like Urban Lumber Network and Bass Thrasher. That will entail meetings to explore and connect new people and opportunities together, always with the intent to drive synergies throughout our portfolio of companies.

There is no replacement for face-to-face meetings when it comes to communicating our truth—business, art, anything. It's about people helping people...it's a powerful thing! Visiting children's hospitals and working with suffering addicts and alcoholics is where I will give and share the best of me and grow the most as a person. I will share my love, artwork, music, book...my friendship. I spent a lot of time at UC Davis Children's Hospital as a kid because my baby sister Nicole had life and death developmental challenges for years, and the doctors and nurses were truly amazing. But the suffering, sadness, and loss of parents losing their babies to cancer or some other sinister death sentence has never left me. I can give comfort to parents in that terrible, scary place. My parents still care for my special-needs sister 24/7. They are heroes to me, as are the parents who stay by their child unconditionally when there will never be cheering crowds, honeymoons, or grandchildren.

My evenings will be focused on book signings, lectures at colleges (most will ban me from campus), then move into the next phase of the evening that will often include limited ticket shows for my visual artwork (oftentimes shows with local talent), and finish the night off with a show with my rock band, Guns of the Revolution. It's all about sharing and learning and growing as a group together. With that said, I may change that at any time if I feel like it's becoming a grind of people demanding more and more until it consumes me. I'm not a starry-eyed dreamer anymore, willing to sacrifice my best for self-serving assholes. I'm not out to get rich and famous. I'm dead serious. I'll drink myself to death fast if that's my intent. I'm heading out to share my message with people who could use another person in their corner, even if it's just my story and a hug that gives them hope to walk through one tough moment. Fame and money are not real. Love and caring for another person are.

Fearless, Grateful & Free

Chris Rockwell
October 17, 2020

CPSIA information can be obtained
at www.ICGtesting.com
Printed in the USA
BVHW010436211020
591324BV00028B/526/J

9 781641 844598